# THE PRESIDENCY AND
# NATIONAL SECURITY POLICY

# THE PRESIDENCY AND NATIONAL SECURITY POLICY

R. GORDON HOXIE

WITH

RYAN J. BARILLEAUX, WALDO W. BRADEN,
RICHARD BROWN, MINTON F. GOLDMAN, DAVID HAIGHT,
GLENN P. HASTEDT, PHILLIP G. HENDERSON,
KENNETH M. HOLLAND, ANDREW F. KREPINEVICH,
ROBERT C. McFARLANE, R. D. McLAURIN,
M. PETER McPHERSON, FREDERICK W. MARKS III,
ROBERT A. RAGAZZO, HAROLD C. RELYEA,
HENRY S. ROWEN, GEORGE P. SHULTZ,
JOHN W. VESSEY, JR., WALLACE EARL WALKER,
JAMES D. WEAVER, AND CASPAR W. WEINBERGER

*Foreword by* BRENT SCOWCROFT

Sponsored by:
CENTER FOR THE STUDY OF THE PRESIDENCY
Proceedings: Volume V, Number 1, 1984

Copyright © 1984
Center for the Study of the Presidency
208 East 75th Street
New York, NY 10021
Library of Congress Card Catalog Number 84-72429
ISBN 0-938204-05-X    Hard Cover
      0-938204-06-8    Soft Cover

"We must be bold and vigilant lest daily cares cloud our longer vision of the task that lies ahead and of the fair fortunes at our command. . . . But this unity, this understanding, this sense of inter-dependence is the heart of the business. Without it we shall make no headway. With it there is no fair ambition we cannot realize."

ANTHONY EDEN
*1951*

*Dedicated To:*

AMBASSADOR RUTH L. FARKAS
   Whose Inspiring Support Contributes Significantly to the
   Center for the Study of the Presidency
   *and*

GORDON GRAY
   Respected Presidential Advisor Who Contributed
   Perceptively to National Security Policy and Organization

# Table of Contents

# Editor's Preface

### Appreciation

This timely volume, *The Presidency and National Security Policy*, was made possible by 22 contributing authors. Their names and careers are noted in the About the Authors section. But beyond that an especial sense of appreciation is due each of them. They range from brilliant young scholars to the principal advisers to the President on national security policy. That all responded affirmatively to the invitation of the Center for the Study of the Presidency to participate, augurs well both for United States security and world peace. The two are interrelated, as set forth by General Brent Scowcroft in his Foreword and by the chapters by George P. Shultz, Secretary of State; Caspar W. Weinberger, Secretary of Defense; John W. Vessey, Jr., Chairman, The Joint Chiefs of Staff; M. Peter McPherson, Administrator, Agency for International Development; Ambassador Robert C. McFarlane, Assistant to the President for National Security Affairs; and the other contributors.

### A Time of Examination

As Secretary of State Shultz perceptively observes in the first chapter, the publication of this volume "will follow the excitement of America's quadrennial exercise of self-renewal" in its Presidential election. It is a time to examine the Nation's priorities and strategies for the ensuing four years. A major part of that concern is in the area of national security policy.

As public opinion specialists Daniel Yankelovich and John Doble recently observed, "Presidential campaigns do more than choose individuals for high office; our history shows many instances where elections have moved the country closer to a decisive resolution of long-standing issues."[1] Indeed Presidential elections have provided mandates for major policy enactments. Such was the case in 1933 with Franklin D. Roosevelt and with Ronald Reagan in 1981. In both instances both leadership and the national mood were related. They always are.

Among the major concerns in the Fall of 1984 are those set forth in this volume, concerns which may well provide a watershed for policy enactments in the ensuing four years. This volume in seeking to assess the Nation's security policies and the President's leadership role therein, can help to chart a course for the 1985–1989 period. The volume not only seeks to examine elements of national strength and the instruments for policy making but also urgent needs, including the need for achieving clearer consensus in the national security policy area.

As this Preface is written in September 1984, we may well inquire as to how America perceives itself and is perceived by others. We should both look back and look ahead. On July 15, 1979 President Carter addressed the Nation about its "crisis of confidence." The American people were not comfortable with President Carter's discerning observations. The Nation's mood was then downbeat. A coinciding of events in the period 1977–1981 had brought a severe deterioration of relations between the two super powers. Detente had reached its high point in the Vladivostock Accords of 1974 between President Ford and the Soviet leader, Leonid Brezhnev. This volume traces the deterioration of those relationships.

By 1980, after the Soviet invasion of Afghanistan, and the holding of American hostages in Iran, the American people looked to new leadership in the restoration of pride and strength. At the same time that President Reagan in 1981 enunciated a program for strengthening the Nation's armed forces, both in Europe and in the United States, a massive vocal anti-nuclear movement arose. It was, as Professor Robert W. Tucker observed, "unprecedented in the breadth of support it appeared to enjoy."[2] In the United States it challenged the MX program of critically needed long range nuclear missiles to counter the awesome Soviet build up. The Scowcroft Commission headed by Brent Scowcroft, the author of the Foreword for this volume, brought perspective on this critical issue. Moreover, the refusal of Western Europe, to be intimidated either by the nuclear freezers or the Soviets, brought the introduction on the soil of *NATO* member nations of medium range missiles to counter those of the Soviets.

Still by 1984 with restoration of the balance between NATO and the Warsaw Pact strongly underway and particularly of the balance between the U.S. and the U.S.S.R., the American people were clearly concerned for the lessening of nuclear tensions. In brief, the American people believe that with the imbalance on its way to be corrected, it is possible to engage in more constructive negotiation. President Reagan himself leads in that view. As Robert C. McFarlane, the President's Assistant for National Security Affairs and the author of a chapter in this volume recently expressed it, "There is no more compelling item on the President's agenda than achieving an equitable, verifiable reduction in nuclear weapons."[3] Appropriate emphasis must, however, be given to the key words: equitable and verifiable.

Yes, in September 1984 the Nation's mood is both concerned and upbeat. When someone said to George Will recently that what this Nation needs is a peace academy, he responded that we already have several that are doing a good job in helping keep the peace. He was, of course, referring to the military service academies. Between 1980 and 1984 their applications for admission have increased by 59%. As a further measure of national renewal, the re-enlistment rate in the Nation's armed forces is today at the highest level since World War II.[4] There is in the Nation a surge of seemingly old-fashioned patriotism.

### The World Climate and U.S.-U.S.S.R. Relationships

Yet the present euphoria must not blind us from a realization of the perilous world in which we live. The bombing today of the American embassy in Lebanon is an example of the fanatical hatred of some terrorist groups. Further, this is a reminder that most of the strife in the world since 1945 has been in developing nations between the forces of radicalism and those of moderation: in Korea, Vietnam, Central America, Africa and the Middle East. In this climate the Soviet Union has sought to create client states, with weapons sales as their principal diplomacy. This is a dangerous business.

But Kremlinologists advise us that potentially more dangerous is the state of Soviet leadership. Now since 1977, beginning with Brezhnev's illness, the Soviet Union has had ailing leadership. It has also been a period characterized by stagnation in the Soviet economy, by the increase of dissidence, and by enormous military build-up. This build-up of air, sea, and ground forces —both conventional and nuclear—is clearly beyond any defensive requirements. It led finally to America's responding build-up.

As Professor Richard Pipes recently observed, "The current crisis of the Soviet's system has two aspects, a political one and an economic one. Speaking in the broadest terms, both arise from a growing discrepancy between the responsibilities assumed by the communist elites at home and abroad, and the human and material resources with which to carry them out."[5]

At least until recent date, the leaders of the malfunctioning Soviet system have been in no mood to negotiate and their actions have been characterized by severe truculence.

This Preface is written shortly after the first anniversary of the shooting down of Korean Airlines Flight 007, with the loss of all 269 aboard. This is a flight this editor has taken often, most recently when participating in the 100th anniversary of diplomatic relations between the United States and Korea. From that tragedy of a year ago and the continuing hostile Soviet mood, one may well ask what are the hopes for world peace and security and for bettering relations between the Soviet Union and the United States?

In this assessment, we begin with the worst. According to Radomir Bogdanov of the Soviet Institute for U.S.A. and Canada Studies, "Our relations are at the lowest point since World War II, and what is very disturbing is that a kind of hopelessness is setting in, a feeling that it is impossible to improve relations with these people."[6]

In this appraisal, Dr. Bogdanov's memory is conveniently short-lived. For example, in the Truman and Eisenhower eras there was on both sides tougher talk than any during the Carter and Reagan periods. Where President Reagan joked in an off-the-record remark of August 11, 1984 about outlawing the Russians, President Truman was dead serious when he wrote as early as January 5, 1946, "I do not think we should play compromise any longer. . . . I'm tired of babying the Soviets."[7] Nor on the Soviet side has any leader been so abusive of any recent President as was Khrushchev in his public denunciations of Eisenhower after the U-2 incident.

Much of the present Soviet discomfit really dates from the detente period of the mid-1970's. In 1975 President Ford had challenged them to sign the Helsinki Accords, recognizing human rights standards. President Carter, early in his own administration, made human rights a major issue in foreign policy. President Carter's human right pronouncements, during his first six months in office, inspired this Tass commentary on the eve of the June 1977 review of the Helsinki agreements: "James Carter has assumed the role of mentor to the U.S.S.R. and other socialist countries. . . . " Tass charged that Carter's criticisms of Soviet non-compliance with the human right portions of the Helsinki convention were "compiled by the enemies of détente."[8]

The Helsinki human rights accords have since aroused the most paranoid fears of the Soviet leaders. In part, they attribute the stirrings for human rights in the satellites, including the Solidarity labor movement in Poland, to Helsinki and the subsequent meetings on European cooperation and security. The three most recent leaders in the Kremlin, Brezhnev, Andropov and Chernenko, were all born before the 1917 revolution and counter revolution. They were especially concerned with Nobel prize winner, Andrei D. Sakarov, and his wife, Yelena G. Bonner, and others in the past decade, speaking out for human rights. There had been no such prior experience.

It is difficult for us to comprehend Soviet attitudes on so many issues because of the difference in our cultural and political heritage. From Plato's *Republic* to the present we have a heritage of democratic ideals, devoid in the Russian experience. We are different people, in different societies, in different systems. In addition to the absence of the Western cultural heritage of free expression, their own heritage is filled with fear of conquest, from the Tartar domination of 1240–1480, to Napoleon, to Hitler. Security, not freedom, dominates their priorities and directs their view towards their neighbors, including Afghanistan. So far as a way out of their own difficulties is concerned, they do not perceive the solution in revolution. As Professor Pipes concludes, "Historical experience since 1917 has caused Russians of every political orientation to fear the collapse of authority even more than despotism. . . ."[9]

As this volume makes clear the Soviets miscalculated American, indeed, world-opinion in their 1979 invasion of Afghanistan. There followed a rapid deterioration of relations with the West: the cutting off of much western technology; the Carter step-up of United States arms build-up; and the boycott of the

1980 Olympics in Moscow. In this climate the United States Senate shelved the SALT II agreement negotiated by the Carter administration.

Inheriting this climate, Ronald Reagan became President of the United States. He did end the grain embargo Carter had imposed, but concurred with the Senate's shelving of the Salt II treaty. While the Scowcroft Commission had been convened in 1983 to consider MX deployment, it also proposed a START program to negotiate on missile reduction.

Ever since being faced down in the 1962 Cuban missile crisis, the Soviets have been building up their armed forces, far beyond any defensive requirements. Back at the time of that confrontation, the United States had 1054 intercontinental ballistic missiles; the Soviets had about 200. Now the United States still has that same number and the Soviets have 1400. Back in the early 1960's the United States had 656 submarine launched ballistic missiles; the Soviet had none. Today, the Soviets have 1,000 while the United States has kept its number about the same. Today, according to Secretary of Defense Weinberger, the Soviets have more nuclear warheads than the United States.[10] It is not the United States numerical increase but rather the modernization and readiness that particularly troubles the Soviets.

Despite Soviet threats, the NATO allies had advised that they would, at the end of 1983, deploy the first of 572 new intermediate range missiles in Europe, unless an accord could be reached on curbing the Soviet intermediate range SS-20's already in place. As a prelude to these Intermediate Range Nuclear Forces (INF) talks in Geneva, there had been vigorous efforts by Secretary of State Shultz in the Summer of 1983 to improve relations with the Soviets. Mr. Shultz and Soviet Foreign Minister Andrei A. Gromyko were to meet in Madrid in September to discuss outstanding issues, including the INF talks. Then Gromyko later in September, was to come to the United States, continuing discussions with Shultz. Beyond that, with satisfactory progress, there could be a meeting with President Reagan. But then came the downing of the Korean airliner; Gromyko's pronouncing a new hard line; and the Soviets walking out of the INF and START talks.

In all probability, the Soviets would have walked out of the Geneva talks anyway. Just as the U-2 incident gave them a pretext to withdraw Eisenhower's invitation to visit the Soviet Union, the Soviets had no intention to accommodate a single Pershing II missile. What happened to their horror was world opinion shifted in favor of the deployment after the KAL shoot down.

"The profound lesson of this Korean airliner tragedy," Dr. Ramon H. Meyers, Senior Fellow at the Hoover Institution, Stanford University, asserts, "is that the Soviet leadership does not conform to the same civilizational and moral values that guide the West." Dr. Meyers warns, "Making concessions in the vain hope that it will elicit a similar response from the Soviets will not bring confidence and trust. Instead it will signal Soviet leaders that it is possible to take advantage of the West."[11]

### The Future

Recognizing the importance of both fairness and firmness in dealing with the Soviets, President Reagan sent Vice President Bush not only to attend the Andropov funeral but also, as indicated in this volume, to make "overtures to the new Soviet leader to ameliorate relations. In the protocol politeness of the funeral, there appeared to be a glimmer of hope for renewed détente. But subsequently all such overtures have been spurned by the Soviets."[12]

Chernenko, son of a Siberian peasant, has the traditional Slavic distrust of the West. With Chernenko in ailing health and publicly heard from on infrequent occasions, there is concern as regards the longevity of his leadership. While retaining his own power as Secretary General of the ruling party, Chernenko has been content for Gromyko to assume the role of public spokesman. This is a curious phenomenon; in Gromyko's 26 years as Foreign Minister with Khrushchev, Brezhnev, Andropov, and now Chernenko, this is the first time he has ostensibly played such a prominent role. In early September 1984 Gromyko indicated a willingness to meet with President Reagan at the White House on September 28th. Secretary of State Shultz has indicated he and President Reagan will convey a very positive message "that the United States desires" a more constructive relationship with the Soviet Union.[13]

There will be no quick fixes in our relations with the Soviets. Bridges between two contending systems cannot be readily built. No President, not even Eisenhower with all his prestige, has made sustained progress in bettering relations with the Soviets. Still, the planet keeps shrinking and the means for its destruction keeps expanding. We must continue to persevere. As Richard Burt, Assistant Secretary of State for European and Canadian Affairs, recently expressed it, "We must be ready to talk with Moscow, but we must be firm and patient in trying to negotiate equitable solutions to the many problems that face us both. Although they may not like it, this is the policy the Russians understand and should respect. It is also the policy most likely to achieve lasting results."[14]

Despite all of the short-term uncertainties as regards Soviet leadership, there is building a horizon of hope in the West. One such example is the budding rapprochement between the two Germanys. Chancellor Helmut Kohl in West Germany, withstood the severe Soviet pressures not to accept the Pershing II missiles. Now, Erich Honecker, to the consternation of the Kremlin, is contemplating becoming the first East German Communist leader to visit West Germany. The Soviets did in early September force the cancellation of Honecker's planned visit. At any rate he and Kohl talk regularly by a special phone. Kohl is determined to enlarge contacts with other Eastern European countries.

This does not mean East German freedom from Soviet domination. As they did in Hungary and Czechoslovakia, the Soviets would crush any uprisings in East Germany, where they station 400,000 troops. Yet a strong love for the Fatherland remains in both Germanys and the human spirit will one day find a way. As Secretary of State Shultz expressed it, "We may not see freedom in Eastern Europe in our lifetime. Our children may not see it in theirs but some day it will happen."[15]

### Challenge and Hope

The United States Ambassador to West Germany, Dr. Arthur F. Burns, observed on June 28, 1984: "President Reagan has done much to restore the faith of Europeans in America's resolve to remain strong and to help nations around the world to protect their freedom."[16] However, this European view is not unanimous. Netherland's opposition to United States arms policies remains outspoken. Greece has considerable anti-American feeling. Spanish membership in NATO remains in doubt.

Today, eastern Europe is restive. With the exception of Czechoslovakia, all of the European Soviet satellites are seeking closer economic ties with the West. Moreover, as in the Soviet Union, the leaders of East Germany, Czechoslovakia, Hungary, and Bulgaria, are in their 70's. They perceived the Soviets differently than a younger generation.

The Soviets have through arms deals made inroads in the Middle East: Syria and Iraq, even Jordan and Kuwait. But the Arabs have a basic distrust of the Soviets. In the Far East the Soviets have lost ground with the two principal powers, China and Japan. Despite active pacifist movements in Japan, the Kremlin's threats on Japan have backfired, enabling Prime Minister Nakasone to strengthen Japan's alliance with the United States. Moreover, China moves closer to the United States. India is the exception, where the Ghandi government is pursuing a 5 billion dollar weapons arrangement with the Soviets.

In Latin America the Soviet penetration is receding. The Soviets are still in shock over the United States intervention in Grenada. Even Marxist Nicaragua and Cuba are making overtures to the United States. Latin American nations including Argentina, Mexico, and Venezuela, are clearly voicing opposition to Marxist inroads in Latin America.

With 25 of the 31 poorest nations in the world, Africa has been viewed by the Soviets as fertile territory. Despite their large arms shipments to these countries, the Soviets are enjoying scant success. American AID programs, as described in this volume by M. Peter McPherson, are more attractive. South Africa has also been a strong counter voice to Marxist inroads. Of recent date, only Ethiopia has succumbed to Communist Party pressures. Soviet influence, even in Angola and Mozambique, is waning. In brief, world-wide, the Soviet penetration is declining.

Yet the task is unfinished. The challenge continues for democratic societies. And the problems which this President faces in the formulation and implementation of foreign policy have confronted every president since Eisenhower. These include problems of achieving consensus. This was a word often used by Lyndon Johnson, but a goal that eluded him. Irving Kristol may have exaggerated the case, but he made the point well when he stated, "One cannot imagine any crisis in world-affairs, short of an overt military attack upon American territory, to which the American Government could respond with the assurance of enthusiastic congressional and popular support."[17]

Much of the divisiveness came out of the Vietnam-Watergate

era. The media have lamentably made more than their own fair
share of the divisiveness, emphasizing the bad news. (For example *The New York Times* index for 1969 has three and one-half
pages in fine print referring to My Lai but only scant reference
to the Communist massacre of 4,800 at Hue at about the same
time). It is little wonder that Professor C. Lowell Harriss concludes, reflecting on such reporting, " . . . it is not reassuring
to be constantly reminded of dominance in foreign affairs journalism of views which have served Americans poorly."[18]

What is needed after all due consideration and debate is consensus. Again as Kristol put it, "Consensus is what sustains an
ideological foreign policy . . . ."[19] Before consensus can be gained
there must be a restoration of trust between the Congress and
the Presidency. This had reached its nadir in the summer of
1974, just prior to the Nixon resignation. The War Powers Resolution of 1973, which as this volume indicates, Nixon and every
subsequent President has deemed unconstitutional, had been
forced on the weakened President Nixon. Sensing its new found
dominance, Congress passed the Budget and Control Act of 1974;
increased its oversight of intelligence operations in 1975; and the
same year terminated covert action in Angola. President Ford
had protested, "Congress has gone too far in trying to take over
the powers that belong to the President and the executive branch.
. . . I'm sure it's a reaction to Watergate and Vietnam."[20]

But the attitudes of individual members of Congress towards
the Presidency, attitudes of distrust bordering on hostility, did
not change with the election of a Democratic President. In October 1979, Stuart Eizenstat, Carter's principal adviser on
domestic policy, concluded, "Moses would have difficulty getting the Ten Comandments through Congress today." By 1980,
Lloyd N. Cutler, Carter's Counsel, declared, "The separation
of powers . . . almost guarantees stalemate today."[21]

Although in the past three years Presidential-Congressional
relations have ameliorated, there is still a long way to go between 535 members of Congress and one President who is and
must be the Nation's commander in chief, chief diplomat, and
the person primarily responsible for national security policy.

By way of example, there have been members of Congress
in this election year who have made misleading charges asserting
the decline of American military readiness. To counter this mischief Assistant Secretary of Defense Lawrence J. Korb, on Au-

gust 24, 1984 issued a detailed public statement indicating that
the United States on that date was prepared to fight a conventional conflict of the intensity of World War II for 30 days; i.e.
twice as long as the United States four years ago was prepared
(15 days) to fight at that level.[22]

But strength is measured in more than armaments. It is also
measured in will, in purpose, in pride. There is much evidence
in 1984 of a resurging patriotism, of a renascent national will.
This is complemented by a vigorous economy, which is unpar-
alleled in creating jobs in the private sector. Moreover, from
the nadir of 1974 we have witnessed over 10 years a restoration
of the leading role of the American Presidency as a political,
as a policy formulating institution. As Ambassador Burns observed it from his Bonn vantage point, "Many Europeans visit
the United States, and they come back with words of astonish-
ment about the dynamism and vitality of our political institutions. We have much to be proud of."[23]

Falsely held, "Pride goeth before a fall." But clearly the flagel-
lation the United States has put itself through over Vietnam
and Watergate should be put behind. We should replace feelings
of guilt and self-recrimination with those of perseverance and pride
in humane service and accomplishment. As Jean-Francois Revel
expressed it, "Clearly a civilization that feels guilty for everything it is and does will lack the energy and the conviction to
defend itself."[24]

More than 30 years ago the British Statesman, Anthony Eden,
wrote this editor regarding the foreign policies of the industrial
democracies: "We must be bold and vigilant lest daily cares cloud
our vision of the task that lies ahead and of the fair fortunes
at our command. . . . But this unity, this understanding, this
sense of interdependence is the heart of the business. Without
it we shall make no headway. With it there is no fair ambition
we cannot realize."[25] In Chapter One, Secretary of State Shultz
reaffirms those principles three decades later: "This partnership — the cornerstone of our foreign policy for 35 years — itself
reflects our ability to combine our moral commitment to democracy and our practical awareness of the crucial importance
of maintaining the global balance of power."[26]

R. Gordon Hoxie
New York City

*September 20, 1984*

# About the Authors

RYAN J. BARILLEAUX, Ph.D., University of Texas at Austin, is Assistant Professor of Political Science at the University of Texas at El Paso. He is a former aide to Senator J. Bennett Johnson. Dr. Barilleaux is the author of works on political theory, including studies in *Presidential Studies Quarterly*.

WALDO W. BRADEN, Ph.D., University of Iowa, is Boyd Professor Emeritus of Speech, Louisiana State University. Dr. Braden is the author or co-author of five volumes and served for 10 years as the editor of the annual volume, *Representative American Speeches*. The former President of the Speech Communication Association, he was also the recipient of the Association's Distinguished Service Award.

RICHARD BROWN, who is associated with Grumman Aerospace Corporation, is a Ph.D. candidate in Politics and International Relations at New York University.

MINTON F. GOLDMAN, Ph.D., Fletcher School of Law and Diplomacy, Tufts University, is Associate Professor of Political Science, Northeastern University. Dr. Goldman has written considerably on Communism and the Soviet Union.

DAVID HAIGHT is an archivist at the Dwight D. Eisenhower Presidential Library at Abilene, Kansas. He has served there since 1971 and is a leading authority on Eisenhower Manuscripts.

GLENN P. HASTEDT, Ph.D., Indiana University, is Assistant Professor of Political Science, James Madison University. His areas of research and teaching are national security policy and foreign policy. He has presented papers on intelligence at the national meetings of the American Political Science Association and the American Society for Public Administration and written on intelligence matters.

PHILLIP G. HENDERSON, Assistant Professor of Political Science, University of Maryland, wrote his doctoral dissertation at the University of Michigan on *Dwight David Eisenhower as Chief Executive: Presidential Policy-Making and Administration 1953–1961*.

KENNETH M. HOLLAND, Ph.D., The University of Chicago, is Assistant Professor of Political Science, The University of Vermont. Dr. Holland has contributed 14 articles to professional journals, mostly on legal and constitutional issues. Forthcoming is his new volume, *Comparative Legal Systems: Western Europe and Japan*. Dr. Holland is a Woodrow Wilson Fellow. He has appeared before the Senate Judiciary Committee as an expert witness.

R. GORDON HOXIE, Ph.D., Columbia University, is President, Center for the Study of the Presidency, and Editor, *Presidential Studies Quarterly*. Dr. Hoxie, formerly President of C.W. Post College and Chancellor, Long Island University, is a Brigadier General, United States Air Force (Ret.). He has served as a consultant to both the Department of State and Department of Defense. He is the author, editor, or contributor to more than a dozen volumes on the Presidency and numerous articles in professional journals.

ANDREW F. KREPINEVICH, M.P.A., Harvard, is Assistant Professor of Social Sciences, United States Military Academy. He has written extensively on national security policy.

ROBERT C. MCFARLANE is Assistant to the President for National Security Affairs. He is co-author of the volume *Crisis Resolution* (Westview Press, 1978).

RONALD MCLAURIN, Ph.D., Fletcher School, Tufts University, is Senior Staff Member, Abbott Associates, Inc. Earlier he served in the Office of the Secretary of Defense. Dr. McLaurin is the author, co-author or editor of 11 volumes and author of numerous articles in professional journals.

M. PETER MCPHERSON is the Administrator of the Agency for International Development. A graduate of Michigan State University, he holds an M.B.A. degree from Western Michigan University and J.D. from The American University. He served as Special Assistant to President Ford, practiced law in Washington, D.C. and was Acting Counsel to President Reagan.

FREDERICK W. MARKS III, Ph.D., University of Michigan, has written for such scholarly journals as *Political Science Quarterly*, *The Historian*, *Diplomatic History*, and *Presidential Studies Quarterly*. Dr. Marks's books include *Independence on Trial: Foreign Affairs and the Making of the Constitution* (1973) and *Velvet on Iron: The Diplomacy of Theodore Roosevelt* (1979). The latter has already been twice reprinted. Currently he is writing a major work on Franklin D. Roosevelt.

ROBERT A. RAGAZZO, a summa cum laude graduate of Fordham University, served as a Fellow at the Center for the Study of the Presidency. Presently he is studying law at Harvard University.

HAROLD C. RELYEA, Ph.D., The American University, is a senior staff member of the Congressional Research Service of the Library of Congress. The author of more than 50 published articles, Dr. Relyea is a leading authority on United States government information policy and practice. His books include *The Presidency and Information Policy* (1981) and *Freedom of Information Trends in the Information Age* (1983).

HENRY S. ROWEN is Professor of Industrial Management, Stanford University and Senior Fellow at the Hoover Institution. He holds degrees from both the Massachusetts Institute of Technology and Oxford University. The former President of the Rand Corporation, he served for two years as Chairman, National Intelligence Council.

BRENT SCOWCROFT, Ph.D., Columbia University, served as Chairman, Department of Political Science, United States Air Force Academy; Military Assistant to the President; and Assistant to the President for National Security Affairs. Recently he headed the Scowcroft Commission on national security policies.

GEORGE P. SHULTZ, B.A., Princeton, Ph.D. Massachusetts Institute of Technology is the United States Secretary of State. He has written extensively in the field of economics and management policy. His most recent volume (with Kenneth W. Dam) is *Economic Policy Beyond the Headlines*.

JOHN W. VESSEY, Jr., is Chairman of the Joint Chiefs of Staff and the principal military advisor to the President. A graduate of the University of Maryland, with his master of science degree from George Washington University, General Vessey is also a graduate of the Industrial College of the Armed Forces. He has lectured and written extensively on national security policy.

WALLACE E. WALKER, Ph.D., Massachusetts Institute of Technology, is Associate Professor of Social Sciences, United States Military Academy. He has written extensively on national security policy.

JAMES D. WEAVER, Ph.D., New York University, is Associate Professor of Politics at Marymount College in Tarrytown, New York. His especial interests are in national security affairs. He has served as an American Council on Education Government Fellow at the Department of Defense.

CASPAR W. WEINBERGER, A.B., LL.B., Harvard, has served since January 1981 as United States Secretary of Defense. Earlier government service (1970–75) included Chairman, Federal Trade Commission; Director, Office of Management and Budget; Counsellor to the President; and Secretary, Department of Health, Education and Welfare. From 1975–80 Mr. Weinberger served as General Counsel, Vice President, and Director, Bechtel Corporation.

# Foreword

It is a particular pleasure to be invited by Gordon Hoxie to write the Foreword for this significant volume: *The Presidency and National Security Policy*. In 1977 I had some modest involvement related to the national security policies of the Ford administration, for the volume *Command Decision and the Presidency*. In part, this new volume is a sequel to that study of national security policy and organization. President Ford had himself written the Foreword for the *Command Decision* volume, noting "Gordon Hoxie has identified constitutional issues which concerned me during my Presidency and which continue to concern me as a private citizen. . . . It seems to me . . . that in the last few years the Congress has become too minutely involved in the day-by-day operation of foreign policy. . . . Moreover, I do question the constitutionality of any legislation authorizing the Congress, by joint resolution, to direct the withdrawal of the armed forces of the United States while engaged in combat or to terminate a declaration of national emergency."[1] For my part, I still share those concerns expressed by President Ford in 1977.

The present volume begins and ends on a fundamental note. One person is primarily responsible for this nation's security: the President. I am particularly pleased that Secretary Shultz has written the first chapter. Therein he counsels "both Congress and the executive branch, [to] exercise our prerogatives with a due regard to the national need for an effective foreign policy. Congress has the right, indeed the duty, to debate and criticize, to authorize and appropriate funds and share in setting the broad lines of policy. But micromanagement by a committee of 535 independent-minded individuals is a grossly inefficient and ineffective way to run any important enterprise." As one who served as national security advisor under President Ford, it is of especial interest to me that Secretary Shultz cites President Ford's continuing concerns on this issue. President Ford summed it all up in his final State of the Union Message when he said, "There can be only one Commander in Chief." Secretary Shultz, like Presidents Ford and Reagan, demonstrates concern about conflicts between the War Powers Resolution of 1973 and the President's responsibilities as Commander in Chief. Every President who has served since its enactment has questioned its constitutionality. In the final chapter, one of the outstanding young scholars who have contributed to this volume, Dr. Kenneth M. Holland, concludes, "Even if the War Powers Resolution were constitutional, Presidents would be forced by necessity to violate it."

Between Chapter One and Chapter Twenty there is a remarkable array of views on the vital issue of The Presidency and National Security Policy. As Julius Caesar referred to Gaul, this volume is divided into three parts: (1) programmatic considerations; (2) historical views; and (3) organization, reform, and strategy.

In Chapter Two, Secretary of Defense Weinberger emphasizes the vital importance of "restoring the military balance with the Soviet Union." He also points out that President Reagan has repeatedly emphasized his determination to negotiate "significant, mutual, verifiable arms reduction agreements with the Soviet Union." Secretary Weinberger supports "arms reduction, not arms control or arms limitation. Reduction has to be the key word and the key goal." He perceives the new advancing technologies as weapons for peace. "They offer the Soviets new incentives to join with us in genuine reductions of both nuclear and conventional forces."

In Chapter Three, with the title taken from the constitutional phrase, "to provide for the common defence," Chairman Vessey of the Joint Chiefs of Staff presents our national defense posture. "Now, we want to make it very clear if deterrence fails we can and will retaliate to any sort of attack, whether it is conventional or nuclear. We will do it in a way that guarantees to our enemies that their wartime objectives cannot be achieved. We believe that if the Soviets understand that, and that if we can employ modern forces to do that, we have a good opportunity to prevent war."

In Chapter Four, Henry S. Rowen, former Chairman, National Intelligence Council, examines Soviet leadership changes, with the important observation that "In an age in which bureaucracies seem to have taken over, the personalities of leaders are still important." Rowen succinctly describes the Soviet military threat: "The military power which the Soviet leadership has at its disposal is formidable. . . . The Soviets have built a strong nuclear weapons establishment rivaling our own and, indeed, one that has been on a faster track. It has created a

modern nuclear threat to Europe and other peripheral areas with
its SS-20 missiles among other weapons. It has fielded an armed
force opposite Western Europe which is large, modern and
growing. Its navy has moved from coastal defense to a capacity
to roam the seas. And it has, in addition built up a powerful
force opposite China." With a stagnant economy, social and
demographic problems, and important leadership issues, the future is clouded for the Soviets. One recourse for them has been
détente. As Rowen points out, "The basis for East-West détente
in the early 1970's was economic interaction indeed, support,
for the Soviet Union in exchange for Soviet restraint on arms
and foreign adventures. It foundered on the Soviet's unwillingness to adhere to their side of the bargain." In a postscript written
in March 1984, Rowen projects "big changes" in the Soviet system
by the end of the decade. The present generation of older leaders
will be gone and "the sense of crisis within the system will be
so palpable as to make such changes politically possible."

In the ensuing chapter, Dr. Glenn P. Hastedt examines the
intelligence community, particularly the CIA, comparing
the Carter and Reagan policies in these matters. By and large,
the Reagan management under William J. Casey comes through
with higher marks than Carter's under Stansfield Turner. Morale in the intelligence community reached a low point with
Turner's drastic personnel reductions. The essay concludes with
the estimate that Casey "will probably leave a more permanent
imprint on the CIA, indeed on the IC (intelligence community)
than any of his predecessors."

In the concluding chapter in Part One on programmatic considerations, Peter McPherson discusses the Reagan Administration's programs of aid for Third World countries. He believes
"it is an interesting historical anomaly that a conservative Republican Administration would end up with a Presidency more involved with foreign aid than has been the case for at least a decade." In a March 1984 Epilogue to his essay Mr. McPherson
emphasizes two critical areas: Central America and Africa. "Central America is severely wounded," he concludes. "Band-aids
will not do. Our proposal [based on the Kissinger Commission's
recommendations] seeks to provide those countries with appropriate materials in sufficient amounts to successfully heal themselves and regain economic and social health." The urgent attention to Central America, however, should not let us lose focus

on the critical conditions of drought and hunger in Africa. A massive aid program is planned for African countries, going beyond food assistance to encourage economic growth. McPherson concludes that the "Administration's underlying commitment . . . is to help people of the third world help themselves — and then leave. We seek friends, not inferiors, partners, not dependents. Most of all, we seek a world at peace."

Part Two, "A Century of National Security Policy", begins with Robert A. Ragazzo's essay on Grover Cleveland and Venezuela. Here is a prime example of an ill-advised, ill-informed program. As a result, " . . . President Cleveland risked a war with Great Britain that the United States probably could not have won. . . . " President Cleveland sought to force Great Britain to submit to arbitration a boundary dispute with Venezuela in an area in which the British had a strong claim. In the course of the dispute, the United States in 1895 made new assertions of predominance in the western hemisphere. It came at a time when American armed forces were woefully inadequate, with only one modern battleship to oppose the world's number one seapower and an army one-sixth the size of that of the British. Fortunately the confrontation came at a time when Britain wanted to make a friend, not a foe, of the United States. Indeed, Ragazzo concludes, "The United States aggressive action was more resented on the European continent than in Great Britain."

Chapter Eight is a penetrating, if controversial, analysis by Dr. Frederick W. Marks of the Hull-Nomura talks of 1941 which preceded the attack on Pearl Harbor. Dr. Marks asserts, "Few episodes in American diplomatic history have been as much misunderstood as the protracted diplomatic exchange carried on between Washington and Tokyo during the year 1941." The talks began in March 1941 when Admiral Nomura was sent as a special ambassador from Premier Konoye. According to Marks, "The *coup de grace* came on November 26 when [Secretary of State] Hull presented Tokyo with a list of demands totally divorced from the context of the past six months and calling for Japanese withdrawal from Manchuko." Marks concludes, "Any reader who has attempted to thread his way through the record of those talks will not be surprised that a task force of Japanese carriers was soon on its way to Hawaii." Marks points out that Japanese anger and frustration was complemented by the success of Japan's partners in the Axis Alliance, Germany and Italy. Hitler was in control of all of western Europe and was seemingly invulnerable in marching across Russia. Japanese proponents of the Axis were in their strongest position on the eve of Pearl Harbor. At that point, war with Japan was the last thing the British wanted. Indeed, the British ambassador to Washington, Lord Halifax, was of the view that the United States had challenged Japan "to the point where she felt compelled to stand and fight."

President Franklin D. Roosevelt fares better in the ensuing chapter analyzing his wartime fireside chats. Beyond the speeches themselves, Professor Waldo W. Braden portrays "how Roosevelt moved from a position of neutrality to the advocacy of support of the allies and eventually to participation in the conflict." Here was no mean accomplishment, " . . . countering the efforts of the isolationists and pacifists, mobilizing the civilians and military for preparedness, supporting the British, French, and Chinese when they seemed to be losing, sustaining his popularity, and winning re-election in 1940 and 1944." After the Teheran Conference of November 1943, at which Roosevelt first met Stalin, he reported to the American people by radio: "To use an American and somewhat ungrammatical colloquialism I may say that I 'got along fine' with Marshall Stalin." Braden concludes Robert A. Divine's assessment of Roosevelt, "a shrewd tactician, a man who displayed great skill in manipulating men and great flexibility in interweaving ideas and principles, even contradictory ones."

The next two chapters focus on the Eisenhower Presidency. The first, by Phillip G. Henderson, focuses on the Eisenhower National Security Council. Based upon recently declassified documents, Henderson takes issue with the "conventional wisdom" of Richard Neustadt, Stanley L. Falk, and others. For example, Neustadt wrote that "Eisenhower seemingly preferred to let subordinates proceed upon the lowest common denominators of agreement. . . . " Henderson concludes, "Traditional scholarship notwithstanding, the Eisenhower system brought about routinization without excessive rigidity and fostered broad advice rather than watered down bureaucratic consensus."

During the Eisenhower years there were a record 366 meetings of the NSC, with the President presiding at 329 of them. Perhaps in more detail than any other President, Eisenhower made the NSC an effective instrument both for policy formulation and implementation. His predecessor, President Truman had kept the NSC at arms length at least until the Korean War. Eisenhower created the position of Special Assistant for National Security Affairs. Throughout the eight years of his Presidency there was an effective relationship between the incumbents in that position, Robert Cutler, Dillon Anderson, and Gordon Gray, and the NSC members. Despite President Eisenhower's strong recommendations to President-elect Kennedy on the vital importance of the NSC, and Gordon Gray's advice to his own successor, McGeorge Bundy, the machinery of the NSC was virtually dismantled at the beginning of the Kennedy administration. Even such a strong Kennedy defender as Theodore Sorensen admitted that "the new administration had not fully organized itself for crisis planning." Future Presidential transition teams can profit from the Henderson essay.

The other Eisenhower essay, that by David Haight on the 1960 U.N. Summit, is likewise based upon previously unpublished documents. Persons reflecting events of the past year in American-Soviet relations may find interesting analogies in the 1960 experiences. In 1983, the Soviets shot down a Korean airliner which had entered Soviet air space and subsequently walked out of the Intermediate Range Nuclear Forces talks in Geneva. In June, 1960, the Soviets walked out of the Ten Nation Disarmament Conference at Geneva and the following month shot down an American plane which allegedly had violated Soviet air space. Khrushchev announced it would be futile to deal with Eisenhower and proposed a post-election summit meeting six to eight months after the election. Then, in October, 1960, he came to New York, where he presented his own disarmament proposals, not only at the United Nations but also on American television. He encouraged the belief that an East-West meeting would be more effective after Eisenhower was no longer President. Since Eisenhower's Vice President was a candidate for the Presidency, it could be inferred that the Soviets believed that the other candidate, Senator Kennedy, would be more effective in improving relations with the Soviets. A number of neutralist leaders proposed a meeting between Eisenhower and Khrushchev while the latter was in New York. In the then climate of Soviet vituperation, the Department of State shared

Eisenhower's opposition to such a meeting. Haight concludes that Khrushchev himself "never seriously considered a meeting with Eisenhower at the U.N. to be feasible. . . . " In brief, the Soviets used it as a propaganda ploy. As for Eisenhower, the author concludes, "It does show that President Eisenhower was clearly in charge of the conduct of U.S. foreign policy during this period." This chapter is especially interesting in light of the current state of United States-Soviet relations.

Dr. Ryan J. Barilleaux's essay, "Kennedy, The Bay of Pigs, and the Limits of Collegial Decision Making," is of special utility for policy planners. Much recent literature recommends a collegial system of decision-making which "eschews a hierarchical decision mechanism for a set of collegially related advisors." (See for example Alexander George's *Presidential Decisionmaking in Foreign Affairs* and Roger Porter's *Presidential Decision Making*.) Dr. Barilleaux questions the soundness of the collegial system by examining decisionmaking in the Bay of Pigs planning. He notes that the National Security Council, which had begun preliminary planning of the operation in the last weeks of the Eisenhower administration, had no real role in the Kennedy planning. Instead, President Kennedy "relied on an informal, select group of his advisors to deliberate on the plan. . . . " Dr. Barilleaux finds three basic weaknesses in collegial planning: (1) Demands on the President's Time and Attention; (2) Lack of Routine Oversight; and (3) Susceptibility to Personality and Charisma. The author notes that Presidents Kennedy, Johnson, and Carter all tended towards the collegial system and "it is likely to be used again in the future." Presidential candidates, as well as policy planners, can profit from this essay.

In the final essay in this section on the historical examination of decision-making, Dr. Minton P. Goldman seeks to examine the considerations which prompted the Soviet military intervention in Afghanistan. He asserts, "The Soviets concluded that, because of an ambivalence in [U.S.] decision making, a perceived willingness to conciliate, and an evident reluctance to use military force in support of foreign policy, President Carter would not try to block their intervention in Afghanistan." Further, he believes, "The Soviets accurately surmised American weakness in west central Asia." Further, "They seemed to have been led by the Carter Administration — quite inadvertently, of course, and despite its signals to the contrary—to believe that a move into Afghanistan would not cause serious or long term damage to their relationship with the United States. . . . "

The concluding section of this volume focuses on organization and strategy. It begins with an essay by Dr. James D. Weaver on how the framers of the Constitution conceived the position of Commander in Chief. Dr. Weaver quotes Hamilton in *The Federalist* that Commander in Chief means "nothing more than supreme command and direction of army and navy, as first General and Admiral of the Confederacy." But, as Weaver shrewdly observes, "Clearly in *The Federalist* Hamilton, desirous for the adoption of the Constitution, was seeking to assuage the anxieties of the anti-federalists." He believes Hamilton and other Framers perceived "the President's Commander in Chief power [as] distinctively expansive and congruent to his other executive responsibilities and prerogatives. . . . " As such, an office had been created which could "motivate and assemble the formation of an integrated command and central apparatus," as competent and valid today as in the first Washington administration.

It is a particular pleasure for me to note the chapter by my former colleague, Robert C. McFarlane, Assistant to the President for National Security Affairs. He clearly and insightfully sets forth the organization and operation of the National Security Council. McFarlane points out that "The NSC system that has evolved over the past four years is designed to bring together four pillars of national security—foreign policy, defense policy, economic policy, and intelligence operations—in ways that support the president's ability to make wise and timely decisions." He notes the President's "fundamental commitment to cabinet government" and the importance of balancing this "with the need for central policy, guidance and control." Interagency coordination is key in the achievement of these considerations. This has led to the establishment of Senior Interagency Groups (SIGs) and Interagency Groups (IGs). Each SIG is chaired by a cabinet member and each IG by an assistant secretary. McFarlane concludes, "The present system is suited to President Reagan's leadership style and to his views on how his administration should be run. The underlying principles of coordination and thorough policy analysis, however, are applicable to any administration.

The challenge is to adapt these to the individual desires and objectives of each chief executive."

Dr. Harold C. Relyea gives us an encompassing essay on emergency powers, with particular reference to the National Emergencies Act of 1976. He observes that emergency power extending beyond Constitutional prescriptions is grounded in Lockean doctrine, which Hamilton set forth in Federalist Paper No. 23. "These powers ought to exist without limitation; because it is impossible to foresee or to define the extent and variety of national exigencies, and the correspondent extent and variety of the means which may be necessary to satisfy them." President Lincoln, during the Civil War, set forth the absolute power of self-defense (*salus populi, suprema* lex): "I felt that measures, otherwise unconstitutional, might become lawful, by becoming indispensable to the preservation of the constitution through the preservation of the nation."

The National Emergencies Act of 1976 seeks to give Congress the means to limit those powers. The Act rescinds all powers obtained by the president and other members of the executive branch through previously declared emergencies. Then it authorizes Congress to terminate future presidential declarations of emergency by concurrent Congressional resolutions, not subject to Presidential veto. It further requires the President, in declaring an emergency, to advise Congress of the provisions of law under which he acts. The President and federal agencies must report to Congress all rules and regulations issued during an emergency, as well as expenditures, and at six month intervals the Congress must consider whether an emergency should be terminated. Here is a law not unlike the War Powers Resolution in its relationship to the authority of the Commander in Chief and like the War Powers Resolution it may be of doubtful Constitutionality. The recent *Chadha* decision by the Supreme Court would suggest that the legislative veto provisions of both the War Powers Resolution and the National Emergency Act are inadmissable.

The ensuing two chapters deal with national security policy and policy-making. In Chapter Seventeen Richard Brown examines the American foreign policy-making process. He notes many proposals to restore to the Department of State its leadership in foreign policy making (including I. M. Destler's proposal to subordinate the position of the National Security Adviser).[2] Nonetheless, Brown concludes that foreign policymaking inevitably gravitates from State to the White House. While stating this principle, he admits in fact that there have been and are still Presidents placing leadership in State: Eisenhower, Ford, and Reagan. He writes:

> The last person to clearly place the leadership in foreign policy at State was Eisenhower, with John Foster Dulles; albeit Ford did it for a shorter period with Kissinger at State and Scowcroft at the White House. Now in the fourth year of the Reagan administration, Reagan is making a clear effort in the same direction. Like Scowcroft who trained him, Robert C. McFarlane is a low-key White House national security adviser. Shultz has earned the respect both of State and the White House. Still this writer believes after Reagan, after Shultz, almost inevitably the balance, the leadership of foreign policy will shift back from State to the White House.

This may or may not happen, depending on the predilections of the next President. A thoughtful President will choose his Secretary of State, Secretary of Defense, and Assistant to the President for National Security Affairs with concern not only for their abilities, but as well for their personalities and ability to work together. The relative balance of authority among them will also depend on the operating style of the President and no particular relationship is therefore inevitable.

In the next chapter Dr. R. D. McLaurin begins with the searching question: "What prevents the United States from pursuing clear-cut interests with equally clear-cut policies as the country is said to have done during the Eisenhower-Dulles period?" Aside from the unique preeminence of Eisenhower as President, McLaurin suggests several factors in the subsequent lessening of clarity and coherence. One of these is that, in the 1980s, the United States no longer enjoys unchallenged military superiority. Another is in ourselves; the lack of consensus that has marred this nation since the late 1960s.

McLaurin proposes the establishment "of a unified department of national security. . . . " While retaining the Secretary of State and Secretary of Defense as administrators of their respective departments and continuing them as cabinet members, he would create a new super cabinet post, secretary of national security, who would be the principal advisor to the President for national security affairs. McLaurin concludes, "A national reallocation of responsibilities in accordance with the matters of contemporary U.S. national security requirements is long overdue."

This is not the first such proposal. Dr. Milton S. Eisenhower, who was perhaps his brother's closest advisor during the Eisenhower Presidency, has proposed two Executive Vice Presidents: one for Domestic Affairs and one for International Affairs. Each would head executive departments and agencies. He proposes, "The Executive Vice President for International Affairs, like his domestic counterpart, should be ranked above the Cabinet, just below the President. . . . He may then deal with the heads of all departments and agencies concerned. He should be the vice chairman of the National Security Council." The two executive vice presidencies would, Dr. Eisenhower contends, give the President more *time* to consider major issues. He quotes Pericles: "Wait for the wisest of all Counselors. Time."[3]

The ensuing chapter by Wallace Earl Walker and Andrew F. Krepinevich considers "The Politics of Defense Policy-Making." The two authors believe, "The most significant U.S. political development" of the past 10 years is "the ascendency of conservatives. . . . " This has contributed to Congressional and Presidential support for strengthening the Nation's armed forces. The authors believe this phenomenon has been aided by conservative think tanks like the American Enterprise Institute, the Georgetown University Center for Strategic and International Studies, and the Hoover Institution, and by a number of influential books.[4] A number of counter-tendencies have also developed. Groups such as the nuclear freeze movement have gained considerable Congressional support, as has the Military Reform Caucus, and institutions such as the Center for Defense Information. The variety and diversity of such groups and the debate over defense and budget deficits have made the task of developing a national consensus extremely difficult. The authors conclude that President Reagan has exercised great skill in moving towards his defense goals in a climate where there is so little consensus.

And so we come to Chapter Twenty which, like Chapter One and so many others, points up the constitutional and political challenges confronting the President as Commander in Chief and in formulating and implementing national security policy. In its breadth and depth from our state of readiness, to the intelligence community, to organization and strategy, highlighting aspects of national security policy for the last 100 years with special reference to Franklin D. Roosevelt and Dwight David Eisenhower, and reviewing our present defense policy, this volume has made a major contribution. We owe a debt of gratitude to each of the contributors to this thought-provoking volume and to the Center for the Study of the Presidency which made it possible. The President stated it well for all of us when he wrote on June 28, 1984, "Let me . . . express my appreciation . . . to the Center for the Study of the Presidency for distinguished service in behalf of our Nation."

BRENT SCOWCROFT
Bethesda, Maryland
September 14, 1984

# PART ONE

# Programmatic Considerations

CHAPTER ONE

# Power and Diplomacy in the 1980s*

**GEORGE P. SHULTZ**
THE SECRETARY OF STATE

Over 20 years ago, President John Kennedy pledged that the United States would "pay any price, bear any burden, meet any hardship, support any friend, oppose any foe, in order to assure the survival and the success of liberty." We know now that the scope of that commitment is too broad — though the self-confidence and courage in those words were typically American and most admirable. More recently, another administration took the view that our fear of communism was "inordinate" and that there were very complicated social, economic, religious, and other factors at work in the world that we had little ability to affect. This, in my view, is a counsel of helplessness that substantially underestimates the United States and its ability to influence events.

Somewhere between these two poles lies the natural and sensible scope of American foreign policy. We know that we are not omnipotent and that we must set priorities. We cannot pay *any* price or bear *any* burden. We must discriminate; we must be prudent and careful; we must respond in ways appropriate to the challenge and engage our power only when very important strategic stakes are involved. Not every situation can be salvaged by American exertion even when important values or interests are at stake.

At the same time, we know from history that courage and vision and determination can change reality. We can affect events, and all we know it. The American people expect this of their leaders. And the future of the free world depends on it.

Americans, being a moral people, want their foreign policy to reflect the values we espouse as a nation. But Americans, being

* *This essay by Secretary Shultz is based upon his April 3, 1984 address before the Trilateral Commission, Washington, D.C.*

a practical people, also want their foreign policy to be effective. If we truly care about our values, we must be prepared to defend them and advance them. Thus we as a nation are perpetually asking ourselves how to reconcile our morality and our practical sense, how to pursue noble goals in a complex and imperfect world, how to relate our strength to our purposes — in sum, how to relate power and diplomacy.

This essay in the new volume, *The Presidency and National Security Policy*, will follow the excitement of America's quadrennial exercise of self-renewal, in which we as a country reexamine ourselves and our international objectives. It is an unending process — almost as unending as the presidential campaign season. But there are some constants in our policy, such as our alliance with the industrial democracies. This partnership — the cornerstone of our foreign policy for 35 years — itself reflects our ability to combine our moral commitment to democracy and our practical awareness of the crucial importance of maintaining the global balance of power. So I consider this an appropriate forum at which to share some thoughts on the relationship between power and diplomacy in the last two decades of the 20th century.

## The World We Face

By the accident of history, the role of world leadership fell to the United States just at the moment when the old international order had been destroyed by two world wars but no new stable system had developed to replace it. A century ago, the international system was centered on Europe and consisted of only a few major players. Today, in terms of military strength, the dominant countries are two major powers that had been in one sense or another, on the edge or outside European diplomacy. But economic power is now widely dispersed. Asia is taking on increasing significance. The former colonial empires have been dismantled, and there are now more than 160 independent nations on the world scene. Much of the developing world itself is torn by a continuing struggle between the forces of moderation and the forces of radicalism. Most of the major international conflicts since 1945 have taken place there — from Korea to Vietnam to the Middle East to Central America. Moreover, the Soviet Union continues to exploit nuclear fear as a political weapon and to exploit instabilities wherever they have the opportunity to do so.

On a planet grown smaller because of global communications, grown more turbulent because of the diffusion of power — all the while overshadowed by nuclear weapons — the task of achieving stability, security, and progress is a profound challenge for mankind. In an age menaced by nuclear proliferation and state-sponsored terrorism, tendencies toward anarchy are bound to be a source of real dangers.

It is absurd to think that America can walk away from these problems. This is a world of great potential instability and great potential danger. There is no safety in isolationism. We have a major, direct stake in the health of the world economy; our prosperity, our security, and our alliances can be affected by threats to security in many parts of the world; and the fate of our fellow human beings will always impinge on our moral consciousness. Certainly the United States is not the world's policeman. But we are the world's strongest free nation, and, therefore, the preservation of our values, our principles, and our hopes for a better world rests in great measure, inevitably, on our shoulders.

### Power and Diplomacy

In this environment, our principal goal is what President Reagan has called "the most basic duty that any President and any people share — the duty to protect and strengthen the peace." History teaches, however, that peace is not achieved merely by wishing for it. Noble aspirations are not self-fulfilling. Our aim must always be to shape events and not be the victim of events. In this fast-moving and turbulent world, to sit in a reactive posture is to risk being overwhelmed or to allow others, who may not wish us well, to decide the world's future.

The Great Seal of the United States, as you know, shows the American eagle clutching arrows in one claw and olive branches in the other. The Great Seal appears on some of the china and other antique objects in the White House and in the ceremonial rooms on the eighth floor of the State Department. On some of the older items, the eagle looks toward the arrows, on others, toward the olive branches. It was President Truman who set it straight: he saw to it that the eagle always looked toward the olive branches — showing that America sought peace. But the eagle still holds onto those arrows.

This is a way of saying that our forefathers understood quite well that power and diplomacy always go together. It is even clearer today that a world of peace and security will not come about without exertion or without facing up to some tough choices. Certainly power must always be guided by purpose, but the hard reality is that diplomacy not backed by strength is ineffectual. That is why, for example, the United States has succeeded many times in its mediation when many other well-intentioned mediators have failed. Leverage, as well as good will, is required.

Americans have sometimes tended to think that power and diplomacy are two distinct alternatives. To take a very recent example, the Long commission report on the bombing of our Marine barracks in Beirut urged that we work harder to pursue what it spoke of as "diplomatic alternatives," as opposed to "military options." This reflects a fundamental misunderstanding — not only of our intensive diplomatic efforts throughout the period but of the relationship between power and diplomacy. Sometimes, regrettable as it may be, political conflict degenerates into a test of strength. It was precisely our military role in Lebanon that was problematical, not our diplomatic exertion. Our military role was hamstrung by legislative and other inhibitions; the Syrians were not interested in diplomatic compromise so long as the prospect of hegemony was not foreclosed. They could judge from our domestic debate that our staying power was limited.

In arms control, also, successful negotiation depends on the perception of a military balance. Only if the Soviet leaders see the West as determined to modernize its own forces will they see an incentive to negotiate agreements establishing equal, verifiable, and lower levels of armaments.

The lesson is that power and diplomacy are not alternatives. They must go together, or we will accomplish very little in this world.

The relationship between them is a complex one, and it presents us with both practical and moral issues. One is the variety of the challenges we face. A second is the moral complexity of our response. A third is the problem of managing the process in a democracy.

## The Range of Challenges

Perhaps because of our long isolation from the turmoil of world politics, Americans have tended to believe that war and peace, too, were two totally distinct phenomena: we were either in a blissful state of peace, or else (as in World Wars I and II) we embarked on an all-out quest for total victory, after which we wanted to retreat back into inward-looking innocence, avoiding "power politics" and all it represented. During World War II, while singlemindedly seeking the unconditional surrender of our enemies, we paid too little heed to the emerging postwar balance of power.

Similarly, since 1945 we have experienced what we saw as a period of clear-cut cold war, relieved by a period of seeming detente which raised exaggerated expectations in some quarters. Today we must see the East-West relationship as more complex, with the two sides engaging in trade and pursuing arms control even as they pursue incompatible aims. It is not as crisis prone or starkly confrontational as the old cold war; but neither is it a normal relationship of peace or comfortable coexistence.

Thus, in the 1980s and beyond, most likely we will never see a state of total war or a state of total peace. We face instead a spectrum of often ambiguous challenges to our interests.

We are relatively well prepared to deter an all-out war or a Soviet attack on our West European and Far Eastern allies; that's why these are the least likely contingencies. But, day in and day out, we will continue to see a wide range of conflicts that fall in a gray area between major war and millennial peace. The coming years can be counted upon to generate their share of crises and local outbreaks of violence. Some of them — not all of them — will affect our interests. Terrorism — particularly state-sponsored terrorism — is already a contemporary weapon directed at America's interests, America's values, and America's allies. We must be sure we are as well prepared and organized for this intermediate range of challenges.

If we are to protect our interests, values, and allies, we must be engaged. And our power must be engaged.

It is often said that the lesson of Vietnam is that the United States should not engage in military conflict without a clear and precise military mission, solid public backing, and enough resources to finish the job. This is undeniably true. But does it mean there are no situations where a discrete assertion of power is needed or appropriate for limited purposes? Unlikely. Whether it is crisis management or power projection or a show of force or peacekeeping or a localized military action, there will always be instances that fall short of an all-out national commitment on the scale of World War II. The need to avoid no-win situations cannot mean that we turn automatically away from hard-to-win situations that call for prudent involvement. These will always involve risks; we will not always have the luxury of being able to choose the most advantageous circumstances. And our adversaries can be expected to play rough.

The Soviets are students of Clausewitz, who taught that war is a continuation of politics by other means. It is highly unlikely that we can respond to gray-area challenges without adapting power to political circumstances or on a psychologically satisfying, all-or-nothing basis. This is just not the kind of reality we are likely to be facing in the 1980s, or 1990s, or beyond. Few cases will be as clear or as quick as Grenada. On the contrary, most other cases will be a lot tougher.

We have no choice, moreover, but to address ourselves boldly to the challenge of terrorism. State-sponsored terrorism is really a form of warfare. Motivated by ideology and political hostility, it is a weapon of unconventional war against democratic societies, taking advantage of the openness of these societies. How do we combat this challenge? Certainly we must take security precautions to protect our people and our facilities; certainly we must strengthen our intelligence capabilities to alert ourselves to the threats. But it is increasingly doubtful that a purely passive strategy can even begin to cope with the problem. This raises a host of questions for a free society: in what circumstances — and how — should we respond? When — and how — should we take preventive or preemptive action against known terrorist groups? What evidence do we insist upon before taking such steps?

As the threat mounts — and as the involvement of such countries as Iran, Syria, Libya, and North Korea has become more and more evident — then it is more and more appropriate that the nations of the West face up to the need for active defense against terrorism. Once it becomes established that terrorism works — that it achieves its political objectives — its practitioners will be bolder, and the threat to us will be all the greater.

## The Moral Issues

Of course, any use of force involves moral issues. American military power should be resorted to only if the stakes justify it, if other means are not available, and then only in a manner appropriate to the objective. But we cannot opt out of every contest. If we do, the world's future will be determined by others — most likely by those who are the most brutal, the most unscrupulous, and the most hostile to our deeply held principles. *The New Republic* stated it well recently.

> [T]he American people know that force and the threat of force are central to the foreign policy of our adversaries, and they expect their President to be able to deter and defeat such tactics.

As we hear now in the debate over military aid to Central America, those who shrink from engagement can always find an alibi for inaction. Often it takes the form of close scrutiny of any moral defects in the friend or ally whom we are proposing to assist. Or it is argued that the conflict has deep social and economic origins which we really have to address first before we have a right to do anything else.

But rather than remain engaged in order to tackle these problems — as we are trying to do — some people turn the concerns into formulas for abdication, formulas that would allow the enemies of freedom to decide the outcome. To me, it is highly immoral to let friends who depend on us be subjugated by brute force if we have the capacity to prevent it.

There is, in addition, another ugly residue of our Vietnam debate: the notion, in some quarters, that America is the guilty party, that the use of our power is a source of evil and, therefore, the main task in foreign policy is to restrain America's freedom to act. It is inconceivable to me that the American people believe any of this. It is certainly not President Reagan's philosophy.

Without being boastful or arrogant, the American people know that their country has been a powerful force for good in the world. We helped Europe and Asia — including defeated enemies — rebuild after the war, and we helped provide a security shield behind which they could build democracy and freedom as well as prosperity. Americans have often died and sacrificed for the freedom of others. We have provided around $165 billion in economic assistance for the developing world. It is of interest to me that M. Peter McPherson, Administrator, Agency for International Development, is the author of one of the chapters in this volume. We have played a vital facilitating role in the Middle East peace process, in the unfolding diplomacy of southern Africa, as well as in many other diplomatic efforts around the globe.

We have used our power for good and worthy ends. In Grenada, we helped restore self-determination to the people of Grenada, so that they could choose their own future. Some have tried to compare what we did in Grenada to the Soviet invasion of Afghanistan. We welcome such comparison. Contrast, for example, the prospects for free elections in the two countries. In Grenada, they will be held this year; in Afghanistan, when? Contrast the number of American combat troops now in Grenada 5 months after the operation with the number of Soviet troops in Afghanistan 55 months after their invasion. The number in Grenada is 0; the number in Afghanistan is over 100,000.

More often, the issue is not the direct use of American military power but military assistance to friends to help them defend themselves. Around the world, security support for friends is a way to prevent crises; it bolsters our friends so they can deter challenges. And it is a way of avoiding the involvement of American forces, because it is only when our friends' efforts in their own defense are being overwhelmed that we are faced with the agonizing decision whether to involve ourselves more directly. Security assistance is thus an essential tool of foreign policy. It is an instrument for deterring those who would impose their will by force and for making political solutions possible. It gets far less support in this country than it deserves.

Central America is a good example. The real moral question in Central America is not do we believe in military solutions, but do we believe in ourselves? Do we believe that our security and the security of our neighbors has moral validity? Do we have faith in our own democratic values? Do we believe that Marxist-Leninist solutions are antidemocratic and that we have a moral right to try to stop those who are trying to impose them by force? Sure, economic and social problems underlie many of these conflicts. But in El Salvador, the communist guerrillas are waging war directly against the economy, blowing up bridges and power stations, deliberately trying to wreck the country's economy.

The conflict in Central America is not a debate between social theorists; it is one of those situations where the outcome of political competition will depend in large measure on the balance of military strength. In El Salvador, the United States is supporting moderates who believe in democracy and who are resisting the enemies of democracy on both the extreme right and the extreme left. If we withdrew our support, the moderates, caught in the crossfire, would be the first victims — as would be the cause of human rights and the prospects for economic development. Anyone who believes that military support for our friends isn't crucial to a just outcome is living in a dream world. And anyone who believes that military support can be effective when its given on an uncertain installment plan is not facing reality.

### Accountability Without Paralysis

The third issue I want to point up is the question of how this country, as a democracy, conducts itself in the face of such challenges.

Over the last 35 years, the evolution of the international system was bound to erode the predominant position the United States enjoyed immediately after World War II. But it seems to me that in this disorderly and dangerous new world, the loss of American predominance puts an even greater premium on consistency, determination, and coherence in the conduct of our foreign policy. We have less margin for error than we used to have.

This change in our external circumstances, however, coincided historically with a kind of cultural revolution at home that has made it harder for us to achieve the consistency, determination, and coherence that we need. The last 15 years left a legacy of contention between the executive and legislative branches and a web of restrictions on executive action embedded permanently in our laws. At the same time, the diffusion of power within the Congress means that a president has a hard time when he wants to negiotiate with the Congress, because congressional leaders have lost their dominance of the process and often cannot produce a consensus or sometimes even a decision.

The net result, as you know, is an enormous problem for American foreign policy — a loss of coherence and recurring uncertainty in the minds of friend and foe about the aims and constancy of the United States.

Particularly in the war powers field, where direct use of our power is at issue, the stakes are high. Yet the War Powers Resolution sets arbitrary 60-day deadlines that practically invite an adversary to wait us out. Our Commander in Chief is locked in battle at home at the same time he is trying to act effectively abroad. Under the resolution, even inaction by the Congress can force the President to remove American forces from an area of challenge, which, as former President Ford has put it, undermines the President even when the Congress can't get up the courage to take a position. As President Ford expressed it, "There can be only one Commander in Chief." Congressional constraints on timely action may only invite greater challenges down the road. In Lebanon our adversaries' perception that we lacked staying power undercut the prospects for successful negotiation. As the distinguished Majority Leader, Senator Howard Baker, said on the floor of the Senate this year:

> [W]e cannot continue to begin each military involvement abroad with a prolonged, tedious and divisive negotiation between the executive and the legislative branches of Government. The world and its many challenges to our interests simply do not allow us that luxury.

I do not propose changes in our constitutional system. But some legislative changes may be called for. And I propose, at a minimum, that all of us, in both Congress and the executive branch, exercise our prerogatives with a due regard to the national need for an effective foreign policy. Congress has the right, indeed the duty, to debate and criticize, to authorize and appropriate funds and share in setting the broad lines of policy. But micromanagement by a commitee of 535 independent-minded individuals is a grossly inefficient and ineffective way to run any important enterprise. The fact is that depriving the President of flexibility weakens our country. Yet a host of restrictions on the President's ability to act are now built into our laws and our procedures. Surely there is a better way for the President and the Congress to exercise their prerogatives without hobbling this country in the face of assaults on free-world interests abroad. Surely there can be accountability without paralysis. The sad truth is that many of our difficulties over the last 15 years have been self-imposed.

The issue is fundamental. If the purpose of our power is to prevent war, or injustice, then ideally we want to discourage such occurrences rather than have to use our power in a physical sense. But this can happen only if there is assurance that our power would be used if necessary.

A reputation for reliability becomes, then, a major asset — giving friends a sense of security and adversaries a sense of caution. A reputation for living up to our commitments can, in fact, make it less likely that pledges of support will have to be carried out. Crisis management is most successful when a favorable outcome is attained without firing a shot. Credibility is an intangible, but it is no less real. The same is true of a loss of credibility. A failure to support a friend always involves a price. Credibility, once lost, has to be re-earned.

### Facing the Future

The dilemmas and hard choices will not go away, no matter who is president. They are not partisan problems. Anyone who claims to have simple answers is talking nonsense.

The United States faces a time of challenge ahead as great as any in recent memory. We have a diplomacy that has moved toward peace through negotiation. We have rebuilt our strength so that we can defend our interests and dissuade others from violence. We have allies whom we value and respect. Our need is to recognize both our challenge and our potential.

Americans are not a timid people. A foreign policy worthy of America must not be a policy of isolationism or guilt but a commitment to active engagement. We can be proud of this country, of what it stands for, and what it has accomplished. Our morality should be a source of courage when we make hard decisions, not a set of excuses for self-paralysis.

President Reagan declared to the British Parliament 2 years ago: "We must be staunch in our conviction that freedom is not the sole prerogative of a lucky few but the inalienable and universal right of all human beings." As long as Americans hold to this belief, we will be actively engaged in the world. We will use our power and our diplomatic skill in the service of peace and of our ideals. We have our work cut out for us. But we will not shrink from our responsibility.

# CHAPTER TWO

# Consensus: The Cement of the Alliance*

## CASPAR W. WEINBERGER
### THE SECRETARY OF DEFENSE

Thirty-five years ago concern for the future of the Western Alliance led to the formation of the Atlantic Institute. In the years that followed, the Alliance has been subjected to many strains and challenges. There have been many claims, that the collective bond was simply an accident of the war and its aftermath of weakness and exhaustion. There have been assertions that it was a bond that could survive neither the economic and political resurgence of Alliance members nor the growing military might of our adversaries. It has been said that when the leadership passed from the generation that learned the hard lessons of collective security in the crucible of war that the need and indeed the existence of the Alliance would perish.

But members of the North American Treaty Organization and members of the Atlantic Institute do not share these prophecies of doom. The Atlantic Institute continues to perform a significant service. It continues to emphasize the need for consensus in the Western Alliance. Its Chairman has posed the question: how we can build, develop, strengthen and maintain the necessary consensus in our own countries to keep the Alliance alive and strong. It is more difficult in NATO countries in many ways because we are each free, independent sovereign nations and we have a wide variety of vigorously expressed opinion. This differentiates us from the Warsaw Pact nations where on the surface, it seems somewhat easier to keep them together, but below the surface I suggest that their strains are far greater than anything we have encountered.

When I read or hear obituaries for the alliance, I am reminded of a private exchange between Metternich and Talleyrand at the opening of the Congress of Vienna in the autumn of 1814. Metternich turned to Talleyrand and said: "Don't speak of al-

---

* *This essay is based upon Secretary Weinberger's address at the Atlantic Institute, Paris, France, December 2, 1983.*

lies, they no longer exist." Talleyrand replied: "There are people here who ought to be allies, in the sense that they ought to think in the same way and desire the same things."

In the wake of this century's second great war, a group of nations concluded that they ought, indeed that they must, "think in the same way and desire the same things." With the dawn of the nuclear age came the understanding that war could no longer be won. It could only be prevented. And with the rise of a Soviet regime eager to subvert freedom also came the need for free nations to join together in convincing the Soviet Union that its aims could not be won by force.

So a new kind of danger had brought forth a new kind of alliance. Raymond Aron, a man of great mind and spirit whose passing the West now justly mourns, spoke of us as "Permanent Allies" — that is, as allies who, "whatever the conflict of some of their interests, do not conceive in the foreseeable future that they could ever be in opposite camps."

In the same essay, Aron went on to make an even bolder statement: "The reinforcement of a permanent ally, he said, "should never . . . arouse jealousy, or alarm." Yet we have all heard the pessimists warn just the contrary. They say that as the strength and confidence of individual members of the Alliance grew, the unity of the Alliance itself would inevitably diminish.

Events have proved that Aron was right and the nay-sayers wrong. The United States, under President Reagan's leadership, has recovered its confidence and its resolve, and European leaders of differing political views have united in their commitment to restoring the military balance with the Soviet Union. Japan has also explored ways of strengthening its own defenses, so we have seen our Alliance grow stronger and more united. Above all, we have seen those "permanent allies" of whom Aron spoke reaffirm the dual strategy of the Western Alliance for Peace: deterrence through strength and arms reductions through negotiation.

The strategy of deterrence really has not changed in the almost forty years it has helped to keep the peace, but what it takes to keep deterrence has changed. In 1979, the members of the NATO Alliance recognized that the Soviet monopoly of longer-range intermediate nuclear forces, and especially their enormous and rapid buildup of the accurate and mobile and therefore survivable SS-20, both in Europe and Asia (and where it is deployed is immaterial because of its mobility) threatened to undermine the whole strategy of deterrence and upset the balance. So the members of the Alliance made a commitment — a difficult decision but one that was taken after thorough consideration and one that there has never been any reason to change — to deploy Pershing II and ground launched cruise missiles in Europe if we could not gain a negotiated alternative that restored the balance. That was a commitment that had to be made and which has been kept and which will restore deterrence. We have stood by that commitment, in the face of threats from the Soviet Union and in the face of difficult political pressures at home.

We have also stood by our determination to pursue peace through negotiations. It is worth noting that during the debate over missile deployment in the Bundestag in the late fall of 1983, Chancellor Kohl's resolution, which was adopted, called for "a continuation and intensification of the East-West dialogue in all fields and on all levels." Likewise, President Reagan has repeatedly emphasized his determination to negotiate significant, mutual, verifiable arms reduction agreements with the Soviet Union. I emphasize arms reduction, not arms control or arms limitations. Reduction has to be the key word and the key goal. President Reagan did not suspend these negotiating efforts despite the fact that the Soviets' brutal murder of 269 innocent people aboard a civilian airliner led many to urge that those negotiations cease; nor has he allowed himself to be discouraged by the Soviet's recent posturing in Geneva.

The estimate I make here in this essay may not yet be the prevailing view. But I really believe right now that the prospects for successful negotiations are better than ever before. Recent history has shown us that the Soviets respond not to blandishments, certainly not to weakness, but to strength, and we are acquiring that strength. What is more, we have shed some of the illusions which accompanied our negotiating efforts of the last decade, without losing our determination to achieve a negotiated solution.

About four years ago, Henry Kissinger made a speech which was, I understand, partly sponsored by the Atlantic Institute. In it he warned that "there is in the West a tendency to treat detente quite theatrically; that is to say, not as a balancing of national interests and negotiations on the basis of strategic reality but rather as an exercise in strenuous goodwill, an exercise in psychotherapy."

It is precisely because we perceive reality more honestly that members of the Western Alliance today entertain hopes that we never would have dared entertain in earlier days. The critically important and really new factor is that we now recognize that we need not trust the Soviet leaders' peaceful intentions to believe that they will not seek a conflict they cannot win. And with this recognition comes a tremendous opportunity to open up new vistas of peace.

This is perhaps not the prevailing wisdom — it may not be wisdom at all — but I really believe that our reinvigorated alliance now is at the threshold of promise and at the frontier of hope. This promise and this hope depend not on some revolution in world politics or some change in human nature, which has never occurred throughout all the centuries, but rather on a revolution in technology — a revolution which could offer new strength and opportunity to nations such as ours, which will not initiate force, but simply seek to defend themselves against aggression.

On March 23, 1983, President Reagan presented a new vision of peace. He asked quite simply:

"Would it not be better to save lives than to avenge them? Are we not capable of demonstrating our peaceful intentions by applying all our abilities and all our ingenuity to achieving a truly lasting stability. I think we are — indeed, I think we must." He went on: "Let me share with you a vision of the future which does offer hope. It is that we embark on a program to counter the awesome Soviet missile threat with measures that are defensive. Let us turn to the very strengths in technology that spawned our great industrial base and that have given us the quality of life we enjoy today."

A defense against ballistic missiles that eliminated the danger of a disarming first strike would dramatically increase the stability of the nuclear balance. A reliable strategic defense, based on a multi-layered system which would not have to be nuclear, but which could detect and destroy thousands of incoming Soviet missiles, would lift the cloud of terror which has hung over us since the beginning of the nuclear age.

In presenting this bold new proposal, the President challenged what Henry Kissinger, in 1979 called "the historical amazing theory that vulnerability contributed to peace and invulnerability contributed to the risks of war." The President has, in short, challenged the conventional wisdom that the threat of devastation is the only ground for peace. And while this is by no means the first time the President has successfully challenged conventional wisdoms, this is by all odds the most important challenge that he had made on behalf of all mankind.

A strategic defense holds out new hope for the future. It also raises, once again, the challenge of meeting a new way of thinking, the challenge of daring to dream dreams, but even more important, to act upon them.

Having said that, let me state as clearly as I can that we in the United States will not lessen by one iota the regaining or maintaining of our strategic modernization program, including strengthening and modernizing all parts of our triad while we explore and probe the frontiers of science for the defense systems. Let no one misunderstand—our pursuit of a reliable defense will not be at the cost of relaxing in any way the need to secure all of the strategic modernization the President seeks. And thus far, Congress has fully approved, authorized and appropriated all the necessary funds for this. We do not give up deterrence, we do not abandon negotiations—but we do seek a third way to keep the peace.

We face similar challenges and opportunities at another technological frontier. Advances are also opening important prospects for improved conventional defense. New classes of conventional weapon capabilities can contribute to direct defense, deep combat, and air defense. New technologies will not only identify and attack both fixed and moving targets with pinpoint accuracy but advances in micro-elements, computer technology, and sensors will enable better coordination and management of our conventional defense.

These new capabilities allow us the prospect of disrupting the very kind of operations Warsaw Pact plans envision: A blitzkrieg that would send ground forces forward in successive echelons, while their air forces conducted offensive operations against our own installations.

Here again is an attempt to use the new emerging technologies which could dramatically enhance deterrence on into the future by convincing the Soviets that their blitzkrieg strategy could not readily overwhelm our conventional defenses. Extremely precise conventional weapons could not only help hold back a first wave of attack, but they could also delay, disrupt, and, increasingly destroy follow-on echelons. In addition, as General Bernard Rogers, NATO's Supreme Commander in Europe, has pointed out, use of these emerging technologies would actually strengthen our whole strategy of forward defense by alleviating one of its disadvantages: inadequate depth.

The NATO Alliance has already taken the first steps toward seizing these new opportunities. At the 1982 summit in Bonn, allied heads of state issued a mandate to strengthen NATO's defensive posture with special regard to conventional forces. They also approved a further initiative on exploiting emerging technologies.*

Both strategic defense and emerging conventional technologies then, offer new hope to an alliance that takes as its starting principle the rejection of force to achieve its goal of successful deterrence through strength. But with opportunity comes challenge, both technological and strategic.

Introducing new technology is never easy. We will always face the chorus of critics who fear that we are pushing the frontiers of technology too far. The hand of these critics will be strengthened each time we test a new system and find some remaining technical problems, each time we venture a new idea and encounter obstacles. And we will encounter obstacles. If we didn't, we are probably not pushing the frontiers of technology far enough.

Some years back, a young French Army lieutenant colonel undertook the rather thankless task of trying to convince his colleagues that mechanized armored forces were the way of the future. The next great conflict, he predicted, would be marked

---

* Editor's Note: The recent removal of Marshal Nikolai V. Ogarkov as Chief of the Soviet General Staff, may be related to his concern for NATO's advancing technologies for conventional forces. In Krasnaya Zvezda, the armed forces newspaper, on May 9, 1984, Marshall Ogarkov warned of, "The sharply increased range of conventional weapons. . . ." He referred to, "This qualitative leap in the development of conventional means of destruction. . . ." He emphasized, "Work on those new types of weapons is already in progress in a number of countries, for example in the United States. Their development is a reality of the very near future, and it would be a serious mistake not to consider it right now." (The New York Times September 13, 1984, pp. A1, A9).

by "movements, surprises, breakthroughs, and pursuits." For his pains, Charles De Gaulle became *persona non grata* in many French military circles as his superiors stood by their reliance on the Maginot Line.

Even when new technology is well understood, we must still confront our human resistance to changing our familiar and comfortable ways. Admiral Lord Nelson, at the Battle of Trafalgar, turned naval strategy upside down by rejecting the doctrine of "line of battle ahead," and relied on maneuver and the concentration of overwhelming force against points of enemy weakness. While his efforts met with success, he may well have paused to ponder and to recall the fate of Admiral Byng, who had unsuccessfully tried a similar strategy some fifty years earlier. It was Byng's subsequent execution that inspired Voltaire's comment, "De temps en temps, il faut tuer un admiral, pour encourager les autres" (From time to time, it is necessary to kill an admiral to encourage the others.)

I wish to reassure the Navy at this point that attached as we are to innovation, we do not feel it is necessary to go this far.

The final challenge we must face is the challenge to our cooperative efforts. In the years ahead, we will need to work together on these new initiatives and many others, even as we hold firm to our abiding aim of deterring war and negotiating arms reduction. We will need to overcome suspicions that our pursuit of new technologies will somehow reduce our commitment to deterrence and arms reduction. It will not. We have to make sure that no one believes that we may reduce our commitments to one another or allow one nation to dominate future decisions about Alliance forces and strategy.

In his March 1983 speech, President Reagan reaffirmed that "as we pursue our goal of defensive technologies, we recognize that our Allies rely upon strategic offensive power to deter attacks against them. Their vital interests and ours are inextricably linked—their safety and ours are one." That is the basis of American policy. America could never exist in a world in which Europe was overrun. Twice within my lifetime, we have gone to war to prevent just that. Our President also emphasized that the hope for defense against ballistic missiles was a hope not just for the people of the United States but for all the Free World, indeed for an entire planet that has lived in fear of nuclear weapons. This is not a plan for "Fortress America."

We should never forget that the Soviets also are pursuing these defensive technologies and have been for several years — at least since 1967. If they should secure these defensive technologies first, then the world would be in great peril. So from every sense of self-protection and survival, we must work to secure this reliable defense against nuclear missiles — not to enable us to destabilize a balance we hope to restore, but to eliminate once and for all the horror that these weapons hold for all mankind.

In the area of emerging conventional technologies, we are already seeing strong evidence of allied cooperation. One important example is the development of the multiple launch rocket system, designed to counter enemy artillery and suppress enemy air defense. France, Germany, the United Kingdom, Italy and the United States are all engaged in a cooperative program for the development of this system to meet agreed requirements of all five participants.

Where do we go from here in this effort to exploit emerging technologies to improve conventional defense? The United States has provided some suggestions for areas where we can exploit the new technologies. Our Allies are now providing their own views and suggestions, which we welcome. This, is, and must be, an Alliance effort. It must be a cooperative effort from design, through manufacture, to deployment. We hope that all Allies will come forward with their own ideas, their own suggestions and their candidates for cooperative programs and we see an important role for the industries of allied countries in carrying out these cooperative ventures.

As we move to exploit these technologies that have been our great source of strength in the past, we must be ever mindful of the need to ensure that this technology does not become available to the Warsaw Pact. If the Soviets are successful in obtaining our best technology, this will not only increase the threat to our forces and our societies but also raise the cost to us of trying to maintain the technological advantage on which our strength depends.

By reducing the threat from nuclear attack, by reducing the effectiveness of conventional blitzkriegs, our new technologies can help convince the Soviets that aggression would not succeed. But they offer far more than a strengthened deterrent. They offer the Soviets new incentive to join with us in genuine reduction of both nuclear and conventional forces.

We are a defensive alliance. We do not start wars. We do not desire to impose our political system by conquest or to exact economic tribute. In a dangerous world that is not of our making, we are simply trying to convince our adversaries that they have no alternative but to join our quest for a lasting peace. A stronger defense against both nuclear and conventional forces can only aid that quest.

But let me warn — and this may seem a surprising warning from a Secretary of Defense — that this quest will require more than strength of arms. It will also require strength of will, of purpose, and of imagination. We need to be bold in our dreams, and very wise in the pursuit of those dreams. Milton asked: "What is strength without a double share of wisdom?"

It is, he said, "vast, unwieldy, burdensome, and proudly secure yet liable to fall. . . ."

We have preserved our Alliance for thirty-five years, disagreeing often, but never forgetting the great gulf that stands between ourselves and those who put no value on human freedom. I believe that our Alliance is truly therefore a permanent alliance, and that it remains the very best hope for peace in very dangerous times. But as we look toward the future, let us hope not just for strength, but for the "double share of wisdom" of which Milton spoke. Above all, let us hope for a wisdom that will enable us to step past the threshold of promise into a better age full of sunlight for coming generations and free of the shadows and horrors of nuclear war.

# CHAPTER THREE

# To Provide for the Common Defence*

## GENERAL JOHN W. VESSEY, JR., USA
CHAIRMAN, JOINT CHIEFS OF STAFF

"War, at this Time, rages over a great Part of the Known World; our News-Papers are weekly filled with fresh Accounts of the Destruction it everywhere occasions. . . . And is our Country altogether free from Danger? . . . if we resolve upon it the very Fame of our Strength and Readiness would be a Means of Discouraging our Enemies; for tis a wise and true Saying, that one Sword often keeps another in the Scabbard. They that are on their Guard, and appear ready to receive Adversaries, are in much less Danger of being attacked than the supine, secure and negligent."

BENJAMIN FRANKLIN'S, "Plain Talk," 1747

Those words from our Nation's past, nearly 240 years ago, could just as well have been written in today's headlines. The world has always been a dangerous, turbulent place; and from the time of Ben Franklin's famous pamphlet, "Plain Talk," to the present, Americans have been concerned about how to have the military forces with the needed strength and prowess to deter aggression or win a war and not be a danger or an unnecessary burden in peacetime for the populace.

### The Constitution and the Common Defence

Our Forefathers at the time of the Revolutionary War were no exception. For, while they recognized the need to be ready to repulse attack, they were reluctant to provide the means to ensure the common defense. They and those before them came to America in the seventeenth and eighteenth centuries to escape military oppression and religious bigotry. Somewhat later,

---

* *This essay is based upon addresses by General Vessey to the Presidential Classroom for Young Americans, Washington, D.C., 5 March 1984; at the 88th Annual National Convention of the Jewish War Veterans of the United States of America, Atlanta, Georgia, 17 August 1983; and the Fourteenth Annual Student Symposium of the Center for the Study of the Presidency, Washington, D.C., April 9, 1983.*

their concerns found expression in our *Declaration of Independence*, in which King George III was accused, among other "injuries and usurpations," of keeping "among us, in times of peace, standing armies, without the consent of our legislatures" and of trying to make "the military independent of and superior to the civil power."

Then, in 1784, after we had won our Independence and after all the British troops had left, the Continental Congress declared that standing armies in time of peace were inconsistent with the principles of a republic. Having said that, the Congress reduced the Continental Army to only 100 officers and men and stationed it as far away as possible from any of the large towns then in existence.

Fortunately, our Forefathers eventually came to accept the fact that security from attack is one of the fundamental objectives of civilized nations and that the *first duty* of government is to protect its citizens. They took care, however, to ensure the cure was not worse than the disease. Our early leaders rightly insisted that the military remain subordinate to the civilian government — a servant, never a master.

Alexander Hamilton, advocating the adoption of the *Constitution* in *The Federalist Papers*, the most famous political essays of that time, called attention to the need to provide for the "common defence." He went on to say, "The whole power of raising armies, is lodged in the legislature, not the executive,. . . . There is an important qualification even in the legislative power which forbids the appropriation of money for support of . . . Armed Forces . . . for any longer period than two years; a precaution which," Hamilton continued, "is a great and real security against the keeping of troops *without evident necessity*."

## The Defense Challenge of Today

That is why today, in 1984, the "evident necessity" of keeping Armed Forces must be justified to the Congress each year so the funds necessary to raise, support and equip the military forces of the United States can be obtained from the people. It all relates to why our military, formed from the society it serves and sworn to support and defend the *Constitution*, embodies the principles by which that society is governed — why our military has been and will remain a servant of the people and never its master, protecting the Nation not policing it.

These fundamentals from our past have been constant throughout our history and they lie at the heart of today's domestic debate on Defense spending. Even though the great principles of this Republic remain unchanged, the world itself has changed. The world of today is far more complex and more dangerous than the world of the 1700's. There are many more nation-states and we are bound to them in many ways and they to us. Economic changes and technological developments have led to far greater interdependence among all nations. At the same time, the pressures from political, religious and ethnic factions within and among them seem greater. Add to this the military might of the Soviet Union and its surrogates, seeking to capitalize on every dispute or to turn instability to its own purposes, and you can see that the world is dangerous indeed.

As President Teddy Roosevelt stated in 1903, we "as a people, whether we will or not, have reached the stage where we must play a great part in this world." We shouldn't shrink from our obligations, "the evident necessity" cited by Hamilton, to sustain the necessary effort to preserve peace and liberty in the face of the challenges of the Soviet system, a system which is the very antithesis of our own values. Even while we negotiate and try to work with the Soviet Union to reduce the risk of war, we absolutely must do what is needed to be done to insure the adequacy of our own defenses.

There is some good guidance in the unity found in King David's words from the 29th Psalm where it reads, "The Lord will give strength unto His people; the Lord will bless His people with peace." Strength and peace are bound together. It is a recognition that a free nation must also be strong to deter the enemies of peace and justice. Those words imply two parallel ideas that contribute to peace. The first, that we be sufficiently strong to deter war and the threat of war. We don't want a war but we don't want to be paralyzed by the fear of war. By deterrence, we seek to preserve peace and freedom and to protect our vital interests by making it self-evidently clear to any potential enemies that they cannot achieve their aims through violence or the threat of violence.

Second, we must seek by every reasonable means to reduce

the risks of war and the dangers of war. Certainly, arms control negotiations are one of the means that we need to pursue. However, we also need to work to reduce the misunderstandings that lead to war. Salvador de Madariaga, the great Spanish philosopher and historian who worked for many years on the old League of Nations Disarmament Commission, said in his memoirs, "Nations don't distrust each other because they are armed; they arm because they distrust each other." So, we need to reduce the distrust among nations.

### Our Defense Posture

Our objectives in this country have been relatively constant since World War II but modern threats to our security now fundamentally endanger our way of life. In the 1950's and the early 1960's we clearly had strategic nuclear superiority; and, our conventional forces, although they were outnumbered by our potential enemies, were technologically superior. Since that time there has been a general shift of power. We arrived at a point early in this past decade where the security of our Nation and that of our allies could no longer be assured, in spite of the great strength of our forces and those of our allies.

Global instability threatened Western interests abroad and endangered our national health at home. Moreover, the unrelenting growth of Soviet military power became an over-riding concern. Today, after two decades of uninterrupted build-up by the Soviets, and almost a decade of neglect on our part, our Nation is now working hard to restore the degree of military power necessary to maintain the peace.

The relentless quest for military superiority by the Soviets has achieved new levels during this past year. Certainly, the Soviets are not 10 feet tall. They have a number of problems of their own. They are really a one-dimensional power — a military power. You don't see a lot of people trying to escape to the Soviet Union, or clamoring for Soviet blue jeans or Soviet computers or Soviet automobiles. Their economy is in serious trouble by their own admission; and their ideology is laid bare even to their friends as being militant and aggressive, devoid of all moral authority. They are the only country in the world surrounded by hostile communist neighbors; but, still, their power has to be recognized.

*Peacetime Strategy*

Our peacetime strategy to counter threats to our security has been constant just as our objectives have been constant. Our strategy is defensive. It reflects the global perspective of United States interests and it is centered on our alliances. It involves having forces deployed in the area where those alliances face potential adversaries — principally Northeast Asia and in Europe. It implies strong naval forces to protect the sea lanes so that we can reinforce those alliances if need be or go elsewhere in the world where our interests may be threatened; and it implies a central reserve of strong, flexible land, sea and air forces that can be moved wherever they may be needed. An armed flexible reserve of strong land, sea and air forces includes a traditional American ingredient, the National Guard and Reserve.

In addition, our strategy implies some uniquely American components: the necessary strategic mobility to get our forces to distant places and an outstanding intelligence system because we are going to have small forces, not large forces, when compared with our potential enemies. So, we must know more about what is going on in the world if we are to make these small forces effective; and we must have the command and control system to be able to control those forces.

Now, we want to make it very clear if deterrence fails that we can and we will retaliate to any sort of attack, whether it is conventional or nuclear. We will do it in a way that guarantees to our enemies that their wartime objectives cannot be achieved. We believe that if the Soviets understand that, and that if we can employ modern forces to do that, we have a good opportunity to prevent war. It is for that reason that the Joint Chiefs of Staff have urged continually that we modernize the strategic nuclear forces of this country to make it clear to the Soviets that they cannot attack this country or threaten its interests with impunity.

*The Nuclear Balance*

The danger to our Nation is great. The Soviets have deployed strategic missiles which are among the most accurate in the world. They have placed those missiles in the world's best-protected missile silos. And, they've aimed them at us. In 1981 alone, as part of this modernization program, they deployed over 1,200 modern, so-called hard-target killing nuclear warheads of the PEACEKEEPER variety. That is more than we intend to deploy in our entire PEACEKEEPER intercontinental ballistic missile modernization program. They deployed roughly the same numbers in 1982 that they did in 1981. They have developed a new strategic bomber that is very comparable to our own B-1, and they have new, modern ballistic missile submarines. We simply have to recognize that the accelerating pace of Soviet modernization and our own slow pace in improving our strategic forces have left us well behind the Soviets in some important measures of military capability.

We as a Nation must deal with the reality of Soviet nuclear weaponry and its destabilizing consequences. We have to make it clear to the Soviets that they cannot threaten nuclear war, or any war, without understanding that we can and will respond in such a way that guarantees that their war aims will not be achieved. If that is clear to the Soviets, I am confident that there will be no war.

The President's bi-partisan commission, the Scowcroft Commission, has made some very sensible recommendations. The Commission said that we must modernize our strategic nuclear forces to counter this dangerous trend and the growing power of the Soviets. The modernization of our strategic forces, including the PEACEKEEPER missile, the TRIDENT submarine, the B-1 bomber, the cruise missiles, and the essential warning systems and command and control are all necesary, and they are necessary right now to ensure deterrence and to keep the peace. In addition to this modernization, our negotiation strategy is tied very closely to our modernization in order to seek verifiable arms reductions. If we give the Soviets the hope that they can wait out the West's political process in order to limit our arms, they simply are not going to negotiate with us at the negotiating table.

### Arms Control

In a speech to the Los Angeles World Affairs Council in April 1983, the President outlined a second important component of our national security policy — that is, the arms control initiatives of the United States. The Joint Chiefs of Staff firmly support the President in his quest for substantial reductions in strategic nuclear arms. But our support for those reductions recognizes that with substantially lower levels of strategic nuclear weapons, the modernization of our own strategic nuclear forces becomes even more important. The Joint Chiefs of Staff believe that we need to modernize all three legs of the strategic triad, and that's underway.

The need to modernize U.S. conventional and strategic forces does not represent tolerance of this ever-increasing spiral of the global arms race. As the President pointed out, the United States is ready to negotiate and has proposed a number of initiatives to reduce the arms race. We have proposed a total ban on chemical weapons, the removal of intermediate-range nuclear weapons from Europe, substantial reductions in the strategic armaments, as well as a reasonable and sensible position for conventional force reductions in Europe.

Concerning the so-called nuclear freeze, the key issue is whether or not we reduce the probability of nuclear war by invoking certain freezes. And I want to tell you that what's behind those movements is exactly what's behind the Joint Chiefs' recommendations to modernize the strategic nuclear forces. We all seek to preserve the peace. The difference is: How do we prevent a nuclear war? There's a fundamental difference in philosophy here. One side believes that by doing something unilaterally, we will show a sign of good faith to the Soviet Union and, therefore, enhance the cause of peace in the world today. If you look at the negotiations we have had with the Soviets in limiting arms in the past, and then look at what the Soviets have done about their arms after these agreements, you will see that it really doesn't make very much sense to depend only on the good will of the Soviets for the security of this country. What I say to you is that I believe that freezing our weapons at a time when the Soviets have more modern weapons than we have doesn't reduce the risks we face; to do so would *increase* the risks for this Nation.

The future holds some hope that we can end the dominance of offensive weapons. The President proposes that we should investigate our technology to see if we can use it to rely on a defense against ballistic missiles — his strategic defense initiative — combined with a limitation on strategic arms and the threat of offensive retaliation. It seems to me that this would be a very American approach. Some have suggested that the President's strategic defense initiative would be destabilizing to the world. That's a myth that has existed in the world for years. The myth is that the Soviets, by signing the Antiballistic Missile Treaty, accepted the doctrine of mutually assured destruction — and mutual vulnerability.

That is a dangerous misperception. Look at what the Soviets have done in terms of defense — both in terms of research against defensive ballistic missiles as well as pouring concrete to make their installations able to withstand nuclear attacks. And look at the defenses they have built in anti-aircraft missiles which can, in turn, be used later perhaps for defense against a ballistic missile attack.

It seems to me that we Americans have one great, controllable variable in the whole arms control business: we can control what is being done about *our* defense. And it is time for the United States to look at that. The President has examined this proposal and directed more research as an important part of our efforts to maintain the strategic balance.

### The Conventional Forces Challenge

Up to this point, I have concentrated on the nuclear balance. However, the Soviets have good reason for increased confidence in their conventional forces as well. They are fielding a range of sophisticated capabilities on land, in the air and on and under the seas. All of these challenge our own forces and the forces of our allies. In the past 15 years, they have added 30 divisions to their army; and that takes them up to more than 180 divisions — more than five times our number. Soviet air power is massive and sophisticated; and, for the first time, they have developed a very strong, "blue water" navy.

Increasingly, their influence has spread well beyond their borders. Their naval power, their airborne forces and, most significantly, their use of surrogates in Third World conflicts seek to outflank our traditional alliances, to threaten our access to strategic materials and to endanger our long-standing friends and allies.

The Soviets are neither our only problem nor the only cause of global instability. Nevertheless, they stand ready to capitalize on the problems in this turbulent world. It is a world which the former Secretary General of NATO characterized as being "perilously close to a new international anarchy." Since World War II, there have been 150 wars and 25 million people have been killed in those wars. If you use the twin criteria that a war is an activity involving significant loss of life with the use of regular armed forces, there are 20 wars going on today.

It is not necessary to look very far beyond our horizons to see the effects of global interdependence and the brutal consequences of armed aggression in the world today. That reality is very close to home. The President asked all Americans to turn their attention to the desperate need for aid for our neighbors to the south. The President made it very clear that we have vital interests in Central America and the Caribbean and we have to regard with great seriousness threats to our legitimate security concerns and those of our friends. We live in this hemisphere. Peace, liberty, security for democracy and economic health for our American neighbors will certainly help us maintain the same benefits for ourselves.

What may not be so well recognized is the way conflict in one part of the world affects everyone else. Take the example of the turbulent African continent. I remember listening to ABC News one day to hear Peter Jennings sum up the world situation by saying, "We begin tonight's broadcast with a nasty little war in a thoroughly inhospitable place. What has been going on until recently in northern Chad has been a civil war. The trouble is there aren't any wars anymore which don't somehow involve the major powers."

Mr. Jennings was only partly correct because *any* war anywhere affects not only the major powers but *every* nation. Libya, for example, which is involved in Chad has gotten itself involved deeply in Africa, and in the Middle East. Its mischief has recently surfaced in this hemisphere, in Central America. In Nicaragua, Libyan support and PLO extremists are active in training and supplying the Soviet-supported Sandinistas.

### Continuing the Revitalization of Our Strength

I return at this juncture to my basic point of peace and strength. Just as peace and the preservation of liberty remain our unending objectives, there will always be those whose only instrument is force. It is therefore essential that we see to the health of our own military strength, to deter conflict and to act as a shield for more peaceful resolution of differences. We must recognize that our willingness to rebuild our strategic forces and our willingness to strengthen our conventional forces all send signals to those who would threaten peace. We must tend to our national power, and not only to the military dimensions of that power but to our diplomatic power, our political strength, and our economic and moral health as well.

I am enheartened to see more consensus in this Nation toward that end and especially toward improving our own forces. We saw a favorable vote in the Congress to support the recommendations of the Scowcroft Commission for the modernization of our strategic nuclear forces. That modernization still hangs very much in the balance and there are a lot of other votes to come; but, Congress needs to support that program if we are to remain a strong nation. We also are beginning to see a growing awareness and concern for the welfare and security of our Central American neighbors under the provisions of the Jackson Plan, named for the late Senator Henry "Scoop" Jackson.

I am especially enheartened by the progress this Nation has made in the last several years in reversing the decline in the health of our conventional forces so evident in the 1970's. Thanks to the support of the American people, the condition of our Armed Forces is good and getting better. I have visited our forces all over the world; and, I want to report my view and that of every one of our field commanders that our Forces are doing well—they are the best I have seen in peacetime. The tougher the job is the better their spirits are; and, that is a good sign for the United States.

Americans can be proud of what the Armed Forces are doing—both the Active Forces and the Reserve Components. They are on the land, on and under the sea, and in the skies, doing remarkable things and doing them very, very well. At the very heart of the improved strength of our Armed Forces is people—good people, who are well-led and well-trained. It is very much as General Creighton Abrams once said. He said, "People aren't just *in* the Armed Forces, people *are* the Armed Forces." And, keeping those people ready for their tasks requires a continuing commitment from our Nation.

We have the values we have today because many of our citizens have been willing to serve in the Armed Forces in the past and to protect the freedoms of this Nation. Very much a part of the willingness and the readiness of soldiers, sailors, airmen and Marines to defend their Nation is the knowledge that the people of this country, during peacetime, during war, and after the guns are silent, will take care of the people in uniform and the veterans — that the Nation will take care of them and their families.

While they are in the service, we will give them the tools of war and the support they need to do their hazardous duties. We will take care of their families if they have to march off to war. We will pick up our wounded and give them good medical care. We will pick up our dead and provide reverent and dignified treatment for the remains and for their graves. We will do what is necessary to get back those who become prisoners of war and we will do whatever is necesary to account for all those who are missing in action. And our forces need to know that the citizens of this country will provide sensible help and care for our veterans when the wars are over.

Anyone who joins the Armed Forces with the idea of getting rich has to be faulted on bad judgment. And, I do not believe you will find very many people in uniform who expect to get rich. However, those who do serve deserve to be able to feed their families and be able to feed them without food stamps. They deserve to be able to educate their children and be rewarded somewhat reasonably for their skills and the extraordinary service they give the Nation. Therefore, the pay and emoluments, including the retirement system, have to continue to attract good people or we simply will not have good Armed Forces.

The Armed Services deserve good equipment, too — good, topnotch equipment, equipment that works and equipment that gives our people an edge over their potential enemies. Our strategy calls for the use of American technology, one of America's strong points. I frequently hear some misguided people say, "Why don't we just buy more, cheaper weapons so that we can buy a lot more of them and then we won't feel so badly if they're destroyed by the enemy." The problem with all that is when the equipment gets destroyed by the enemy so do the people who are operating the equipment. We value human life more than we value things. Our citizens don't want young Americans in combat with cheap, bargain-basement, ineffective weapons.

In that respect, I am happy to see that the Reserve Components — American's great militia heritage — are getting a sensible share of modern equipment. It is essential that we keep all of our Reserve Forces strong because the National Guard and the Reserves figure more prominently in our strategy today than they ever have. They need support from the people, and, particularly, they need support from their employers. The health of our Reserve Components is important for the security of the Nation.

At the same time, it is very important for us in uniform to recognize that the taxpayer deserves a fair shake in this whole equipment exercise, too. He deserves to have us buy good equipment — equipment of value that's worth the price and equipment that is effective but not "goldplated." By the same token, the members of the Armed Forces and the taxpayers deserve a fair shake from American industry and American labor by having them produce quality equipment; and, certainly, the Nation deserves the highest levels of integrity and honesty from American industry in seeing that only a fair price is asked.

## The Role of the Joint Chiefs of Staff

There is another element in providing for the "common defence." It is how we organize and lead our forces. Let me address the role of the Joint Chiefs of Staff in security policy. Suggestions have been made that if the Joint Chiefs of Staff were simply reorganized, the defenses of this country would be improved to the point that we would be able to spend considerably less for defense.

The Joint Chiefs have examined their own organization; they have examined very closely the law that governs the activities of the Joint Chiefs, and have come to some conclusions. Our first conclusion is that the people who wrote the duties of the Joint Chiefs in Title 10 U.S. Code wrote the right duties. The duties of the Joint Chiefs are very simple. The first duty is that they are the principal military advisors to the President, the Secretary of Defense, and the National Security Council. The second duty is to provide strategic plans and strategic direction to the Armed Forces of the United States; and the third is to provide logistic plans to support those strategic plans and to assign logistic responsibilities to the Armed Forces of the United States. The remaining areas are to establish unified and specified commands for the control of the Armed Forces of the United States; to review the material and personnel requirements to support the strategic plans of the United States; to provide policies for the education of the Armed Forces of the United States; to provide for the membership on the U.N. Military Committee; and to perform such other duties as the President may direct.

The longer you examine those duties, the more you can see that they are, in fact, the right duties for that senior body of military advisors to the President and the Secretary of Defense. The question is: Do they carry out their duties as well as they can? Only history will tell. Do they carry them out as well as we would like? The answer is that they could do better because the Chiefs are fallible human beings. But are they trying to do better? Yes, they are working hard to provide the best defenses possible for this Nation.

Now, the other thing we determined as we examined that operation is that there are three very important relationships. They seem quite obvious looking at the law; yet even we did not understand those relationships until we had examined the problem in some detail. The first relationship is between the Joint Chiefs as a body and the President and the Secretary of Defense. As you look at that relationship through history, you will see that the Chiefs may have met once a year with the President, and sometimes they did not meet at all with the President. We decided that we would try to get the President of the United States and the Secretary of Defense to tend to this relationship, to see if it could be improved. I want to tell you that the current body of the Joint Chiefs of Staff has met with the President as a group on a regular basis. So the relationship has, at least, been tended. Only history will tell if the relationship produced the right thing for the United States.

The other relationship that is important is the relationship among the Joint Chiefs as a body: the Chairman, the Chiefs of Staff of the Army and the Air Force, the Chief of Naval Operations, and the Commandant of the Marine Corps. If the relationship is to serve those duties outlined by the law, it must include great trust and confidence in each other and understanding by each of the other's important duties. Each one of those Service Chiefs has some very important full-time duties: building an Army, building a Navy, building an Air Force, building a

Marine Corps — making sure that the Army, Navy, Air Force, and Marine Corps can fight. But the Chiefs have to be able to rise above that particular set of duties and get together to address that other set of JCS duties that's laid out in the law. It requires a careful tending of the relationship.

The third relationship that is important is one between the Joint Chiefs as a body and another body of people — the nine commanders of the Unified and Specified Commands who command the Armed Forces of the United States — who, by law, would be the commanders in the battles that our Armed Forces might fight. They are the ones who must make the plans which the Joint Chiefs must review, plans which must be in accordance with the strategic direction of the Joint Chiefs. So that relationship needs careful tending. I can't speak for that relationship in the past years, but I want to tell you that this particular set of Chiefs has paid a lot of attention to that relationship. We've had each of those Commanders come in and personally brief their concepts of operations and military plans to the Joint Chiefs. It's been a particularly productive exercise because it has helped the Chiefs understand what has been good and what has been bad about the strategic direction that they have given to the Armed Forces of the United States in the past. We, in turn, can alter that strategic direction if it's necessary to do so.

So, I would say, as we look at these debates about how best to organize the Joint Chiefs, we must remember those three relationships. I suggest that there is very little we could write in the legislation about those relationships; because those relationships depend upon those three groups of people. This particular group of Chiefs has attempted to build on what has been done in the past, and I would say to you that those relationships are good today.

### A Continuing Commitment to Defense

All these factors lie at the heart of our military health — good people, good equipment, good training and support, and dedicated leadership. I am buoyed by the progress that I have seen. Yet, at the same time, I am concerned about our willingness to continue to provide for our security. We inherited from our Forefathers the liberty and freedom that we enjoy today. They, at their particular time in history, did their parts to assure our security and they pledged their lives, their fortunes and their sacred honor just as the signers of the *Declaration of Independence* did. We have reaped the benefits of their commitment and sacrifices; and, now, it is time that we pay the price, not only for ourselves but for the people who will come behind us.

Every lesson of history that I see tells us that if we want to preserve both peace and liberty, we must stay strong. As Benjamin Franklin said in the closing lines of "Plain Talk," "We have yet a time before us which may afford a good and almost sufficient Opportunity if we seize it and improve it with becoming Vigour." If our Nation provides properly for its military health, for its economic and political health and, above all, its spiritual health, I am confident our Nation can continue to keep the peace and preserve the blessings of liberty for ourselves and for our posterity.

# CHAPTER FOUR

# Soviet Changes: What Should We Expect*

**HENRY S. ROWEN**

CHAIRMAN, NATIONAL INTELLIGENCE COUNCIL

An important concern in the intelligence community is the change that is taking place in the leadership of several key nations. In an age in which bureaucracies seem to have taken over, the personalities of leaders are still important. We recognize this in our selection of presidents and it is true elsewhere. And foreign leaders have been changing rapidly: In the Soviet Union Andropov has replaced Brezhnev, in West Germany Kohl has succeeded Schmidt; in Japan someone will replace Suzuki [Nakasone, as it turns out].

The most important of these leadership changes is that in the Soviet Union during the past seven days following Brezhnev's death. This change has long been anticipated, yet because of the absence of an organized procedure for the devolution of power in that society, the transfer of political power there is an uncertain business. It seems to have been accomplished this time, however, with remarkable speed and assuredness. This suggests that a strong leadership will emerge quicker than in earlier successions.

This outcome, if it in fact sticks, will offer both challenges and opportunities. These will derive from the underlying realities that face the new Soviet leader and that face us as well.

The most salient of these facts is first the success of the Soviet Union in carrying out the greatest military buildup in history and the projection of this power abroad directly or through proxies throughout Africa, to the edges of Asia, and to the Western Hemisphere. Second, and equally important, is the

---

* This essay is based upon Chairman Rowen's November 17, 1982 remarks in the Harry J. Sievers Lecture Series jointly sponsored by the Center for the Study of the Presidency and Fordham University. After two years as Chairman, Rowen returned to Stanford University, where he is Professor of Public Management at the Graduate School of Business and Senior Fellow at the Hoover Institution on War, Revolution, and Peace. There in March 1984 he wrote the postscript.

fact that this power rests on an economic system which is in deep — and deepening — trouble.

First on the new leadership.

It is a remarkable thing that in the 65-year history of Soviet Union this is only the fourth time that supreme power has passed and only the second time that there has been anything approaching the deliberate selection of a new leader. When Lenin died, it turned out that Stalin, despite Lenin's warnings against him, was able to use the seemingly administrative post as the Secretary General of the Communist Party to gather the essential elements of power in his own hands. In so doing, of course, he changed the originally more limited nature of that position. When Stalin died, there was a competitive process lasting some weeks, which produced a triumvirate. It took some two years for Khruschev to gather supreme power in his own hands. Then, when he misplayed his hand, Brezhnev displaced him. And now, Yuri Andropov has arrived to replace Brezhnev in a transition which is presented as an orderly one, although we have only limited comprehension of the struggle for succession which took place during Brezhnev's long twilight.

There are three sets of circumstances which we can expect of General Secretary Andropov.

The first of these is his history. He is no stranger. He first came to Western attention as Ambassador in Hungary in 1956 and played a key role in suppressing the brave Hungarian people's effort to regain their freedom. Performance there earned him a title — "The Butcher of Hungary." Later he spent fifteen years running the dreaded and all powerful KGB, vastly expanding both its capacities throughout the world and the subtlety and force with which it controlled, indeed, crushed internal dissent. It was, significantly, under his leadership that psychiatry was perverted to the disposition of troublesome dissidents. Moreover, he has now come to power supported by two of the most threatening elements of the Soviet state, the military and the Secret Police.

Those forces have been dominant in Soviet society for a long time. Since at least the Cuban missile crisis, while engaging us in a so-called detente and a series of arms limitation talks, the Soviets steadily increased Soviet strategic and conventional power while we either stood still or lost ground until today the Soviets make claim to military superiority and are widely and generally accorded no less than parity. A combination of growing military power and active intervention abroad has brought Soviet arms and Cuban troops to far away Angola and Ethiopia, and has brought Soviet troops into Afghanistan.

Any realistic hopes that a genuine detente with the Soviet Union might survive practically disappeared with these developments and vanished when a genuine workers' revolt occurred in the Soviet empire and was met with repression. The cry, "Workers of the world unite," makes the leaders in the Kremlin tremble. They fear that it might even happen in Russia.

The military power which the Soviet leadership has at its disposal is formidable. I will spare you the details. It is sufficient to say that the Soviets have built a strong nuclear weapons establishment rivaling our own and, indeed, one that has been on a faster track. It has created a modern nuclear threat to Europe and other peripheral areas with its SS-20 missiles among other weapons. It has fielded an armed force opposite Western Europe which is large, modern and growing. Its navy has moved from coastal defense to a capacity to roam the seas. And it has, in addition, built up a powerful force opposite China.

Whatever else can be said of Brezhnev, he cannot be faulted for having left the Soviet Union militarily weaker than he found it.

This is not to say Andropov inherits a comfortable security situation. Despite the lagging defense efforts of the United States and its allies, we remain formidable. I believe that Andropov or anybody else would have to think many times and weigh the potential consequences and dangers very carefully before risking the response which the NATO powers can make. The main question before us is not who would survive or would win in a conflict in which there would probably be only losers, but how we can seize the opportunity which now presents itself to defuse risks and mitigate threats.

The main bases for optimism are the problems which Andropov inherits. Soviet agriculture has suffered crop failures in four successive years and is unable to feed the nation; Soviet society suffers from declining health with alcohol addiction running rampant; corruption is massive and reaches the top of the system; there is a suppressed but growing dissidence; ethnic conflicts are likely to be intensified in the years ahead.

The key to the drive for military power has been the ability of the Soviet economy to provide small but steady improvements

in the economic base and to the standard of living. Until recently, the Russian economy operated well enough to support
the acquisition of more and more guns.

We now recognize that an important element in Moscow's
ability to keep this strategy alive through the 1970s was help
from the West, in the form of credits to buy equipment, technology, and food. In addition, the Russians helped themselves
by acquiring Western technology through espionage, and by
earning hard currency through exports of oil, arms and gold.

The Soviet economy is now in a period during which annual
growth rates will be in the 1 percent to 2.0 percent range. Higher
energy costs and declining rates of labor productivity, economic
bottlenecks, and underinvestment in non-military industry are
major causes of this declining performance. In addition, due
to low birth rates during the 1960s among ethnic Russians and
other Slavs, the Soviet Union has a shortage of workers in key
regions. During the decade, the work force in the Russian
Republic — which accounts for 60 percent of the country's total
industrial output and 75 percent of total military output — will
shrink by 1,300,000.

It is in large part to compensate for these problems that the
Russians have turned to Western equipment and technology.
Their need for our equipment and technology is greater now
than it was during the heyday of detente. But their ability to
import equipment and technology is declining rapidly due to
a shortage of hard currency:

a. Oil Prices are dropping
b. Gold prices are low (due, in part, to heavy Soviet selling).
c. The market for Soviet arms is softening.
d. Western banks are reluctant to extend credit to the Soviet
   Union — or its satellites.
e. Four consecutive poor harvests have forced the Russians to
   divert billions of dollars from equipment and technology
   purchases to grain.

But despite this, military expenditures continue to grow with
the share of GNP for defense now at around 13–14 percent.
Given current and future economic conditions, maintaining
historical rates of growth in defense spending will be economically and politically more difficult. Nevertheless, we expect that
Soviet defense spending will continue to grow, although pos-

sibly at a lower rate than in the past. If so, the defense share of GNP could increase to 15 percent in 1985 and more by the end of the decade. In short, it's difficult to see how Moscow can continue its arms buildup without hurting its economy unless it can get help from the West.

For Kremlin leaders, the trick will be to keep the old strategy going for a while longer by finding enough money to support growing — or even current — levels of defense spending while fending off disaster in the civilian sectors. One option would be to order a tightening of belts, using more police power if necessary to keep the lid from blowing. A second option would be to "starve" the satellites to help the Motherland, for instance by reducing the subsidies the Soviet Union now provides Eastern Europe by selling oil at roughly half the world market price. Another would be to find alternate sources of hard currency. Most obvious is increased exports of raw materials including natural gas, minerals, and increased exports of chemicals. They might also try to get credits from old lenders and new ones, such as Middle East governments and try to gain access to wealth without spending hard currency through increasing influence — politically, economically or militarily — in the Persian Gulf region where so much of the world's oil wealth exists.

Kremlin leaders have not confronted these problems squarely and have not adopted a coherent response. Andropov is the first Soviet leader to take power at a time when his country can portray itself as the world's number one in military power. If U.S. will is perceived as weak, the ability of Moscow to intimidate is enhanced. Governments might respond to Soviet threats by extending credits at low rates of interest — or by selling things to the Soviet Union and its satellites at favorable prices; for instance oil which commands hard currency in world markets.

Only ideology and military power provide the cohesion necessary to hold the Soviet empire together. These forces have been challenged in Eastern Europe and may be inadequate in the future in the moslem and other disparate parts of the empire. Around the world, in Poland, in Cuba, in Vietnam, the Communists' system is a failure and is maintained only through the use of force. The western system of freedom of political choice and freedom of market has proven its superiority.

What the Soviet system needs is clear: Above all, it needs to be freed from the dead weight of the central controllers. It needs to be decentralized, to allow managers real authority in making decisions, to allow prices to influence consuming and manufacturing decisions, to allow individual farmers (or at least small groups) to make crucial choices in the countryside. And so on. Will Andropov move in this direction? How much freedom of action will he have? We don't know. Nor, in all probability, at this point does he.

If he does not move, or move much, in these directions, we think we know what will happen; nothing, economically. The system is stagnant. Only market-type reforms will enable it to get on a higher growth path. Yet such reforms are resisted because they can occur only with the loss of power of local political and bureaucratic cadres. These cadres were central in the Brezhnev era and they are also important to Andropov. If he wants to move the system out of the doldrums, he has to weaken their power and yet they, together with the military, are crucial to the maintenance of the system.

The only other important option for economic improvement open to Andropov, one that is less promising in its effects but one that may appear less risky, is to undertake to get help from the West. The Soviets have been here before — as have we. The basis for East-West detente in the early 1970s, was economic interaction, indeed support, for the Soviet Union in exchange for Soviet restraint on arms and foreign adventures. It foundered on the Soviet's unwillingness to adhere to their side of the bargain. Now a decade later, Andropov inherits an internal situation which is even worse than Brezhnev faced.

Therefore we can expect to hear Western voices calling for a softer line, more trade and credit to encourage and strengthen those in the Kremlin inclined to pursue economic and social goals rather than military and imperialist ones, and far less effort to redress our own defense deficiencies. Yet we do not know that there is a peace party in the Kremlin or, if there is one, that it has any clout. We do know that Andropov came to power with the support of the military and the secret police. It is not unreasonable to expect that he and his colleagues might hope to get that which they tried to get and didn't quite bring off in the 1970s: both sustained Western economic benefits *and* sustained exploitation of Soviet imperial power. In this situation, it's just as likely that any reassurances we offer about possibilities for peaceful cooperation would be perceived as signs of weakness and lack of resolve or taken as an opportunity to lull us into complacency and create renewed opportunity for extending military superiorty.

We have a policy and the President reaffirmed it after Brezhnev's demise. It is to seek conciliation from a position of firmness and strength. It is to seek reduction in the armaments that threaten all of us. It is not to subsidize or to make our technology available to those who threaten us but to be open to trade on market terms. We have begun during the last year initiatives in arms control. President Reagan has outlined our approach to four important items — negotiations between the United States and the Soviet Union on intermediate-range nuclear weapons, known as INF, and those on strategic nuclear arms reductions, known as START; the negotiations on mutual and balanced reductions of conventional forces in Europe (MBFR), and the continuing process of discussion and negotiation stemming from the Final Act of the Helsinki Conference on Security and Cooperation in Europe. In addition, the United States is trying to prevent the spread of nuclear weapons; to eliminate the menace of chemical weapons (a case in which the Soviet Union is a clear violator of international agreements); to study the possibility of imposing further limits on the military use of outer space; and to develop new measures to minimize the risks of war by miscalculation.

As we face the future, it is important to remember the origins of the present situation. Over a period of more than 25 years the Soviet Union claimed immunity from the United Nations Charter rules against aggression, and the rest of the world tacitly accepted its claim. That course is no longer tolerable. Soviet expansion and the Soviet Union's growing military power threaten the international system. That system cannot continue to accept the Soviet practice of aggression through the use of its own forces and those of its proxies and satellites, whether organized as armies, guerrillas, armed bands, or terrorists, backed by the implicit threat of its growing nuclear forces. During the 1970s, a period when the United States nuclear arsenal was held relatively stable, the Soviet Union expanded its nuclear forces far beyond any conceivable requirements for deterrence and defense. We must give priority to our security and to that of other democratic nations in the world.

Having said all of this, I do not want to end on too pessimistic a note. With our European allies, our basic congruence in values dominates our occasional differences. We have been through a period of difficulty and largely as a result of Secretary Shultz's efforts we have reached an agreement on a better approach to our economic relations with the Soviet Union. Perhaps the new Soviet leadership will recognize that its interests lie in reducing the level of arms and in improving the material welfare of its people. We will be more than willing to join in reciprocal arms reductions efforts. And, if the new leadership elects to tend to its own affairs at home and to interfere less in the affairs of others, it would no doubt also find the path open to wider and mutually beneficial economic relations with the West.

All of these good things can happen; we need to keep our minds alive to these possibilities. Meanwhile, let us keep our powder dry.

### Author's Postscript March 7, 1984

By now General Secretary Andropov is no longer with us. What did he accomplish? We will only know later, if ever, actions initiated by him that are not now evident. But it is clear that he did little to deal with the fundamental problems facing the Soviet system. Efforts to tighten discipline, lessen absenteeism, reduce corruption may have had an effect but they were short-lived. Their evanescent effect can be attributed to Andropov's short tenure, but it is more plausible to believe that they would not have succeeded had he been in power longer.

General Secretary Chernenko now faces these problems. As a member of the leadership that was most closely associated with Brezhnev, there is little reason to expect radical changes under his leadership. Given his age and apparent condition of health, he may not be with us long either. So, probably before the decade of the 80s is over, the Soviet leaders will have another opportunity to choose someone who might bring about big changes. And perhaps by then the sense of crisis within the system will be so palpable as to make such changes politically possible.

### Editor's Postscript — June 18, 1984

It has now been four months since Konstantin U. Chernenko succeeded Yuri V. Andropov as Communist Party first secretary. These four months have not brought a thaw in Soviet–U.S. relations; quite the contrary.

In retrospect we can see the high point of renewed detente was reached five years ago today, when Brezhnev and President Carter signed the SALT II treaty. Thereafter, deteriorating relations had precluded the United States Senate from ratifying the treaty. In December 1979 the Soviets had invaded Afghanistan. The following month President Carter, denouncing the Soviet actions in Afghanistan, had cut U.S. grain sales to the Soviets and suspended the sale of high-technology equipment, such as computers; moreover, he organized a partial boycott of the summer Olympic games in Moscow. Another aftermath of the Afghanistan invasion had been the arrest and exile in Gorki of Andrei D. Sakharov, the Nobel Prize-winning father of the Soviet hydrogen bomb.

Tensions had again increased between the Soviets and the United States in December, 1981, with the crackdown by Poland's puppet regime on that country's Solidarity labor union. The Soviets are terrified by the prospects of the workers uniting not only in the satellites but even in the Soviet homeland.

In 1982–83 Soviet efforts to bully West Germany, Britain, Italy, and the Netherlands from accepting new U.S. Pershing II and cruise missiles failed. To show their anger the Soviets in 1983 had broken off all formal talks with the Americans and their allies on both conventional disarmament and nuclear arms limitations.

During this period Andropov's health had deteriorated and after August 1983 he ceased attending public functions. The following month the Soviets' shooting down of an unarmed Korean airliner with the loss of 269 aboard, after it had strayed into Soviet airspace, had heightened Soviet-U.S. tensions. Despite this, President Reagan and his emissary, Vice President Bush, who had attended the Andropov funeral, made overtures to the new Soviet leader to ameliorate relations. In the protocol politeness of the funeral, there appeared to be a glimmer of hope for renewed detente. But subsequently all such overtures have been spurned by the Soviets, who are in a truculent mood, demanding withdrawal of U.S. missiles from Western Europe as a condition on renewing Geneva talks on missile limitations. Leading this hostile monologue is Foreign Minister Andrei A. Gromyko. In his 26 years as Foreign Minister with Khrushchev, Brezhnev, Andropov, and now Chernenko, Gromyko had never before exercised such a prominent role. Clearly Chernenko is not well, and he lets Gromyko do the talking, while retaining his own power as General Secretary of the ruling party. Son of a Siberian peasant, Chernenko has the traditional Slavic distrust of the West.

In retrospect it may well be that the Soviets' recollections of the 1975 Helsinki accords may be even more distressing to the Soviets than the more recent U.S. arms build-up. At Helsinki, in exchange for a guarantee of the post-World War II European boundaries, the Soviets, seemingly with little concern, had become a signator to standards of human rights. From that day forth the peoples of eastern Europe have found a source of hope which deeply troubles the Soviet leaders. The old men in the Kremlin in their memories, lived near enough to the Russian Revolution to have a paranoid fear of a counter revolution. Sakharov and Solidarity have become apparitional symbols.

# The Intelligence Community and American Foreign Policy: The Reagan and Carter Administrations

GLENN P. HASTEDT
ASSISTANT PROFESSOR OF POLITICAL SCIENCE
JAMES MADISON UNIVERSITY

WITH

R. Gordon Hoxie
EDITOR, PRESIDENTIAL STUDIES QUARTERLY

It is an often made observation that Vietnam marked the end of a long-standing elite consensus on the nature and purpose of American foreign policy. The successive Carter and Reagan administrations are testimony to the dimensions which have come to mark the ensuing policy debate. The Soviet invasion of Afghanistan brought about a narrowing of the differences between these two administrations. It did not bring about a complete reconciliation of their starting positions, or provide a foundation for establishing a new consensus.

The fundamental foreign policy differences between the Carter and Reagan adminstrations — along with their points of uneasy congruence — are well illustrated in their handling of the intelligence community. Since the Church Committee in 1975 held its well publicized hearings on the Central Intelligence Agency (CIA), the intelligence community has become a focal point in the debate over the future shape and direction of American foreign policy. Different definitions of the nature of America's role in the world, and of the sources of threat to it, produce different answers to the question of what do we want an intelligence community to do.

An examination of the Carter and Reagan administration's handling of the intelligence community reveals that while very real differences separate them, there are also strong elements of continuity. This examination will proceed in four parts. First, the make-up of the intelligence community will be described.

Second, the philosophical differences between these two administrations will be discussed by examining their different definitions of the "intelligence problem" facing the United States today. Third, the nature of the intelligence function will be analyzed. Fourth, the Carter and Reagan administrations will be compared in their handling of the intelligence function. In this discussion intelligence will be examined as organization, raw data, analysis and estimates, covert action, and counterintelligence.

## The Intelligence Community

The concept of a community implies similarity and likeness. It suggests the existence of a group of actors who share common concerns and possess a common outlook on events. In these terms the intelligence community (IC) is a community only in the loosest sense. More accurately, it is a federation of units all varying in their degree of institutional autonomy, the nature and extent of their contribution to the intelligence function, and their political clout. Before describing the current make-up of this community, two points need to be stressed. First, the notion of an intelligence *community* is neither inherent in the definition of intelligence nor the sole organizational form employed by states. Second, the IC is not a static entity. Its composition, as well as the relative importance and roles of its members, has varied over time as new technologies have been developed, the international setting changed, and bureaucratic wars were won and lost.

The National Security Act of 1947 created the CIA and assigned it the responsibility of coordinating the intelligence activities of other departments and agencies. It did not use the term intelligence community nor identify those departments and agencies to be coordinated. The status of charter member is best conferred upon the CIA; the State Department's intelligence unit, the Bureau of Intelligence and Research (INR); and the intelligence units of the Armed Forces. All were given institutional representation on the National Security Council (along with the newly created Department of Defense which at the time lacked a centralized intelligence capability) by the 1947 National Security Act. Additionally, the State, War, and Navy Departments had been designated in 1946 by Truman to constitute the Central Intelligence Group, the immediate institutional fore-runner of the CIA.

Three institutions which have a long standing but lesser presence in the intelligence process are the Federal Bureau of Investigation (FBI); the Treasury Department; and the Atomic Energy Commission (AEC). While the FBI's counterintelligence role has remained constant, significant changes have occurred with regard to the other two. Accounts of the Treasury Department's early involvement in the IC stress its drug enforcement role. This is no longer the case. By the time of Ford's Executive Order, Treasury had come to be charged with the overt collection of foreign financial, monetary, and general economic information.[1] All reference to its drug enforcement role had been dropped.

The fate of the AEC is somewhat different. The task of evaluating, collecting, and providing technical information on foreign nuclear energy programs has remained a part of the IC's concerns. It is the organization which no longer exists. The AEC gave way to the Energy Research and Development Administration in the Ford administration which, in turn, gave way to the Energy Department under Carter. Each of these agencies was designated by executive order to be a member of the IC and given responsibility for energy matters. Though considered for dismantling by Reagan, the Energy Department retains its place in the IC according to his executive order.

The first major addition to the IC occurred in 1952 when Truman issued a presidential directive transforming the only recently created Armed Forces Security Agency into the National Security Agency (NSA). NSA operates as a semiautonomous agency of the Defense Department and is charged with 1) maintaining the security of U.S. message traffic and 2) interpreting, traffic analyzing, and cryptanalyzing the messages of other states. In 1961 the Defense Intelligence Agency (DIA) joined the IC as its newest major member. DIA emerged as part of the centralization process occurring within the Defense Department. The major objectives behind its creation were to unify the overall intelligence efforts of the Defense Department, and to more effectively collect, produce, and disseminate military intelligence.

Over the years DIA has emerged as the principal challenger to the CIA in the preparation of intelligence estimates. DIA's challenge to the CIA's status as first among equals has reached a new height in the Reagan administration. Both the Reagan transition team and the Senate Select Intelligence Committee called for the upgrading of DIA's estimating capabilities so that it might more effectively challenge the estimates produced by the CIA.

A 1972 recommendation by the Fitzhugh Committee led to the further centralization of functions within the military establishment. The Defense Mapping Agency and the Defense Investigative Service were formed out of the three separate mapping and investigative services of the Army, Navy, and Air Force. These units now serve as lesser members of the IC.

Changes have continued to occur at the fringes of the IC. The Carter and Reagan Executive Orders designated the staff elements of the Director of Central Intelligence (DCI), who is also the head of the CIA, as a member of the IC where the Ford Executive Order made no such reference.[2] The only difference between the Carter and Reagan structuring of the IC lies in Carter's adding the Drug Enforcement Administration to it and Reagan's removing it from formal memberships in IC.

### Defining the "Intelligence Problem"

#### Philosophical Starting Points

Party platforms in the U.S. are not noted for their value as programmatic guides to action. Bargaining, compromise, and posturing more than the consistent application of a philosophy to policy problems guides their composition. Surprisingly, this truism does not hold with respect to how the 1976 Democratic and 1980 Republican platforms conceptualized the "intelligence problem." These two platforms accurately foreshadowed the general philosophical thrust that the Carter and Reagan administrations would bring to bear in their respective dealings with the IC. The 1976 Democratic platform was the first to ever make an explicit reference to the intelligence problem. One paragraph in length, it reflected a fundamental suspicion of the IC as it then operated. It stated that:

> Our civilian and military intelligence agencies should be structured to provide timely and accurate information and analysis of foreign affairs and military matters. Covert action must be used only in the most compelling cases where the national security of

the U.S. is vitally involved; assassination must be prohibited. There should be full and thorough Congressional oversight of our intelligence agencies. The constitutional rights of American citizens can and must be fully protected, and intelligence abuses corrected, without endangering the confidentiality of properly classified intelligence or compromising the fundamental intelligence mission.[3]

The intelligence problem was defined in the Democratic platform as one of control and the correction of past abuses. Covert action must be greatly restricted, assassinations prohibited, disclosures and oversight made effective and thorough, and the protection of constitutional rights guaranteed. The focus was essentially external. It was on the relationship between the IC and the outside world, including the American political system. The requirements of the intelligence function and the problems that the IC faced in performing its assigned mission were left unaddressed. In its place there is only the exhortation that the ingelligence function must be accomplished in a timely and accurate fashion.

The intellectual roots of this perspective, and the reasons for its serving as a reliable guide to action, are twofold. First, this statement accurately reflected the image of the CIA presented to the public at large through the mass media in the early 1970s. It was an outsider's view of the IC, one in which the charge that the CIA was a rogue elephant held a great deal of validity. It was a perspective which Carter, the novice in intelligence matters and the self-professed Washington outsider, could be attracted to.

Secondly, Vice President Walter Mondale and his former senatorial aide, David Aaron, quickly established themselves as the driving force behind CIA legislation in the Carter administration. Mondale's views on the CIA were formed during his service on the Church Committee and were quite consistent with the general spirit of that committee's investigation. Above all, Mondale appeared to be deeply suspicious of covert operations for fear that they would violate American civil liberties.

This generally negative outlook inspired by Mondale remained constant during the Carter administration. The Iranian crisis brought an outburst of anger on Carter's part over the performance of the IC, and a changed conception of the intelligence function. Despite Mondale's misgivings, the centerpiece of this new outlook was an increased emphasis on covert action capabilities plus a desire to lessen Congressionally mandated reporting requirements. The fundamental suspicions remained. Carter's 1980 State of the Union Address, described by Ray Cline as the most balanced reference to intelligence made by Carter during his presidency,[4] attests to the continuance of the negative outlook which characterized the Carter administration's approach to the IC.

> We also need clear and quick passage of a new charter to define the legal authority and accountability of our intelligence agencies. We will guarantee that abuses do not recur, but we must tighten our controls on sensitive intelligence information, and we need to remove unwarranted restraints on America's ability to collect intelligence.[5]

Interestingly, the 1980 Democratic platform devoted only one sentence to the intelligence problem. Placed at the end of a paragraph on defense, it pledged to "further improve intelligence gathering and analysis."[6]

The 1980 Republican platform devoted a full nine paragraph section to the intelligence problem. Unlike the 1976 Democratic platform, its focus was on the state of affairs existing within the IC and the problems it faced in performing its mission. The section began by asserting the deteriorating ability of the IC to supply governmental leaders with timely and accurate analysis. Iran and the underestimation of Russian military strength were cited as two especially critical failures. The loss in morale, and of public confidence in the IC, were also decried. So too was the hesitancy of foreign intelligence services to cooperate with U.S. agencies. The need to remake the IC into a "reliable and productive instrument of national policy" was next pledged with a number of specific steps in that direction being outlined:

— reestablish the President's Foreign Intelligence Advisory Review Board
— propose legislation to allow intelligence officers to operate safely and efficiently abroad
— support legislation to invoke criminal sanctions against those who make disclosures of the identity of U.S. intelligence officials abroad, sources, or methods
— support amendments to the Freedom of Information Act and the Privacy Act to allow for meaningful background checks
— provide a capability to help influence events vital to our national security interest

—  provide a method of generating alternative intelligence estimates[7]

Constraints on, and the control of, IC actions received mention only in the concluding paragraph. The platform pledged to prevent the reoccurrence of abuses, but asserted the need to repeal "ill considered restrictions sponsored by the Democrats." Such restrictions had eroded U.S. capabilities and made easier the efforts of Russia, who, as the platform earlier had noted, operated by a different set of rules than did the U.S. Under Carter and his CIA Director, Admiral Stansfield Turner, covert operatives, which had numbered in the thousands in the 1960's had been reduced to about 300. The Republican platform forecast a return to vigorous covert operations, "a capability which only the United States among major powers has denied itself."[8]

The views expressed in the Republican platform are consistent with the view of the IC held by conservatives and many ex-intelligence officers. A late entry into the debate on the CIA, and long a minority view, this position gradually gained in respectability as the 1970s came to an end. With the Reagan candidacy the advocates of these views were given their first solid political base to work from in presenting their interpretation of the intelligence problem.

Initially no driving force comparable to the Mondale and Aaron tandem emerged within the Reagan Administration to shape its approach to intelligence matters. Instead, a general consensus existed among all the parties on the need for change in the direction put forward by the platform. Differences of emphasis and priorities did exist within this consensus. They have repeatedly emerged into public view as different factions have vied for leadership in forging policy. The early lead was taken by those associated with the Reagan transition team and the Heritage Foundation. The transition team was headed by William J. Casey, as Chairman, and Edwin Meese III, as Chief of Staff. The Casey-Meese recommendations called for significant changes in the structure and operation of the IC. Casey, a New York attorney, who had served in the Office of Strategic Services in World War II, was named as DCI with Cabinet rank (first in CIA history). Admiral Bobby R. Inman, who had served as the NSA Director since 1977, was named as Casey's Deputy. Inman had already emerged as a leading force within the IC.

While an advocate of change, Inman did not endorse the sweeping changes sought by the transition team, nor did Casey countenance the view that Inman was the real head. With Inman's resignation, Casey, whose leadership had been low key, took charge. Philosophically he enumerated the changes that had been urged by the Reagan transition team during his chairmanship.

## Political Realities

The translation of philosophy into policy has not been a smooth process for either administration. According to press accounts, both the Carter and Reagan Executive Orders became surrounded in controversy. Carter's Executive Order is generally acknowledged to have been held up for months due to strenuous objections by the Defense Department to Stansfield Turner's bid for taking power, complete control over the IC's budget, and the stripping of NSA and the National Reconnaissance Office (NRO) out from under its control. The final compromise gave Turner much of the budgetary and tasking powers that he sought. It also protected the prerogatives of other IC members by building into that authority appeal procedures. The NSA and NRO remained under Defense Department control.

Conflict surrounding Reagan's Executive Order was less visible within the administration than it was in executive-legislative negotiations over its content. That is not to say, however, that conflicts cannot be presumed to have existed within the administration. Inman's resignation just months after the Executive Order was issued suggests the existence of an ongoing dispute over priorities and programs in that quarter.

Congressional objections to Reagan's Executive Order as it was originally proposed centered on provisions permitting the CIA to infiltrate and influence domestic groups. Under the Carter Executive Order the FBI, and not the CIA, was permitted to do this but only with the permission of the Attorney General. As it finally emerged, the Reagan Executive Order was in its fourth draft and incorporated fifteen of the eighteen major revisions proposed by the House and Senate Select Intelligence Committees. Included was a retention of the Carter ban on infiltrating domestic groups.

Such compromises on Reagan's part were not necessary from

a legal point of view; an Executive Order does not require Congressional consent. They reflected the changed political environment in which the intelligence problem—however it is defined—has to be approached. Congressional acquiescence to a proposed course of action has now become crucial to the successful operation of the IC and the accomplishment of the intelligence function. Intelligence has become a public issue and the arena in which decisions on it are made has been fundamentally transformed. The IC in general, and the CIA in particular, have become public bureaucracies.

### Definitions of Intelligence

As with the concept of power, intelligence is simultaneously a term with a self-evident meaning and one which proves to be exceedingly difficult to define with precision. Official definitions of intelligence have either been so broad as not to be useful, or have been made irrelevant by governmental policy decisions. Academic definitions have been on the whole more revealing, but no consensus has emerged in the literature on its exact meaning.

The National Security Act of 1947 adopted a definition of intelligence which stressed its informational character. It assigned the CIA the following tasks:

(1) To *advise the National Security Council* on intelligence matters of the government related to national security.

(2) To make recommendations to the National Security Council for *coordination of intelligence activities* of departments and agencies of government.

(3) To *correlate and evaluate* intelligence and provide for its appropriate dissemination within the government.

(4) To perform for the benefit of existing intelligence agencies such *additional services* as the NSC determines can be efficiently accomplished by a central organization.

(5) To perform *other functions and duties* relating to national security intelligence as the National Security Council may direct.[9]

Yet virtually from the outset, policy makers and the CIA adopted a far more expansive definition, one which included covert action, domestic activities, and counterintelligence. The 1955 Hoover Commission defined intelligence as dealing with "all things that should be known in advance of initiating a course of action."[10] Reagan's Executive Order did not attempt a definition of intelligence, an omission it shares with Ford's Executive Order. Carter's Executive Order merely states that intelligence is foreign intelligence and counterintelligence. These two terms were respectively defined as follows:

> *Foreign Intelligence* means information relating to the capabilities, intentions and activities of foreign powers, organizations or persons, but not including counterintelligence except for information on international terrorist activities.
>
> *Counterintelligence* means information gathered and activities conducted to protect against espionage and other clandestine intelligence activities, sabotage, international terrorist activities or assassinations conducted for or on behalf of foreign powers, organizations or persons, but not including personnel, physical, document, and communcations security programs.[11]

These definitions were also adopted by the Reagan administration and differed only slightly from the language found in Ford's Executive Order.

Three academic efforts at defining intelligence are noteworthy for their analytical rigor and completeness of discussion. The first is the classical definition of intelligence presented by Sherman Kent in 1949.[12] He defined intelligence to be knowledge, activity, and organization. As knowledge, intelligence could take on one of three forms: strategic, current-reportorial, or speculative-evaluative. Organizationally, intelligence could either take on a national (central) dimension or a departmental one. Intelligence as an activity encompassed seven functional stages progressing from the recognition of a problem to the presentation of findings.

Harry Ransom's 1970 work constitutes a second significant contribution to the study of intelligence.[13] He conceives of the intelligence function as providing the information required for decision or action. It is interchangeably process and product. Ransom stresses that because of the interdependence of the acquisition, interpretation, and use of information, it is a process with no clear starting or ending point. Like Kent, Ransom relies on the concept of functional stages to categorize intelligence as a process. Viewed as a product, Ransom sees intelligence as being either strategic, tactical, or counterintelligence.

The most recent approach of note is that taken by Roy

Godson.[14] Though sharing Kent's basic terminology, Godson sees Kent's effort as only a partial study of intelligence, one restricted to an examination of analysis and estimates. He sees intelligence as compromising four symbiotically related elements: clandestine collection, counterintelligence, analysis and estimates, and covert action. It is asserted that these four functions have been associated with the concept of intelligence by most governments regardless of whatever differences in organization, tactics, or focus may have separated their handling of the intelligence function.

The approach to be followed here will borrow from all three of these definitional efforts in recognizing that intelligence is a multidimensional concept. It will share with Ransom and Kent the assertion that intelligence is best conceived of as "the endeavor to get the sort of knowledge upon which a successful course of action can be rested."[15] With Godson it will recognize that as it is presently understood and organizationally constituted, any discussion of intelligence must address the issue of covert action. Accordingly, the Carter and Reagan administrations will be compared along five dimensions in their approach to intelligence. Intelligence will be viewed as organization, raw data, analysis and estimates, covert action, and counterintelligence.

## Intelligence as Organization

### Structural Comparisons

A discussion of the organization of the intelligence community and the intelligence function must proceed along two lines. The first focuses on its formal structure. The second addresses the operating styles and managerial attitudes of its top administrators. It is the first dimension which receives the most attention in the press and in the drafting of legislation. As Richard Betts notes, such structural changes tend to generate only marginal changes in the operation of the IC.[16]

With the counsel of such veteran students of national security affairs as Gordon Gray, Robert D. Murphy, and William J. Casey, President Ford had created analytical teams, with a Team A from the defense community and Team B from outside. Team B took a hardline on the Soviet Union. Team B critics of CIA estimates of Soviet military strength were equally

critical of estimates generated by the Office of National Estimates (ONE) and its successor, the National Intelligence Officer (NIO) system. More significant changes often occur at the
level of operating procedures. Here Betts notes that the tendency
is to fluctuate between styles which stress the centralization of
power and those which seek to foster competition among the
members of the IC. It is along this second dimension that the
differences between the Carter and Reagan administrations are
the most pronounced.

The Carter administration made no fundamental changes in
the organizational structure of the IC. The Carter administration largely settled for changing the designations of officials and
moving functions from one office to another. Four structural
changes deserve comment.[17] First, Carter abolished the President's Foreign Intelligence Advisory Board (PFIAB). (This was
the organization that had recommended creation of Team B).
In place of PFIAB, Carter established a smaller Intelligence
Oversight Board which had functions roughly similar to those
of the PFIAB. Second, Carter returned to the practice of placing
the national estimating function within a corporate body and
housing it within the Directorate of Intelligence. He did so by
placing the NIOs within a newly created National Intelligence
Council (NIC). Third, in a move which appears to be more
symbolic than substantive, Carter designated the national estimates staff a community asset. This placed it on a par with the
collection tasking and budgetary functions. To emphasize its
new community-wide nature, the Deputy Director of Intelligence (DDI) was given the new title of Director of the National
Foreign Assessment Center.* Lastly, the Carter administration
returned to the practice of subordinating those departments concerned with analyzing weapons intelligence to the Directorate
of Intelligence. This took them out of the Directorate of Science
and Technology, leaving it solely responsible for developing intelligence collecting and dissemination technology.

The Reagan administration has yet to make a major structural change in the organization of the IC. The Reagan transition team asserted the need for such changes, and they may yet
occur. William Casey, however, has stated that the time is not
right for a structural upheaval, and does not appear to be par-

---

* *Organizational charts identify him as Deputy to the DCI for National Intelligence.*

ticularly interested in pursuing the matter. Adhering to a pledge in its platform, the Reagan administration has reconstituted the PFIAB. The only other change of note is the removal of the NIC from under the control of the DDI and its placement under the personal direction of the DCI. This is a move criticized by some who feel that positioned this way the estimating process is too vulnerable to political pressures.

## Operating Styles

Turner came to the IC as an outsider and left it as an outsider. Unlike his predecessor, George Bush, or his successor, Turner made little effort to gain the confidence of the intelligence professionals who served under him. Nor did he become their advocate in public. His managerial style approached that of Downs' zealot: he was loyal to a relatively narrow range of policies, and he sought power both for its own sake and to accomplish these goals.[18] By the time of his departure, he had alienated both members of the Cabinet and the intelligence community professionals. Two traits stand out in Turner's managerial style. First, he isolated himself from his subordinates. Turner placed a layer of personal assistants drawn from his Navy days between himself and the intelligence professionals that he directed. Communication flowed largely downward. Oral reports were discouraged, and written reports became the preferred method of interaction. Turner was also known to rewrite estimates and send them forward for action rather than returning them to the NITC for redrafting.

The second trait was a mistrust for the career intelligence officer. One area where this mistrust surfaced was in his handling of personnel cutbacks. These cutbacks had begun, during the brief period in the Nixon Administration when James Schlesinger was DCI, and were then held by many observers to be not unreasonable. What virtually all observers agree upon is the objectionable manner in which they were continued under Turner. "Purge" is the term one most frequently encounters in descriptions of Turner's handling of these cutbacks. The Halloween Massacre of 1977 eliminated 800 spots in one cut. Reportedly included in the cuts were the station chiefs in Bonn, Vienna, London, Ottawa, and three in Latin America.[19] All were careerists with over thirty years service. These actions plus the constant rumor of further cuts demoralized the IC and led to a flood of early retirements among middle level and senior officials.

Casey came to the post of DCI with a very different set of priorities and managerial style. Casey neither sought to become an intelligence czar, a charge leveled against Turner, nor a Dulles-like superspy. Cline suggests that the low profile managerial role model established by John McCone may best describe Casey's perception of his job.[20] Evaluations on how he has fared in this have been mixed with political bents but by 1984 were increasingly affirmative. Turner has accused him of being a wanderer, hopping from one topic to another and leaving the CIA directionless. Others assert that Casey skillfully delegates authority; has his interests and pursues them, leaving capable subordinates to handle details elsewhere. His deputy is John McMahon, a CIA veteran, much respected; McMahon has had experience in both analysis and covert operations. Casey's espionage chief, John Stein, is also a much respected professional, who succeeded Max Hugel, who had been a campaign aide. Although no charges were brought against Hugel, Casey's initial espionage chief had been a center of controversy and had early-on resigned. Like Stein, the chief of the Directorate of Intelligence, Robert Gates, is highly regarded. In what Casey sees as his most important managerial task he appears to be succeeding. Accounts suggest that the Max Hugel affair notwithstanding, Casey has been successful in his morale building efforts. After a controversial initial period, he has emerged with much needed leadership.

Both administrations have exhibited a number of similarities in their approach to staffing the IC, and have encountered similar problems. Each administration has been accused of appointing intelligence amateurs to high level posts. This clearly was the case with Turner, and appears to have been one of the necessary qualifications for the job of DCI in the Carter administration. The other qualification was a reputation for personal loyalty. Theodore Sorensen, Carter's first choice for DCI, possessed these traits along with a substantial body of political expertise.

The ill fated Sorensen nomination is representative of the general frustrations that liberal critics of the CIA have experienced in seeking to tame that institution. Sorensen had expressed a willingness to make the CIA's budget public and a conviction

that covert action be undertaken only in the most extreme circumstances. The telling blow levelled at his nomination was the
charge that Sorensen had misused secret material in the preparation of his book on the Kennedy years.[21] Liberal critics see
a double standard in the manner in which the CIA has aggressively pursued its radical critics such as Agee and Snepp compared to the apparent reluctance with which it has pursued former
agents such as Terpil and Wilson.

The charge of amateurism is less true with regard to Casey,
yet it still has some merit. Casey had served in the OSS for five
years and was a member of Ford's PFIAB. Hence he was not
without experience in intelligence matters. Moreover, he is a
scholar and a prodigious reader. His experience in intelligence,
however, was not nearly as current or extensive as was that of
the other front runner for the post, Bobby Inman. Casey's appointment as DCI had followed his successful managerial role
in the Reagan-Bush 1980 election campaign. Having come to
the aid of the Reagan candidacy when it was in need, Casey
was given his choice of top governmental positions and opted
for DCI.

The Carter and Reagan administrations have also shared a
series of unprecedented and embarrassing setbacks in making
high level appointments. Most of these problems have centered
around the lack of qualfications of those nominated. One case
where this was not the problem was with Carter's reported choice
of Lyman Kirkpatrick as the CIA's Deputy Chief. Opposition
to his appointment stemmed from his role in investigating illegal
CIA drug testing programs while serving as the CIA's Inspector
General.

Carter was immediately confronted with the charge of
amateurism with his appointment of Sorensen as DCI. Turner
would also be vehemently attacked by former career intelligence
officers for his appointment of outsiders to key posts. As aforementioned, Casey received early criticism with his appointment
of Republican businessman Max Hugel to the post of Deputy
Director of Operations. Press accounts suggest that three factors
governed this decision. First, Casey planned to take an active
role in covert operations matters; therefore, the need for a professional to head the Operations Directorate was lessened. Second

was a desire to build CIA bridges back to the business community. Finally, there appears to have been the belief that as an outsider, Hugel could inject fresh ideas and innovative spirit into the clandestine service.

It should also be noted that the Reagan administration has broken some new ground in its replacement of Inman with career professional John McMahon. Tradition had been that the top two spots in the IC would be occupied by one civilian and one ex-military figure. Casey and McMahon constitute the first all-civilian team to head the IC. The Casey-McMahon team appears to be functioning well. By 1984, Casey, who has had the steadfast support of President Reagan, had clearly won the support of the CIA professionals and the Agency's morale, badly damaged in the 1970's, had been restored.

### Intelligence as Raw Data

The sources of intelligence are varied. At the most basic level a distinction exists between overtly and covertly collected data. These categories may, in turn, be subdivided according to the collection methods employed. The major difference between the Carter and Reagan administrations centers on the relative weight they have given to the different subcategories of covert intelligence: human intelligence (HUMINT) versus technologically derived data. This latter category consists of electronic intelligence (ELINT), photographic intelligence (PHOTINT), and signals intelligence (SIGINT).

Compared to technologically derived data, HUMINT has two main advantages. It is comparatively less expensive, and it holds out the prospect of uncovering the intentions of the other side. An intelligence official accurately summed up its major weakness:

> nobody has ever believed a piece of HUMINT, no matter what its pedigree, unless he found it compatible with his personal predisposition.[22]

A second weakness centers on the time frame within which HUMINT operates. To be successful, HUMINT requires the adoption of a long-term perspective. Resources must be put into place, and allowed to develop contacts and access to data. Presidents, confronted by political challenges to their leadership, and a seemingly endless series of international crises, have a far shorter perspective. They often become impatient with the security considerations necessary to run an effective HUMINT operation, placing results over the practice of good trade craft.

Data gathered through technological means has as its strong suit the aura of authenticity and objectivity associated with scientific undertakings. It appears to the policy maker as concrete, objective, and incapable of manipulation by the enemy for purposes of deception.[23] Its primary weakness is that technologically gathered data tends to overwhelm the analyst. Far more data is collected than can be effectively analyzed. A second weakness is that it cannot deal with the matter of intentions. It can potentially answer the question of what is happening but never the question of why it is happening.

Deep personnel cutbacks in the clandestine service plus Turner's preference for (some would say obsession with) satellite intelligence caused HUMINT to come out decidedly second best in the first part of the Carter administration. This changed with the fall of the Shah. Events in Iran brought home with great force the need for insight into the motivations of actors. In a November, 1978 news conference, Carter admitted that his administration had overemphasized ELINT and neglected HUMINT. No charge of imbalance has been leveled at the Reagan administration. It has by all accounts accelerated the restoration of personnel slots, and recruitment of personnel in an effort to rebuild a HUMINT capacity. Casey was initially faced with a shortage of competent professionals and has engaged in a vigorous recruitment program. The 800 clandestine operatives Turner had sacked had by 1984 been replaced by Casey, in part by recalling retired officers.[24]

### Intelligence As Analysis and Estimates

The analysis and estimates function is the process of making sense out of the raw data at one's disposal. The ongoing debate has been over whether to integrate intelligence and policy, or to keep them separate. The dominant position was put forward by Kent.[25] He asserted that policy making and analysis must be kept separate. The purpose of analysis was to give policy makers warning of impending action and to plot long-term trends. It cannot be expected to predict specific events. In 1949 political scientist, Willmoore Kendall, put forward the opposing position.[26] He argued that analysis cannot be kept value free or separate from policy making. Analysis must articulate and evaluate policy options, and force the policy maker to confront alternatives.

More recently, former DCIs Richard Helms and William Colby have put forward contrasting views of the analysis and estimating function.[27] Helms has argued that the IC must be seen as a staff function of the President and nothing else. As such, it should not release sanitized estimates to the public, or present information which could be used to oppose administration policy. Colby has adopted the opposite position. He favors public reports, sees the IC as having a responsibility to the entire government and not just to the President, and does not oppose the release of information which contradicts administration policy.

The analysis and estimates function as practiced in the Carter and Reagan administrations does not fit neatly into any of the above positions. This is not surprising; reality seldom matches up perfectly with theory. Elements of the above debates, however, have surfaced as these two administrations have grappled with the question of how best to manage the analysis and estimates function.

Structurally, the Reagan administration is moving in the opposite direction from the Carter administration in two respects. It is moving away from centralization to a competitive system of analysis and estimates. Both the Reagan transition team and the Senate Select Intelligence Committee had called for such a move. Both advocated the upgrading of DIA's estimates. Second, while it has retained Carter's NIC it has moved it out from under the control of the DDI and placed it under the personal direction of the DCI. Where the Carter administration was producing a dozen National Intelligence Estimates a year, under Casey's direction the Reagan administration had by 1983 increased this to 50 annually.[28] At the same time the CIA was working on an additional 800 projects ranging from Third World population trends to assessments of Soviet weapon systems. Both leadership and money have contributed to the increase. The analytical budget has increased 50% and the number of analysts has been restored to the level of the early 1960's.[29]

Similarities between the two administrations are noticeable when one moves from structure to process. Both have been charged with the politicalization of the analysis and estimating function. There is an element of validity to these charges. Turner did rewrite estimates and send them on up the policy process rather than back down for reworking. Turner and Casey have both rejected estimates as inadequate. Says one professional, "Casey had good instincts on the process of producing National Intelligence Estimates."[30] The fact that these estimates did not support administration policy at the minimum created an impression during the Turner years of political pressure being placed on the analyst to produce the desired estimate.

Far from adhering to a prescribed position, however, Casey has encouraged dissenting and minority positions. The dissent is no longer relegated to a footnote. This is important since often the minority position turns out to be the correct one. Conventional wisdom is also being challenged. For example, a new review of Soviet anti-ballistic systems presents a far more alarming position than past assessments.[31]

The charge of politicalization is, however, also somewhat of a misnomer. Political reality makes impossible Kent's injunction to keep policy making and analysis separate. The real question is how to best integrate them. The starting point must be with policy makers making clear what their concerns are. This involves the laying out of collection priorities and terms of reference for the analyst. The policy maker must inject himself or herself into the intelligence function if it is to produce desirable results. This almost by definition politicizes the process. In the absence of such guidance, the analyst may produce accurate estimates, but they run the risk of being held irrelevant by the policy maker and dismissed. Casey, according to an expert has worked to make reports "shorter, blunter and more timely."[32]

Policy makers must guide analysis if the product is to be of use to them with any predictability. To label this interaction of policy maker and analyst as politicalization is to not understand the estimating function. There is nothing in this process of providing direction which absolves intelligence professionals of the responsibility of presenting estimates contrary to administration policy if that conclusion is warranted by the data at their disposal. The analyst must do so and the policy maker must accept that it will happen. There is no degree of separation or integration which can force the policy maker to accept that estimate. One can, however, increase the odds of its acceptance if one is addressing the policy maker's concerns in the estimate, and if both are speaking the same language.

What has occurred in the Carter and Reagan administrations is not the politicalization of analysis; it is the publicization of the product of analysis. Increasingly intelligence estimates are being either purposefully made public or leaked to the public in an effort to effect the resolution of an ongoing policy debate. Unlike the politicalization of the analytic process, the publicization of its product is neither inevitable nor desirable. It instead reflects the changed political atmosphere within which the IC now operates.

This more visible environment makes impossible a return to the anonymity sought for it by Helms, but does not make necessary the degree of openness argued for by Colby. The degree to which the product of the intelligence estimating process should take on a public nature is a question which does not yet have an answer. The answer to that question does, however, lie partly under the control of policy makers. The Reagan administration has moved both directions on this question. On the one hand it has taken steps to reduce the publicness of the intelligence product. Leaks have been plugged up. The practice of issuing sanitized versions of select estimates has been ended. It remains to be seen to what extent those actions will have their desired impact, or if they will just alter the process by which estimates are made public. Both the winning and losing side in the policy debate must decide that it is best to keep the intelligence product out of the public eye. Yet, the temptation to expand the arena of conflict and bring in new allies is great. On the other hand its use of photo intelligence involving fighting in Central America and communications intelligence on Russia's shooting down of the Korea jet liner indicates some willingness to go public with intelligence.

Casey has been successful in reducing bickering among the agencies in the IC by actually encouraging dissenting views in a winnowing process. Moreover, he has created a Weekly Watch Report and for even more timely reporting a "typescript memorandum" for the President and other key officials. He personally sees the President at least twice a week.

## Intelligence As Covert Action

Covert action is an area of intelligence activity for which publicly available data are scarce. Consequently, it is an area where judgements must be put forward cautiously. To understand the debate which rages here one must first understand that in many respects covert action is a uniquely American concept. Roy Godson notes that even in translation it is difficult to find in the intelligence lexicon of other states. Absent elsewhere is the distinction between covert and overt which forms the heart of this concept. The Soviet Union, for example, uses the term "active measures" to refer to all attempts at influencing people regardless of its method.[33]

Evidence suggests that there is not as large a gap separating the Carter and Reagan administrations in this area as one might expect. The Carter administration came into office with an established bias against covert action. In addition to the factors cited previously for this opposition, including the Church Committee in the Senate and Mondale's role therein, one might add the findings in the House of the Pike Committee's investigation into covert action. Its negative evaluation of covert action as a policy tool could only reinforce this Carter-Mondale perspective.

The Carter administration also inherited a covert action capability which had been the object of cutbacks since the Nixon years when a feeling existed that too much money was being spent on intelligence. Cline suggests that no increases in spending occurred from 1970–1974, and that given inflation a decrease in spending actually took place.[34] While these cuts hit personnel in all areas, they hit especially hard at the covert action capability. Schlesinger, as Nixon's DCI cut 1,800 from the CIA, with all but 200 coming from the Operations Directorate. As commented upon above, Turner continued in this tradition with his own brand of personnel cutbacks.

By midterm a change occurred within the Carter administration. Following over a year of what the press labeled as intense internal debate, there began a move to augment the U.S. covert action capability. The most visible step in this direction was

Carter's proposing legislation which would have made it easier for the CIA to engage in small covert operations. He proposed increasing the types of operations which did not require presidential approval, not banning the use of clergy and academics as agents, and permitting Americans to be spied upon abroad under certain circumstances.

But Carter scarcely got the build-up underway. Starting with about 300 covert operatives, the Reagan administration has increased this to more than 1000.[35] It has built up the covert action capability and the pursuit of less restrictive conditions governing its use. The primary difference between the two administrations lies in their fundamental attitude toward covert action. The Carter administration sent out mixed signals. Accounts suggest that Carter did not engage in any wholesale termination of covert action programs despite his stated opposition to them. In fact, prior to events in Iran, Carter approved a Special Coordinating Committee (SCC) recommendation that the CIA keep its paramilitary capability. Implementation of this recommendation appears to have floundered on the continuing opposition of Mondale and others in the administration to the CIA having such a capability. Shackley charges Turner with deliberately and consistently whittling away at this capability because of his dislike for the decision.[36]

Casey is a firm believer in covert action and Reagan is not afraid to use it. If anything, press reports suggest that the Reagan administration may have been too enthusiastic in its initial approach to covert action. The *Economist* reports on two African covert action operations proposed by Casey and Hugel which it states the House Select Intelligence Committee viewed with scant enthusiasm.[37] One was to have been directed at Qaddafi, and the other at the struggle for control of the Western Sahara. Congressional opposition caused their abortion. The repeated reports of CIA sponsored covert action programs in El Salvador and Nicaragua, and their accompaniment with highly overt naval maneuvers, are another indication of the Reagan administration's greater enthusiasm for covert action. The difficulties that it early encountered in generating public support for such a course of action attests to the depth of the "outsider" view of intelligence represented by the Carter administration's approach to intelligence. The waning of these difficulties in 1983–84 suggests that the Reagan administration may be making headway in translating rhetoric into action on a scale that it feels is necessary by covert operatives in sensitive areas of Africa, Asia, and Latin America. In point of fact the most controversial covert action, that in Nicaragua, was not of the CIA's seeking. Its 1983 efforts to turn the Nicaraguan effort over to the Pentagon was firmly rejected by Secretary of Defense Caspar Weinberger and the Joint Chiefs of Staff, who wanted no part of guerilla operations.[38] By contrast, however, with the Clark Amendment of 1975 which cut off such operations in Angola, the Boland-Zablocki resolution of 1983, which would have done the same thing in Nicaragua, was defeated.*

### Intelligence As Counterintelligence

Counterintelligence occupies a no man's land within IC. Once the power base of James Angleton, counterintelligence at the end of the Carter administration was without a vigorous institutional advocate among the operating units of IC. This was a situation which the Reagan administration perceived as dangerous. It perceived threats to U.S. national security going unmet because they fell into gaps between organizational jurisdictions.

The reasons for this state of neglect were many. First, of all the elements of the intelligence function, counterintelligence is the most difficult to define. Is it merely a police activity concerned with protecting national security secrets? Does it extend to protecting America's privately owned industrial secrets? Is terrorism within its jurisdiction? Does it include taking action to counter the moves of others, or is it solely a defensive and preventive undertaking?

A second reason for this inattention was the prominent role counter-intelligence has played as a source of tension between the FBI and the CIA. To address the question reopens old wounds, not all of which have completely healed. Thirdly, there also appeared to be an almost institutional aversion to counterintelligence by the CIA. Its roots lay in Angleton's obsessive

---

* *Editor's Note: In May 1984 Congress did cut off covert aid to the 10,000 anti-Sandinista rebels, known as* contras. *Since the cut-off, volunteers have aided the* contras *as have U.S. religious, political and relief organizations and empathetic Latin American countries. At the same time Secretary of State Shultz was assiduously negotiating with the Sandinistas.*

search for a mole in the CIA's midst and the scars that this journey into a "Wilderness of mirrors" left on its collective memory.[39] Under Casey, the increase in counterintelligence "is free of the non-productive, self-destructive mole hunting of years past. . . ."[40]

Nonetheless there remains our societal distrust and suspicion of programs directed at spying on Americans. The potential of such programs for abuse is held by many to far exceed their potential contribution to the intelligence function. The Carter administration shared this skepticism and distrust for counterintelligence, and it was virtually a nontopic during those years. The sole action taken in this area was to centralize oversight responsibility within the SCC. This centralization of authority appears not to have been granted in order to improve counterintelligence capabilities, but to prevent the feared abuses associated with it.

Counterintelligence has been very much a real topic of concern in the Reagan administration. The perceived need to identify and counter hostile actions, set the parameters for review of counterintelligence policy. Available evidence suggests that the Reagan response to this perceived failing lies in the creation of a new organization with broad powers to collect information, and a central records system which the FBI and CIA could draw upon. However, no major change in the counterintelligence system has yet occurred. Holding back such a move is Congressional and, even to an extent, administration opposition.

The suspicions of counterintelligence associated with the Carter administration are still held by many in Congress. The new political environment in which intelligence decisions are made does not allow Congressional concerns to be dismissed. As with the case with its Executive Order, political reality dictates that the Congressional perspective be incorporated into any presidential directive on counter-intelligence.

Internal disputes which plagued the Carter administration, to a degree continued into the Reagan administration; they played a role in Inman's resignation. However, it would be improper to view Inman's resignation as a rejection of counterintelligence revitalization efforts. A consensus does exist within the administration on that point. As it related to counterintelligence, Inman's resignation stemmed more from a difference of opinion over the direction it should proceed, the priority it should have, and the political costs such an effort would entail in the way of publicity, leaks, and premature public disclosures. A counterintelligence review continues within the Reagan administration, and it may prove to be the area of the most marked substantive differences between the Carter and Reagan administrations.

With all of the vast amounts of information gained by technology, such as cameras in space and infrared sensors, there is no substitute for the human operation. In this area the most significant accomplishments of the Reagan administration CIA has been the restoration of agents behind the Iron Curtain and in other strategic areas. Predictions ranging from Poland to Argentina to Grenada have been on target.

## The Future and Conclusion

In 1984 the CIA under Casey is moving rapidly into three areas in association with other federal agencies: drug trafficking, international terrorism and theft of U.S. technology.

The Intelligence Community budgets and personnel in the Reagan administrations have been greatly augmented. Yet by contrast with the Komitet Gosudarstvennoy Bezopasnosti (KGB) they are small. True, the KGB mission transcends that of the American IC. It includes areas performed by the Federal Bureau of Investigation, a coastguard, and an enormous border patrol. But in the areas confined to those of the IC its personnel and monetary support far exceed its American counterparts. Nor does it have a Congress or a free press investigating it. Still its recent score card has not been good. In 1983, 135 Soviet intelligence agents defected or were expelled from 20 countries. France alone expelled 45 accused of clandestine search "for technological and scientific information particularly in the military area."[41]

With all of the accomplishments of the current DCI, his relations with Congress, until recent date, have shown scant improvement. Indeed, they acutely worsened in April, 1984 with the imbroglio over the mining of Nicaraguan harbors. Martin Tolchin of *The New York Times* termed this the "worst rupture" in the history of CIA Congressional relations.[42] Senator Barry Goldwater, the Republican Chairman of the Senate Select Committee on Intelligence, termed the mining "an act of war." Senator Patrick Moynihan, the Democratic vice chairman of the committee, resigned that post in protest. The committee took the view that the operation was in violation of the Oversight Act of 1980 which requires the agency to keep both the Senate and the House Intelligence Committee, "fully and currently informed," on any "significant intelligence activity."[43]

In this instance Casey proved more politically astute than most persons recognized. After Casey on April 26th came close to an apology, Moynihan withdrew his resignation. The following day the Senate committee staff met with Ernest Mayerfeld, deputy director of the CIA's Office of Legislative Liaison, and other agency staff to work out guidelines for more effective working relationships. According to reports, "Mr. Moynihan is pleased with the new agreement" which Casey readily signed. However, another Senator on the committee termed it "a face saving device for the committee." The Senator, who asked not to be identified, added, "The agency people are probably laughing at us, and will carry on as before."[44] The Congress laughed back in May by cutting off funds for covert aid to the *contras*.

Philosophically the gap between the Carter and Reagan administrations approaches to the IC is great. The political reality of managing it has served to lessen the distance that each has been able to move from its predecessor. Carter's Executive Order differed from Ford's primarily in the explicitness with which it treated the issues of responsibility, restrictions, and oversight. As it finally emerged from the drafting process, Reagan's Executive Order contained many of the prohibitions found in Carter's. It major differences were ones of streamlining and emphasis. The negative thrust of Carter's Executive Order was replaced by more positive, or at least neutral, terminology.

While political reality has lessened the distance that might be expected to separate these two administrations, it has not negated the impact these two widely divergent philosophical starting points have had on intelligence policy. Whether one looks at intelligence as organization, raw data, analysis and estimates, covert action, or counterintelligence, the Carter administration pursued a policy of centralizing power and minimizing the potential for abuse inherent in the intelligence function. Only grudgingly did it begin to define intelligence requirements in terms of matching an external threat to U.S. security. It never completely overcame its negative and skeptical view of intelligence.

The Reagan administration has so far consistently defined intelligence requirements primarily in terms of the Soviet threat. Within each category of intelligence discussed here, it has sought to build up U.S. capabilities. For its part, the Reagan administration has been less inclined to accept that danger of abuse many see as inherent in its plans. Inheriting an agency of low morale, it has built a renewed esprit. Pragmatically there are these differences. The Reagan administration not only stepped up covert and counterintelligence operations, but it has also significantly increased efforts to combat illegal drug importations and to safeguard American high technology advances from being purloined. Such actions have gained support.

Nonetheless, the realities of political constraints on the IC in the 1970's continue on into the 1980's. So also does the debate launched in 1975 by the Church Committee. It will crescendo in the 1984 election.* Through it all is woven both the national concern and the political climate. In that climate Casey, to some, remains controversial. Albeit, he will probably leave a more permanent imprint on the CIA, indeed on the IC, than any of his predecessors. Indeed, as Robert S. Dudney and Orr Kelly recently concluded, ". . . Casey has elevated the. . . [CIA] from a state of disrepute during the 1970's to a newfound position of power and influence on foreign policy. . . .[He] is likely to be remembered as the man who put the CIA back on its feet when that seemed like an impossible mission."[45]

---

* Editors Note: This was precisely what was happening as this volume went to press. The subject of covert operations was raised by President Reagan, responding to questions on terrorist bombings in Lebanon. According to Hedrick Smith of The New York Times it became the subject of "one of Mr. Mondale's most blistering criticisms of the President."

Former President Carter entered the fray, demanding an apology for any implication that his own administration had reduced covert action capabilities. President Reagan not only proferred such an apology but also publicly assumed responsibility. He did so in his capacity as Commander in Chief, as related to the September 20, 1984 assault on the American embassy, as he had for the more devastating October 23, 1983 bombing of the American Marine compound at the Beirut International Airport. (The New York Times, September 27, 28, 29, and October 3, 1984).

Still the issue of prior administrations' reduction of covert operations remains. As this chapter indicates, Carter's CIA Director, Stansfield Turner, had with Mondale's guidance drastically reduced CIA covert operations. It was only after the Afghanistan invasion of December 1979 that Carter began the restoration of covert support during his last year in office.

# CHAPTER SIX

# The A.I.D. Program*

## M. PETER McPHERSON
ADMINISTRATOR, AGENCY FOR INTERNATIONAL DEVELOPMENT

You may well ask, why a conservative Republican Administration has been more supportive of a foreign aid program than has been the case in Washington for at least a decade.

I am not really here to argue the case as much as I am to state the facts. Last year, in 1981, for example, with the active and aggressive support of the President, for the first time in three years we got a foreign aid bill enacted by the Congress, and not merely another continuing resolution.

Last year in the first budget proposed by this President, the bilateral program was larger than the spending had been for foreign aid the year before. And now in every budget — there have been three budgets — the President has proposed more money for foreign aid for bilateral programs.

When the President went to Cancun, both while he was there and upon his return, he proposed that A.I.D. be charged with sending task forces to Third World countries and that those task forces be Presidential Task Forces. We have aggressively used that principle ever since.

A few months ago he appointed me his Special Representative for Relief and Reconstruction in Lebanon — really an expansion or a throw back to Marshall-type plans which have become almost a traditional function of foreign aid.

The fact is that under a conservative Republican Administration the foreign aid program has been strongly supported and has become, I believe, a more effective institution for that reason.

An institution like this — the Center looking at the Presidency — would be very interested in why this anomaly would be the case, and particularly with this President. In different times he has been very critical of foreign aid and the institution

* *Editor's Note: This address and question period are from Mr. McPherson's lecture, November 11, 1982, in the Harry J. Sievers Memorial Lecture Series jointly sponsored by Fordham University and the Center for the Study of the Presidency.*

of the Agency for International Development. There are basically two reasons for this.

One is that the foreign aid program under President Reagan
has been modified so as not to become an international welfare
program, but a self-help program. Philosophically, the President believes very deeply in the self-help aspects of the foreign
aid program.

Second, the foreign aid program has become a very important part of the foreign policy of the United States. Now and
in the past it had been that, but clearly more so in this Administration whose foreign policy has been complementary to meeting
the basic needs of poor people around the world.

It may be a little immodest, but I think I had a little to do
with being able to move the program and to get the support
of the White House. Over the last eight or nine years I had the
good fortune to at one time or another to be an assistant deputy
to both Ed Meese and to Jim Baker, and to be the President's
lawyer during the transition in the early days. But the facts are
that it was not so much a matter of personalities as the chemistry
of the issues and the needs of the institution.

What happened first in the modification of the foreign aid
program? Well, one of the very early things we did was turn
back to the U.S. Treasury some $28 million. Not everybody
in town was comfortable with that. Some were saying, "We
worked hard for that money, why are you turning back $28 mil-
lion?" What we did was this. We went through our program
and identified projects that simply were bad projects. They just
weren't giving the Third World anything. The money was not
being spent in a worthwhile manner. That certainly caught the
President's eye.

So we had a Rose Garden Ceremony. A great big check. Pictures on the front page of the *Washington Post*. It was quite an
affair. It caught the President's attention as to how this program
might become efficient.

A few months later when we were really putting on a big push
for that bill, at a meeting with Republican Congressional leaders,
someone asked, "Mr. President, you campaigned against foreign aid, why are you supporting it now?" He said, "Well, this
is our program. All those bad parts of the program are gone
now — that $28 million McPherson turned back. We made the
program, we think, a more efficient program."

However, we also shifted the philosophy of the program. I do not mean it was shifted in a partisan way. In different years it had been this way, but in recent years began to drift away from this kind of philosophy. We have come to view ourselves as development bankers if you will. We said we want to give money to a country that has a policy context that will make good use of the money. If the policies of the country are not good, then the money will just be wasted. The examples are not dramatic, because this a careful diplomatic problem. But the facts are when you look around the world and see which countries the monies have been shifted to, we have become development bankers. We have moved away, as I indicated earlier, from being an international welfare program to being a self-help program — to training, to institution building, and that kind of thing.

All these ideas about self-help projects really culminated in the Cancun Task Force concept. The President devised the idea himself, saying, "Let's send small groups of experts to foreign countries that are Presidential Missions to look at the policies of those countries. We want to help those countries do a better job with what they've got."

We have used that stamp of approval and it has resulted, frankly, in very effective programs as a result of Missions to Peru, Thailand and other places. This self-help emphasis is perfectly consistent with traditional conservative and liberal support for foreign aid on Capitol Hill. Capitol Hill liberals, I believe, basically accept the self-help approach — "Teach people how to fish, and not give them fish."

There is a second reason why the program has caught the imagination of the President and the Secretary of State. There has been a more complete integration of the foreign aid policy with the overall foreign policy of this country without compromising its basic integrity. I think that is perfectly consistent.

But too often historically, A.I.D. has had a sort of stand-offish relationship with the State Department. It has felt that if it gets too close it will be submerged. That is a reasonable fear. On the other hand, those foreign policy interests of the United States should be met by our foreign aid program and at the same time the A.I.D. Administrator should be a spokesman for foreign policy. But I conceded very early that it is critical in a town of fiefdoms like Washington, D.C. to have a very senior Cabinet official involved in protecting development interests.

So I was not Administrator for more than a day or two before I had an opportunity to meet with then Secretary Haig. I said, "The law says I report to the President, but as a practical matter I really report to you. Why don't we formalize that—at least informally anyway? Let me start coming to your daily under secretaries' staff meeting and become a part of the wider State Department community."

Well, that worked beautifully in terms of protection and in terms of getting a bigger voice at the White House and in achieving greater integration of the foreign aid program into the foreign policy of the country. We did not compromise our basic humanitarian goals. For example, we still have a program in Bangladesh for almost $200 million a year. And Bangladesh is certainly not a critical point for the foreign policy of this country, but it is for our humanitarian interests.

By not compromising those humanitarian goals our liberal friends and traditional supporters of foreign aid on the Hill are satisfied—more than satisfied, because people like Matt McHugh are really very supportive.

It was interesting to see when we did get that Foreign Aid Appropriation Bill passed through the Congress, to see how the struggle between the traditional supporters of foreign aid and the Jack Kemps of Congress affected how the bill finally emerged. Jack Kemp argued for more military assistance and Economic Support Fund money, and traditional supporters of foreign aid argued for more development assistance and for more money for the IDA and the World Bank. The balance that was finally struck between those forces was reflected in the monies we got and explains why, in the end, we had the substantial Republican and Democrat support for the bill.

That coalition—the balance of foreign policy interests with humanitarian interests is a balance we need to continue to strike. My point, obviously, is that the Administration's interest and the broader support in the Congress came about because of the closer correlation of the foreign aid bill with the foreign policy interests of the country.

Another example of all this is Lebanon, which for some is maybe an item of interest in itself. The President looked to the A.I.D. program to be the instrument to coordinate the Government-wide effort for U.S. contributions to the reconstruction of Lebanon. We were in some ways a reasonable institution to do it, but it was a broader role than we have had in recent years. But it fit very logically in that we are now very much a part of the foreign policy community at large and would not be working sort of adversely to that interest there. After all, as important as the reconstruction of Lebanon is from a humanitarian point of view, it is also a political issue of grave importance. It is critical for the physical reconstruction of the country to go hand in hand with its political reconstruction.

We have, in terms of our efforts there, begun to mount an increasingly effective international effort. The World Bank is now in Lebanon doing a brief study. While the United States has obviously played the largest role thus far, and will continue to be a major participant, we expect additional donors to contribute importantly in the near future.

Just to close then, I think it is an interesting historical anomaly that a conservative Republican Administration would end up with a Presidency more involved with foreign aid than has been the case for at least a decade.

I would welcome any questions you might have.

QUESTION: How is foreign aid integrated with our foreign policy in Guatemala, Honduras, and El Salvador?

THE ADMINISTRATOR: The whole Caribbean Basin Initiative is a combination of humanitarian, economic and political interests of the United States. Those countries are our neighbors. They are long-time natural allies and friends. We think that we more than other countries — other political donors — are the more likely people to help them, more than the Europeans for example. Moreover, we want to help them. Their economies are quite important to our economy relative to the African countries. Accordingly, it is in our self-interest to help them. Hence, the free trade zone and that kind of thing.

However, we believe as well, that the political instability in Central America is a major foreign policy concern to this country and, in the longer term, to Mexico, and others also. All combined we have been charged as the Agency to administrate a substantially larger economic assistance program in Central America and the Caribbean.

For example, it is A.I.D.'s responsibility to administrate the land reform program in El Salvador — a program that we think is important. There are some concerns and problems with it, but we think it is important for the political stability and the economic growth of that country. In short, those things all blended together in Central America, and we now have a much larger program than we had three to four years ago.

Q: You mentioned the fact that A.I.D. was helping Lebanon to rebuild politically. What is the political focus of the United States there?

T A: Well, we think that stability in Lebanon is important for stability and peace in the Middle East. If we try to put all the facts together all the time it would be difficult to sort out. So we compartmentalize it. But the facts are: working out a solution in Lebanon will have a significant impact on reaching a solution in the region as a whole. We have a very important role to play.

Q: I want to know what the political focus is in Lebanon. What do we hope to accomplish politically?

T A: Well, Lebanon with all its so-called confessions — its religious groupings — is a very fragmented society. At the same time there is total upheaval in the society — at least at times. This means that if there is truly a wise and well thought-out program, there is some opportunity for change — for change to help bind some of those wounds. We need to be sensitive to the fact that Shiite Moslems are a predominant group in Southern Lebanon and as we are involved in reconstruction we need to be sensitive and not inadvertently exclude them. But rather in our reconstruction effort we need to make them feel more a part of the whole Government in Lebanon. The President of Lebanon is a man interested in economics and is involved. We think he will use our money and the other donor money to economically and politically bind his country together.

Q: I have sort of a philosophical question. I notice many of the countries who receive aid are developing countries who have an upper class which is receiving most of the countries' income where a fair amount of corruption is going on. Middle-class American taxpayers are supporting economic aid, which is good, but probably more of this burden should fall on the wealthy classes of those countries who are evading that responsibility. How do you reconcile that? How much leverage does the A.I.D. program give you in the taxation system of these countries to improve government administration so that they are sharing what should be their own burden?

T A: We think that a foreign aid program has a responsibility to talk with countries in which it works about exactly these issues. Since 1973 A.I.D. has been under a statutory mandate to direct its programs toward the poor majority in the countries. We are not supposed to be concerned about economic growth overall in the country. We are to be concerned about the kinds of growth that allow the poor majority of the country to get at least some of the benefits of that growth. And we believe we do that.

But to speak more generally to your question, we try to talk with governments and structure our discussions so as to make them mean something in terms of policies. The policy that most commonly hurts the poorest people in many countries is the prices that farmers are paid for their products. It is particularly true in Africa, but it is true in many other countries around the world as well.

Farmers almost always are the poorest people in a country. They have the least access to medical care, to education, to these kinds of things. By and large their per capita income is smaller than almost everybody else in the country. But they do not have the ability to express themselves well politically or to threaten the political status quo very often. They cannot riot and overturn governments.

Usually, there is no effective form of political expression to champion their cause, which means they can be politically exploited by urbanites who do. What do the urbanites do? They pressure their governments to pay the farmers less than world market prices so they can have cheap food. In fact, it ends up being a tax on the poorest people in the country for the benefit of the people that are marginally better off. We think that is just not equitable. We talk about that a lot. The President's task forces to several of these countries have made that a major issue. We do not answer everything, but we try our darndest.

Q: Can you tell us what forms aid is taking? Give us some brief examples.

T A: Sure. Fifty percent of our programs are in agriculture. In agriculture we usually provide assistance by creating agricultural extension systems, by going out to show farmers how to do things better, and research to create new varieties of crops that will grow in the climates, soils, and conditions, etc. It involves education and training — showing people how to be better farmers.

We are doing a lot in terms of health care. We are doing major research in malaria vaccine. It looks like it might pay off. In the last couple of years we have been able to develop a mixture that addresses diarrhea which kids contract. This could have more of a revolutionary impact on the mortality rate of kids than has occurred for almost two or three decades.

We are involved in some energy work, but 50 percent is in agriculture.

Q: Who is in charge of this program on behalf of your agency in Lebanon?

T A: I have a man by the name of Butler, who was my Mission Director in Peru. Just a few months ago we restructured it, and put him in charge of it.

Q: One more question, do you use the National Catholic Relief Services expertise and long experience to any extended degree?

T A: Oh, sure. We use them extensively. And I am well aware of the organization, because when I was a Peace Corps volunteer in Peru the counterpart in Latin America, Caritas, is one I worked with very closely.

I lived and worked in a little barriata outside Lima. It was called El Monton, because it was built on the old Lima garbage dump. It is a classy place! My chief companion in the place was a Catholic priest — a good Irish Catholic priest named Malone. The rural Methodist McPherson and Catholic Malone had a good time. We did a lot of good things together. Caritas was an important part of what we did there.

Q: Would you start with Genesis so we can better understand the scope of your discussion and the significance of it? What is the charter and mission of the Agency for International Development. And a couple of sub-questions. What part of your program is related to major capital programs — to dams, roads, and construction of that sort? You have already appropriated my well thought-out question about fishing — eating fish and learning how to catch fish.

T A: A.I.D.'s basic mission is to help poor people in developing countries and to increase their standard of living, basically through economic growth in these poor countries.

We do that under this Administration mostly by creating better crops, by training, by building institutions to help people. We are not in the business anymore — 15 years ago we were to a fairly large degree — of creating major infrastructure projects.

In Lebanon, where we will be involved in these kinds of projects, it will be the first time in a large way in a long time. The World Bank is basically an international donor agency that builds roads, that builds dams, and that kind of thing. Our business is more technical assistance if you will — teaching how to do that sort of thing. Does that answer your question?

Q: Do you contribute funds to the national budget of the countries in which you operate that might be used for purposes other than the ones intended?

T A: We try not to. We think that by and large the best use of our money is through these projects which I have just described. However, there are examples. Perhaps it would be worthwhile for me to expand on the integration of foreign policy with the whole program. There are examples where the balance of payments and the economic situation of the country is so disastrous and the country is of such significance to us politically that we do get in the business of writing checks. That's true today in the Sudan. It just has a very dire economic situation. It is very important to the overall situation in Egypt and the Horn of Africa and so on. And we are all but writing checks to them. It is also true of some of the countries of the Caribbean Basin right now, where the prices of sugar and of bauxite and the raw materials which support their economies are poor. Thirty or forty percent of the people are out of work down there.

Q: Are you in competition with the IMF in Costa Rica?

T A: No. We view ourselves as being complementary to and supportive of the IMF. In Costa Rica we are providing some budgetary support, but we have been very insistent that we are going to make modest investments until Costa Ricans can come to terms with the IMF. We have to be very sure that we do not undercut the hard discussions that the World Bank and the IMF have with these countries, and that they do not undercut our hard discussions.

Q: Did you say that aid for Bangladesh is only for humanitarian reasons and there is no political involvement at all? Can you have a policy that is only humanitarian and not have a political involvement?

T A: I think Bangladesh is probably a pretty good example of where our interest is almost totally humanitarian. I think virtually everybody here remembers the terrible days of the floods and the other disasters that came upon them almost immediately at the time of separation from Pakistan. We came in with a tremendously large food assistance program. Since then we have made major contributions to growth in Bangladesh. I would argue that the foreign policy interests of the United States in Bangladesh are not significant. We believe that our major interest in that country is humanitarian. We believe those people are trying to do something.

Q: Do you really think since you mentioned Lebanon there is a possibility to help Lebanon without Soviet-Palestinian problems. How much can we do?

T A: I think that there will be no major economic reconstruction of Lebanon unless there is a reasonable political stability. And the Palestinian problem — how they are dealt with — is obviously part of the overall political equation. The Palestinians need to be dealt with. And an important part of our foreign aid in Lebanon is going to help Palestinians.

Q: No. I meant the political situation with the Palestinians.

T A: I guess my response is that you have to work out the problems of all of the groups in Lebanon — including the Palestinians to have political stability. Without political stability there can be no economic reconstruction.

I did not answer your question?

Q: Are the political problems in Lebanon ever going to be solved so that Lebanon will really be rebuilt?

T A: Well, we are trying. We are trying. We think that the President of Lebanon is trying and the Lebanese people are trying. I have been in Lebanon three times in about three months. It is my belief that some progress is being made there.

Q: Would you say something about current U.S. policies concerning relevant channeling of U.S. resources in concessional assistance to our multilateral versus our bilateral forms. And what would be the rationale for that particular policy you have?

T A: While it is true that this conservative Republican Administration has more actively supported bilateral programs than previous Administrations, some serious questions have been raised about multi-lateral approach. But we have been committed to meeting our IDA commitment.

IDA for those of you who may not know is the "soft loan window" of the World Bank to which the U.S. committed a certain amount of money during the Carter years. And we are now living through that in the Congress. The Congress, frankly has not voted us the amounts we really thought we ought to have despite our request and active support by the President and Secretary of Treasury Regan and others.

There is another factor. We believe that we must meet that IDA commitment, and I think we will. The world believes we will; they just wished we would do it faster.

There is another thing that is worth mentioning. And that is it may turn out that IDA may be a better program because it has less money. Let me explain why I think that is true.

I have a great deal of respect for Tom Clausen. We work closely and well together. He has been very helpful to me in our program. But the World Bank grew about 12 times in about as many years — IDA, the entire World Bank system. It experienced enormous growth. And what the World Bank did was to give its regional people country targets so that for Pakistan, say, you had to have so many hundreds of millions of dollars for programs that year.

The problem with that is at the same time the World Bank was trying to get Pakistan or Peru, for example, to do things better. To pay their farmers more — in other words, to have a change of policy. But the manager of the portfolio had to get the loans out there. He had no ability to impact upon the policy change sought, because the country in question knew darn well near the end of the fiscal year the Bank would authorize the loans. Under tighter budgets it seems to me the Bank may be in a better position to get more self-help from the countries than they were before. I wish to separate these comments from my earlier comments on our commitment to deliver the IDA money, because we think that it is important to deliver the money.

Q: By far the largest portion of the Bank's capital investments go through IBRD loans rather than IDA. For the poor countries that is not very obtainable. So IDA is critical from one particular point of view. I'm not going to argue with you the point of budgets, because that might well be the case. But the fact is that the Bank's portion of the total funding for the poorest of the countries which is the IDA soft window is 18 or 20 percent of its total lending program. And of course, IDA is a concessional program and not a bank loan program anyway.

T A: I think that Tom Clausen's principal concern is not the IBRD fund, but the IDA fund. And it is in IDA money that the Bank has frequently had too much money to push.

Q: What portion of AID aid goes to Egypt and Israel?

T A: We have about $6.5 billion a year in foreign assistance bilateral and multilateral. Out of that Egypt gets a billion and Israel gets $785 million. Those two countries alone have almost one-third. Now the monies they get are so called Economic Support Fund monies which do not have the 1973 statutory prescription on them. So I do not have any problems with that prescription, because that prescription applies to directed programs.

But the facts are this is a very heavy chunk of the whole. From my comments a moment ago on the ability of the IDA to talk policy, you can extrapolate my concern about Egypt a little bit. Egypt is a big program, and it has fundamental policy issues to face.

About a month before Sadat was assassinated, I had the opportunity to spend about an hour with him in Alexandria. Egypt has the same problem of not paying the farmers enough, because the Cairo people can riot and that kind of thing. And, indeed, they did in 1977 when they raised prices. I talked to him about this.

I told him, "You know Mr. President, my father thinks that you and the people of Egypt are a marvelous people." His eyes lit up and he said, "Well, why is that?" I explained, "He is a wheat farmer in the Midwest, and he thinks it is great that you are willing to pay him and his neighbors twice as much for wheat as you are willing to pay your own farmers for wheat. He does not quite understand why you do this, since you have to import wheat."

And that is what happens. Their farmers end up not producing, because they do not get paid enough. And Egypt has to import grain from people like my father to make up the difference. They will pay us twice what they will pay their own farmers.

Q: There is some implication there.

T A: Anyway, the policy dialogue suffers a little bit with a billion dollars a year going in there.

Q: Sir, that is correct of Egypt, but of other countries like Tanzania and Kenya, the resources are not there to bring in the United States there nor are resources there to increase the producer prices. In that case, would A.I.D. be willing to supplement the monies paid to farmers? The market boards are still there. They are still paying a low price. They are unwilling to extract more from the urban dwellers? Is A.I.D. going to help in such a case?

T A: Well, those are subjects and foreign policies which I am very familiar with, and apparently you are as well. The production of agriculture in Tanzania has gone down steadily for many years. We think that it is very clearly related to the fact that Tanzania has set the price substantially below world market value. We think—a lot of people think, like the World Bank, the IMF and others—that certain interest groups in a country get special treatment because they are political problems. We do not have to look around very much ourselves to see that this is not unique to developing countries. But we think that the Tanzanian situation needs to be addressed.

The Kenyan situation is parallel, but with more movement. It looks like the Kenyan Government is getting ahead of it a little bit.

Q: Given the context of this conservative Republican Administration's foreign policy what role does a nation's human rights policy play in the allocation of foreign aid? What role should it play in terms of promoting and enhancing the development of basic, fundamental human rights in developing nations? Should foreign aid be used as a method—in effect a big stick—to extend the human rights of Third World nations?

T A: I think foreign aid should be used as a method to encourage basic human rights. It should be used as a method to encourage democracy. And the means with which that tool is used is a matter of some public discussion. Should it be public?

How strongly should it be developed relative to other concerns? I do not have any doubt at all that we must continue to be interested in human rights and democracy.

I happen to think that it is very difficult to have sustained economic growth with any equity — over more than just a decade or half a decade — without some semblance of democracy. If you do not have some degree of political expression and not too much coercion on the part of government authorities, you do not keep the process moving upward. It does not need to be American-style democracy, but there needs to be some kind of political expression.

I do not want to beat my example of farmers to death, but the reason you have tremendous agricultural production in America is because farmers have political clout. And with political clout, they demanded and got research on crops, extension systems, and land grant colleges. They got the tools. And with those tools which they got by way of the ballot box, they built a system equalled by almost nothing else this country has produced.

Q: The mission of A.I.D. is to help poor countries. Is that kind of a vague definition? Does it matter whether the countries are sympathetic to the United States' forms of democracy? Before you send money, does it matter as far as human rights and what that country is doing to its own people?

T A: A lot of factors need to go into that. You have to look at human rights concerns. You have to look at what they are doing for themselves; whether they are willing to make economic sacrifices; whether they are willing to do the right things to make economic growth go — the development bankers concept I talked about in my speech. The foreign policy interest of the United States, by statute and by the judgment of this Administration, should be taken into consideration, for example, the votes that countries cast at the United Nations. Unfortunately, I never find that things are quite black and white. Very few countries have black records from our point of view that we can say, "Oh, boy, we do not want to give them anything." There are so many factors that come into play, that you cannot make easy and quick decisions, but these things should all be weighed.

Q: What percentage of our national resources — however you would like to define that — are given to your program?

T A: 0.02.

Q: 0.02. How does that compare with the investment of the other countries in similar investments in similar objectives or programs?

T A: We are about thirteenth or fourteenth in the world on a per capita income basis, if you define things in terms of economic assistance. If, on the other hand, you define it more broadly in terms of the United States' contribution to international security and to economic growth — in other words, if you add defense; and if you put in our contribution to the United Nations, put in all those organizations to which we contribute, our percentage exceeds all others.

Q: My next question was suggested by what you said about your father's wheat. How much of the money that is appropriated for foreign aid may indeed come back in the form of foreign purchase of American products?

T A: About two-thirds.

Q: So, we ourselves benefit.

T A: Directly.

Q: At one time population was a concern. You do not hear much about it any more and the Agency for International Development has a priority in that area. I understand you to say that the priority at the present is to try to develop countries economically, which is certainly consistent with the point of view of the Barbara Wards and others. Are there any other conditions attached to aid that tend to touch upon population questions?

T A: Our population program is still a very substantial program. It has had a lot of discussion about it in the early days of the Administration. Frankly, I believe in it deeply and was quite a fighter for it. The program has basically remained intact.

I feel strongly that countries and people need to want to have that help and that it cannot be forced upon them. In other words, you cannot say, "Either you have a family planning program in your country or we are going to cut off all the other economic assistance we give you." But I think we do know that the increase in population correlates fairly directly to how much economic progress people will make.

We make sure that this program is a voluntary program, both in terms of countries and in terms of individuals involved. By legislative suggestion of a year ago, we are expanding and experimenting how we might increase the effort in terms of natural family planning.

Q: Does that represent a change in policy from the past?

T A: Natural family planning?

Q: It was alleged in the past that A.I.D. conditioned the implementation of some kind of a national family planning policy upon a country.

T A: The record is a little bit unclear, but I have made our policy about that explicit.

Q: Could you just give us some examples of the program. For instance, we know that Egypt and Israel and El Salvador are major recipients of aid, who else are major recipients?

T A: On a short-term basis, Turkey is a major recipient: $350 million dollars for FY 1982. They have gone through an austerity readjustment and we expect that that program will dramatically trail off in the near future.

I have mentioned Bangladesh with $200 million. And that has been a long-term, year-after-year effort. The Horn of Africa: Kenya and Sudan have been big programs.

In Asia, the Philippines, Indonesia and Thailand are not programs the size of Bangladesh, but they are good-sized programs. Our major growth has been in Africa. Most people do not understand that the situation there is so much worse on the average than in Asia and in Latin America.

The average life-span in Africa is about 15 years less than you would have in Asia. You have a per capita food production that has gone down for ten years. Africa has really got basic problems. In addressing our humanitarian as well as our foreign policy needs — our total economic assistance in the last three years to Africa has gone up 41 percent.

Q: How about South America? What about programs there? Do we have any aid to Paraguay?

T A: Very small, a couple of million dollars a year. Paraguay, if they can pull it off right, has got a gold mine on its hands.

They have got a dam that is in the process of being built that will supply electricity to Brazil and Argentina. The thing will just make everybody a whole lot of money in the country.

Q: I have come across a good number of African leaders who are disgruntled with aid assistance. For instance, in agriculture the F.A.O. has been in Africa for a very, very long time. Yet, there is so much hunger. There is no food. They wonder what they have been doing. And taking into consideration the political system in this country, have you given a thought as to how effective your program will be, say, after the Administration is voted out. You know? Will they still support your program, because in agriculture it takes a long time for any program to be effective.

T A: Well, I hope so. I think, in fact, that there is a broad consensus in the Congress for what we are doing in Africa. We have increased our program to Africa, as I have said, by 41 percent. I think it is very important. In fact, I don't suppose you saw it, but Tuesday or Wednesday I had an op-ed piece in the *Christian Science Monitor* in which I laid out what I thought the problems in Africa were and why we particularly need to work at it.

The African countries, frankly, can do more for themselves. They have got to pay the farmers more. They have got to put less medical care into the big city hospitals and more out in the bush. They have got to do a bunch of things for themselvs. But over and above that we have got to deliver aid in the fashion that I think we are now beginning to.

Every region has unique problems. There are no solutions that are totally fitted for everyone. The Sub-Saharan area of Africa traditionally grows grain, sorghum, and millet as its staple food. There has been virtually no research done to increase production of sorghum and millet. We have got the miracle rice and wheat, but we do not have the miracle sorghum and millet. Because no one has ever really cared. They were poor peoples' crops and those poor people were off in Africa. Who cared about it?

It is the same thing with goats. No one has virtually done any research to figure out how to increase milk and meat production of goats. Basically, because they are poor peoples' animals. But we have got a major project in each of those areas that we think in half-a-dozen years may produce better varieties — better strains — of both the animals as well as the crops. And we think that a sustained effort like this will have an impact, but more important is what African countries will do for themselves.

GORDON HOXIE: Before we conclude, may I ask a question myself? This is related to the other questions in terms of the measure of support. What countries to which we can attribute our efforts at least in part, Peter, have risen to the level where they no longer need support or that support is being phased out? Can you give us an example of that?

T A: Let me answer it first in general terms and then in terms of specific countries.

It is hard when you read *The New York Times* and other papers day-after-day — the problems and the revolutions — to grasp the amount of progress that the world has really made.

Let us look at the world as it was, say in 1955. In 1955 much of Asia — India, Pakistan, Thailand, and so forth — had an average life-span of 40. Maybe 45, but no more than that. Today, it is at least ten years more than that in large part due to lower child mortality, but the average length of life is really 10 or 15 years longer. The revolutionary impact of this lengthening of the average life span is really something that is hard to calculate in this relatively plush society.

In the mid-1950s, only one percent of the kids in Nepal ever went to school. One percent! Today, at least 70 percent get into school sometime.

Almost everybody here remembers seeing the pictures of the starvation in India, for example. In the mid-1950s that was a fairly common thing. Well, last year India was nearly self-sufficient in food — at least in grain. And that is really revolutionary. A.I.D., through a variety of means, contributed to each one of those things. We really have a great deal to be proud of. By the way, I might argue, this progress occurred in the 1960s and part of the 1970s when we were not on the international welfare kick: When we were building institutions, training, creating miracle rice and wheat. Well, that is the general picture.

As to specific countries, we had a large program in Brazil. We had a program in Mexico. We had programs in Singapore, Korea, and others. It was not that many years ago after the

Korean War when South Korea was viewed as a basket case —
much as Bangladesh currently is.

The facts are: countries will follow wise economic policies of
their own, if there is a decent amount of outside economic assistance, and if we continue the trade we have going — if we do
not get too restrictive. And if the United States can also make
its contribution by keeping interest rates at affordable levels,
the world will continue to prosper.

I want to tell you here that you as citizens who continue to
pay your tax dollars, you have done an awful lot to make that
possible.

*Epilogue*
M. PETER MCPHERSON
March 1984

In my remarks of November 11, 1982, I made the statement
that under a conservative Republican Administration the foreign aid program has been strongly supported and has become
a more effective institution for that reason.

Since that time the Reagan Administration has acted to
strengthen the validity of that statement. It has also held to the
belief that such assistance must basically be of a self-help nature
and integrated with the foreign policy goals of the United States.
While maintaining that course, the Administration has not turned
its back on the humanitarian aspects of assistance.

Clear evidence of this resolve is present in two areas of the
world where problems have reached crisis proportions since my
meeting with your group in 1982. I refer to Central America
and Africa. In both instances, the co-mingling of the self-help
approach and humanitarianism is present.

There can be little doubt that the crisis in Central America
is of deep concern. Its outcome will bear heavily on the future
of our neighbors in that region and on the vital interests of the
United States.

Following through on the National Bipartisan Commission
on Central America recommendations the Administration has
proposed legislation titled "The Democracy, Peace and Development Initiative for Central America." It is a five-year program that embodies specific goals. These include: bringing to

an end the downward spiral of production; achieving a positive economic growth rate and the needed jobs that will accompany the growth; increasing agricultural production, greater participation by the people in the benefits of such growth including substantial increases in primary education enrollments; a significant reduction in the rate of infant mortality; the provision of modern family planning services to stabilize population growth; an increase in the rate of construction of low-income housing and attendant sewer and water infrastructure. Another major goal is the strengthening of democratic institutions to achieve substantial progress toward broad participatory democracy and legal systems that protect individual human rights.

It is a major undertaking and it will be costly. However, when compared to the ultimate cost of doing too little too late, the price of doing enough — and doing it now — will be modest.

Its success will also hinge on the adoption of policies by the governments of that region that will promote sound, broad-based economic development. This is vital. The combination of external resources and sound policies will produce progress. Central America is severely wounded. Band-aids will not do. Our proposal seeks to provide those countries with the appropriate materials in sufficient amounts to successfully heal themselves and regain economic and social health.

While much of the attention of the Western Hemisphere is centered on Central America, economic problems, drought and wide-spread hunger continue to plague huge numbers of people in sub-Saharan Africa. In fact, African food production has declined by over twenty percent per capita between 1961 and 1982.

Underlying Africa's inability to cope with these factors is a burgeoning population and a generally poor system of economic policies that are not oriented toward producer incentives and growth. Agricultural research institutions and basic infrastructures are weak and deficient.

Food assistance alone does little to prevent the recurrence of such emergencies. Thus, the Administration is proposing a two-pronged approach to the crisis. First is a supplemental appropriation to help relieve the immediate food emergency needs. This is in addition to current levels of food assistance. Second, an Economic Policy Initiative for Africa to stimulate a coordinated, multi-lateral effort to effect policy reform that will encourage economic growth. The latter, long-term initiative calls for the establishment of a $500 million five-year fund directed to those countries which have indicated a willingness and ability to establish comprehensive growth-oriented policies, primarily in the agricultural sector. It would also call for the strengthening of donor coordination with other countries to provide broader support for policy reform. The World Bank is willing to play a leadership role in this effort. Several U.S. private and voluntary organizations have already responded in a positive way.

As you can see, both in Central America and Africa, the Administration is aggressively taking the lead. In both instances there is a strong inter-relationship between self-help and humanitarianism.

Our philosophy at A.I.D. is principally focused on self-motivated, self-sustaining economic assistance. Transferring resources alone is not productive. Development requires, among other things, generating and spreading useful knowledge; strengthening institutions which are keyed to the real needs of the people; placing practical technology in the hands of the poor; reinforcing the strength of indigenous small private business; and instituting internal policies in which these development factors can emerge and flourish.

We have fashioned our policies relating to foreign assistance to address these needs. We have set forth what we call the 'four cornerstones' of policy.

First, through policy dialogue and reform, we seek to achieve agreement with host governments on the nature of key policy constraints to basic development and on practical changes that can be addressed. While taking care to observe the sensitivities of host governments, we believe it only reasonable that internal policy reforms are taken where needed to enhance the probability of developmental success.

Second, our policies of assistance include the building and strengthening of local institutions within a host country to mobilize the human and other resources needed for self-sustained economic growth. Such institutions help individuals gain access to the skills and the services needed to increase their productivity and income. They increase the country's utilization capacity and the effectivenss with which aid resources foster development that can be sustained after external assistance is withdrawn. Democratic institutions also provide the people with a greater voice in decision-making as well as the determination of their own destinies.

Third, as a matter of policy, we are placing increased emphasis on research, development, and transfer of appropriate technology to third world countries. This includes the priority sectors of A.I.D. concentration — agriculture, energy, health and population, and human resources development.

Fourth, we are stressing the contributions that the indigenous private sector can make to solving key development problems. Free and competitive markets offer the best means of achieving the objective of helping third world nations meet the basic human needs of their poor majority through sustained, broadly-based economic growth. The allocation of resources through competitive markets is more likely to be fair, efficient, and more equitable than allocations made by governments.

The principal goal of the emphasis on market solutions to development problems is to promote the economic security and independence of the people of the third world. In particular, this applies to the freedom of individuals to earn their livelihood by producing goods and services and marketing them for a fair price.

In order to provide a better focus for the organization, implementation, and coordination of the private sector initiative, we have established the Bureau for Private Enterprise within the structure of A.I.D.

As we look to the future, we will press for further strengthening of indigenous private sectors and reliance on market forces.

We will refine and strengthen our efforts to stimulate the establishment of recipient country internal policies that encourage broad-based economic development with emphasis on the needs of the poor.

We will move with a sense of urgency on the distribution of the inexpensive and easily administered therapy known as Oral Rehydration that dramatically reduces child mortality from diarrheal dehydration. This malady is the leading cause of death among children under five years of age in the less developed countries.

We will aggressively pursue the development and transfer of appropriate technologies in health, agriculture, population, and education.

We will continue our trend of the past three years to increase the size and quality of training and education programs we support for third world students.

In November of 1982 we were maintaining a viable assistance program in Lebanon. I spoke to you of our efforts and hopes for the people of that nation. Positive goals were being accomplished by a dedicated A.I.D. staff in cooperation with the government. Our people were truly on the front lines in our effort to help establish stability for the benefit of the people — particularly the poor — in their desire to improve their opportunities for a better life.

However, the broader factors of political and military strife that have beset that nation have made it impossible to continue A.I.D. presence. Our mission has been reluctantly withdrawn. I remain hopeful that this is only a temporary interruption. When peace is restored I am confident at this time that we will return to help the people help themselves in the restoration of their country, their lives, and their opportunities.

In all our efforts, it is important to understand this Administration's underlying commitment. It is to help people of the third world help themselves — and then leave. We seek friends, not empires; partners, not dependents. Most of all, we seek a world at peace.

PART TWO

# A Century of National Security Policy: From Cleveland to Reagan

# CHAPTER SEVEN

# Grover Cleveland and Venezuela: The Perils of Moralism

**ROBERT A. RAGAZZO**
CENTER FELLOW
HARVARD LAW SCHOOL

American politicians and statesmen have often practiced foreign policy as if they were on crusade, and Grover Cleveland was just such a crusader. In 1893, he acted according to the highest standards of political morality in his treatment of the Hawaiian problem.[1] The Venezuela-British Guiana border controversy presented Mr. Cleveland with the opportunity for a repeat performance. In his eagerness to stand by a small American neighbor, Cleveland attempted to force the British to submit to arbitration the question of title to a South American jungle even though the British clearly had the better claim to the disputed territory, international law hardly sanctioned American intervention, and American self-interest could be implicated only by the wildest contortions of the Monroe Doctrine. In so doing, President Cleveland risked a war with Great Britain that the United States probably could not have won; moreover, it forcefully demonstrated the perils of an overly moral approach to foreign policy.

The origins of the border controversy date back to 1810, when Venezuela achieved independence from Spain with ill-defined borders. Four years later, Holland ceded to Great Britain the territory which would eventually become the colony of British Guiana and which lay on Venezuela's nebulous eastern boundary.[2] The British explorer, Sir Robert Schomburgk, surveyed the disputed boundary line for the British in 1841 and placed Point Barima, which guarded the mouth of the important Orinoco River, on the British side.[3] The Venezuelans responded by claiming, without much evidence of conquest or occupation, the Essequibo River as their eastern boundary and thus laid claim to over one-half of what the English considered to be British Guiana.[4] In 1844, Lord Aberdeen, disposed to be conciliatory on a matter of much greater relative importance to the Venezuelans, proposed that the Schomburgk line be amended by conceding Point Barima to Venezuela.[5] Venezuela rejected this offer, and the negotiations were abandoned until Venezuela was able to end twenty-six years of domestic turmoil in 1876.[6] Subsequently, Britain made various compromise overtures, but Venezuela, hoping for a windfall after the discovery of gold in the disputed region rejected the British proposals and insisted upon arbitration. The British would not agree to arbitration of the area east of the Schomburgk line because "Venezuela's claims were grossly distorted and arbiters are sometimes inclined to split the difference."[7] Moreover, British settlers had long lived in the area claimed by Venezuela.

The matter rested in limbo when President Cleveland began his second term in March of 1893. For two years, Venezuela made repeated attempts to secure aggressive American support for arbitration of the border dispute.[8] How little Mr. Cleveland was initially moved is illustrated by his conciliatory reference to the boundary question in his annual message of 1894: "Believing that its early settlement, on some just basis honorable to both parties, is in the line of our established policy to remove from this hemisphere all causes of difference with powers beyond the sea, I shall renew the efforts heretofore made to bring about a restoration of relations between the disputants and to induce a reference to arbitration."[9] Within six months, President Cleveland would be demanding arbitration rather than inducing a reference to it.

The mounting pressure of public opinion may be one factor which caused the President's caution to so abruptly become rashness.[10] The Venezuelans helped to instigate this pressure by employing William L. Scruggs, the former American minister to Venezuela under President Harrison. Mr. Scruggs circulated a pamphlet ("British Aggressions in Venezuela, or the Monroe Doctrine on Trial") which successfully enlisted American patriotic fervor on behalf of the Venezuelan cause.[11] As the title of the pamphlet implied, Scruggs, albeit skillfully, had only presented the Venezuelan side of the story. Moreover, Americans still enjoyed pulling the British lion's tail. Both houses of Congress passed unanimously a joint resolution urging Cleveland to recommend "most earnestly" to Great Britain and Venezeula that they settle the dispute by arbitration.

The British also contributed, albeit unwittingly, to the pressure for a more aggressive American policy by their part in the "Corinto Affair." On April 27, 1895, Great Britain landed troops in Nicaragua to force the government of that nation to pay an indemnity for expelling a British consul from the port of Corinto. Although the British left one week later with payment in hand, the incident was not soon forgotten. Walter Gresham, then American Secretary of State, correctly explained that American honor had not been slighted and the Monroe Doctrine had not been implicated because the British had never intended to occupy Nicaragua on a permanent basis.[12] Nevertheless, the Toledo *Blade* proclaimed: "Had James G. Blaine been Secretary of State this past year, Americans would not now be hanging their heads in shame."[13]

Nor was public opinion inflamed only from abroad. Senator Henry Cabot Lodge (R-Mass.) exclaimed with regard to the boundary dispute: "All that England has done has been a direct violation of the Monroe Doctrine, and she has increased and quickened her aggressions in proportion as the United States has appeared indifferent. . . . The supremacy of the Monroe Doctrine should be established at once — peaceably if we can, forcibly if we must."[14]

If the *Blade* had wished for a new, more forceful Secretary of State, the quirks of fate provided one by requiring the death of Walter Quintin Gresham on May 23, 1895. President Cleveland, having decided that "there was nothing left for us to do consistently with national honor but to take the place of Venezuela in the controversy," signaled his change of attitude by promptly appointing his Attorney-General, Richard Olney, to fill Mr. Gresham's post.[15]

One scholar has described Olney as "a man of prompt and energetic decision."[16] Faced with the possibility that the federal mail deliveries might be obstructed by the Pullman strike of 1895, Olney had instructed the United States Attorney for California as follows: "See that the passage of regular trains carrying United States mails . . . is not obstructed. Procure warrants or other available process from the United States Courts against any and all persons engaged in such obstruction, and direct marshall to execute same by such number of deputies or such posse as may be necessary."[17] Here, clearly, was a Secretary of State who would not take kindly to British dawdling on a controversy over forty years of age. President Cleveland believed that Mr. Olney was the perfect man to give expression to his newly formed desire for a more aggressive American approach to the Venezuelan problem: "I have always considered it a providential circumstance that the Government then had among its Cabinet officers an exceptionlly strong and able man in every way especially qualified to fill the vacant place."[18]

When Mr. Olney replaced Walter Gresham, he inherited the task of composing a note to the British concerning the Venezuela-British Guiana boundary dispute. His note was sent in the form of a letter to the American minister to the Court of St. James, Thomas Bayard, under the date of July 20, 1895.[19] Olney begins with a passage that betrays his sympathy for the Venezuelan position: "Out of moderation and prudence, Venezuela has contented herself with claiming the line of the Essequibo River as the true boundary between Venezuela and British Guiana."[20] Venezuela's claim to the Essequibo line was wildly extravagant, as a comparison to the boundary line determined by the Tribunal of Arbitration in 1899 clearly indicates. The British had been warned at the outset of Mr. Olney's hostility to their cause; they could not have known that he was just warming up.

After an examination of the history of the controversy, Secretary Olney remarks that the American government must decide "to what extent, if any, the United States may and should intervene in a controversy between and primarily concerning Great Britain and Venezuela."[21] He concludes that international law permits a third party to intervene "whenever what is done or proposed by any of the parties primarily concerned is a serious and direct menace to its own integrity, tranquility, and welfare."[22]

We must now consider in what way the integrity, tranquility, and welfare of the United States was implicated by a border controversy over title to a South American jungle. One scholar suggests that if Britain were allowed to command the Orinoco River through possession of Point Barima, "she would be in a position to control much of the internal trade of a vast region."[23] The argument in rebuttal is convincing: "In view of the British footholds in the Caribbean, it seems difficult to believe that the balance of power or the capacity of Britain to do harm would have been much affected by her possession of the territory around Point Barima."[24] Moreover, as noted above, Great Britain had been willing to cede Point Barima to Venezuela since 1844.

Thus, present strategic considerations did not allow Mr. Olney to convincingly demonstrate that American welfare was at stake in the case at hand. This able Boston lawyer decided to make his case on the Monroe Doctrine. He claimed instead that any violation of the theory of the Monroe Doctrine adversely affected the welfare of the United States. Quickly passing over the non-colonization principle, which he said had, "long been conceded," the Secretary quoted the non-interference principle in full and rested his case on it.[25] In Olney's words, the essence of this principle was that "no European power or combination of European powers shall forcibly deprive an American State of the right and power of self-government and of shaping its own political fortunes and destinies." Such a policy "in effect deprives Venezuela of free agency and puts her under virtual redress." Olney then attempted to gain some leverage over the British by asserting that the original pronouncement of the Monroe Doctrine "was unquestionably due to the inspiration of Great Britain, who at once gave it an open and unqualified adhesion which has never been withdrawn."[26] Professor Dexter Perkins observed, "This statement . . . would have made George Canning turn in his grave."[27]

In an attempt to demonstrate the connection between American welfare and the non-interference principle, Mr. Olney gives a strategic and a moral argument. Strategically, the Secretary postulates a kind of domino theory. If the United States allows even the smallest transgression of the non-interference principle by one European nation, others will be encouraged to follow suit, and "the ultimate result might be the partition of South America between the various European powers."[28] As a result, "our only real rivals in peace and enemies in war will be found located at our very doors." This would force the United States to incur the "evils of immense standing armies and all the other accessories of huge warlike establishments" to prevent its dismemberment.[29] Secretary Olney's position "could hardly have been imagined by one who approached the controversy with the slightest pretension to calm and dispassionate judgment."[30] It is doubtful that such a partition of South America was possible even in 1823.

Neither did Mr. Olney's moral argument demonstrate any nexus between American welfare and European respect for the non-interference principal. Olney declares: "The people of the United States have a vital interest in the cause of popular self-government."[31] Yet, it is impossible to discover any connection between American interest in popular self-government and General Crespo's dictatorial regime in Venezuela.[32] Olney's contention that any transgression of the non-interference principle, however slight, placed American welfare in jeopardy is untenable.

Furthermore, considering Mr. Olney's insistence that European observance of the non-interference principle must be absolute, we should have been led to expect that Britain's violation would be a small one. In fact, it is non-existent. Olney completely rewrote the doctrine of James Monroe as he applied the non-interference principle to the case at hand. The Secretary states: "Though the dispute relates to a boundary line, yet, as it is between states, it necessarily imports political control to be lost by one party and gained by the other."[33] As noted above, Olney had described the essence of the non-interference principle as prohibiting any European power from depriving an American state of the right and power of self-government. Incredibly, he equates British jockeying over the position of a boundary line with attempted overthrow of the Venezuelan government. We must therefore conclude that Olney did not satisfy the canon of international law that a nation's welfare must be significantly at stake before it can intervene in a dispute primarily concerning two other nations.

Such considerations, however, did not deter Richard Olney. The Secretary was not quite finished rewriting the Monroe Doctrine. He claimed, in an often quoted passage, that Britain must accept American intervention because: "Today the United States is practically sovereign on this continent, and its fiat is law on those subjects to which it confines its interposition." He went on to explain why: "It is not because of the pure friendship or good will felt for it. It is not simply by reason of its high character as a civilized state nor because wisdom and justice and equity are the invariable characteristics of the dealings of the United States. It is because, in addition to all the other grounds, its infinite resources combined with its isolated position render it master of the situation and practically invulnerable as against any or all other powers."[34] Herein, Secretary Olney shows the impartial nature of his lack of respect for the dead. If he had earlier disturbed the peaceful resting of Canning's spirit, he must now have caused President Monroe to turn in his grave as well. The Monroe Doctrine can in no way be held to assert that, in the western hemisphere, America's fiat is law on those subjects to which it confines its interposition.

Olney pronounced America's fiat: Great Britain must submit the boundary question to binding arbitration.[35] Olney reasoned that Great Britain might be violating the non-interference principle by exercising control over territory which might be Venezuelan. If the United States had a right to prevent violations of the non-interference principle, it had a right to determine if any violations were extant and remedy them through arbitration. Secretary Olney concluded his note by directing the British to reply, before the President's annual message in December, as to whether they would submit to arbitration or "greatly embarrass the future relations between the United States and Great Britain."[36]

The belligerent tone of the above note, which sounded more like an ultimatum, can be viewed as a function of Richard Olney's personality.[37] Montgomery Schuyler has described Olney as "the family despot to whose least whim all around him were forced to accommodate themselves or suffer the penalty of his displeasure."[38] However, we must remember that Olney's note was part of a team effort and, as such, was intended as an expression of the Cleveland administration's adoption of a more aggressive stance on the boundary dispute. Mr. Cleveland certainly communicated his complete satisfaction with Olney's remarks on the Monroe Doctrine when he said: "In no event will this American principle ever be better defined, better defended, or more bravely asserted than was done by Mr. Olney in this despatch."[39]

Lord Salisbury, the British Foreign Secretary, badly misunderstood this change in the Cleveland administration's policy. Secretary Olney had delivered "words that were the equivalent of blows" to the British, confident that now "England would sit up and listen respectfully when the United States suggested arbitration."[40] Lord Salisbury, however, was not shaken from his lethargy. On August 7, 1895, when Bayard read Olney's note to him, Salisbury expressed "regret and surprise that it had been considered . . . necessary to present so far-reaching and important a principle and such wide and profound policies of international action in relation to a subject so comparatively small."[41] Clearly, Lord Salisbury was not impressed. He further angered Cleveland and Olney by not complying, albeit by accident, with the request to send an answer prior to the President's annual message.[42] When the British reply finally arrived in Washington, it did nothing to assuage the anger of the President or his Secretary of State.

Lord Salisbury's answer was in the form of a letter to the British minister to Washington under the date of November 26, 1895.[43] Contrary to Cleveland's wishes it did not reach Washington until after Congress had convened in December. As we have seen, Olney's note contained multiple errors. Lord Salisbury uncovered them one by one "much as a learned professor would pick to pieces a college freshman's theme."[44] The British Foreign Secretary began by denying that the Monroe Doctrine had been violated: "The British Empire and the Republic of Venezuela are neighbors, and they have differed for some time past, and continue to differ, as to the line by which their dominions are separated. It is a controversy with which the United States has no practical concern. . . . It has nothing to do with any of the questions dealt with by President Monroe. It is not a question of the colonization by a European power of any portion of America. It is not a question of the imposition upon the communities of South America of any system of government devised in Europe."[45] We have already commented on British conformity to the Monroe Doctrine and, therefore, on the basic soundness of this assertion.

Next, Lord Salisbury challenged the contention that America's fiat was law. With regard to the demand for arbitration, he replied: "Whether, in any particular case, arbitration is a suitable method of procedure is generally a delicate and difficult question. The only parties who are competent to decide that question are the two parties whose rival contentions are in issue."[46] Secretary Olney had commanded the British to accept arbitration. The British repeated their offer to arbitrate claims west of the Schomburgk line, but not east of it.

Having previously accepted the validity of the Monroe Doctrine for the sake of argument, Lord Salisbury now challenged the contention that it was a canon of international law: "International law is founded on the general consent of nations; and no statesman, however eminent, and no nation, however powerful, are competent to insert into the code of international law a novel principle which was never recognized before."[47] The view that President Monroe was not competent to make international law by unilateral proclamation is undoubtedly correct. Indeed, the Monroe Doctrine, being merely a statement of a President which was never passed as a law by Congress, has nothing to do with American domestic law.

However, Lord Salisbury possessed some sense of American devotion to the Monroe Doctrine. He declared that, although the Monroe Doctrine could not be considered part of international law, the British nevertheless looked favorably on the principles advanced by James Monroe and concurred with "the view . . . that any disturbances of the existing territorial distribution in that hemisphere by any fresh acquisitions on the part of any European state would be a highly inexpedient change."[48] The essence of Lord Salisbury's reply, therefore, was that America had no cause for concern because Britain simply had not violated the Monroe Doctrine.

This reply by the British Foreign Secretary has received unduly harsh treatment at the hands of the critics. Professor Perkins claims that Lord Salisbury's "superior dogmatism and patronizing self-confidence jeopardized the peace between America and Great Britain."[49] However, Secretary Olney had arrogantly demanded arbitration in an area long settled by the British. Any negative reply would have increased his already considerable wrath. Lord Salisbury's reply was exceedingly more diplomatic than the original note, and Olney's bluster was superimposed on a very poorly argued position. Any blame for jeopardizing the peace must rest squarely on the shoulders of the American President and his hand-picked Secretary of State.

In any event, the peace was clearly jeopardized by President Cleveland when he delivered a special message to Congress on December 17, 1895 by way of reply to Lord Salisbury.[50] The President declared that the Venezuela-British Guiana border dispute had "reached such a stage as to make it now incumbent on the United States to take measures to determine with sufficient certainty for its justification what is the true divisional line between the Republic of Venezuela and British Guiana."[51] Cleveland proposed, and the Congress later approved by unanimous vote, the creation of a commission to make such a determination.[52] He concluded the message by declaring that "it will . . . be the duty of the United States to resist by every means in its power . . . the appropriation by Great Britain of any lands . . . which after investigation we have determined of right belongs to Venezuela."[53] Thus, since the British would not agree to arbitration, Grover Cleveland would run his own boundary line and defend it by force of American arms.

Professor Perkins succinctly describes the conditions under which President Cleveland had just declared himself prepared to fight a war with Great Britain: "The American navy had just one modern battleship to pit against the great navy of Britain. The army was about one-sixth the size of the British."[54] The exposed position of Canada hardly served to equalize the balance.[55] What motives explain Cleveland's willingness to fight a war on these terms?

The explanation given by Mr. Olney in his note is not convincing; the British posed no danger to the non-interference principle pronounced by James Monroe. During a series of lectures at Princeton after the turn of the century, President Cleveland also identified defense of the Monroe Doctrine as the motivating force behind his Venezuelan policy. He asserted that forcing the British to submit to arbitration was necessary because British actions constituted "an actual or threatened violation of a doctrine which our nation long ago established, declaring that the American continents are not to be considered subjects for future colonization by any European power."[56] Although a better case can be made from the American point of view by relying on the non-colonization principle, it would seem that British jockeying over the position of a boundary line, which might have resulted in a miniscule increase in Britain's South American holdings, cannot be equated with anything so grand as "colonization." Moreover, when a President and his Secretary of State cannot agree on which principle of the Monroe Doctrine Britain has in fact been violated, it is fair to conclude that we must look beyond the Monroe Doctrine to discover the true source of American motivation.

President Cleveland's Venezuelan policy has been viewed as a response to the depression of 1893.[57] It may be that Cleveland had identified overproduction as the cause of this depression and moved to alleviate the problem by securing American access to Latin American markets, which involved denying the Orinoco River to the British.[58] Here we must recall that control of the Orinoco did not add much to the British position in South America and that the British had been disposed to concede Point Barima since 1844. In addition, "the business leaders of New

York were among the earliest critics of the President's policy
. . . as English holders of American securities began calling their
capital home, American holders liquidated in their turn."[59] The
economic effects of an aggressive foreign policy over the boundary
dispute were bound to be mixed. It is unlikely that President
Cleveland would have risked a war in which America would
be the inferior belligerent by far under these circumstances.

Perhaps, as alluded to above, the President's position on the
border controversy was a response to the hostility of public
opinion toward passive administration policy. Professor Blake,
after suggesting as much, concedes that "courage, honesty, and
duty were basic qualities with the President and he challenged
England on the Venezuela issue only after he became personally
convinced that the Monroe Doctrine was at stake and that it
was his duty to maintain it."[60] Cleveland had established that
courage, honesty, and duty were indeed among his basic qualities by risking his political fortunes to ensure just treatment of
Hawaii in 1893.[61] There is no reason to believe that the intervening two years had done anything to increase the President's
respect for public opinion. Popular attitudes may account for
the swiftness of the change in administration policy and for the
belligerency of its tone. They do not account for its substance.

Although we have disputed Professor Blake's conclusion that
defense of the Monroe Doctrine explains the behavior of Cleveland and Olney, his focus on the basic integrity of the President, which was certainly shared by Olney, provides the best
explanation for the seemingly irrational tactics of the Americans.
Cleveland and Olney were not motivated by practical considerations of economic welfare and popularity; rather, they were
influenced by considerations of morality.[62]

As noted above, Olney demonstrated his sympathy for
Venezuela in the opening passage of his note to Salisbury by
applauding Venezuela for "moderation and prudence" which
formed no part of her policy on the boundary question. The
point is not that the Tribunal of Arbitration, by vindicating the
Schomburgk line, ultimately proved that Olney and the
Venezuelans were in error but that Olney sincerely believed he
was defending the legitimate claims of a small American nation
against the transgressions of a mighty European power. The
words of President Cleveland on the threat posed by the British
Lion show an equal concern for the rights of the underdog: "If

fisticuffs and forcible possession are resorted to, the big, strong neighbor rejoices in his strength as he mauls and disfigures his small and weak antagonist."[63] As a result, Cleveland demanded that the British submit to binding arbitration, which he termed "the refuge which civilization has builded among the nations of the earth for the protection of the weak against the strong."[64]

This approach accounts for the willingness of Cleveland and Olney to risk war on highly unfavorable terms. Truly moral men do not abandon their moral convictions for reasons of military logistics. However, as Professor Campbell is quick to point out, "American interests marched with the dictates of justice — that was one of the rewards of virtue."[65] Without hypocrisy, Cleveland and Olney could secure the benefits of extra markets and popular support from their platform of justice.

In the final analysis, the peace was not disturbed because the British capitulated. They did so, in contrast to the Americans, for practical reasons of foreign policy. Emerging from a century of "splendid isolation," England needed allies, or at least friends, in her competitions with the Franco-Russian alliance and Germany. Her best prospect was her racial cousin across the Atlantic.[66] War became utterly inconceivable after January 3, 1896, when Emperor Wilhelm of Germany sent a telegram to President Kruger of the Transvaal to congratulate him on the defeat of the Jameson raid and the "independence" of his country.[67] Britain was forced to capitulate because her primary interests lay in Africa not South America.[68]

On January 12, 1896, Lord Playfair proposed to Ambassador Bayard that all settlements, Venezuelan as well as English, be exempt from arbitration, but that all territory between these settlements be divided by a court of arbitration.[69] The crux of the Anglo-American dispute had been, since July 20 of the previous year, whether the British would bow to the American demand for arbitration. Although Lord Playfair had not agreed to unconditional arbitration, the British had finally conceded the legitimacy of American intervention in her border dispute with Venezuela and consented to arbitration in principle. On February 2, 1897, Great Britain and Venezuela finally signed a treaty providing for a Tribunal of Arbitration to settle their boundary dispute. This treaty stipulated that all territory would be subject to arbitration but adverse holding for fifty years would make a good title.[70] In October of 1899, the Tribunal handed down its decision. Point Barima went to Venezuela; otherwise, Sir Robert Schomburgk's line was closely followed.

The verdict of history must be that President Cleveland and Secretary Olney stood behind a screen of moral idealism that was unjustified. Over a forty-year period, Great Britain had not attempted to exploit Venezuela's weakness. The Tribunal of Arbitration ended the controversy with the solution Britain had offered at its beginning. From America's perspective, the Monroe Doctrine could be applied to the dispute only through gross distortion.

Moreover, even had the moral position of Cleveland and Olney been sound, they committed the United States to a war she could not have fought successfully. Such conduct on the part of public statesmen is unconscionable. This is not to suggest that moral principles are not worth fighting for unless the relative balance of power lies in one's favor. Rather, the point is that the moral principles must be of sufficient magnitude to justify the enormity of the sacrifice. The cause of freedom was hardly implicated by a controversy over title to a limited piece of South American real estate. The necessity of keeping moral principles in perspective was a lesson a later generation of Americans would learn painfully in Vietnam.

Fortunately, the British were not disposed to punish the lack of American diplomatic decorum. The ironic result of the border crisis was Anglo-American rapprochement. Richard Olney "twisted the Lion's tail."[71] In reply, Lord Salisbury "patted the Eagle's head."[72] It is just possible that Dame Fortune smiles on those who act, however rashly, from the best of moral motives.

Actually, the United States aggressive action was more resented on the European Continent than in Great Britain. Both official and newspaper opinions in France, Germany, Austria-Hungary, Italy, Spain, Holland and Russia were hostile to this new assumption of United States predominance in the western hemisphere. Latin American views were mixed regarding the United States protector role. Venezuela, of course, was supportive, as were Columbia and Brazil (which had a somewhat similar boundary dispute with French Guiana). Peru and the Central American countries displayed varying degrees of support for the Cleveland-Olney assertions. However, Mexico, Argentina, and Chile greeted the American position with hostility and suspicion.

The distrust in Latin America for the growing Colossus of the North surfaced in the poorly attended Congress of American States meeting in Mexico City in 1896. As Julius W. Pratt concluded, "To have a powerful protector was all very well, but it was clear that some of Uncle Sam's neighbors were growing fearful that the protector might lay claim to certain rights of overlordship."[73]

# CHAPTER EIGHT

# Facade and Failure:
# The Hull-Nomura Talks of 1941

## FREDERICK W. MARKS III

Few episodes in American diplomatic history have been as much misunderstood as the protracted diplomatic exchange carried on between Washington and Tokyo during the year 1941. It would require more than a chapter in a book to place the Hull-Nomura talks in their proper perspective against a backdrop of previous parleys, all of them fruitless and all for a similar reason, albeit with less explosive results.[1] Nevertheless, if the following essay succeeds, even partially, in penetrating some of the mythology surrounding Roosevelt's final days of peace, it will have served a useful purpose.

As 1941 dawned, the Gaimusho (Japan's foreign office) found itself in control of most of China's coastal area, most of her populace, and the bulk of her slender industrial apparatus. At the same time, even though Chiang Kai-shek had retreated to the remote reaches of Chungking, his Nationalist armies gave no sign of surrender, and because Washington was their principal underwriter, Tokyo still hoped to engage the United States in serious talks leading to a mutually acceptable compromise. Roosevelt, appearing interested as always, received Admiral Nomura in March as a special ambassador from Premier Konoye.[2] Another round of talks would enable the White House to satisfy all shades of opinion. Isolationists and pacifists could be encouraged to look for genuine accommodation, while hard-liners could be assured that the talks were merely intended to give Tokyo a graceful means of retreat; they would be accompanied by ever-increasing economic pressure.

For some time, Japan had invited the aid of the Catholic Church as an intermediary, and it now enlisted the service of two Maryknoll priests: Bishop James E. Walsh, Superior General of Maryknoll (the Catholic Missionary Society of America), and his vicar general or treasurer, the Reverend James N. Drought. After visiting Tokyo in late 1940 and conveying to Japanese leaders a sense of what they felt Washington might be willing to accept, they went to Roosevelt with an outline of what they thought Japan might be persuaded to offer. Two additional representatives came to the United States to serve as liaison between Washington and the Japanese cabinet. The first of these, T. Wikawa, headed Japan's largest banking group and, with the rank of minister plenipotentiary, remained in touch with Premier Konoye by private code. Related by blood or marriage to ex-premier Wakatsuki as well as to the head of the Domei News Agency, he had risen from the rank of finance commissioner in New York to become minister of finance and then to draft Japan's foreign exchange law. Colonel Hideo Iwakuro, who arrived a few weeks after Wikawa, bore the unassuming title of military attaché and did not speak English, but he could negotiate in French or German and was assistant to General Muto, chief of the powerful Military Affairs Bureau of the War Department. According to Joseph Grew, American ambassador to Tokyo, Iwakuro was exceedingly influential in military circles and had the complete confidence of the Japanese secretary of war.[3]

Initially, Drought served as a bridge between Wikawa, whom he saw directly, and Roosevelt, whom he reached through Postmaster General Walker. When Iwakuro entered the picture, Nomura was not far behind, and it was out of this group that there emerged Drought's celebrated Draft Understanding of April 16. Among its salient features were the following: the United States was to recognize Manchukuo, allow greater scope for Japanese immigration, and support demands for British withdrawal from Hong Kong and Singapore; Japan would withdraw from China in recognition of that country's independence and territorial integrity; she would also refrain from exacting any war indemnity and would endorse the doctrine of the Open Door, to be more precisely defined at a later date. Chiang and his rival, Wang Ch'ing-wei, were to merge their governments, and both Japan and the United States were to oppose the transfer of any territory in the Far East, including the Philippines. Secretary of State Hull agreed to accept the Draft Understanding as "a basis for the institution of negotiations" with the exception of its clauses on immigration, Hong Kong and Singapore, and with the further proviso that Japan would assent to four general principles for which the United States had long contended; namely, the territorial integrity and sovereignty of all nations; non-interference in internal affairs of other nations; equality of commercial opportunity; and nondisturbance of the Pacific status quo except by peaceful measures.[4]

Once the Hull-Nomura talks began in earnest, Drought made seventeen visits to Washington, ranging in duration from several days to several weeks, and before he was finished he had spent most of May, September, and November on the Potomac.[5] Bishop Walsh, who personally delivered two of Konoye's messages to the president, kept a close watch on the Japanese side. He passed two months with Wikawa during summer and fall at various locations in the vicinity of Tokyo. At the request of Eugene Dooman, second in command at the American embassy, he also transmitted many messages from the Gaimusho to the State Department with an eye to narrowing differences which seemed to bar the way to a final settlement.[6]

The major issues in dispute can be reduced to four: American economic opportunity in China and Manchukuo; allowance for Japanese troops to remain in China as a barrier against Communist inroads and for the shielding of Manchukuo; Japan's neutrality in the event of American entry into the European war; and American recognition of Manchukuo. The last of the four was accepted by both parties as an automatic part of any peace agreement, and as regards the first and third points, Japan proved willing to concede everything.[7] She had never ceased promising that once the war ended in China, America would receive ample economic opportunity, and before the talks ended she proved willing to set this down on paper. As for the Axis, Tokyo was technically bound to fight if and when the United States should enter the war, but the language of the Tripartite Pact was such that she could interpret it freely. This she promised to do in return for tolerance of her stake in North China and Manchukuo. On November 21, she offered to put such an interpretation of the Pact in writing which, allowing for the premium she placed upon "face," was a momentous concession. No one can be certain she would have honored this promise or any other, but the likelihood is great. This was the opinion of Downing Street, and the prospect seemed real enough to cause considerable concern on the part of high German officials.[8] There is no compelling evidence to the contrary.

Troops proved to be the sticking point. Yet, even here the Japanese took the position by late May that they would be willing to withdraw up to 90% of their occupation force within two years and restrict the remainder to specified zones in North China. Hull dashed any hope of compromise by insisting upon a *one* year withdrawal of *all* forces with the suggestion that Chiang or an international commission by given the task of halting Communist penetration. On September 13, Japan went a step farther by offering to withdraw the remaining 10% after "a certain period." Hull, however, stood firm on immediate withdrawal of all troops. This might have been the last word, but it was bruited that Konoye would accept a Chinese police corps in North China under Japanese officers and might agree to a specific withdrawal date if Roosevelt would attend a Pacific summit conference as originally anticipated. Many, including Walsh and Grew, believed that if Konoye went to Hawaii as the first premier ever to leave his country on an official visit, he would deliver what he promised.[9]

What is surprising is that the Japanese were willing to go as far as they did when the history of the American side from the start had been one of backing and filling. Professor Paul Schroeder has demonstrated that as Nomura offered more and more in the way of concessions, Hull offered less and less until Japan finally moved into southern Indochina, providing Roosevelt with an excuse for further stalling. Hull had been the first to back away from the Draft Understanding on stipulations involving immigration and British withdrawal from Hong Kong and Singapore. This, in turn, invited similar retreat on the part of Nomura, who immediately became vague on the question of the Axis and stationing of troops. Thereafter, Hull initiated each mutual departure from the expected basis for agreement.[10]

Typically, Hull insisted on May 16 that Nomura return to the Draft Understanding while he himself drew even farther away from it. In the early rounds of negotiation, he focused on the issue of troops; but when Japan promised to withdraw most of its forces in two years, he shifted to the question of unity in Japanese politics and argued about whether the government of Prince Konoye was actually in position to honor its promises. When this was answered in an extraordinary way, he moved on to economics until Japan offered to do in China exactly what the United States was doing in South America. Seemingly satisfied on this point, he then agreed to accept the Draft Understanding substantially intact, only to return to the troop issue (even as he admitted in private the need for Japan to station forces in the north). Each time the Japanese offered a concession, he raised the ante. On July 7, he introduced a demand for *public* rejection of the Axis Pact, something the United States had promised as early as January it would not do. Finally, on October 8, after Tokyo indicated that even the question of troops in North China might be negotiable, Hull took the extreme position that he would not sign any agreement until Tokyo proved its seriousness by withdrawing some of its troops *in advance*. Drought, maddened by White House tactics, called them "contemptible."[11]

It is generally assumed that the president was sincere in his approach to Japan.[12] Yet why, if he was bargaining in good faith, was Drought brought to complain on July 7: "We have now gone three and a half months without offering any official counter-statement"? If he had been serious, why did he encourage the idea of a summit meeting on August 17 and again on the 28th only to retreat from it? On the 17th, having just returned from his meeting with Churchill at Argentia, he suggested that Nomura consider a specific date, October 15. On August 28, he backed away from Hawaii as a site, naming Juneau, Alaska, as more convenient. He was still "keenly interested," he told Nomura, "in having three or four days with Prince Konoye." In the meantime, press leaks had begun to cause Foreign Minister Toyoda acute embarrassment. His country had extended an unprecedented invitation without receiving the courtesy of an answer, and he urgently requested announcement of a definite meeting date such as September 20. Inexplicably, Roosevelt now came to a dead halt. There would be no meeting, he told Nomura, until major principles had been settled. On the following day, September 4, he announced the closing of the Panama Canal to Japanese shipping.[13] Toyoda and Konoye were thus left dangling.

One can go further. Why did FDR allow his subordinates to offer the idea of a *modus vivendi* on November 18–19 only to fall back on generalities two days after the Japanese accepted and advanced a specific proposal? It is true that Japan's offer of November 20 included an unsatisfactory proviso that the United States must halt all aid to China — must cease all measures "prejudicial" to "peace between Japan and China." But instead of objecting, Hull chose to add two requirements of his own: that Japan vacate *all* of Indochina instead of just the southern portion, and that she receive only enough oil to meet her *civilian* requirements.[14]

Why, one may also ask, did Roosevelt interpret the Japanese advance into southern Indochina beginning July 2 solely in terms of aggression? While it placed Tokyo in a better position to threaten Singapore and Manila, it also helped her to secure her food supply at a time when Britain had closed off an alternate source of rice in Burma. Maxwell Hamilton, chief of the Far Eastern Division at State, viewed the advance as basically defensive in light of anticipated intensification of American and British economic pressure. Two weeks earlier, Washington had instituted a new phase of trade restriction affecting east coast and Gulf ports. Japan, in short, had her back to the wall. She foresaw bloodshed.[15]

Why, finally, did Hull confine himself to such vague terminology? Why did he use the term "Indochina" several times when he plainly meant only the southern half of Indochina, and why did it take him ten months to indicate that complete and immediate troop withdrawal from all of China was a *sine qua non*?[16] The proposal he submitted on May 31 was nebulous with respect to both the Axis Pact and troops remaining in North China. Three and a half months later, when Nomura finally agreed to consider a time limit on troops remaining in North China, Roosevelt ordered Hull to return to general principles and "reemphasize my hope for a meeting [with Koneye]." Nomura was positively stunned when presented on October 2 with another spate of generalities. Accused of stalling, it was at this point that Roosevelt countered with his radical insistence on *prior* withdrawal of troops as a token of good faith.[17]

It is ironic that Japan should be the one whose good faith was called into question when neither Hull nor presidential adviser Stanley Hornbeck nor Roosevelt himself ever regarded the Drought-Walsh initiative as anything but a ploy. From the outset, Hornbeck and Hull advised against serious negotiation, and when Roosevelt told Churchill in August that he felt he could "baby" the Japanese along for another thirty days, this is just what he meant. It is what he had been doing since the fall of 1939, indeed his strategy became so obvious at times as to be almost comic.[18] Although Japan presented important new proposals on April 9, Hull used subsequent sessions with Nomura to concentrate less on specifics and more on general questions such as democracy versus the inherent evil of Hitlerian Germany.[19] Again and again, he cited America's exemplary conduct in Latin America without acknowledging the slightest difference between one hemisphere and another. Repeatedly, he arraigned Nazism and propounded the advantages of free trade.[20] By June, therefore, the dialogue was reduced to trivia and Hull folded his tent for a six-week summer vacation. Nomura sought him out at the Greenbrier resort in West Virginia only to be told he was unavailable on a doctor's excuse.[21]

Long-suffering Bishop Walsh confessed to being "a little mortified" by the administration's foot-dragging. "If the thing is finally done," he wrote, "it will not be due to their good management." On November 7, we may observe Hull holding forth on the virtues of the Pan-American system. A week later, he is to be heard maintaining the preposterous fiction that talks with Nomura had not yet got beyond the "exploratory" stage! Contributing to the carnival atmosphere was a simultaneous series of parallel talks. Grew had been conversing with Toyoda; Welles had fallen to squabbling over minor points with Minister-Counselor Wakasugi; Roosevelt had been seeing Nomura at frequent intervals, while both Dooman and Ballantine had entered into an exchange with their opposite numbers. Nor does this include conferences between Hamilton and Wikawa.[22]

The *coup de grace* came on November 26 when Hull presented Tokyo with a set of demands totally divorced from the context of the past six months and calling for Japanese withdrawal from Manchukuo.

Any reader who has attempted to thread his way through the record of these talks will not be surprised that a task force of Japanese carriers was soon on its way to Hawaii. Even if Hull never admitted, as he did, along with Undersecretary of State Sumner Welles, to a deliberate policy of stalling, the record reveals numerous devices employed since the fall of 1939 to cover the face of American intransigence.[23]

As spring blossomed into summer and summer gave way to fall in 1941, Tokyo had less reason than ever to surrender. Hitler, in full control of nearly all western Europe, had expelled Britain from Greece and Libya, Tobruk excepted, and gone on to throttle Russia. Never had Japanese proponents of the Axis been stronger. In August, an attempt was made on the life of ex-premier Hiranuma, principal diplomatic adviser to the emperor, and he barely escaped. In September, a bullet passed within inches of the premier himself. Grew took to carrying a revolver.[24]

Some historians have pinned the blame on Nomura, stressing his relative inexperience or echoing Hull's charge that the admiral did not possess an adequate command of English: "I frequently doubted whether he understood the points I was making."[25] But why, one must ask, did Hull continue to negotiate with a person who demonstrated such difficulty with communication? Many have accepted Hull's thesis that Nomura erred in presenting the Draft Understanding to Tokyo as an American proposal when it was merely a paper drawn by Drought, one which Hull had agreed to accept "as a basis for starting conversations" and subject to four principles for which the United States had long contended.[26]

In point of fact, Drought's Draft Understanding of April 16 was nothing if not an American proposal. It had been drawn on the initiative of American clergymen in collaboration with the president of the United States and his advisers. The Japanese had made it perfectly clear to Drought, and through Drought to Roosevelt, that they were sending a plenipotentiary and that FDR was expected to designate his own representative to work with Wikawa and hammer out an agreement. The Japanese government would approve said agreement in due time and the president would then call a conference to seal the compact before the eyes of the world.[27] Wikawa's presence in Washington, in fact the whole idea of a Draft Understanding, with emphasis on the word "understanding," was intended by Tokyo to assure agreement with the United States before the tendering of a formal proposal. As Drought put it to Joseph Ballantine, Hamilton's assistant, "the Japanese would want some intimation that the Japanese proposals would be substantially acceptable to this [the U.S.] government." If America accepted unofficially, the Japanese cabinet would give formal endorsement, hopefully before Foreign Minister Yosuke Matsuoka returned from a trip to Berlin and Moscow. The pro-Axis Matsuoka would then be faced with a *fait accompli*.[28] Walker warned Hull on March 17 that "Prince Konoye, Count Arima and Marquis Kido [Lord Keeper of the Privy Seal] are endangering their lives by these negotiations. Obviously, they will not confide in the Japanese embassy at Washington until they are certain of substantial agreement with the two persons" (Wikawa and Iwakuro).[29] The next day, Walker again warned Hull that the Japanese wanted either "substantial change introduced or substantial approval given" to the Draft Understanding "so that Tokyo can immediately instruct its Embassy to submit the Draft officially upon which both governments can announce an 'Agreement in Principle.' " The idea was so crucial to Walker that he mentioned it a third time to Hull. It was therefore a warrantable expectation on Japan's part that when Hull authorized Nomura to submit the Draft Understanding to Tokyo as "a basis for the institution of negotiations," it constituted a morally binding agreement, and not at all what Hull later claimed.[30]

Originally, when asked by Nomura if the United States could approve the Draft, Hull replied encouragingly that some points would need modification or elimination, but he could see "no good reason why ways could not be found to reach a fairly satisfactory settlement of all the essential questions presented." Drought referred to this wording when on May 12 he recalled "our assurance that there will be no substantial modifications in the proposed 'understanding' " and it is why Nomura told his superiors that Hull had agreed "in general." Here was anything but a misunderstanding based on language barriers. According to Walker, Hull actually assured Nomura there would be no substantial modifications, and according to Konoye, Hull accepted Japan's second tentative plan (the Draft Understanding) as a basis for discussion, which amounts to the same thing.[31]

One reason why Hull's initial response to the Draft Understanding was so misleading is that there was a difference between what he initially said and what he had been told to say. On March 7, Hornbeck, who believed there was no use negotiating with men whose word could not be trusted, informed him that although Roosevelt wanted him to engage in talks with Nomura he must be reserved and keep the ambassador guessing; the United States was in no hurry. In April, he was instructed to remain as vague as possible and confine his talk to generalities such as the desirability of trade liberalization or the merits of the Declaration of Lima. If asked whether he could accept the Draft Understanding, he was to say it could be "a starting point for discussion." In other words, Roosevelt and Hornbeck wished to remain noncommittal while giving the impression of interest. Hull was advised to state that if Tokyo approved the

Draft, he would study it "sympathetically" and "feel optimistic that on the basis of mutual good will our differences can be adjusted."

Needless to say, in the language of diplomacy where "no" may be interpreted to mean "yes," differences resolvable in an atmosphere of good will cannot be very substantial. Inadvertently, Hull ended by promising a good deal more than his instructions permitted. For the phrase "starting point" he substituted the word "basis" which carries an entirely different meaning. On June 10, Hornbeck reined him in with a reminder that he had succeeded in bringing himself "to a negotiation" ("no matter how it may otherwise be technically described"). Almost as if some invisible wire had tightened around his neck, Hull now ceased to direct his attention to substantive matters. By June 20, the Japanese leadership was complaining that he seemed more interested in silk purchases or a bus line franchise than in the major points at issue. Drought agreed, telling Walker that "it makes us look perfectly ridiculous."[32]

Another stock criticism of Nomura is that he did not let Tokyo know immediately of Hull's insistence on four general principles as a condition for considering the Draft Understanding. Such an omission pales, however, against the backdrop of the summer's talks. Japan could have paid lip service to Hull's principles. But from the beginning, it was specifics that counted. Even if Nomura *had* been less proficient in English — and this may be doubted in view of his former residence in Britain and the United States, not to mention his 1939 talks with Grew — and even if there had been a genuine misunderstanding as to the nature of the Draft Understanding, this alone could never have been decisive. One or two mistakes on Nomura's part do not explain Hull's stalling. They do not account for his flight from specificity. Any failure in communication was due to ignorance of another kind. Roosevelt misunderstood Japan's relationship with China even as he misunderstood the aims of the Soviet Union. Conversely, Japanese leaders never seem to have grasped the true nature of Roosevelt.

Some have shifted the blame to Walsh and Drought, claiming they were meddlesome amateurs who exaggerated on both sides the concessions each was willing to make. Admittedly, the "Preliminary Draft of an 'Agreement in Principle' " which Drought first circulated to Hull via Walker on March 17 implied the with-

drawal of all Japanese troops when it provided for China's absolute independence. It also stipulated that Japan would sever all
trade with Germany and stop shipments to countries *trading* with
Germany. Neither of these provisions appeared in the Draft Understanding of April 16. But neither did there appear the earlier
provisions for a Japanese Monroe Doctrine and a dividing of
the Pacific into two zones of naval influence. In any case, it
was the latter document which Hull accepted as the "basis" for
discussion, not the former.[33]

While the priests were not professional diplomats, neither were
they "self-appointed" in the sense often implied. They were chosen
by Japan and accepted by Roosevelt. Their mission was self-
starting only insofar as a telegram from publisher-philanthropist
Robert Cuddihy to former Vice Minister of Foreign Affairs Set-
suzo Sawada got the ball rolling. Letters of introduction from
Lewis Straus helped keep it in motion. Before leaving Tokyo
in December of 1940, the priests had conferred with Foreign
Minister Matsuoka on two occasions and helped him draft a
speech to the America-Japan Society. Although their meeting
with the premier was cancelled at the last minute, they called
on General Muto. They met the vice minister for foreign affairs
and were introduced to Prince Saionji's grandson, the head of
the Domei News Agency. They also saw Wikawa and called
on Taro Terasaki, chief of the American desk at the Japanese
Foreign Ministry. Several times, they visited their old friend,
Sawada, who had recently held a position comparable to that
of Welles in the United States. Nothing was left to chance. It is
especially significant that once they had the confidence of the
Japanese, the Roosevelt administration welcomed them as an
important channel of negotiation. Hull asked Drought to remain on top in Washington, and Walsh was requested by the
American embassy in Tokyo to serve as go-between. The bishop
made frequent visits to the embassy in the fall and stayed in
touch with Grew through Dooman. Roosevelt himself encouraged the priests and thanked them for their help.[34]

Drought, who is said to have been an "innocent abroad," and
"as wrong about Japan as any person could be," had worked
as a young missionary in China and written a Hakka grammar
which later became a standard text.[35] As treasurer of a great
religious society with large interests in Japan, he also had ample
opportunity for diplomatic contact. Typical was a letter he ad-

dressed to Ambassador Horinouchi protesting the 1939 bombing of a Maryknoll center in China. He knew how careful the Japanese had been to protect non-combatants, he said, and was keenly aware of why their people were at war; sensitive to the larger issues, he had consistently tried to represent the Japanese viewpoint to the American people. Nevertheless, this latest incident in which a Maryknoll father had been wounded, might be misconstrued:

Our relations must be conducted with frankness and on a basis of honorable self-respect, and I am sure that I should be wanting in both, and unworthy of your esteem were I to fail to invoke your particular consideration to the injuries suffered by our Father and the property losses sustained by our Society.[36]

Walsh, one of six men to found the first American Catholic mission in China, had lived in that country for eighteen years. After acquiring a fair command of Chinese calligraphy, he had found time to write several books on subjects related to China, including *Observations in the Orient* and *The Young Ones* (stories about Chinese children). Among his published works, which included a number of plays and innumerable articles, was a biography of Father McShane containing a section on Oriental psychology.[37]

Together, Walsh and Drought articulated the Japanese outlook more accurately than anyone at the highest echelons of State. With a healthy respect for the eastern mind, they could appreciate Japan's insistence upon secrecy as well as the grave risk of assassination her leaders were running.[38] As Walsh remarked in 1940, "we deal in the Orient with superior civilizations, with essentially good people; with fine sensibilities." Drought explained the futility of Hull's preaching in a single sentence: "Orientals put a different value on speech than we do." Far better than any of Roosevelt's other advisers, he understood Japan's fear of communism and her usefulness as a potential makeweight against Russia. He was also aware of the fact that American cooperation might be parlayed into Japanese support in the struggle against Hitler.[39]

Unique in the annals of American diplomacy, Drought composed lengthy memoranda detailing problems and outlining solutions *from Japan's point of view*. Using the term "our" to mean "Japanese," he laid out Tokyo's best approach to the United States in terms of American psychology. Japan would be well advised, he argued, to compare her desire for a friendly government in China to Woodrow Wilson's preference for Carranza over Huerta in Mexico; she should borrow from the corpus of Pan-American thought to describe her Pan-Asian League; she should continue to claim her own version of a Monroe Doctrine for the Far East. If the Maryknoller had his way, Matsuoka would have tried to dispel lingering fear of a Japanese deal with the Axis by broadcasting to the American people on Christmas Eve, 1940.[40] He foresaw the appeal that a Pacific summit conference would have for Roosevelt and assured Japanese leaders that even if such a meeting proved only moderately successful it could do nothing but good as it would "break down the present tension and permit Japan to consolidate her position, *with or without American approbation.*"[41] This, perhaps as much as anything else, explains why Roosevelt withheld his consent. Realizing the need for different nations to have different systems of government, Drought considered a cosmopolitan outlook so vital for peace that he included in his "Preliminary Draft of an 'Agreement in Principle' between the United States and Japan" the following:

The governments of the United States and of Japan recognize that the diversity of cultural and consequent (sic) political and social forms prevailing among advanced nations [is] . . . inescapable . . . only a perverted will can distort as an incitement to conflict . . . this natural diversity which, when properly appreciated and encouraged, is one of nature's gifts for creative human and international progress . . . among nations the political form of constitution . . . [is a] private domestic concern.

He has been accused of being pro-Japanese and "going over" to Tokyo. In fact, he was one of a handful of diplomats capable of seeing things for what they really were.[42]

The Hull-Nomura talks entered their final phase with Drought and Walsh receding into the background, their place taken by men sworn to fight. Unknown to Roosevelt, a mammoth task force was girding for action at an island rendez-vous far to the north of Honshu. Six carriers with 423 planes, 2 battleships, 2 heavy cruisers, 11 destroyers, 28 submarines, and 8 tankers were practicing for the most daringly successful attack in recent naval history.

Inasmuch as Tokyo struck without warning — Nomura did not deliver his declaration of war until twenty minutes after the fact — FDR declared December 7 a day that would "live in infamy." Ever since, it has been associated in the popular mind with an element of murderous deceit. Nevertheless, if there was treachery, one must conclude that it was not the Japanese who led their adversary on, not they who broke their word, nor they who slapped their adversary in the face. Hull not only arranged to snub Nomura when he came calling to West Virginia. Similar presumption led him to make an unprecedented demand for a change in the Tokyo cabinet. Yoshie Saito, adviser to the emperor, protested strenuously at the 38th Imperial Liaison Conference held on July 10:

> Hull's "Oral Statement" contains especially outrageous language. For instance it says . . . "there are differences of opinion within the Japanese government . . . we cannot make an agreement with a Japanese government of that kind" . . . His attitude is one of contempt for Japan. I have been in the foreign service for a long time. This language is not the kind one would use toward a country of equal standing; it expresses an attitude one would take toward a protectorate or a possession. These words are inexcusable.

The foreign minister concurred:

> Hull's statement is outrageous. Never has such a thing occurred since Japan opened diplomatic relations with other countries . . . I was truly amazed that he [Nomura] would listen without protest to a demand that Japan, a great world power, change her cabinet.

It seems to have been Hull's insulting manner which stung the most: "The United States did nothing about our proposal for forty days." At the Imperial Conference of December 1, it was said that Roosevelt had not only refused to make a single concession; he had added new demands. He wanted a complete and unconditional withdrawal from China, the withdrawal of recognition of Nanking, and reduction of the Tripartite Pact to a dead letter. This, Tojo pointed out, "belittled the dignity of our Empire." Even the distinguished Hara Yoshimichi, President of the Privy Council, a man who continued to argue against war with the United States, was brought to admit before his colleagues on that same day: "The United States is being utterly conceited, obstinate, and disrespectful."[43]

None of the above need be taken to mean that Roosevelt lacked a valid reason for refusing compromise. It can be argued that if Konoye's troops had been permitted to march out of China under the flag of victory, they might have gone into action elsewhere, and to the serious detriment of America. Roosevelt himself seems to have been of this persuasion, even though many, including British leaders, disagreed. War with Japan was the last thing Whitehall wanted. When Prime Minister Churchill told his people in February, 1942, that American belligerency was something for which he had toiled unremittingly, he was referring primarily to the Atlantic theater. While British leaders may have preferred war in the Far East to American neutrality, they generally disapproved of Roosevelt's take-it-or-leave-it attitude.[44] As late as October 18, 1941, the Foreign Office took the position in cables to Lord Lothian that Britain had been willing to follow the American policy of maximum economic pressure, but "we should still prefer if possible to keep Japan out of the world conflict and to detach her from the Axis."[45] Churchill did object to the Japanese version of a *modus vivendi* under consideration in late November, but this was because it called for a break in the supply line to China, not because it held out hope for a compromise. All agreed that the Chinese coolie must not be deserted as long as he continued to hold down large numbers of Japanese, but while no one wanted a subservient China, the fear was that Roosevelt was not giving Japan sufficient opportunity to distance herself from the Axis.

On this point, good men may disagree. The crux of the issue lies in the fact that FDR's methods at their best frustrated the normal process of communication. At their worst, they violated common canons of courtesy, not to mention fair dealing. So devious was he on occasion, and so successful in concealing the true nature of the Hull-Nomura talks, that individuals on each side of the bargaining table have ever since been saddled with a burden of blame which is in no way theirs. Here again, British opinion is worthy of note. Informed observers at the Court of St. James never accepted the notion of Japan's attack as a stab in the back. Oliver Lyttleton, Minister of Production and a leading member of Churchill's War Cabinet, told the American Chamber of Commerce that the United States had not been driven to war by Tokyo but rather had challenged her to the point where she felt compelled to stand and fight. Lord Halifax, then serving as ambassador to Washington, concurred with Lyt-tleton, noting that this was an idea Americans seemed unable to grasp.[46] Indeed. Halifax and Lyttleton were face to face with a mindset which even the passage of forty years has done little to alter.

# The Roosevelt Wartime Fireside Chats: A Rhetorical Study of Strategy and Tactics

**WALDO W. BRADEN**
BOYD PROFESSOR EMERITUS OF SPEECH
LOUISIANA STATE UNIVERSITY

## *Introduction*

Today many persons have little memory of Franklin D. Roosevelt, Wendell Willkie, Harry Truman, Douglas MacArthur, and many other World War II personalities. When they hear a Reagan speech referred to as a "Fireside Chat," they are puzzled. In the present essay it is my hope to recapture some of the moods that surrounded World War II by concentrating upon fifteen of the Fireside Chats that F.D.R. delivered between September 3, 1939 and June 12, 1944.

A generation that listens to country-western singers and late night, far-out disc jockeys has little understanding of what the radio meant to persons in the thirties and forties. In those distant days radio sets pulled the families together. Around the living room, the members assembled to listen to favorite entertainers, popular commentators, or even church services. Mount Pleasant, Iowa, for example, seemed very much a part of the great world when a rich voiced announcer or commentator came through the speaker from New York, Washington, Chicago or Denver. Hush settled around the circle in an effort not to miss the humor of Amos and Andy, Jack Benny and Rochester, Burns and Allen. Elmer Davis, Boah Carter, and H. L. Kaltenborn gave dimension and importance to the news. In that company Franklin D. Roosevelt could hold his own with "with a warm and vibrant voice that breathed confidence in the future and arrested and held the attention of his listeners."[1]

Roosevelt succeeded in projecting himself into those little gatherings all over the country and in making his listeners fantasize that they too were sitting in the White House and listening in on frank and important conversations. Robert Sherwood commends Roosevelt "for his superb ability to use the first person plural" and for speaking "simply, casually, as a friend or relative."[2] In tones that conveyed warmth, calmness, good humor, exuberance, concern, or fortitude, he conversed (never giving the impression of reading) in a manner of a friend or neighbor, face to face, over the kitchen table or in a town meeting. Restricted by his physical handicap, he gave special attention to his voice control, facial expressions, and head movements as well as his straightforward colloquial English. He maintained rapport with his "fellow Americans" who came to anticipate important news and frank counsel from their leader. Prior to 1939, he had trained the American public to look forward to his radio talks. Between 1933 and 1939, he presented thirteen Fireside Chats and had appeared on the air many other times. With a lively sense of communication, Roosevelt made Americans feel that he was eager to share his thoughts, and he assured them that it was his duty as President to inform them about what was happening in Washington or on the numerous war fronts. Into his broadcasts, he slipped in many reminders that he was taking them into his confidence. For example he said:

"Let us sit down together again, you and I, to consider . . . "
"Tonight my single duty is to speak to the whole of America."
"I think it is a matter of fairness that you hear the facts."
"I am very anxious that the American people be given the opportunity to hear."

Perhaps some background information is in order concerning the twenty-eight Fireside Chats so designated in the Roosevelt Papers. Varying in length from approximately 1,500 to 4,500 words, these radio talks were delivered usually between nine and ten-thirty p.m. from the Diplomatic Reception Room of the White House. But contrary to their label the setting had no fireplace and no easy rocker. The President sat in a straight-backed chair at a small table facing the several microphones. Often present was a small gathering of invited listeners, sometimes including members of his family, visiting dignitaries, and other guests. Harry C. Butcher, manager of the CBS Washington office, provided the label "Fireside Chat" to augment the idea that the President was informally talking.[3] In the initial announcement of the first talk, Roosevelt emphasized that

The Constitution has laid upon me the duty of conveying the condition of the country to the Congress assembled at Washington. I believe I have a like duty to convey to the people themselves a clear picture of the situation at Washington itself whenever there is a danger of any confusion as to what the government is undertaking.

In explaining the first Fireside Chat, delivered March 12, 1933, that was devoted to the banking crisis, F.D.R. set forth his purpose: "to use the radio to explain to the average men and women of the Nation" why "their money was tied up in some bank." He continued, "It was my endeavor to explain these things in non-technical language, so that the great mass of our citizens who had little or no experience with the technicalities of banking would be relieved of their anxiety. . . ."[4]

For all presentations F.D.R. maintained tight control of the preparation, deciding when to speak, preparing initial memos about what he wanted to say, determining the strategy, reviewing the several drafts as they moved along, recasting the language, and approving the final reading copy. Many speeches went through seven or eight drafts. His principal speech writers from 1940 through 1945 were Samuel I. Rosenman, Robert Sherwood, and Harry Hopkins. Archibald MacLeish, Librarian of Congress, sometimes helped. Other knowledgeable persons were called upon to work on given speeches or to give counsel. Drafts were sometimes reviewed by cabinet members, including those of State or War or trusted advisers such as Bernard W. Baruch or Felix Frankfurter. Facts were checked and rechecked.[5] Rosenman writes, "There was no pride of authorship. . . . Whatever language and and whomever's language did it best was the language we wanted."[6] Roosevelt and his speech helpers sought to maintain an oral quality. Sherwood speaks of Roosevelt reading a draft aloud "to see how it sounded and to detect any tongue-twisting phrases that would be difficult on the radio."[7]

*It is the central goal of this chapter to discuss how Roosevelt moved from a position of neutrality to the advocacy of support of the allies and eventually to participate in the conflict.* His rhetorical problems involved maintaining morale, avoiding hysteria, countering the efforts of the isolationists and pacifists, mobilizing the civilians and military for preparedness, supporting the British, French, and Chinese when they seemed to be losing, sustaining his popularity, and winning re-election in 1940 and 1944. Unfolding events sometimes placed Roosevelt in the awkward position of seeming to be inconsistent and even dishonest. How could he insist that he "hated war" and at the same time move toward total mobilization?

### Before Pearl Harbor

From September, 1939, until December 7, 1941, Franklin D. Roosevelt met "his severest test as a leader of public opinion because he faced bitter opposition" from the isolationists, such as William E. Borah and a citizenry that was eager to avoid the conflict. Sol Bloom, a long time U.S. Representative and chairman of the House Foreign Affairs Committee, writes that during these years Roosevelt had "to prepare the American people for war. . . . It was a problem of education. . . of how to get all of us ready in mind and spirit" to enter the conflict.[8] A part of Roosevelt's strategy was appointing Republicans to key positions to help build bi-partisan support. Among those so appointed in 1940–41 were William Allen White, Frank Knox, Henry L. Stimson, and Harlan Fiske Stone.

To paraphrase Donald Bryant, Roosevelt's task involved adjusting "people to ideas and ideas to people." Expressing another alternative, one of the Republican appointees, Henry L. Stimson, Secretary of War (1940–45), the former Secretary of State (1929–33) under Hoover, felt that F.D.R. should have brushed "aside the contemptible little group of men who wailed of 'warmongers', and in the blunt strokes of a poster painter . . . demonstrated the duty of Americans in a world issue." Stimson criticized Roosevelt's "honeyed and consoling words" and thought that "the President directed his arguments altogether too much toward his vocal but small isolationist opposition, and not toward the people as a whole."[9]

Bloom and Stimson present the choices open to the President in 1939. His options provide context for the four Chats delivered prior to December 9, 1941. As early as October 5, 1937, in his famous Quarantine Speech delivered at a bridge dedication in Chicago, Roosevelt was made dramatically aware of his rhetorical problems when he attempted to warn Americans of the seriousness of the developments in Europe. Rosenman says, "The reaction . . . was quick and violent — and nearly unanimous. It was condemned as warmongering and saber-rattling."

Reflecting the attitudes of his boss, Rosenman concludes that F.D.R. made "this mistake of trying to lead the people . . . too quickly, and before they had been adequately informed of the facts or spiritually prepared for the event."[10] Certain words in this statement that reflect F.D.R.'s rhetorical goals are "*lead* the people . . . *informed* of the facts . . . *spiritually* prepared." [italics added] It is evident that Rosenman, close to the President, was well aware of the rhetorical problems and recommended a strategy of Bloom instead of Stimson. On January 31, 1939, at a confidential conference with the Senate Military Affairs Committee, Roosevelt articulated the strategy that he pursued in the months before the attack on Pearl Harbor. To the senators he said: "We don't want to . . . frighten the American people at this time or any time. We want them to gradually realize what is a potential danger, and I always translate things . . . in terms of the past. It is a fair way of putting most things."[11]

*September 3, 1939.* On the evening of the day Great Britain and France responded to Hitler's attack on Poland, by declaring war on Germany, F.D.R. gave a fifteen minute Fireside Chat. He repeated that he stood for peace and hated war, but he insisted that he had better information than his critics and that "the most dangerous enemies of American peace" were "those who, without well-rounded information . . . undertake to speak with assumed authority . . . to give the nation assurances . . . which are of little present or future value." In his final sentences, after repeating that "the Nation will remain a neutral Nation," he suggested, "I cannot ask that every American remain neutral in thought as well. Even a neutral has a right to take account of facts." These sentences represented a first step toward his ultimate decision, which many believe he had already made.

*May 26, 1940.* Nine months later after German forces had entered the Netherlands and Belgium (May 10), occupied the French city of Sedan (May 14), and commenced to push the British and French forces toward the sea, Roosevelt returned to the people with a second Fireside Chat in which he suggested that "the aggressors" were driving "women and children and old men" from their homes. Discrediting his American critics, he accused them of "closing their eyes from lack of interest or knowledge" to what was happening and he called them "partisans," guilty "of the dissemination of discord," and exploiters of "prejudice through false slogans and emotional appeals." Most of his speech he devoted to showing that the nation was prepared "to defend a way of life, not American alone, but all mankind." In these thrusts he built sympathy for the people of France and the Low Countries, discredited his critics, and gave notice that the country was prepared to protect itself.

*December 29, 1940.* Seven months later he gave his third war Fireside Chat. To stress its importance, he explained in his opening sentences that it was "not a Fireside Chat on war," and that "never before since Jamestown and Plymouth Rock has American civilization been in such danger as now." Indeed, this stark pronouncement had shock value. Worried about allied reverses in Europe and Asia, he advocated that the United States become "the great arsenal of democracy," indeed a happy choice of phrase because it became a slogan of the war. Denying at the moment any intention of sending American troops to Europe, he advocated supplying arms to the British, the Greeks, and the Chinese. To emotionalize his presentation, he resorted to a selfish appeal, saying that these nations by resisting the enemy would keep war "from our firesides." Adding another powerful fear appeal, he warned that "the Nazi masters of Germany might enslave the whole of Europe and then . . . use the resources of Europe to dominate the rest of the world." He blasted the Nazis as a "gang of outlaws," "pious frauds," and an "unholy alliance of power and pelf." To characterize their method he included such phrases as "living at the point of a Nazi gun," as "evil forces which have crushed and undermined and corrupted," and as "shooting and chains and concentration camps . . . the very altars of modern dictators." Discrediting his opposition, he called them "secret emissaries" who sought "to stir up suspicion and dissension . . . to turn capital against labor and vice versa . . . to re-awaken long slumbering racial and religious enmities" and to "exploit for their own ends our natural abhorrence of war."

He concluded that "these trouble-breeders" hoped "to divide our people into hostile groups and to destroy our unity and shatter our will to defend ourselves." Loading the scales heavily on his side, he accused his critics and opponents of being "enemy agents," "evil forces," "American appeasers," and "defeatists." Of course, in his denunciations by lumping together enemy spies,

American Nazis, America Firsters, pacifists, and his Republican critics, he implied guilt by association, knowing that many of his listeners would make no subtle distinctions among those who opposed him. Elevating his own position Roosevelt associated with it: "the plain truth," "willingness to hear the worst," "gallantry, the Monroe Doctrine, realism, human dignity, compassion for war victims, democracy," and "this nation which we love and honor." Through an emotional sweep, Roosevelt sought to unite his partisans and to make questioning his position unpatriotic.

*September 11, 1941.* The sinking of the destroyer Greer by a German submarine off Iceland became the occasion for a fourth Fireside Chat and the next step toward total commitment. Speaking that night a stern, determined Roosevelt moved ever nearer to all-out war. Anticipating the rationalizations of his critics, he explained, "She [Greer] was flying the American flag. Her identity as an American ship was unmistakable. . . . The German submarine fired first upon the American destroyer without warning and with deliberate design to sink her." To stress the seriousness of the encounter he reviewed four other aggressions on the high seas: three sinkings and an attempt to stalk an American battleship. Roosevelt saw in these episodes justification to move openly against the Axis; consequently, he advanced a traditional American argument: the Nazi government had committed "an act of piracy" against the American flag; it had violated the freedom of the sea. Furthermore, it had engaged in a "conspiracy" to seize governments in South America. By premising his case upon violations of freedom of the seas and the Monroe Doctrine, Roosevelt brought into play two traditionally strong biases of Americans since "the earliest days of the Republic."

To stir hatred of the Nazi leader, Roosevelt associated Hitler with such acts as "his intrigues, his plot, his machinations, his sabotage," "world mastery," "Axis domination," "acts of aggression," "Nazi dominated world," and "ruthless force." In this address Roosevelt included one of his most telling slogans, "When you see a rattlesnake poised to strike, you do not wait until he has struck before you crush him." To neutralize being called a warmonger, he rationalized that it was his "obligation," his "obvious duty" to warn that "when German and Italian vessels of war enter the waters, the protection of which is necessary for American defense, they do so at their own peril." Spiking what his critics might say and shifting blame to Hitler, Roosevelt concluded, "The aggression is not ours; ours is solely defense."

However, still much aware of his critics, he directed a pointed remark at them and at Hitler: "No tender whispering of appeasers that Hitler is not interested in the Western Hemisphere, no soporific lullabies . . . can long have any effect on the hard-headed, far sighted, and realistic American people."

The construction of this speech shows that Roosevelt continued the same caution that had marked his utterances since his Quarantine Speech of October 5, 1937. Even at this late moment, dictated by the sinking of an American destroyer, he repeated his calculated position — insisting that he wanted peace, but that the Axis had forced him to alter his policy. Some may question whether F.D.R. was sincere and honest. And it is true that many writers suggest that Roosevelt really did hope for peace and that he did "hate war." In his defense it should be observed that with the flows of reports from the battlefronts of the human suffering and the ruthlessness of the Axis onslaught, the President and his advisers had determined that the United States could not long avoid active participation in the world-wide conflict.

## Pearl Harbor

*December 9, 1941.* The attack on Pearl Harbor brought the fifth wartime Fireside Chat. Roosevelt detractors contend that F.D.R. manipulated the Japanese into firing the traditional first shot, or that at least he knew of the possibilities of the strike and did nothing about it, and that through diplomacy he could have forestalled the attack on Pearl Harbor. [See Chapter Eight] Although the writer does not believe this theory (and many reputable historians support this position), it is not the purpose here to argue this point; instead the focus continues to be upon the rhetorical strategy and tactics of Roosevelt.

The speech that he made to Congress, December 8, 1941, perhaps the best oration of his career, is tighter, more direct, and more moving than his Fireside Chat the following night to the American people. The message to Congress was five and a half minutes long, while his following radio speech took a half hour.

In explaining to the people why he had asked the Congress to declare war against Japan, he traced the aggression of the Axis power, admitted the seriousness of the attack on Pearl Harbor, warned that "the road ahead . . . lies hard work," and "the United States can accept no result save victory, final and complete." Although he denounced the Axis, he now made no reference to his domestic critics. In a sense, he had outlasted his opponents by letting dramatic events quiet them, smother their arguments, and make counter-strategies appear unpatriotic and dangerous. Sounding his theme for the remainder of the war, he said "Every single man, woman, and child is a partner in the most tremendous undertaking of American history." The partnership theme suggesting inclusiveness and involvement of the total citizenry became the prevailing theme of his remaining Fireside Chats, not as a leader or boss or superior, but as a fellow American, speaking of united effort and common purpose.

These two speeches, delivered immediately after Pearl Harbor, show a significant quality of the Roosevelt rhetoric. Roosevelt incorporated a dramatic, dynamic quality through his simple words, short declarative sentences and the parallel structure. In speaking to the people via radio, he demonstrated these qualities by quickly summarizing the aggressions of the Axis powers in nine sentences — all worded in parallel form.

> In 1931, ten years ago, Japan invaded Manchuko — without warning.
> In 1935, Italy invaded Ethiopia — without warning.
> In 1938, Hitler occupied Austria — without warning.
> In 1939, Hitler invaded Czechoslovakia — without warning.
> Later in 1939, Hitler invaded Poland — without warning.
> In 1940, Hitler invaded Norway, Denmark, the Netherlands, Belgium, and Luxembourg — without warning.
> In 1940, Italy attacked France and later Greece — without warning.
> And this year, in 1941, the Axis powers attacked Yugoslavia and Greece and they dominated the Balkans — without warning.
> And now Japan has attacked Malaya and Thailand — and the United States — without warning.
> It is all of one pattern.

Roosevelt had presented four Fireside Chats to prepare for

actual declaration of war. In those speeches he avoided the suggestion of the likelihood of that drastic final step attempting to lessen the sting of his critics that he was "a warmonger," but he could hardly be accused of using "honeyed and consoling," words as Stimson later charged. With caution and deliberation these speeches show that he moved step by step toward his objective: suggesting first that the people need not remain neutral in spirit; second, that the United States was preparing to defend its interests and territory; third, that the United States should be "the arsenal of democracy"; and fourth, that the United States forces would protect its vessels on the high seas. Only "the sudden criminal attack perpetrated by the Japanese" brought the climax: a declaration of war.

### After Pearl Harbor

*February 23, 1942.* In the weeks following Pearl Harbor, the daily reports of the Japanese sweep in the Far East, the American losses in the Philippines, the British losses in Burma, the U-boats' deadly precision in the Battle of the Atlantic, and torpedoing of British mighty *Prince of Wales* bewildered and devastated American morale. Reporting the purpose of the speech of February 23, 1942, Rosenman suggests that "the President was . . . concerned lest a spirit of defeatism settle over the American people."[12] Robert Sherwood hints at another objective; that is, Roosevelt concentrated on "purely American misfortune and promised soon we and not our enemies will have the offensive."[13] Sherwood further observes that the President "was wonderfully skillful and forceful in directing it [attention] elsewhere"—away from the British misfortunes.

Demonstrating his awareness of the importance of timing, Roosevelt chose to give "a report to the people" shortly after Washington's birthday. The analogy between Washington's experience and the present struggle enabled Roosevelt to forecast hope for the future. In a key argument he suggested, "Washington's conduct in those hard times had provided the model for all Americans ever since." Any one who since the first grade has heard repeatedly how Washington overcame adversity at Valley Forge and in his battles with the British could rationalize that the events of 1942 were indeed another Valley Forge and that just as Washington had overcome—so Americans in World War II would overcome the enemy. The identification with Valley Forge, the Revolution, and the oft-quoted words of Thomas Paine encouraged Americans to hope for better times.

Of course, Roosevelt took advantage of his ability (and that of his speech writers) to report graphically in simple terms the campaigns of our far flung forces. For his Chat of February 23, 1942, in advance he had advised listeners to have maps available when he talked. As a result many newspapers in their daily editions reproduced map drawings. In his opening sentences Roosevelt directed, "I have asked you to take out and spread before you a map of the whole earth, and to follow me in the references which I shall make to the world–encircling battle lines of this war." While speaking, he occasionally inserted, "Look at your map again," or "Your map will show that it would have been a hopeless operation." His specific details, his ease of manner, his conversational tone, and his warmth conveyed to Americans that they had ringside seats at the unfolding of great events.

The careful composition and extensive revisions produced a moving quality. The Roosevelt writing team leaned toward short, declarative sentences, often arranged in parallel form. They knew that the repetition of key words and phrases resulted in an attractive cadence. They worked for energy, movement, and drama, in their portrayal of military and naval engagements in the air and on land and sea.

The fast moving exposition clarified the dimensions of the conflict, the seriousness of the threat to Americans and their allies, and the necessity for unity and sacrifice at home. Stressing the enormity of the problems facing the Allies, Roosevelt declared, "It is warfare in terms of every continent, every island, every sea, every air-lane in the world." The repetition of the word "every" tied the sentence together and pyramided its impact. Having his listeners follow him on their world maps, he advanced his argument and demonstrated why defense of the Philippines was unwise. Frankly admitting the "obvious initial advantage" of the Axis powers, he advanced the American strategy: "Our first job is to build up production so that the United Nations can maintain control of the seas and attain control of the air — not merely a slight superiority, but an overwhelming superiority." At this time Roosevelt also showed that he was still sensitive about the attitudes of the isolationists and the anglophobes. Consequently, he directed some strong remarks toward them:

> The Americans who believed that we could live under the illusion of isolationism wanted the American eagle to imitate the tactics of the ostrich. Now, many of those same people, afraid that we may be sticking our necks out, want our national bird to be turned into a turtle. But we prefer to retain the eagle as it is — flying high and striking hard.

By associating the *ostrich* and the *turtle* with the isolationists, he knew that he had contrasted two highly loaded negative symbols with "the eagle as it is — flying high and striking hard," a most revered American symbol that in power ranked next to "the stars and stripes" and "Uncle Sam". The traditional eagle with outstretched wings triggers the encompassing American myth.

He further denounced "Axis propagandists," "Americans who, since Pearl Harbor have whispered or announced 'off the record' that there was no longer any Pacific Fleet," and those that deal in "the realm of rumor and poison." Characterizing the opposition, he called them "fifth columnists — selfish men, jealous men, fearful men."

Throughout this broadcast he continued to follow the strategy of minimizing the reports of losses by associating them with "weird rumor" and with "fifth column" reports. Further, to lessen American sacrifice he suggested that it did not compare with that of the Allies. For example he said:

> The British and the Russian people have known the full fury of Nazi onslaught. There have been times when the fate of London and Moscow was in serious doubt. But there was never the slightest question that either the British or the Russians would yield. . . .
>
> Though their homeland was overrun the Dutch people are still fighting stubbornly and powerfully overseas.
>
> The great Chinese people have suffered grievous losses; Chungking has been almost wiped out of existence — yet it remains the capital of an unbeatable China.

Statements such as these made it difficult for any American to complain about sacrifice at home or abroad.

Roosevelt directed concern away from the perplexing problems of the moment. Throughout his development, he shifted attention away from serious losses toward a hope for the achievement of future goals. Finding it difficult to question the President who seemed calm, confident, and determined, the average listener drew upon his strength and believed that "the conquering spirit" would prevail.

*April 22, and September 7, 1942.* F.D.R. devoted two Fireside Chats in 1942 to the problems of inflation. Each one, delivered immediately after he had forwarded a message to Congress, was intended to bring pressure upon congressmen to enact wage and price controls and at the same time to counter the special pleading of labor unions, farmers and industrialists who were complaining about restrictions on the economy. Rosenman reported that Roosevelt expressed his strategy as follows: "I certainly would like to tell the people something about what is going on at the fighting fronts. I'd like to show them the kind of sacrifice their sons are making — maybe in that way we can get them to realize how important it is to back up those boys by any sacrifice necessary."[14]

But the objectives of any presidential wartime speech were never simple. In this speech Roosevelt included some carefully worded propaganda for our fighting allies overseas. Aware of Axis plans to take over some French possessions, he spoke directly to the French people:

> "The United Nations will take measures, if necessary to prevent the use of French territory in any part of the world for military purposes by the Axis powers. . . . The . . . French people understand that the fight of the United Nations is fundamentally their fight, that our victory means the restoration of a free and independent France. . . . "

Rosenman suggests that F.D.R. also included "propaganda both for Russians and against the Nazis by complimenting "the crushing counter offensive on the part of the great armies of Russia."

Roosevelt combined a two-fold attack on those who chose to speak out against his policy or did not want to cooperate. He inferred that they either sympathized with the enemy or were not willing to pay the price that had been leveled upon "the workers of France and Norway and Netherlands," "the farmers of Poland and Denmark and Czechoslovakia and France," "the businessmen of France and the women and children who Hitler is starving." Not to cooperate was intended to bring a severe self rebuke to anyone who wanted to keep his self respect. In this speech he again utilized the argument of more or less, forcing his listeners to compare their lives with sacrifice of those abroad: "Not all of us have the privilege of fighting our enemies . . . Here at home everyone will have the privilege of making whatever self denial is necessary."

F.D.R. labelled as opponents those who did not want to cooperate with the program of "keeping the cost of living down." Turning to highly negative strong language, he referred to those of "the faint of heart," those "who put their own selfish interest above the interest of this Nation," "those who pervert honest criticism into falsification of fact," "self styled experts," "a few bogus patriots who use . . . the press to echo sentiments of the propaganda in Tokyo and Berlin," and "the handful of noisy traitors — betrayers of Christianity itself — would be directors who in their hearts and souls have yielded to Hiterlism."

After waiting all summer for Congress to enact legislation to control wages and prices, on September 7, 1942 Roosevelt gave Congress an ultimatum to enact the necessary legislation by October 1. A second time he turned to the voters to bring pressure upon congressmen, but at the same time he also wanted to inform the public as to why restraints on inflation were necessary. He skillfully sandwiched the plea for sacrifice on the home front between reports of sacrifices and activities on the war front. For the first time in many months FDR was able to speak optimistically about the war on four fronts: Russia, Pacific, Mediterranean and Middle East, and the European front.

To personalize his appeal, he included a story about the heroism of Lieutenant John Powers:

> You and I are "the folks back home" for whose protection Lieutenant Powers fought and repeatedly risked his life. He said that we counted on him and his men. We did not count in vain. But have not those men a right to be counting on us? How are we playing our part "back home" in winning this war?
>
> The answer is that we are not doing enough.

In these five sentences, F.D.R. demonstrated succinctly a major facet of his wartime strategy. When he says, "He [Powers] said that we [the American people] counted on him and his men," Roosevelt brought into play a powerful appeal. He enhanced his argument by asking, "But have not these men a right to be counting on us?" The heroism of Powers implied the answer, putting pressure upon the listeners at home to match by words and deeds the efforts of the fighting men. When he concluded that "We are not doing enough," he gave energy to his words "count on" — in a way a person would speak of an obligation or contract with his neighbor.

Implicit in the Roosevelt strategy was the suggestion that those on the battlefields or in the occupied countries were doing so much (the greater) that it behooved those at home to attempt to match those sacrifices — admittedly smaller in magnitude. This tactic placed the listener in a difficult position: not to act was a severe wrench on self respect and suggestion of betrayal of those in uniform. This line was intended to encourage participation in the war effort, to silence the opposition, to keep enlistments high, to justify sacrifice, to make restrictive laws and regulations bearable, to sell savings bonds, and to maintain morale in general.

*October 12, 1942.* After returning from a trip "of inspection of camps and training stations and war factories," (September 7 to October 1, 1942) Roosevelt delivered his fourth Fireside Chat of 1942. Rosenman and Sherwood, who both worked on the speech offer different views of its purpose. As the content of the speech suggests, Rosenman explains that the President hoped to gain "adequate manpower for civilian production" and "to find more young men" for the "fighting forces."[15] The suggestion concerning the lowering of the draft age to eighteen supports this observation. Hinting at another goal, Sherwood suggests "the main purpose of the trip [probably also the speech] was, of course, for political influence on the Congress and on the Congressional elections."[16] Similar to other Roosevelt utterances the motivations were complex.

This speech is an excellent example of the President attempting to give "the people the facts."[17] To explain why he made the trip, he said, "The Commander in Chief cannot learn all of the answers . . . in Washington. And that is why I made the trip. . . . I can tell you very simply that the . . . trip . . . permitted me to concentrate on the work . . . without expending time, meeting all the demands of publicity. And — I might add — it was a particular pleasure to make a tour of the country, without having to give a single thought to politics." Of course this last thought was to thwart those who might accuse him of political motivations. Building his credibility he emphasized that he had made "firsthand observations." For example he said:

> "I saw only a small portion of all our plants, but that portion was a good cross section . . . "
>
> "In one sense my recent trip was a hurried one, out through the Middle West, to the Northwest, down the length of the Pacific, and back through the Southwest and South . . . . I had the opportunity to talk to the people who are actually doing the work. . . ."

The listeners gained assurance in having the President share with them his personal observations, taking his fellow Americans into his confidence about his conclusions. In his broadcast Roosevelt could shift from explaining defeats to reporting positive results: increased production on the home fronts, the training of "our fighting forces," the planning of "the Joint Staff of Army and Navy," the unity among the allied forces, expanding shipping of war materials and the promise of a new offensive against Germany and Japan. In a sense he turned the tables on "our enemies," saying,

> "The 'War of Nerves' against the United Nations is now turning into a boomerang. For the first time, the Nazi propaganda machine is on the defensive. They began to apologize to their own people for the repulse of their vast forces at Stalingrad and for the enormous casualties they are suffering. . . ."

By this tactic he exuded a confidence well understood and typical of the Americans' belief in their invincibility in battle.

The Roosevelt strategy centered around involving all Americans and again stressing the inclusiveness of the war effort. In opening he asserts "This whole Nation of 130,000,000 free men, women, and children is becoming one great fighting force. . . . Each of us [is] playing an honorable part in the great struggle to save our democratic civilization." Later he rephrases the idea as follows: "In a sense, every American because of the privilege of his citizenship, is a part of the Selective Service." Few families escaped having members come under Selective Service. His strategy was to make the citizen feel that he must match the sacrifice at home with that of "our fighting forces" throughout the world. The appeal is not as direct as it is in other speeches, but his references to "the Selective Service" is a strong indication of the argument of more or less.

Roosevelt summarized the great demands for manpower in a direct and forceful way in numerous places in his development:

"We have had to enlist many thousands of men for our merchant marine."

"I am impressed by the large proportion of women employed."

"In order to keep stepping up our production, we have had to add millions of workers to the total labor force."

"The school authorities . . . should work out plans to enable our high school students . . . to help farmers. . . ."

"I believe that it will be necessary to lower the present minimum age limit for Selective Service from twenty years down to eighteen."

It is entirely possible that F.D.R. hoped to prepare the nation for the lowering of the draft age. He skillfully lessened the shock concerning this necessity by saying, "I can very thoroughly understand the feelings of all parents whose sons have entered our armed forces. I have an appreciation of that feeling — and so has my wife." Of course he was referring to his own sons all of whom were in uniform. Herein he again attempted to share in the experiences and sacrifice of the war.

To make his main concern more acceptable, Roosevelt attempted to take the sting out of his proposal through inserting into challenging context. Roosevelt gave the good news before getting around to the bad news or contrasting lesser goals with greater goals or suggesting small sacrifices seem acceptable in light of greater sacrifices made by Allies or the troops overseas.

## 1943

During 1943 Roosevelt delivered four Fireside Chats: on May 2, 1943, he spoke about the seizing of the coal mines; on July 28, he made a progress report on the war including the downfall of Mussolini; on September 8, in a minor effort he opened the Third Loan Drive and on December 24, he made a major address preparing the formation of the United Nations.

*May 2, 1943.* One of his most dramatic speeches was given on May 2, 1943, when he announced the government take-over of the coal mines. After reporting a two week inspection tour, covering twenty states, he turned his attention to the miners. To turn the screws on idle workers, he said: "I want to make it clear that every American coal miner who has stopped mining coal . . . is obstructing our war effort. . . . A stopping of the coal supply even for a short time, would involve a gamble with the lives of American soldiers and sailors and the future security of our whole people."

Making his appeal even more telling, he said a little later: "You miners have sons in the Army and Navy and Marine Corps. You have sons who at this very minute — this split second — may be fighting in New Guinea . . . China, or protecting troop ships. . . ." Then he inserted two stories about coal miners in the services from Pennsylvania and another from Kentucky.

The reason for his delivering of this chat is somewhat in doubt because just before he went on the air he received word that John L. Lewis was sending miners back to work. In light of this development the speech seemed pointless as a means to bring pressure on the miners. But it is entirely possible that he wanted to make it difficult for any other group to follow the strategy of the miners. He expressed his determination to keep the war moving forward and to prevent inflation. "There can be no one," he said, "among us — no one factor — powerful enough to interrupt the forward march of our people to victory."

This type of assurance and confidence became important forces in keeping morale high and not "to let the cost of living continue to go up as it did in the first World War."

*July 28, 1943.* In the remaining three appearances, Roosevelt commenced to discuss post war plans. Rosenman indicates that the President had planned to speak as early as July 11, but the resignation of Mussolini delayed the talk until July 28, 1943. At this time he seemed to have two objectives. In announcing Mussolini's demise, Roosevelt made clear that the Allies intended to help the Italian people regain self government. This approach was intended as propaganda to other enemy peoples that might choose to surrender. Likewise it was expedient to maintain the morale of large numbers of Italian-Americans concentrated in several American cities. Second, he included a progress report on the war and plans for G. I. benefits for returning servicemen. As he had done previously, he continued his unity theme: "For the two of them [the fighting front and the home front] are inexorably tied together."

*December 24, 1943.* He delivered his most important talk of the year at 3:00 p.m., December 24, from the Franklin D. Roosevelt Library at Hyde Park. The importance that he attached to this occasion is reflected in the facts that the speech went through eight drafts, and that he departed from his usual custom and spoke in the afternoon. In addition to being broadcast on four networks it was given world wide coverage to troops and allied peoples via the facilities of the Office of War Information. This speech became his last important Fireside Chat.

Christmas messages from Roosevelt had become a regular occurrence either broadcast from Washington or Hyde Park. For speeches he usually gave a short greeting with a religious tone, sometimes a prayer. But upon his return from the Teheran Conference he immediately talked to congressional leaders about a report to the American people. At a press conference he expressed the conviction that the trip "was in every way a success, not only from the point of view of the conduct of the war, but also for the discussions that I hope will have a definite and very beneficial effect for the post war period." In discussing this coming Fireside Chat, Rosenman reports that the President told his speech staff that F.D.R. wanted to report "in a Fireside Chat on Christmas Eve, and tie in the objective of permanent world peace discussed at Teheran with the natural message of Christmas — peace on earth, good will to men."[18]

The speech of course was in keeping with his custom of sharing his experiences and insights with the people, and it fit well into his objective of maintaining morale and of preparing the citizens for the serious losses that were likely to come with the invasion of France.

Strengthening his credibility, Roosevelt related that he had just returned "from extensive journeying in the region of the Mediterranean and as far as the borders of Russia," stressing that he had conferred with Churchill, Stalin, and Chiang Kai-shek, at meetings in Cairo as well as Teheran. He personalized what he had done and seen. For example, he said that the two conferences had given him his "first opportunity to meet Generalissimo Chiang Kai-shek and Marshall Stalin — and sit down at the table with these unconquerable men and talk with them face to face." Later he said, "To use an American and somewhat ungrammatical colloquialism I may say that I 'got along fine' with Marshall Stalin." His openness and his eagerness to tell about his trip gave his radio listeners the warm feeling of being included in the great events and served to forestall criticism that he had made secret agreements with the other powers.

The constructive portion involved three aspects. First, he gave assurances of the unity that exists among the allies and their leaders. Second, he announced that General Eisenhower had been given command "to lead the combined attack from other points," meaning, of course, France. Third, he announced the plans of the four great powers to establish an organization to maintain the peace once the war was over.

From a propaganda point of view, the speech had three objectives. By stressing the great goals for the future, he also prepared for the somber future: "The war is now reaching the stage where we shall all have to look forward to large casualty lists — dead, wounded, and missing." Second, his praise of allied leaders — calling Churchill, "this great citizen of the world;" Chiang, "a man of great vision, great courage and a remarkable keen understanding of the problems of today and tomorrow;" Stalin, "a man who combines a tremendous, relentless determination with a stalwart good humor" — served to cement good relations with them and to suggest to the world that the United Nations were united. Third, he no doubt had hoped to create consternation among the enemy by giving evidence of a unified command of the forces of the Allies.[19]

### Strategies Summarized

This paper has concentrated upon Franklin D. Roosevelt's wartime rhetoric; that is, his adjustment of his ideas to the allied peoples and the allied people to his ideas. It of course makes no claim of presenting a complete analysis of his total wartime efforts. It has asked the question: how did he move Americans from neutrality to total participation in the great conflict?

Prior to Pearl Harbor he devoted four Fireside Chats to "educating" his "fellow Americans" many of whom were totally opposed to involvement in the war. In a sense F.D.R. followed the strategy of letting developing events dictate his rhetorical choices. Each speech became a response to a dramatic happening. After seeing his popularity reach a low mark in the 1938 congressional elections, he sought to reestablish his creditability by stressing his reliance on "first hand" reports and his eagerness to share them with the public. At the same time he was attacking his opposition by attributing to them sinister motives, thereby implying guilt by association.

After Pearl Harbor, he frequently turned to three principal strategies. First he made a great plea for togetherness and unity, in order to gain total dedication of Americans. In stark negative terms, he warned, "No one — among us [is] powerful enough to interrupt the forward march of our people to victory." In his rhetoric he closely linked the fate of Americans with that of Allied peoples on the battle fronts. Hence he sought to promote consubstantiality among liberty loving peoples.

In a second major strategy, F.D.R. repeatedly utilized the topic (topoi) of degree that makes use of comparison and contrast. In discussing the heavy demands of a war economy, he asked Americans to compare their inconveniences and burdens with the greater sacrifices of the armed forces and our allies. By magnifying the sacrifices abroad, he forced Americans to minimize their discomforts at home. Hence he made it difficult for groups not to cooperate and not give their best efforts.

As a third major strategy, F.D.R. pursued a rhetoric of optimism. Never glossing over bad news or the seriousness of the Axis threat, F.D.R. met these challenges with a hopeful attitude, pointing to victory and a better world. He exuded optimism through his openness, confident delivery, and well chosen words. He never let the home folks, the armed forces, or the allied peoples lose sight of the overall objectives. In his speeches he complemented the efforts of Winston Churchill.

Roosevelt and his speech writers were master phrase makers who had a good sense of what would attract and hold attention, and of how to stir the imaginations. Of course they likewise knew that the success of any public utterance is reflected in those nuances that linger on with the listeners and in its quotability, particularly in the media; consequently they sought ways to make the Fireside Chats vivid and impressive.

Sometimes Roosevelt phrases were clothed in magnificent words and at other times in the idiom of the street. Long remembered were such choice sentences, as the following:

"We seek to keep war from our firesides." (Sept. 3, 1939)
"There will be no black-out of peace." (Sept. 3, 1939)
"Ours is a high duty, a noble trust," (Dec. 29, 1940)

"We must be the great arsenal of democracy." (Dec. 29, 1940)

"When you see a rattlesnake poised to strike, you do not wait until he has struck before you crush him." (Sept. 11, 1941).

"It is warfare in terms of every continent, every island, every sea, every airlane in the world." (Feb. 23, 1942)

"We glory in the individual exploits of our soldiers, our sailors, our marines, our merchant seamen." (Sept. 7, 1942)

"There can be no one among us — no one faction — powerful enough to interrupt the forward march of our people to victory." (May 2, 1943)

Imbued with democratic ideals, Roosevelt pursued his rhetorical ends through sharing, openness, forthrightness, and confidence. He kept before his listeners reminders of their obligations to those who made greater sacrifices and of the worthiness of the ultimate goals. Clothing his presentation in effective language, he gave dignity and majesty to his cause. Obviously, he must be viewed as a superior rhetorican — "a shrewd tactician, a man who displayed great skill in manipulating men and great flexibility in interweaving ideas and principles, even contradictory ones."[20]

# CHAPTER TEN

# Advice and Decision: The Eisenhower National Security Council Reappraised

**PHILLIP G. HENDERSON**
ASSISTANT PROFESSOR OF POLITICAL SCIENCE
UNIVERSITY OF MARYLAND BALTIMORE COUNTY

The resignation of Secretary of State Alexander Haig on June 25, 1982 provided a dramatic climax to one facet of the seemingly perennial struggle for control over foreign policy waged between the White House and the once preeminent State Department. In the midst of the now customary feuding between Cabinet Secretaries, Assistants to the President for National Security Affairs, and White House staff, it is constructive for us to take a closer look at the comparatively tranquil Eisenhower years when the two principal advisory and administrative organs — the Cabinet and the National Security Council — worked in tandem with remarkable success in providing an orderly and effective forum for Presidential policy-making. Certainly, Eisenhower himself must be credited with providing the leadership necessary to blend the often disparate elements of the nation's foreign affairs and defense establishment into a cohesive framework. But equally important in explaining the relative harmony between the White House and the Cabinet departments is recognition of the contribution of certain organizational features of the Eisenhower era.

This paper will focus on some of the important organizational innovations of the Eisenhower years on the premise that many of the problems that have plagued post-Eisenhower administrations could be averted or at least mitigated through the adoption of similar principles of administration. In demonstrating the importance of these administrative innovations, however, it is necessary to simultaneously challenge some common misconceptions regarding policy-making processes during the Eisenhower years.

## Traditional Assessments of Policy Processes During the Eisenhower Years

On the basis of traditional scholarship, one would likely conclude that national security policy-making processes during Eisenhower's Presidency were static, inflexible, and incapable of producing broad consideration of policy alternatives. Eisenhower's principle advisory organ, the National Security Council, presented a popular target for administration critics. Members of the Council were often depicted as compliant and courteous rather than probing — exhibiting a reluctance to highlight differences of opinion in front of the President.[1] Some writers believed that the Council functioned as a legislative committee with members going beyond an advisory capacity and actually voting on issues. It was suggested that Eisenhower's decisions (frequently characterized as Council decisions) were not based on deliberate measuring of opposing views against each other, "but on a blurred generalization in which the opportunity for choice had been submerged by the desire for compromise."[2] Approved statements were allegedly so broad that they did not address specific problems adequately. The vagueness was sufficient to allow each protagonist of a different line of action to find justification for his own view.[3]

Beyond these perceived weaknesses in Council operations, the President himself was portrayed as a reluctant decision-maker who was more interested in achieving consensus than in tackling complex problems head-on. Richard Neustadt, in his classic work *Presidential Power* noted that "Eisenhower, seemingly, preferred to let subordinates proceed upon the lowest common denominators of agreement than to have their quarrels — and issues and details — pushed up to him."[4]

Richard Tanner Johnson, in his widely cited study on Presidential management styles, suggested that Eisenhower had undermined his own authority by using his elaborate administrative machinery as a protective shield. In comparing the decision-making styles of Truman and Eisenhower, Johnson wrote:

> . . .While both Truman and Eisenhower respected staff machinery and utilized what we have called the formalistic approach, Truman's machinery was geared as an aggressive apparatus for acquiring and conveyng information to the top: in contrast, Eisenhower arrayed

his staff machinery like a shield. Truman wanted alternatives to choose from. Eisenhower wanted a recommendation to ratify. When Ike could not work through his set procedures, or when the shield failed him or when his associates quarreled or confronted him with a difficult choice, he grew disheartened and angry.[5]

Eisenhower's formalistic approach to decision-making was characterized by "the absence of thorough going deliberations in formulating policy."[6] Eisenhower, by Johnson's account "usually remained silent in the discussion" of issues at NSC meetings.[7] Indeed, the President "was often a hazy figure in the background of the decisions of his Administration, he delegated broad authority to his advisors and backed them up." The more Eisenhower delegated authority, Richard Neustadt cautioned, "the less he knew, and the less he knew, the less confidence he felt in his own judgment."[8]

Using newly available archival evidence, a more enlightened view of Eisenhower's national security policy-making unfolds. Recently declassified White House documents will be used to demonstrate the invaluable role of the National Security Council as a forum for debate and decision-making during the Eisenhower years. Traditional scholarship notwithstanding, the Eisenhower system brought about routinization without excessive rigidity and fostered broad advice rather than watered down bureaucratic consensus. Eisenhower encouraged, indeed demanded input from his department heads, but he maintained a healthy skepticism and open disdain for unbridled parochialism. Finally, new documentation makes it clear that Eisenhower, far from being a victim of his own elaborate machinery, was remarkably adept at gathering advice and information from a variety of sources and in drawing upon this broad base of information to make decisions that were at times boldly detached from the counsel of administration insiders.

## Organization of the Eisenhower NSC

Under Eisenhower's leadership, the National Security Council became the principal forum for the formulation and implementation of national security policy.[9] He created the position of Special Assistant to the President for National Security Affairs, expanded the professional staff to its largest number of permanent positions in the history of the NSC, and established two major NSC adjuncts: the Planning Board and the Operations Coordinating Board.[10] Through these mechanisms, R. Gordon Hoxie observes, Eisenhower "institutionalized the NSC and gave it clear lines of responsibility and authority."[11]

Eisenhower's administrative innovations reflected his commitment to the use of organization as a concomitant to informed policy-making. In defending his reliance on a highly structured system, Eisenhower wrote:

> Organization cannot make a genius out of an incompetent, even less can it, of itself, make the decisions which are required to trigger the necessary action. On the other hand, disorganization can scarcely fail to result in inefficiency and can easily lead to disaster. Organization makes more efficient the gathering and analysis of facts, and the arranging of the finding of experts in logical fashion. Therefore organization helps the responsible individual make the necessary decision, and helps assure that it is satisfactorily carried out.[12]

To assist the President in administering the NSC, Eisenhower's Special Assistant for National Security Affairs was named the principal executive officer of the Council with responsibilities for determining (subject to the President's approval) the Council agenda, briefing the President in advance of Council meetings, presenting matters for discussion at Council meetings and supervising the overall operations of the NSC staff and Council.[13] In these activities, the Special Assistant was expected to serve as a neutral facilitator and coordinator, not as a policy advocate. As Dr. Hoxie notes, the Special Assistant's low profile was consistent with Eisenhower's emphasis on "teamwork" as an indispensable element in the administration's national security organization.

> He made clear at the outset that under his personal direction the Secretary of State was to be the "channel of authority within the executive branch in foreign policy." It would have been unconscionable to Eisenhower (as to Dulles) that the Special Assistant for National Security Affairs, who served as the executive officer in vitalizing the NSC, could in any way come between the President and the Secretary of State. Eisenhower made the Secretary of State, the Secretary of Defense, and the Secretary of the Treasury a triumvirate to review national security plans and operations on the premise that diplomatic, military and economic affairs were necessarily related.[14]

## The Planning Board and Policy Formulation

The Planning Board became an integral part of the Eisenhower NSC system, meeting 640 times in the first five years of the administration. The Board incorporated Eisenhower's desire for continuous policy planning. The Planning Board normally met twice a week for sessions lasting three or four hours. Board members devoted most of their time to debating, refining and drafting policy papers for consideration by the President and the Council.

NSC papers were usually assigned by the Planning Board to the department or agency with primary responsibility for implementation of the policy under consideration. The responsible agency had freedom to call on all other agencies for assistance in producing a draft of the policy report. Frequently, the CIA had input on policy papers because of its role as spokesman for the intelligence community. Likewise, the Treasury Department and Bureau of the Budget were likely to have substantial input on the many policy papers requiring an evaluation of costs and resources.[15]

A typical NSC paper contained several sections: a "General Consideration" of the problem at hand; a list of "Objectives" of U.S. security policy; a statement of options or "Courses of Action" dealing with methods of achieving the stated goals and often subdivided into categories such as political, economic and military; and a final section consisting of a "Financial Appendix" detailing the estimated costs of putting a new program or policy into effect.[16]

Upon completion of the first draft, the policy paper was presented to the Planning Board for open discussion. The Special Assistant to the President, who chaired all Planning Board meetings, opened consideration of a paper with his own criticisms and comments based on extensive work by his staff. The paper was then placed before the entire Board for input and debate. From all accounts, these debates were generally spirited and rigorous. S. Everett Gleason, a career civil servant who served on the Staff of the NSC under both Truman and Eisenhower, described the procedure of the Planning Board as "informal and democratic."

Any Planning Board member is free to speak to any issue which may arise whether or not this issue is within the precise sphere of his department's official responsibility or is presumed to be his area of expertise.[17]

Most reports were discussed at several sessions of the Planning Board and revised between meetings on the basis of the Board's discussions. A conscientious effort was made to ensure that differences of opinion were not glossed over. Where disagreements existed, policy "splits" were written into the Planning Board drafts prior to submission to the Council for debate and resolution. Gleason indicates that these splits were based on conviction and substance, and were consistently preferred over watered-down versions that disguised differences. Far more than representing mere verbal quibbles, the splits in the policy paper reflected genuine differences with respect to intelligence estimates or policy recommendations.[18]

The papers prepared by the Planning Board were distributed at least ten days prior to the Council meeting in which they were discussed. This assured that the Under Secretaries or Assistant Secretaries who had participated in Planning Board discussions would have an opportunity to brief the head of their department with regard to issues that would be brought before the Council. Robert Bowie, who served as the State Department's representative on the Planning Board, observes that the preparatory staff meetings held at the State Department provided an opportunity

> for thrashing out positions and expressing competing views, before the Secretary, so that he could reach a judgment about what position he wanted to take at the NSC meeting the next day.[19]

Then, in the Council meeting, the principal advisors to the President confronted one another. Consequently, Bowie notes, the President "got a pretty good exposition of the competing points of view within the Executive branch."[20]

## The Role of the NSC Support Staff

Standing apart from the Planning Board with its policy formulating role, was the support staff of the NSC, which consisted of an Executive Secretary and several professional assistants. Whereas the Planning Board was comprised of individuals from the departments and agencies who were responsible for developing policy ideas for consideration by the Council, the staff of the NSC was a permanent, career oriented cadre of professionals charged with preserving continuity. Hence, while the Planning Board often served as an agent for change, the staff was designed to foster "institutional memory." Its task, in the words of one participant, was "to remember, not to recommend."[21]

The NSC staff reviewed policy papers with respect to coherence, completeness and applicability in light of past experience. Through integrated evaluation of the status of all national security programs, the staff identified gaps in national security policy and brought to the attention of the Council important issues or anticipated developments that were not receiving sufficient attention.[22]

In a sense, the NSC staff emulated the qualities of "neutral competence" traditionally associated with high ranking civil servants at the old Bureau of the Budget. The staff provided a government-wide perspective, untainted by the parochial outlook that occasionally surfaced among departmental and agency representatives on the Planning Board. "At the very least its existence meant that there was available to the President (through the Special Assistant) an independent source of analysis of departmental recommendations."[23] A similar balance was struck within the Operations Coordinating Board between permanent staff officers, who provided continuity in operations, and staff officers on assignment from the Board's member agencies, who contributed expert advice based on departmental experience.

Eisenhower believed that the supporting staff, unlike the Planning Board and Council, would remain relatively stable in its composition across different administrations. Over time, however, the professional staff of the NSC has become increasingly politicized. More and more, the staff has come to resemble the particular outlook and perspective of the President's Assistant for National Security Affairs. Generally speaking, there are fewer departmental and agency representatives, with less government experience and more of an academic perspective on national security issues than during the Eisenhower years.

### Regular Meetings as a Cornerstone of Policy Development

Soon after Eisenhower took office, his advisory panel on national security stressed the importance of direct Presidential participation in the successful operation of the National Security Council. Although President Truman presided at the first NSC meeting and occasional meetings thereafter, he did not regularly attend sessions of the Council until the beginning of the Korean War. His abstention was based in part upon the concern that his presence might inhibit free discussion and in part because Truman questioned whether Congress had the constitutional authority to require the President to seek advice from the statutory members of the NSC before reaching decisions on certain subjects.

Truman's early absence from the Council table deprived him of the opportunity to hear first-hand the views of Council members, to ask questions of them, and to engage personally in the interchange of ideas. Even when Truman was present, at least one participant, General George Marshall, believed that "he was not a force at the table to bring out discussion."[24]

In recognition of the importance of active Presidential participation in Council affairs, a special Study Group appointed by the President recommended that he should attend Council meetings as regularly as possible, and as chairman

> should ask for views around the table, exercise leadership so as to bring out conflicts and so that all agencies which later have to do the job will feel they have participated.[25]

Regularly scheduled, well attended and Presidentially directed Council meetings became a hallmark of the Eisenhower era, but these features gave the appearance to some of excessive routinization and formalism. Yet these ingredients served an invaluable "clearing-house" function for the administration by providing a regularized forum in which the President's principal advisors on national security were brought up to date, through briefings, policy reports and open discussion of the most important issues of the day.

Eisenhower's first Special Assistant for National Security Affairs, Robert Cutler, notes that the clearing-house aspect of the Council was especially valuable in the early stages of the Eisenhower administration.[26] Regular meetings of the Council afforded personnel without previous government experience an opportunity to gain firsthand knowledge of how the Washington bureaucracy operates along with detailed information on national security policy. Participants were also exposed on a regular basis to the President's own thinking on policy. This exposure combined with written directives prepared on the basis of the President's statements left less latitude for bureaucratic improvisation at the implementation stage. As Dillon Anderson, a prominent NSC participant suggests, Eisenhower wanted the department heads who had the responsibility for carrying out policy to have the opportunity to advise him before he decided what policy would be. The President "invited a lot of give and take" from departmental representatives before making his decision. But having participated in a decision by stating their views, representatives from the departments "damn well knew what it was and there'd be no fuzzing up as to what the President's decision had been."[27]

Despite these important advantages to frequent utilization of the NSC as a policy forum, Presidents in the post-Eisenhower era have not followed suit in employing the Council on a regular basis. Even in the comparatively active Nixon and Ford administrations, the Council was convened only 125 times[28] or about one-third the number of meetings which took place during the comparable eight year period of the Eisenhower Presidency. Indeed, during Eisenhower's tenure as Chief Executive there were 366 regular and special meetings of the National Security Council. The President presided over 329 of these meetings — nearly 90 percent of the total.[29]

It comes as no surprise in light of the Eisenhower experience that one of the principal recommendations of President Jimmy Carter's reorganization study on "National Security Policy Integration" called for more carefully structured meetings of the National Security Council and more precise mechanisms for recording and carrying out agreements. The "Odeen Report," named after Chairman Philip Odeen, argued that more full meetings of the type utilized by Eisenhower would keep officials from the departments informed about policy which in turn would make policies more bureaucratically enforceable.[30]

### Debate and Decision-Making in the Eisenhower NSC

Eisenhower's National Security Council system was organized to satisfy the President's desire for systematic presentation of alternative viewpoints. In defending his reliance on the formal components of his decision-making apparatus Eisenhower said:

I have been forced to make decisions, some of them of a critical character, for a good many years, and I know of only one way in which you can be sure that you have done your best to make a wise decision. That is to get all of the people who have a partial and definable responsibility in this particular field, whatever it may be. Get them with their different viewpoints in front of you, and listen to them debate.

I do not believe in bringing them in one at a time, and therefore being more impressed with the most recent one you hear than by earlier ones. You must get courageous men, men of strong views, and let them debate and argue with each other. You listen, and you see if there is anything that has been brought up, any idea that changes your own view or enriches your view or adds to it. Then you start studying. Sometimes a case becomes so simple that you can make a decision right then. Or you may go back and wait two or three days, if time is not of the essence. But you make it.[31]

Eisenhower was perplexed by the charge that he disliked controversy and preferred a watered down consensus to heated debate of an issue.

I have never in my life, except on a court martial, seen a vote to decide a question. Some people have alleged that my way of making decisions — and this was actually quoted — was to insist on unanimity, and if there was a divided or minority opinion, I'd send all of them back and say, "Get it unanimous." Then I'd adopt it. Well, I could not think of anything more ridiculous and more wide of the mark than this. All my life is a refutation of such a theory, and why someone dreamed it up, I don't know.

As a matter of fact, there was a writer [Alexander DeConde] who speculated on exactly how much my assistants made my decisions for me or helped me, or how much I deferred to them. Well, this is one of those things where you become inarticulate when you try to refute it. . .

. . .Now this one writer of whom I spoke, he certainly never came to see me. He never came to any man who was really close to me. Yet he wrote with great authority. And so did some columnists. . .

When really scholarly people reach conclusions on somebody else's book or column as their authority — they don't seem to me to be very true to the scholarly tradition. They ought to go to better sources than that.[32]

Turning to better sources does indeed provide us with a vastly different impression regarding Council operations. Declassified minutes to the National Security Council meeting of August 30, 1956,[33] for example, richly illustrate the breadth of Council debate. After an opening discussion of the Suez situation and other significant world developments, the Council turned its attention to a far ranging discussion of NSC Planning Board Paper 5612 which focused on "U.S. Policy in Mainland Southeast Asia." The ensuing debates were significant in identifying finely honed differences of opinion between various advisors on the Council. At least four major "splits" can be identified from the debates of the August 30th meeting. Although these differences were not always dramatic, they demonstrate, unequivocally, the fact that important policy disagreements were not glossed over as has often been charged. Instead, alternative viewpoints were set forth in lucid fashion by the Planning Board and subjected to what Robert Cutler has described as the "acid bath" of Council debate.

The Joint Chiefs of Staff registered two important splits to the Planning Board document at the August 30th meeting. The first point of disagreement centered on a provision in paragraph 2 of the Planning Board document which stated that "The loss of the Southeast Asian mainland could thus destroy the possibility of establishing an equipoise of power in Asia."[34] The JCS believed that this sentence improperly implied that "establishing an equipoise of power in Asia" was or should be the U.S. objective in the area.[35] The President indicated his approval of an alteration in the wording of the sentence to read: "The loss of the Southeast Asia mainland could thus have far-reaching consequences seriously adverse to U.S. security interests."[36] In accepting the recommendation of the Joint Chiefs, the president agreed that the "equipoise of power" language could be construed broadly to reflect an American commitment to maintaining a balance of power in the area.

After granting his approval to alternative language for paragraph 2 of the Planning Board document, the President and Council members turned their attention to another, even more critical change proposed by the Joint Chiefs of Staff in the wording of paragraph 19 of the Planning Board document. This paragraph provided for the use of military force in Southeast Asia under the condition

> that the taking of military action shall be subject to prior submission to and approval by the Congress unless the emergency is so

great that immediate action is necessary to save a vital interest of the United States.[37]

The Joint Chiefs proposed rewording this statement to read

> The Congress should be requested to give to the President advance authority to act quickly in times of crisis, including the use of armed forces. The grant of such authority should be publicized.[38]

Hence, the Joint Chiefs sought to solicit from Congress a "Gulf of Tonkin" styled resolution long before its time, and without the pretext of a Tonkin Gulf-like incident. The Chiefs argued that full knowledge that the President had been given authority by Congress to act, with military force if necessary, would serve as a strong deterrent to Communist aggression. But while the President agreed with the Chief's objection to the equipoise language in an earlier paragraph of the document, he did not accept the second change for fear that the language of the paragraph, if accepted as government policy, might "commit the United States to military intervention in Southeast Asia too readily."[39]

Secretary of State Dulles, addressing himself to Special Assistant Dillon Anderson, asked for clarification of paragraph 19.

> Was it conceivable that under this paragraph as presently worded, U.S. armed forces could intervene to assist a state of mainland Southeast Asia without having either a mandate from the UN or the cover of the SEATO treaty? If this were the case, then the purport of paragraph 19 went beyond anything that could be described as constitutional.[40]

Anderson explained to Dulles that in his view

> military action by the United States, as set forth in paragraph 19, would not take place prior to submission to and approval by the Congress, unless the emergency was so great that immediate action was necessary to protect our vital interests.[41]

The minutes show, however, that Anderson's response did not satisfy Dulles. The Secretary of State reemphasized that

> if the paragraph conceivably could mean that the President could decide to intervene with our armed forces in the absence of any cover of UN or SEATO action, such a move went beyond the constitutional powers of the Presidency.[42]

The President agreed with Dulles' argument stating that he

did not believe that he could constitutionally go as far as paragraph 19 would suggest if it were modified to include the proposed language of the Joint Chiefs of Staff. More importantly perhaps, in language foreshadowing the spirit of the War Powers Act of 1973, Eisenhower said:

> except in the event of a direct attack on the United States itself or the armed forces of the United States, we could not possibly go to war without a declaration of war by the Congress.[43]

In rejecting the language presented by the Joint Chiefs, Eisenhower reiterated his belief that no concept of the vital interests of the United States could justify his intervening with military force except a direct attack on the United States or on U.S. forces.[44]

After concluding the debate over the President's prerogatives regarding the use of military force in Southeast Asia, the Council discussed several other important issues on August 30th. One important split involved different positions on behalf of the State Department and the Defense Department with regard to the question of distinguishing between allied and neutral nations in the administration of military and economic aid.

The essence of the State Department position on the trade issue was that it did not wish to lay down as a fixed policy statement the principle of preferential treatment for countries formally aligned with the United States. Secretary of State Dulles noted that:

> It might well happen that some country aligned with the United States in some kind of collective security pact would not actually be in need of military or economic assistance, whereas some other country which was in a neutralist posture might need our help to prevent itself from being absorbed into the Communist orbit.[45]

Responding to Dulles, Acting Secretary of Defense, Reuben Robertson, expressed concern that if the United States proceeded "to give military assistance to neutral nations like Burma, nations allied with us will assume that this assistance will be given to Burma at their expense."[46] Admiral Radford added that it was the view of Congress that the U.S. should give military assistance only to dependable allies.

Dulles then insisted that paragraph 11 of the policy paper under consideration should not consist of a fixed rule or statement of policy that would actually prevent the United States from providing military assistance to neutral countries like Burma if it proved to be in the strategic interest of the nation to do so.

The President stated that while he was sympathetic with Secretary Dulles' desire to avoid an iron-clad rule, he also agreed with the Defense Department that "other things being equal, the United States should extend preferential treatment to allies over neutrals."[47]

The debate over the question of preferential treatment to allies over neutrals prompted Dulles to offer a modification in the wording of the Defense Department's language to make it clear that although preferential treatment would "normally" be given, there would be room for exceptions. Eisenhower approved Dulles' proposal and the Record of Action incorporated the more flexible language as government policy.

Among other splits of opinion debated by the Council on August 30th were provisions concerning the degree of support the U.S. should provide to the armed forces of Laos and the type of aid, if any, that should be extended to Burma. The former issue pitted the Defense Department and the Joint Chiefs of Staff against representatives of the State Department, the Office of Defense Mobilization and the Bureau of the Budget. The issue of aid to Burma found the State Department and Office of Defense Mobilization opposing Treasury, Budget and the Joint Chiefs. These divisions clearly illustrate the fluidity of coalitions on the Council. When added to the previously discussed debates of the Council they also serve to illustrate the depth of discussions which took place at a typical Council meeting.

The minutes of the NSC meeting of August 30, 1956 provide important insights with regard to the Council's role in debating and refining issues and in assisting the President in resolving complex problems through consideration of policy options. For a closer look at the President's pivotal role at council meetings it is instructive to turn for a moment to records of the 363rd Council meeting which took place on April 24, 1958.[48] The minutes to this meeting illustrate Eisenhower's rather formidable skill for raising probing questions, pinpointing central issues, and facilitating critical debate in his efforts to arrive at sound decisions.

The April 24th meeting began with a presentation by William H. Holaday, the Director of Guided Missiles. Holaday's report included a recommendation that the number of Inter-mediate Range Ballistic Missiles (IRBMs) be increased from 8 to 12 squadrons (120 to 180 missiles) by 1963. Eisenhower questioned the wisdom of increasing the number of first-generation IRBMs to 180 since much more would be known about the effectiveness of first generation THOR and JUPITER missiles by 1960. It may be, the President argued, that "some time about 1960 we may have to say that we are going to scrap some of these missiles."[49] Eisenhower was particularly concerned that improved second generation IRBMs would be available in the not so distant future, making the purchase of more first generation missiles a questionable investment. Dr. Killian, the President's Science Advisor, voiced the opinion that the question of second-generation missiles raised by the President was indeed the key question in the debate.

After addressing the issue of producing more first generation IRBMs, the President questioned Mr. Holaday about the reasons for producing two types of aerodynamic missiles known as MACE and REGULUS. Mr. Holaday offered the explanation that REGULUS missiles were ship launched while the MACE series was land-based. Apparently not satisfied with Holaday's explanation, the President asked whether REGULUS could not be launched from the land as well as from ships. Mr. Holaday responded that REGULUS could be used as a land-based mis-sile but that it would be more costly than the MACE system to use in a land-based capacity.

The President then suggested that REGULUS missiles ought to be modified so that they could be used on land or at sea, and the MACE Program discarded. Secretary of Defense Quarles interjected that MACE had a special guidance system which made it particularly effective for tactical use, whereas REGULUS was adapted to radio control and was not as effective for shifting land operations. The notes of the NSC discussion indicate that Eisenhower remained skeptical about the need for both systems despite Quarles' explanation.

In line with the general thrust of his questions, the President said:

> It would seem that we must anticipate some very hard thinking if in four or five years time we are to avoid presenting a bill to the public for these military programs which will create unheard of inflation in the United States.[50]

Secretary of State Dulles lent support to the President's arguments in a manner that provides a striking contrast to traditional images of the Secretary's zeal for prosecuting the Cold War.
Dulles prefaced his comments to Council members by challenging
the notion that the United States should strive to be the greatest
military power in the world. The Secretary of State was particularly concerned that most discussions of the Council seemed
to suggest that the U.S. should have the most and the best of
everything. "Was there no group in government," Dulles asked,
"which ever thought of the right kind of ceiling on our military
capabilities?"[51]

Dulles noted that the President had often quoted George
Washington on the desirability that the United States possess
a "respectable military posture." The Secretary of State suggested
that a ceiling should be imposed when the government had
reached a level of "respectable" military readiness. "In the field
of military capabilities," Dulles told Council members, "enough
is enough."[52] Failure to recognize this fact would lead to a situation in which all of the nation's productive capability would be
centered in the military establishment. The President voiced
agreement with Dulles, adding that too much defense spending
"could reduce the United States to being a garrison state or ruin
the free economy of the nation."[53]

Though in the end Eisenhower approved the Defense Department's proposal for increasing the operational capability of
IRBMs from 8 to 12 squadrons, he did so only after satisfying
himself that the request was neither premature nor unnecessarily redundant. Eisenhower's decision appears to have surprised Special Assistant Robert Cutler, who expected on the basis of the remarks made by both the President and the Secretary
of State, that approval would be withheld or at least delayed
pending further study. But as was characteristic of Eisenhower's
approach to decision-making, his tough questions and comments
reflected a commitment to weighing the broader implications
of policies under consideration by the Council while simultaneously testing the strength of conviction of the policy advocates
themselves. As Presidential aide Robert Bowie suggests:

> Eisenhower often directed probing questions at Council members,
> not so much to play devil's advocate, as to make sure the person
> had given careful thought to the problem at hand.[54]

Despite his approval of the Defense Department's IRBM proposal, the President by "thinking aloud" before Council members, left no illusion regarding the thorough scrutiny that would be given to questions of military procurement. Records of White House meetings held outside the formal Council setting further illustrate the President's active leadership role in combatting parochialism and steering debate towards the broader economic and security interests of the nation. At a conference on the defense budget on March 20, 1956, for example, Eisenhower raised several questions about duplication of research and development among the three branches of the armed services.[55] The President opened the meeting, which was attended by three representatives from the Defense Department and three from the Bureau of the Budget, expressing concern that "nothing in the defense budget is ever eliminated."[56] Noting that this was hardly a new phenomenon, the President added that it took the Army 50 years to get rid of horses after they had become obsolete.

In a White House meeting with the Joint Chiefs of Staff the following day, Eisenhower said that while he did not expect the Chiefs to abandon their basic convictions or conclusions about security needs, he did expect that activities "will be conducted on a spartan basis, and with awareness of the essentiality of a sound economy to true security."[57] He warned the Chiefs of the adverse effects of fluctuations which would result from attempting too much for a short period, and then having to cut back deeply.

In line with his desire to relate national security policies to projected costs and potential impact on the economy, Eisenhower instituted a requirement early in his administration that a financial appendix appear at the end of all proposals submitted to the NSC for consideration. The financial appendix, by placing a new burden on departments to justify their programs on economic as well as security grounds, became a subject of controversy in the administration. The special Assistant to the Joint Chiefs of Staff for National Security Affairs, General F. W. Farrell, expressed his displeasure with the requirement in a letter to Robert Cutler written in June of 1957.

> . . . While recognition of the financial facts of life is extremely important, it seems to me that the Planning Board could well overplay its Watch Dog of the Treasury role . . . It is essential to realize that NSC documents have significance other than as budget safe-

guards . . . We should not take it on ourselves to do all the Budget Bureau's work for it . . .[58]

Cutler responded to General Farrell with a lucid defense of the budget practices of the NSC's Planning board.

In its planning operations, the Board should be just as much concerned with the effect of defense plans on the economy as with defense plans on themselves. To have this concern, and constantly exercise it, is not solely a Budget [Bureau] function. Budget is not an originator but an appraiser and executioner. The Planning Board, to adequately serve President Eisenhower must integrate the economic as fully into every policy as the politico-military. The Planning Board is not a planner for the ideal, but for the intensely practical.[59]

Cutler's letter to Farrell accurately captured the President's commitment to hard-nosed economic analyses in judging the acceptability of national security policy proposals. Undoubtedly, the resulting integration of domestic and economic considerations is of fundamental importance in explaining Eisenhower's success in keeping the defense budget from spiraling out of control in the Cold War environment of the 1950s.

## *The Augmentation of Formal Channels*

Although the National Security Council served as an invaluable forum for Presidential decision-making, Eisenhower was not a captive of the Council. The President frequently augmented formal Council sessions with less formal meetings in his office. During the months of May and June 1959, for example, the President held at least six small group advisory meetings and several additional meetings with his Special Assistant for National Security Affairs to discuss pressing problems.[60] As the schedule in Appendix II indicates, these meetings dealt with a wide array of important issues including test suspension of nuclear weapons, the Berlin problem, nuclear powered aircraft, and the Jackson Committee report on NSC operations. Attendance at these meetings was strictly limited relative to regular NSC meetings with a maximum of ten individuals invited to participate.

In addition to these small, informal meetings in the President's office, Eisenhower made fairly extensive use of outside consultants to supplement formal NSC machinery. During the first two years of the administration, the President utilized outside consultant groups on at least six different occasions. These groups dealt with such topics as continental defense policy, petroleum policy, and basic national security policy.

Within a month following his inauguration, the President invited seven individuals from different walks of life and different regions of the nation to act as consultants to the NSC. This group, which became known in administration circles as the "Seven Wise Men," included, among others, the President of Cornell University, the Head of Pacific Gas and Electric, and a prominent scientist from St. Louis who had played a major role in the Manhattan Project.[61] By design, these men were all Washington outsiders who were completely disassociated from the departments. All seven were given security clearances and received intensive briefings from CIA, military and State Department officials. Eisenhower called upon this group of advisors to provide a fresh perspective, untainted by bureaucratic biases.

Some critics have suggested that the reports of outside consultants and panels were filed away and not acted upon, but this clearly was not the case. Rather, the reports of advisory groups were critically reviewed by the NSC Planning Board before being sent to the Council for consideration and action. The President and the Council would approve, modify, or reject reports in part or in whole. Recommendations of the Technological Capabilities Panel (1954–1955), for example, were presented by the Chairman, Dr. James Killian of the Massachusetts Institute of Technology, at a long Council meeting. Various portions of the recommendations were considered and acted upon at fourteen subsequent Council meetings.[62] Similarly, the recommendations of the Securities Resources (Gaither) Committee (1957–1958), were presented by the Chairman of the Committee and his principal assistants at two Council meetings. Portions of the committee's recommendations were acted upon at thirteen subsequent Council meetings. One consequence of the Gaither Panel's report was to put more emphasis on the alert and dispersal of Strategic Air Command bombers in order to lessen their vulnerability to a Soviet attack.[63]

The famous Open-Skies proposal for American and Soviet aerial inspection of each other's territories was formulated by another administration advisory group known as the Quantico

Panel. At the encouragement of the President, Nelson Rockefeller set up and directed the Quantico Panel to explore various ideas for recommendations that the United States might submit at the Geneva Summit Conference in July 1955 with regard to the topic of arms control. The Quantico Panel "groped for a formula that would allow the U.S. to retain its nuclear arsenal while making it clear that its primary purpose was peace."[64] The Quantico report went to the President on June 10, 1955 and he read it with enthusiasm. Although the proposal was not accepted by the Soviets, it was one of the many innovative and far-reaching proposals that evolved from Eisenhower's utilization of advisors and consultants who served the President from outside the formal channels of the administration's national security machinery.

### Policy Implementation in a Dynamic Environment: The Evolution of the Operations Coordinating Board

Just as departmental input was institutionalized at the policy formulation stage by the Planning Board, the departments were given an instrumental role in policy implementation by way of the Operations Coordinating Board. The Operations Coordinating Board was created by Executive Order on September 2, 1953 to coordinate the implementation of NSC policies "in an imaginative and effective manner and in accordance with the Council's wishes."[65] In addition, the OCB was charged with reporting on the progress that appropriate departments and agencies had made in carrying out NSC policies. The objective of the OCB, in the words of Sherman Adams, was to prevent the execution of a policy from "falling between the chairs." "It was meticulous hard work, the follow-up that ensued after decisions had been made."[66]

The OCB did not have the authority to direct or order agencies and departments to implement policies in a particular fashion. Rather, its plans, actions and recommendations were based on agreement between the chiefs or deputy chiefs of the major departments. Hence, the OCB relied on collegiality and consensus building to shape implementation processes.

Prior to the creation of the OCB, the implementation of policy directives from the NSC had been entrusted to one department or agency, normally the State Department. Although other departments and agencies were nearly always involved in the implementation of policy, arrangements for coordination were generally ad hoc in nature.[67]

The OCB was initially chaired by the Under Secretary of State. The Board's other members included the Deputy Secretary of Defense, the Director of Central Intelligence, the Director of the United States Information Agency and a representative of the President. Heads of other agencies were invited to send a representative to OCB meetings when the OCB was dealing with matters bearing directly on their responsibilities. Membership on the OCB was constituted at the Under Secretary level to ensure that Board members would have sufficient authority within their respective agencies to direct the implementation of agreements reached within the OCB.

In the selection of the OCB's professional staff an effort was made to strike a balance between permanent staff officers and staff officers detailed from the OCB member agencies. The former provided continuity while the latter fostered insights derived from personal experience inside the agencies.

Formal weekly meetings of the OCB were preceded by an informal luncheon at 1:00 p.m. every Wednesday. At the luncheon meeting members were free to bring up any matters that they considered appropriate for discussion. No agenda was utilized although members of the Board frequently gave advance notice of topics they wished to discuss.[68]

While the Planning Board was sometimes criticized for relying heavily on the use of staff papers, OCB discussions at these informal luncheon meetings were seldom conducted on the basis of such papers. Rather, the luncheons served as a forum in which OCB members consulted informally with other ranking government officials on a wide spectrum of concerns related to the Board's activities. Agreements were reached during the luncheon on some matters. Others were referred to an appropriate OCB working group for study and recommendations. Some matters were referred to relevant agencies for decision outside the OCB framework.

Following the informal luncheons, the OCB would convene for its formal meeting at 2:15 p.m. In contrast to the luncheons, the formal OCB meetings were guided by a written agenda. Operation plans for implementing national security policy were discussed, revised and approved at these meetings. The chairman of the working group responsible for preparing operation plans along with an Assistant Secretary from the agency charged with implementing the policies under consideration were usually in attendance to answer questions and report on developments.

Operation plans usually contained a section listing the objectives of a given policy; a statement of actions agreed upon; an enumeration of agency responsibilities for implementation; statements of the agency programs for carrying out the plan as prepared by the agencies responsible for implementation; and a section on proposed actions on which there was not agreement between the agencies.[69] Preparation of operation plans helped participating departments and agencies identify, clarify, and resolve differences of policy interpretation or operating responsibility. By exposing operating difficulties, the plans provided a basis for practical recommendations for more effective implementation of policies. Once approved, operation plans set forth useful guidelines for agency operations in Washington and abroad, with particular attention focused on activities that required interagency coordination.

In addition to preparing plans for the operationalization of policy, the OCB was required to report to the National Security Council on the progress of the departments and agencies in implementing policies. These "Reports to the NSC," were submitted every six months and included information on actions taken to implement policy along with a discussion of difficulties in operations that impeded the attainment of objectives authorized by the NSC.[70] Supplementing these detailed semi-annual reviews were weekly progress reports which provided ideas for change or modification of policies.[71]

The Operations Coordinating Board was not a rigidly structured organization. Rather, it was the subject of study and revision throughout Eisenhower's term of office. Near the end of his first term, for example, a study was initiated by the President to analyze the OCB with an eye toward recommendations for reorganization and improvement. The study, which was directed by Nelson Rockefeller, recommended that the OCB be given command authority and that the Special Assistant to the President for National Security Affairs be made the Chairman of the Board and backed by an independent staff.[72]

Rockefeller's report drew special attention to the difficulty of trying to distinguish, in practice, between policy and operations.

An attempt had been made to draw such a distinction by physically separating the Planning Board and the Operations Coordinating Board. In a memorandum to Sherman Adams, White House aide William Jackson summarized the problem:

> Situations . . . are brought into OCB and other interdepartmental mechanisms for discussion and possible resolution under the assumption that these are within the scope of "coordination and operations" although they really represent situations in which a policy decision has to be made. One of the basic difficulties with the OCB has been that its role in these cases which involve policy conflicts has not been defined . . .[73]

In recognition of the problems brought about by separating the activities of the Planning Board and the Operations Coordinating Board, President Eisenhower issued an Executive Order on January 7, 1957 which designated special Assistant Robert Cutler as a representative of the President on the OCB and Vice Chairman of the Board. The merger of Cutler's responsibilities as Chairman of the Planning Board and Vice Chairman of the OCB offered growing recognition of the important interrelationship between policy formulation and policy implementation.

On February 25, 1957, Eisenhower issued a revised Executive Order which for the first time formally placed the OCB within the structure of the NSC. The White House Press release announcing this formal merger stated that the time had come to establish "a closer relation between the formulation and the carrying out of security policies."[74] In line with this action the offices of the OCB staff were moved into the Executive Office Building in space adjacent to the offices of the NSC staff.[75]

A final step towards integration of the OCB into the NSC framework was taken on January 13, 1960 when Eisenhower designated his special Assistant for National Security Affairs, Gordon Gray, as the new chairman of the OCB. In his letter to Gray confirming the appointment, Eisenhower wrote:

> In view of your continuing responsibility as the principal supervisory officer of the work of the National Security Council in formulating national security policies including those assigned by me to the OCB for coordination, you are in a position to provide impartial and objective guidance and leadership to the Board.
>
> The new assignment is one step which I feel should be taken toward enabling the President to look to one office for staff assistance in the whole range of national security affairs.[76]

In a letter written on January 19, 1960, Secretary of State Christian Herter extended his personal congratulations to Gordon Gray for his new role as OCB Chairman. Though the appointment of Gray meant that a State Department representative would no longer chair the OCB, Herter expressed hope that Gray would continue to utilize the State Department's facilities for OCB luncheons and Board meetings. "In this way," Herter wrote, "perhaps, I may be able to drop in on your luncheon meetings from time to time."[77]

In his response to Herter, Gray underscored his intention to continue the harmonious working relationship between the White House and State Department that had characterized the Eisenhower years.

> I will keep constantly in mind the predominant interest and responsibility of the State Department in most of the matters which come before the Board.

> Your gracious offer for the use of the Board of the Department's facilities for luncheons and Board meetings is accepted with alacrity. Please know that it would give all of the members of the Board the greatest personal pleasure if you will drop in on luncheon meetings from time to time, and beyond that, it would give us added incentive to do our work well.[78]

In a transition memorandum written one year after he became chairman of the OCB, Gray noted that the change had been an improvement for a variety of reasons. By naming the Special Assistant as chairman, the President had in effect eliminated a situation in which a protagonist was also expected to be an "impartial chairman."[79] Furthermore, the new arrangement allowed for more direct involvement of the President in OCB affairs through his Special Assistant.[80]

In a letter to the President written during the final days of the administration, Gray noted:

> The Board is an evolving mechanism, changing its procedures and organization as it gains in experience and in response to changes in the world situation.

> In the eyes of the highest officers of the departments that do business through the Board it has become an increasingly effective mechanism.[81]

## John F. Kennedy and the Demise
### of the Eisenhower System

Perhaps no modern President presents a more striking contrast to Eisenhower in his approach to national security organization and policy-making processes than his successor, John F. Kennedy. As Kennedy's close aide and advisor Theodore Sorensen commented:

> Kennedy brought to the White House unusual first-hand knowledge of the foreign, domestic, legislative and political arenas but no experience in the Executive Branch. He was always more interested in policy than in administration, and would later admit that "it is a tremendous change to go from being a Senator to being President . . ."
>
> He continued to reshape executive procedures throughout his term, but from the outset he abandoned the notion of a collective, institutionalized Presidency.[82]

Kennedy persisted in his belief that the informal management style of Franklin Roosevelt would serve him equally well in dealing with the bureaucracy of the 1960s. With open disdain for Eisenhower's efforts to institutionalize departmental representation through such mechanisms as the Planning Board and Operations Coordinating Board, Kennedy sought to "deinstitutionalize" and "humanize" policy-making processes by eliminating the formal machinery of the Eisenhower years. Hence, Kennedy, by Sorensen's account

> abolished the practice of White House staff meetings and weekly Cabinet meetings. He abolished the pyramid structure of the White House staff, the Assistant President-Sherman Adams-type job, the Staff Secretary, the Cabinet Secretariat, the NSC Planning Board and the Operations Coordinating Board, all of which imposed, in his view, needless paperwork and machinery between the President and his responsible officers . . . He paid little attention to organization charts and chains of command which diluted and distributed his authority . . .[83]

These actions were taken despite pleas from Eisenhower and his associates not to act too hastily in abandoning the organizational innovations of the previous eight years. Gordon Gray, Eisenhower's Special Assistant for National Security Affairs during the final three years of the administration, advised his successor McGeorge Bundy to avoid hasty decisions to abolish the machinery developed by Eisenhower. In a White House memorandum, Gray summarized his remarks to the incoming Special Assistant.

> I confessed some personal bias for I said that I felt that my reaction to the suggestion that the OCB [Operations Coordinating Board] be abolished would be perhaps the same as his to the suggestion that now the College of Arts and Sciences at Harvard be abolished . . . I constantly reiterated that I was simply asking for avoidance of hasty decisions and that the main point was that the functions assigned to the OCB were vital in Government and that it did not make sense to me to abolish the agency and then find it necessary to recreate it. This could be an unhappy waste of time and resources. I said even the suggestion that it might be abolished had an eroding effect on the structure especially in the lower echelons of the department.[84]

Gray's plea apparently had no impact on Bundy or the President. Not only was the OCB abolished, the National Security Council itself seemed to fall into disfavor with the new President. As Theodore Sorensen notes in his memoirs:

> At times he [Kennedy] made minor decisions in full NSC meetings or pretended to make major ones actually settled earlier . . . He strongly preferred to make all major decisions with far fewer people present, often only the officer to whom he was communicating the decision . . .

> For brief periods of time, during or after a crisis, the President would hold NSC meetings somewhat more regularly, partly as a means of getting on record the views of every responsible officer (who might otherwise complain that he wasn't consulted and wouldn't have approved), but mostly to silence outside critics who equated machinery with efficiency.[85]

In 1961, a Kennedy aide mentioned to former Special Assistant Robert Cutler that the administration's intention had been to first dismantle the Council machinery that Eisenhower had developed, and then to build new Council machinery of the kind President Kennedy wanted. But the aide candidly admitted: "We've been so damn busy since we got down here, Bobby, that we've never had time to get on with the second step."[86]

Sorensen acknowledges that the lack of formal decision-making processes led to difficulties at times. In his assessment of the administration's advisory processes during the Bay of Pigs, for example, Sorensen notes that

> Only the CIA and the Joint Chiefs had an opportunity to study and ponder the details of the plan. Only a small number of officials and advisors even knew of its existence; and in meetings with the President and this limited number, memoranda of operation were distributed at the beginning of each session and collected at the end, making virtually impossible any systematic criticism or alternatives . . . No strong voice of opposition was raised in any of the key meetings, and no realistic alternatives were presented . . . No realistic appraisal was made of the chances for success or the consequences of failure.[87]

Sorensen concedes that the gaps in planning "arose in part because the new administration had not fully organized itself for crisis planning." And while Kennedy himself believed that "no amount of formal NSC, Operations Coordinating Board or Cabinet meetings would have made any difference," Sorensen suggests that not all of the President's associates agreed with this assessment.[88]

As Gary Wills has noted elsewhere, General Maxwell Taylor is among those who faulted Kennedy's national security policy processes for producing the decisions that led to the Bay of Pigs fiasco. General Taylor believed, according to Wills, "that it was a lack of bureaucratic procedure and expertise that doomed the landing. The military was blamed for an operation it did not control. It was asked to advise from the sidelines with only partial glimpses of the total plan."[89]

Bernard Shanley, who served as Special Counsel in the Eisenhower administration, offers a similar appraisal of Kennedy's advisory processes. By destroying the Planning Board and OCB, Shanley suggests, Kennedy, in effect, destroyed the backbone of the NSC.

> The staff work was just not done properly so when these issues came before the National Security Council, they were not properly staffed or prepared for decision. That is what happened in the Bay of Pigs . . . The President had done away with the OCB and the staff work wasn't there.[90]

Lyndon Johnson, like Kennedy, did not allow the NSC to take on the institutional role it had under Eisenhower.[91] Consequently, the bureaucracy charged with enforcing administration decisions, was cut off from the process of policy formulation and consultation on implementation. In place of the formal Planning Board and OCB meetings utilized by Eisenhower to bring participants into the policy-making arena, Johnson relied on informal mechanisms such as the famous "Tuesday Lunches" to iron out policy. Townsend Hoopes suggests that the informality of the Johnson system exacted a heavy price with regard to policy outcomes.

> The decisions and actions that marked our large-scale military entry into the Vietnam War in early 1965 reflected the piecemeal consideration of interrelated issues . . . the natural consequence of a fragmented NSC and a general inattention to long-range policy planning. Consultation, even knowledge of the basic facts, was confined to a tight circle of Presidential advisors, and there appears to have been little systematic debate outside that group.[92]

## The Eisenhower NSC System in Perspective

In 1961, the Senate Subcommittee on National Policy Machinery, in reviewing the origins of the National Security Council, concluded that the purpose of the Council was "at least as much to make the Presidency serve the needs of the departments as to make the latter serve the former."[93] Consistent with these goals the Eisenhower NSC staff consisted primarily of career officials directed by the Special Assistant for National Security Affairs who was instructed by the President to serve as a neutral coordinator of advice and information with a passion for anonymity.

Eisenhower's first Special Assistant for National Security Affairs, Robert Cutler, was so little seen or heard in Washington that Samuel Lubell entitled his February 1954 *Saturday Evening Post* article on the Special Assistant "The Mystery Man of the White House."[94] Cutler offered a cogent explanation for this characterization in his memoirs.

> Before I came to the White House I had been speaking a great deal on a variety of subjects. But an "anonymous" Assistant to the President has no charter to speak for his chief in public. The President and I made an early arrangement, from which I never departed except on the President's permission, that as to my official duties (other than to explain mechanical aspects of the Council) I should

keep my trap shut. No speeches, no public appearances, no talking with reporters.[95]

In prophetic fashion, Cutler warned against efforts to expand the policy role of the Special Assistant or enlarge his staff.

> . . . Since the Special Assistant has direct access to the President, an NSC staff operation of the kind suggested would tend to intervene between the President and his Cabinet members, who are responsible to him for executing his policies. Grave damage could be done to our form of government were there an interruption in the line of responsibility from the President to his Cabinet.

> For the foregoing reasons, I have opposed the interposition at the apex of government, responsive to the President's Special Assistant of a large staff which would concern itself with the formulation of national security policy. The Special Assistant may need a few more staff assistants . . . But I would think it inadvisable formally to give him greater responsibilities or formally to increase his functional prestige . . .[96]

Eisenhower's second Special Assistant for National Security Affairs, Dillon Anderson, shared with Cutler a low profile approach to serving the President.

> I undertook to indicate to him the policy alternatives and the differences, if any, in the departmental views. But I became mindful early in the game that the only way I could be of continuing service to him was to keep out of an effort to suggest policy to him . . . I could have plugged my own views. But I felt it was not the right thing for me to try to get in between the President and his Secretary of State on foreign policy matters . . . And during my period of service there I enjoyed the most cordial relations with Foster Dulles, and with Wilson and with Radford, because they knew that I was not trying to use my proximity to the President to end-run them on any of their subjects.[97]

The post-Eisenhower experience has been strikingly different. Indeed, although the Senate Subcommittee on National Policy Machinery warned explicitly against efforts to base foreign policy coordination on a "superstaff" in the White House,[98] the practice of nearly all post-Eisenhower administrations has been geared toward precisely this type of centralization. Corresponding with this trend in White House centralization, there has been a marked surge in policy-entrepreneurship among prominent NSC staff. No longer are Assistants to the President for National Security

Affairs neutral coordinators with a passion for anonymity. Instead, they have become policy advocates who often find themselves in direct confrontation, not just with the Secretary of State, but the Secretary of Defense and other department and agency heads. Increasingly, Presidents find themselves in a self-imposed quandary over whom to listen to. While Eisenhower used the NSC to coordinate policy with the permanent career officials in the departments, modern NSC staff have sought at times to subvert the departments. In his memoirs, Henry Kissinger describes one such conflict which came about during the India-Pakistan crisis of 1971. This crisis, according to Kissinger, was marked by "a bureaucratic stalemate in which White House and State Department representatives dealt with each other as competing sovereign entities, not members of the same team."[99]

Although the administration of Gerald Ford witnessed a brief return to the Eisenhower standard of a low profile Special Assistant, Jimmy Carter was quick to revive the practice, which had become so pronounced during the Nixon years, of appointing a highly visible National Security Advisor. Indeed, Zbigniew Brzezinski, in his memoirs, boldly asserts that an activist President needs a conceptualizer or policy advocate in the White House.[100] Brzezinski concedes, however, that his dual role of "protagonist as well as coordinator of policy" fueled the image of an administration "in which the National Security Advisor overshadowed the Secretary of State" with "adverse consequences not only for me personally but more significantly for the President himself."[101]

Kenneth W. Thompson, in his incisive review of Brzezinski's memoirs, suggests that the principal lesson of the Security Advisor's account is that "no Secretary of State could possibly be the President's principal advisor on foreign policy under the organizational system Brzezinski describes."[102]

> In organizing his power, Brzezinski is frank to say that he saw the President as many as six times a day, summarized discussions with Secretaries Vance or Brown including his disagreements with their recommendations, conveyed messages from the President to the Secretaries, sent the President a weekly NSC Report ("a highly personal and private document for the President alone"), used the SCC [Special Coordination Committee] . . . "to shape our policy toward the Persian Gulf, on European security issues, on strategic matters, as well as in determining our response to Soviet aggression,"

. . . outlined all major Presidential speeches on foreign policy, cleared with relevant NSC staff all major cables with policy implications, approved foreign travel by Cabinet members, and established the Situation Room as the locale where most decision-making in the joint area of national security policy took place.[103]

Indeed, Carter's foreign policy decision-making system, was in Brzezinski's own words "formally the most centralized of all in the postwar era" with the National Security Advisor himself at the hub of that system.[104]

Interestingly, the most visible of all Special Assistants for National Security Affairs, Henry Kissinger, concedes in his memoirs that "a President should make the Secretary of State his principal advisor and use the national security advisor primarily as a senior administrator and coordinator to make certain that each significant point of view is heard."[105] Kissinger's prescription seems quite appropriate — particularly in light of the relative success of this formula during the Eisenhower years.

## Conclusion

Under Eisenhower's leadership, the National Security Council provided an important forum for identifying key issues and facilitating systematic analyses of policy options. Formal meetings assisted the President in his decision-making by exposing him to a broad array of information and opinions. More importantly, perhaps, Council members were exposed on a weekly basis to the President's own thinking on national security issues and to his policy directives once decisions had been made.

Studies of Eisenhower's advisory processes in the field of national security policy seldom make reference to efforts by the President to augment formal Council machinery with informal advisory channels. Yet, the administration was marked by a far more dynamic and flexible character than has been commonly assumed. White House records demonstrate that the President utilized a variety of sources to gather and assess information. Furthermore, the President and his advisors sought on a continuous basis to improve the formal machinery of the Council, as evidenced in the evolution of the Operations Coordinating Board.

Of the six Presidents who have served since Eisenhower, none have utilized the National Security Council as extensively and few have used this body as effectively in the formulation and implementation of policy. More than any of his successors, Eisenhower realized the importance of respecting the authority of the executive departments by resisting the tendency to centralize and isolate policy-making in the White House. Departmental representation was built into the Eisenhower system through institutionalized channels such as the NSC Planning Board and the Operations Coordinating Board. Eisenhower drew extensively on his staff while carefully guarding against staff dominance. Nowhere was this more clear than in his explicit limits on the role of the Special Assistant to the President for National Security Affairs. It seems clear, in retrospect, that Eisenhower's formal advisory processes are better suited to the multiple demands placed on modern Presidents than the informal, ad hoc approach to policy-making utilized by some of his successors. As we continue to refine our understanding of modern Presidential policy-making, we will surely profit from our continued study of the Eisenhower years.

## Appendix I
## ATTENDANCE AT N.S.C. MEETINGS AS OF JANUARY, 1957

### A.  SEATED AT TABLE

*Statutory Participants*

1.  The President
2.  The Vice President
3.  Secretary of State
4.  Secretary of Defense
5.  Director of O.D.M.

*General Standing Request*

6.  Secretary of Treasury
7.  Director of Budget
8.  Special Assistant for
     Disarmament

*Ad Hoc Standing Request*

9.  Attorney General
10.  Chairman of A.E.C.
11.  Director of F.C.D.A.

*Non-statutory Participants and Observers*

12.  Chairman, Joint Chiefs of Staff
13.  Director of Central Intelligence

*General Standing Request*

14.  Special Assistant for Oper. coordinating
15.  Director, U.S.I.A.
16.  Director, I.C.A.

*Staff*

17.  Special Assistant for Nat. Sec. Affairs
18.  Executive Secretary, N.S.C.
19.  Deputy Exec. Secretary, N.S.C.

### B.  NOT SEATED AT TABLE

*Occasional*

20.  Assistant to President
21.  White House Staff Secretary
22.  Chairman, Council Foreign
      Economic Policy

*Less Frequent ad hoc*

23.  Secretary of Army
24.  Secretary of Navy
25.  Secretary of Air Force
26.  Chief of Staff—Army
27.  Chief, Naval Operations
28.  Chief, Air Staff
29.  Commandant, Marine Corps

Source:   White House Office, Office of the Special Assistant for National Security Affairs,
NSC Series, Administrative Subseries, Folder: NSC Organization & Functions (11),
Eisenhower Library.

## Appendix II
## MEETINGS WITH PRESIDENT DURING MAY & JUNE 1959 OF THE SPECIAL ASSISTANT FOR NATIONAL SECURITY AFFAIRS

Monday, May 4—11:15–11:40
 President's Office
Tuesday, May 5—8:30–9:30
 Meeting with President (Herter, Quarles, Dulles, Killian, McCone)
Monday, May 11—10:15–11:30
 President's Office
Friday, May 15—10:45
 Meeting with President (Dillon, Murphy, McElroy, Taylor, Dulles, Goodpaster)—
 *Berlin/Germany*
Monday, May 18—9:00–9:40
 President's Office
Monday, May 25—10:50
 President's Office
Tuesday, May 26—11:45–12:20
 Meeting with President—*Defense Construction*
Monday, June 1—10:00–10:30
 President's Office
Monday, June 1—2:15–3:00
 President's Office
Monday, June 8—9:30–10:30
 Meeting with President—*Test Suspension*
Monday, June 8—11:45
 President's Office
Tuesday, June 9—3:00–4:15
 Meeting with President (Vice Pres., McElroy, Dillon, Gates, Holaday, Lemnitzer,
 Burke, White, Killian) *Air Defense*
Friday, June 12—9:00
 President's Office
Wednesday, June 17—9:00–9:30
 Meeting with President (Dillon, McElroy)—*IRBM's to Greece*
Thursday, June 18—10:30
 Meeting with President (Dr. Killian & Dr. Brooks)—a.s.w.
Monday, June 22—10:00
 President's Office
Monday, June 22—10:30
 Meeting with President (Consultants)
Tuesday, June 23—11:40
 Meeting with President—*Nuclear Powered Aircraft*
Wednesday, June 24—9:00–10:00
 Meeting with President (McElroy, Pugh, Loper, Sides, Boyd, McCone Stewart,
 Dunning, Killian, Goodpaster) *Immediate Long-Range Effects of a Massive Nuclear Exchange*
Wednesday, June 24—5:15–6:45
 President's Study—*Jackson Committee Report*
Thursday, June 25—After NSC
 Meeting with President—*Intelligence Activities in Berlin*

Source: White House Office, Office of the Special Assistant for National Security, Presidential Subseries, Box 4, Meetings with the President 1959 (1)
*Editor's Note: Gordon Gray was the Special Assistant.*

# Dwight D. Eisenhower, Nikita Khrushchev and the U.N. "Summit" Assembly of 1960

DAVID HAIGHT

ARCHIVIST, DWIGHT D. EISENHOWER PRESIDENTIAL LIBRARY

The idea of an East-West summit as a means of easing the cold war was a popular topic in international diplomacy during the late 1950s despite the meager accomplishments of previous summit meetings involving the Western Powers and the Soviet Union.[1] More than two years of patient, if often tedious and uncertain diplomatic maneuvering by the governments of the United States, Great Britain, France and the Soviet Union appeared to bear fruit with the scheduling of the Paris four power summit in May, 1960. The furor over one errant American reconnaissance aircraft shattered the product of these efforts.

Sentiments for a summit meeting between President Dwight D. Eisenhower and Soviet Premier Nikita Khrushchev did not die at Paris, however. For a brief time, the convening of the Fifteenth United Nations General Assembly in September aroused hopes for a meeting of the two men. In retrospect, it is clear that these hopes were unrealistic although developments during the Assembly did encourage the belief that a United States-Soviet Union summit would be easier to obtain when Eisenhower left office.

President Eisenhower believed that unless Khrushchev changed his attitude, a meeting with the Soviet ruler at the United Nations would be futile, and he viewed moves promoting such a meeting as threats to the United States' prestige and almost as personal insults. He therefore worked actively behind the scenes to defeat a draft United Nations resolution calling for an Eisenhower-Khrushchev meeting. Eisenhower saw the cold war in moral terms — as a contest between right and wrong, between freedom and slavery, and saw nothing but sinister motives behind Khrushchev's behavior at the United Nations that fall.

On the other hand, the sketchy record of Khrushchev's activities during this period suggest that the Ukranian's blustery behavior reflected his shaky political position at home and increasing criticism of his policies by Communist China. He apparently saw no reason to resume talks with Eisenhower but did want to leave the door open for establishing relations with the next American president.

Summit sentiments persisted during the deterioration in US-Soviet relations following the U-2 incident and the failure of the Paris Summit Conference. In June, the Soviets walked out of the Ten Nation Disarmament Conference at Geneva, asserting that the disarmament question would have to be referred to the United Nations General Assembly that fall. Tensions increased in July when the Russians shot down an American RB-47 reconnaissance plane which allegedly violated Soviet air space. The Soviets unsuccessfully tried to secure the U.N. Security Council's condemnation of the United States for the U-2 and RB-47 flights. Both countries expelled certain of the other's diplomatic personnel amid accusations of espionage. Khrushchev did not, however, attempt to press the Berlin issue which had appeared so critical during the past year. Instead, he indicated publicly the futility of dealing with Eisenhower on this and other problems and expressed his hope for a four power summit meeting to be held in 6 to 8 months (Eisenhower would no longer be President then). Meanwhile, the outbreak of violence in the Congo threatened to suck the United States, the Soviet Union and the United Nations organization, itself, into a dangerous confrontation in Africa.

The summer of 1960 was a hard one for President Eisenhower. He was embarrassed by the withdrawal of invitations to visit the Soviet Union and Japan, and by the continuing furor over the U-2 incident. Despite the increasingly belligerent Soviet rhetoric directed at the United States, the American President privately vowed to continue cultural exchanges and exchanges of visits with the Soviet Union as much as possible and to avoid cutting off disarmament and nuclear testing talks.[2] Publicly, however, with his foreign policy facing increased criticism at home during the beginning of the 1960 presidential campaign as well as abroad, by September, President Eisenhower appeared to have lost the initiative in waging the cold war.

Premier Khrushchev, on the other hand, appeared to seize

the initiative on August 1 when the Soviet Government gave the summit concept a new twist by calling for an 82 government summit discussion of disarmament to be held during the United Nations General Assembly.[3] The Soviets' call for a massive U.N. summit conference strongly implied a trip by Khrushchev to New York. Speculation began to focus on the Eisenhower Administration's response. Would the President go to the U.N. and if so, would he meet Khrushchev? President Eisenhower gave his first public response to Khrushchev's proposal in an August 10 press conference. When queried about Khrushchev's possible attendance at the U.N. Eisenhower commented that Khrushchev's suggestion was "obviously a propaganda thing." Eisenhower would, however, go to New York if he thought it necessary. When asked about the possibility of meeting Khrushchev, the President replied:

> Well frankly. . ., I have considered the possibility so remote that I haven't given it a thought. If I were to come to the conclusion that if it was useful for me to see him why I would of course invite him to come down if he chose. But I haven't given it the kind of thought that would allow me to make a decision at this time.[4]

Privately, the Administration gave Khrushchev and the U.N. considerable thought. Despite the potential international significance of the upcoming General Assembly, Secretary of State Christian Herter gave the President essentially negative and unimaginative advice — make a quick trip, speak in general terms about peace, avoid Khrushchev, and return to Washington. Herter feared that if the President announced his plans to attend too far in advance then Khrushchev would certainly come. Eisenhower shared this concern. He remarked that "this business about his announcing he will go, the next thing you know, maybe Castro will be coming up." The President did, however, display the ability to rise above this "avoid Khrushchev" mentality. He noted that if he went to the U.N. people would expect him to talk about such problem areas as the Congo and Cuba.[5]

Henry Cabot Lodge, then in the process of resigning as U.S. Representative to the United Nations in order to become Richard Nixon's running mate in the 1960 campaign, recommended that Eisenhower go ahead and announce in a low key way his intentions to attend the General Assembly instead of delaying and following Khrushchev in a "me too" manner.[6] The President declined to commit himself in early August to a trip to the U.N. He reasoned that his administration had to put a good speech together before he could say yes and that it took five to six weeks to prepare a good final version of such a speech.[7]

On September 1, Khrushchev kicked off a two day trip to Finland by declaring "it would be a great honor" to head the Soviet delegation to the U.N. General Assembly. His announcement reiterated his hopes for a general summit discussion of disarmament in New York.[8] While still in Finland, Khrushchev was quoted as saying "It would be good if General Eisenhower and Prime Minister Macmillan appeared at the U.N."[9]

Thus, when Khrushchev embarked on his 10 day voyage to New York on September 9, he appeared to be in a strong position. The Soviet Premier did not enjoy smooth sailing, however. At home, Khrushchev, too faced increasing fire from real or potential political opponents. The military was upset over reductions in forces, pension cuts, and still resented the dismissal of Marshal Zhukov from the Presidium in 1957. Stalinist elements within the Kremlin advocated a harder line toward the West.[10] To Khrushchev's critics in the Soviet Government, the U-2 flight and President Eisenhower's maladroit admission of responsibility for the flight confirmed the failure of Khrushchev's attempts to improve relations with the United States. These critics denounced Khrushchev's favorable view of Eisenhower held prior to the U-2 incident.[11] Khrushchev's political vulnerability, resulting in part from the U-2 affair, encouraged Communist China to exert pressure on the Soviet ruler to reverse his relatively moderate policies toward the West. The continuing deterioration in Sino-Soviet relations made it imperative for Khrushchev to assert his country's leadership over the communist world.[12] U.N. Secretary General Dag Hammarskjold's peacekeeping operation in the Congo frustrated Soviet efforts to gain influence in Africa through support of Patrice Lumumba as the sole ruler of the Congo.

One historian has stated that one of Khrushchev's primary motives in coming to the U.S. was to secure a meeting with Eisenhower.[13] British Prime Minister Harold Macmillan referred cryptically in his memoirs to indications which he received through diplomatic channels that Khrushchev might be using the disarmament and Congo issues as a cover for seeking a meeting with the President.[14] Although Khrushchev, while in

New York apparently hinted at a willingness to meet the President, available evidence, including Khrushchev's public statements, suggest that he never seriously believed such a meeting to be feasible. Instead, he continued to promote a four power summit to be held after a new American president was elected.[15] Most accounts have emphasized Khrushchev's efforts to assert his leadership over the communist world, to undermine Western dominance in the U.N. General Assembly, to embarrass President Eisenhower, to impress the representatives of new African and Asian states, and to promote Soviet objectives in the Congo, as reasons for his attendance.[16]

President Eisenhower certainly took a dim view of Khrushchev's intentions. The American President was convinced that Khrushchev intended to use the U.N. for propaganda purposes.[17] Top advisers within the Administration, including White House Staff Secretary, General Andrew Goodpaster, and Secretary Herter, concurred in this assessment and both advised the President to oppose turning the United Nations into a propaganda circus.[18]

Almost as soon as Khrushchev announced his intentions to attend the U.N., Eisenhower received advice on how to deal with the Soviet leader. C. D. Jackson, a Time Incorporated executive and presidential adviser on psychological warfare, warned Eisenhower of "a concentrated propaganda barrage of incredible concentration and ferocity" at the United Nations. Deploring what he saw as vacillating statements about the President's plans emanating from the State Department, Jackson urged Eisenhower to make some dramatic statements in a speech to counter Khrushchev's plans to "raise hell with the United States' position throughout the world."[19] The President replied that he was ready "to stand in whatever breach Mr. Khrushchev can create by the lies, distortions and deceit that he will use at the U.N." Eisenhower told Jackson that if he could effectively refute the false Soviet charges and place America's case before the world through a speech at the U.N., he would be ready.[20]

On the other hand, Herter suggested that the United States encourage the Western powers to boycott the General Assembly. He urged the President to authorize the State Department to recommend to foreign governments that heads of state and government not go along with Khrushchev. Eisenhower noted his apparent agreement by annotating Herter's memo "OK

DDE."[21] The State Department did send the British Government a note advising that President Eisenhower did not plan to attend the General Assembly and that hopefully heads of other western governments would also refuse to attend.[22] Presumably similar messages were sent to other western governments. Any hopes for a universal snubbing of Khrushchev were soon dashed by events.

Khrushchev's proposed summit session appeared to begin taking shape when one head of state after another announced his intentions of coming to New York. First the heads of Soviet satellite states in Eastern Europe — Gheorghe Gheorghiu-Dej of Rumania, Wladyslaw Gomulka of Poland, Janos Kadar of Hungary, Antonin Novotny of Czechoslovakia, and Todor Zhikov of Bulgaria. Then commitments from the unaligned nations of Africa and Asia began to filter in — first President Sukarno of Indonesia, then President Josef Tito of Yugoslavia and President Gamel Abdel Nasser of the United Arab Republic announced. Tito and Nasser, while denying any plans to form a bloc, saw the upcoming assembly as an opportunity to advance the concept of non-alignment by mediating between the East and the West. Prime Minister Nehru also decided to come as did the heads of many African states, including Kwame Nkrumah of Ghana and Sekou Toure, of Guinea.[23]

Meanwhile, during those days immediately preceding the beginning of the General Assembly, Khrushchev increased his criticism of the U.N. peacekeeping mission in the Congo. On September 13, he asserted that the colonialists were carrying out their policies in the Congo through Dag Hammarskjold who was personally blocking a settlement there.[24] He continued, also to tout his proposal for a high level discussion of disarmament.

How should the Eisenhower Administration cope with these events? Khrushchev's increasingly sharp attacks on Dag Hammarskjold appeared to pose a threat to the stability of the United Nations organization while the flood of foreign leaders heading for New York seemed to play into Khrushchev's hands. The Eisenhower Administration held little hope that Khrushchev's appearance could improve relations between the United States and the Soviet Union. In a September news conference, Eisenhower condemned the use of the U.N. as a forum for propaganda and expressed doubt that any meeting with Khrushchev would take place.[25] Other Administration spokesmen also sharply criticized Soviet intentions.[26]

While there was virtually no disagreement within the Administration as to the negative impact of Khrushchev's trip to the U.N., the President and his advisers remained uncertain as to the appropriate response to Khrushchev. By early September Eisenhower had decided to address the General Assembly but he continued to ponder the timing of a visit. He considered addressing the Assembly after the 1960 election.[27] Herter, believing that a presidential appearance at the U.N. would be more effective if done in December and not in competition with Khrushchev, told General Andrew Goodpaster that it would be better to let Khrushchev have the stage at first. Goodpaster was concerned that the Administration avoid the appearance of panic.[28]

By September 8, the President decided, contrary to Herter's advice, to go to the U.N., make the first speech even if Khrushchev were there, and then leave. Eisenhower reasoned that by waiting around he would let Khrushchev get the jump on him. He thought it would be better to be rebutted by Khrushchev than the other way around. Eisenhower decided to give a positive and constructive speech, and not merely a polemic against Khrushchev. When informed of the President's decision, Secretary Herter reiterated his opposition and expressed his concern that Khrushchev would think that by beckoning a finger he could call together the many heads of state.[29] The President did not, however, change his mind. The decisions by the heads of many non-aligned states to attend had rendered the proposed Western boycott ineffective, and Khrushchev's increasingly harsh attacks on Dag Hammarskjold influenced Eisenhower's decision to change tactics.

Eisenhower now had to inform his British ally of his decision and approved the following message which was telephoned to Macmillan:

> In view of the situation brought about by recent developments over which we had little or no control I have had to change my plans about going to the United Nations and of course would quite understand should you decide to come.[30]

The beleagured President wanted Macmillan to come and help him withstand Khrushchev's expected propaganda assault on the West and on the United Nations. Macmillan, perhaps with visions of laying the groundwork for a future summit confer- ence, agreed to come. The United States and Great Britain were soon bolstered by decisions by Canadian Prime Minister John Diefenbaker and Australian Prime Minister Robert Menzies to join them.

In mid-September a summit meeting with Khrushchev was probably about the last thing on Eisenhower's mind. The Depart- ment of State, however, aware that summitry was still alive as a topic of public discussion and diplomatic maneuvering, pre- pared a paper entitled "The Future of Summitry" which was transmitted to the President on September 15. After noting that the leaders of several countries had commented on the possi- bility of another summit with varying degrees of encouragement, the paper analyzed the various types of summit formats, their rationale, and the pros and cons of each one. It concluded by recommending that whenever direct conversations between the President of the United States and the Premier of the Soviet Union were desirable, these should be sought in the guise of informal exchanges or attendance at the U.N. rather than at formal summit conferences. It recommended a study of the pos- sible role of simultaneous attendance at the U.N. as a desirable alternative to other forms of summitry. This type of meeting might avoid or at least reduce the excessive publicity, use of enormous numbers of government personnel, risks to prestige and other disadvantages connected with formal summit confer- ences.[31] President Eisenhower's files contain no record of his thoughts on this paper but he certainly did not consider applying the paper's suggestions to the current session of the U.N. General Assembly.

As the convening of the Assembly neared, the Administra- tion decided to confine the movements of Khrushchev, Fidel Castro, Janos Kadar, and Mehemet Shehu of Albania to Man- hattan. Public statements issued by the White House and State Department emphasized security as the reason for the restric- tions.[32] Other considerations were also apparent in the decision — U.S. non-recognition of Albania, Hungarian viola- tions of human rights, and efforts to let Khrushchev know he was unwelcome.[33] These restrictions evoked protests from the affected governments, stirred up criticism from speakers during the sessions and contributed to the tensions surrounding the Fifteenth U.N. General Assembly.

The Assembly opened amid much turbulence which was punctuated by Khrushchev's antics — his publicized embrace of Fidel Castro, his impromptu balcony news conferences, as well as rumors of the Soviet leader's desire to meet with Eisenhower. Shadowing this opening was the spector of chaos in the Congo and the feared intensification of the cold war.

With this pervasive tension as a backdrop, President Eisenhower took the rostrum at the U.N. on September 22 to become the first head of state (although speaking second after the Brazilian delegate) to address the Assembly. The President gave a well-received speech which emphasized U.S. support for Dag Hammarskjold's peacekeeping mission in the Congo and presented a U.S. policy of support for U.N. aid to Africa aimed at opposing Soviet influence in that continent. He also discussed disarmament at length, emphasizing of course the United States' position on international inspection and verification. He called for restricting military activities in outer space. Keeping his comments regarding the Soviet Union brief and moderate in tone, Eisenhower did not mention the U-2 incident but did criticize Soviet opposition to a full investigation of the downing of the RB-47 aircraft. He said nothing about resuming summit talks.[34]

Many contemporary observers agreed that the President made a constructive presentation.[35] Even Khrushchev was reported as saying he considered Eisenhower's address to be conciliatory.[36]

Nikita Khrushchev's 15,000 word speech to the General Assembly on September 23 contrasted greatly in tone to Eisenhower's address. After welcoming the newly independent African states to the U.N. and extolling the Soviet Union's efforts to improve the international situation, the Soviet Premier lambasted the "aggressive intrusion" into Russia by the American U-2 aircraft. He asserted that the United States had elevated violations of international law into a principle of deliberate state policy. Khrushchev voiced additional criticism, denounced colonialism, and proposed general and complete disarmament while blaming lack of progress toward this goal on the United States. He also reiterated his hopes for a summit conference to be held in a few months to discuss Germany. He attacked Dag Hammarskjold and called for the replacement of the Secretary General with an executive organ consisting of three individuals. Each would represent one of the three major blocs of nations in the world as seen by Khrushchev — the Western powers, the socialist states, and the neutralist countries.[37] Khrushchev later called for Hammarskjold's resignation, but said nothing in any formal Assembly session to indicate a desire to talk to Eisenhower.

After addressing the General Assembly, Eisenhower conferred privately with 13 heads of state or other delegation leaders during two trips to New York on September 22–23 and again on the 26. Yugoslavian President Josef Tito, meeting President Eisenhower for the first time on September 22, told the American President that he understood the United States' position vis-a-vis the Soviet Union. He thought, however, that it was necessary to overcome existing obstacles and stated that the sooner the USSR and the US resumed their conversations the better. To Tito the greatest responsibility of the part of the nations was to see that the major powers came together as soon as possible. Eisenhower expressed agreement and thought that world opinion expressed through the assembly of nations would demand this. Eisenhower hoped that something might get started at the U.N. but he did not look for anything dramatic.[38]

Three days after Nikita Khrushchev's speech before the General Assembly, Eisenhower met with Prime Minister Nehru of India, and their conversation suggested the two men's differing attitudes toward Khrushchev. Eisenhower told Nehru that he found nothing constructive in Khrushchev's speech and saw Khrushchev as desiring only to find out how many nations he could get committed to himself. The President said that the central problem for the General Assembly to consider was disarmament (he and Khrushchev agreed on that) and said that the United States could go along with any reciprocal verifiable disarmament proposal. Nehru stated that the Russians had already agreed to the concept of inspection in principle and that the issue now was the number of inspections which might be conducted. Eisenhower, not in a conciliatory mood, asserted that the frequency issue was a serious one. The President said that the United States was willing to disarm but must find a way to check on this disarmament. Nehru replied that disarmament and controls were tied up in one package, a view sympathetic to Khrushchev's position. In closing the meeting, Eisenhower stated that he did not see how any American president could go to a summit meeting with Khrushchev without assurances ahead of time that the Soviet leader would talk constructively. Nehru only commented that the situation was exceedingly complicated.[39]

President Eisenhower returned to Washington on September 27 to take care of unfinished business. On September 29 he had to travel to Denver to attend the funeral of his mother-in-law. While returning, he learned of a new problem arising from the United Nations General Assembly.

On September 30, Indonesian President Dr. Achmed Sukarno submitted to the Assembly on behalf of the delegations of Ghana, India, the United Arab Republic, Yugoslavia, and Indonesia the following draft resolution:

> Deeply concerned with the recent deterioration in international relations which threatens the world with grave consequences
>
> Aware of the great expectance of the world that this assembly will assist in helping to prepare the way for the easing of world tensions
>
> Conscious of the grave and urgent responsibility that rests on the United Nations to initiate helpful efforts
>
> requests as a first urgent step the President of the United States of America and the Chairman of the Council of Ministers of the Soviet Socialist Republics to renew their contacts interrupted recently so that their declared willingness to find solutions of the outstanding problems by negotiation may be progressively implemented.[40]

This resolution was drawn up at a "tea party" hosted by Tito and attended by Nasser, Nkrumah, Nehru, and Sukarno at Tito's headquarters on September 30. Two days earlier Nasser forshadowed the formal draft resolution by publicly urging Eisenhower and Khrushchev to meet under the aegis of the U.N. to set up guidelines for disarmament.[41]

Did Khrushchev encourage the neutrals to introduce this resolution? Eisenhower believed so although available evidence does not prove that he did. What it does show is that Khrushchev conferred privately with Tito on September 29. Shortly afterwards, Tito talked to Nasser and Nehru. The resolution was introduced the next day. Despite his public blasts at the United States, Khrushchev nourished summit hopes by dropping hints at receptions that he would be willing to meet with the President if the meeting could be arranged by a third party. On September 29 when asked if he was prepared to meet with Eisen-

hower, Khrushchev replied that if he said yes "it would sound
as if he was begging for a meeting," but he added, "I am here
in New York not in Moscow."[42]

Krushchev may have actually wanted without expecting a
meeting with Eisenhower. By obtaining such a meeting, Khrushchev could have returned home with an achievement of sorts.
He could have pressed his views on disarmament upon the President. If Eisenhower were not receptive then Khrushchev could
again put the onus of failure on the American President as he
had done at Paris. Khrushchev may also have wanted to embarrass President Eisenhower. The harsh tone in his public rhetoric suggests a personal bitterness which was not entirely feigned.
Having previously held favorable views of Eisenhower, Khrushchev was placed in an awkward position by the U-2 incident,
and the resulting political pressure probably severely limited
the Soviet ruler's negotiating position. In conversations with the
United States Ambassador to the Soviet Union, Llewellen
Thompson, immediately prior to embarking for New York,
Khrushchev emphasized Eisenhower's assumption of responsibility for the U-2 flight as a source of his bitterness. Khrushchev
told Thompson that he was convinced Eisenhower did not approve the May 1 flight and that he (Khrushchev) had left Eisenhower a way out of the dilemma arising from the fallen plane.
Instead, not only had Eisenhower assumed responsibility for
the U-2 flight, he had also sent another plane (the RB-47) across
the Soviet frontiers.[43]

The neutralist leaders appear to have had a number of motives in submitting the resolution. Khrushchev's hints were a
factor as was a genuine desire on the leaders' part to calm down
the cold war tensions. This desire was expressed in speeches
before the Assembly by Nasser, Nehru, Nkrumah, Sukarno,
and Tito, and was reiterated by Nehru and Tito in private
meetings with Eisenhower.[44] But probably uppermost in the
minds of Tito and some of the others was the opportunity
presented by such a move to enhance their stature as leaders
in a movement of unaligned nations. For Tito, the resolution
was the latest of his many efforts, exerted since the early 1950s
to promote the concept of non-alignment between East and West.
For the five leaders as a group, the year 1960 marked the height
of their international prestige.[45]

President Eisenhower should not have been completely surprised by the submission of this resolution, for there had been considerable public speculation about a possible meeting with Khrushchev. Even Press Secretary James Hagerty had suggested that the President could not refuse such a meeting.[46] Eisenhower, however, was irked because he had met with four of the five sponsors of the resolution and none had specifically mentioned this proposal, although Tito had clearly expressed pro-summit sentiments in his meeting with the President.[47] Eisenhower was insulted at the idea of the neutralists placing himself and the United States on the same level as Khrushchev and the Soviet Union. He did not understand how nations could be neutral between free and not being free or between right and wrong with the United States clearly right and the Soviet Union wrong. He told Jordan's King Hussein that the communists regard man as an educated mule to be directed by the state. While Khrushchev used the U.N. as a tool for his own purposes, the United States tried to use it for human progress.[48]

Eisenhower's view of the proposed resolution remained completely negative. He did not believe that any meeting with Khrushchev could accomplish anything and was certain that U.N. approval of this resolution would embarrass the United States. He thought the resolution so illogical that it had to be contrived, and sensed Khrushchev's influence behind it.[49]

Spokesmen for the Department of State shared the President's opposition. Secretary Herter never believed an Eisenhower-Khrushchev meeting to be possible. Charles Bohlen, Herter's adviser on Soviet affairs, told the President that if he received Khrushchev without the Russian showing a change in attitude, it would convince the Soviet leadership that the Soviet Union was so powerful that it could treat the United States with contempt and at its own choosing, return to the "spirit of Camp David." The Soviet Union needed to show its good faith through positive acts such as the release of the two surviving fliers downed in the RB-47 aircraft.[50] Vice President Nixon, in the midst of his presidential campaign, urged the President not to see Khrushchev and that he (Nixon) be informed of any decisions in this matter.[51]

At least one Administration official hoped that an Eisenhower-Khrushchev meeting could be arranged under certain conditions. Secretary of the Treasury, Robert Anderson, a conservative Texan whom Eisenhower considered to be prime presidential material, suggested that the President send a note directly to Khrushchev mentioning the resolution. This note should refer to the Western governments' statement following the Paris summit meeting and state that the United States Government was always ready to talk if the Soviet Union would show evidence of sincerity about easing tensions and discussing disarmament. While pointing out that these matters were not bilateral in nature, the note should urge that the United States and the Soviet Union do something. If the Soviet Union were to show its sincerity by such actions as the release of the two RB-47 fliers then the two countries' foreign ministers could meet to see what could be done. Thereafter, a personal meeting between Eisenhower and Khrushchev could be arranged.[52]

Eisenhower and Herter dismissed Anderson's suggestion for a direct reply to Khrushchev. Eisenhower noted that Khrushchev had virtually cut off relations between the two men and such a reply would give Khrushchev a chance to counterattack in a press conference. The President and his advisers strained to respond adequately. Herter referred to a suggestion within the State Department that the President invite all five neutralist leaders to a meeting in Washington. Since this would have brought Nasser and Tito to Washington it was rejected, presumably because of political considerations. The President, thoroughly angry at the neutralist leaders and deeply suspicious of their motives, thus ignored an opportunity to test his personal diplomacy in a positive manner on these men. Determined not to enhance the five leaders' stature as representatives of a non-aligned bloc, Eisenhower decided that his approach should consist of a brief answer to the five and a public statement emphasizing the sincerity of the United States in negotiating with the Soviets.[53] On October 2 the President told a contingent of State Department officials to make sure that this resolution did not pass.[54]

Later that day, Eisenhower met with Harold Macmillan and Australian Prime Minister Robert Menzies to discuss the U.N. situation. Eisenhower opened by saying he could not understand why the rest of the world had not been shocked at this call for a two man summit. He was especially disappointed at Nehru's support of the resolution. The group then proceeded to discuss a proper response to the neutralists. Macmillan, harboring hopes of picking up the pieces of the shattered Paris summit meeting, presented a statement calling for a resumption of four power discussions. An extended discussion of the theory and practice of four-power summitry followed, with the President pointing out that the four powers met simply because of their participation in World War II and could not speak for other nations. British Foreign Secretary Lord Home noted that the four powers possessed the bulk of the armaments in the world, a fact which therefore provided another basis for four-power meetings. Menzies, sympathetic to the United States' position, commented that the resolution was a dangerous one which put the President and Khrushchev on the same basis, and was clever propaganda. Herter did not favor another summit meeting but wanted to make it clear who broke up the last one. Macmillan, persisting, asked that they not close the door on a future meeting. He summarized his conversation with Khrushchev and reported that the Soviet leader favored a renewed meeting of the four powers early in the following year. The President agreed that it would be necessary to leave the door open.[55]

The meeting closed with an agreement on the appropriate response to the neutralists. Eisenhower's letter, sent to each of the five, referred to the Western powers statement following the Paris summit conference which indicated readiness to participate in negotiations anytime. This offer was still good. After citing actions by the Soviets which had increased tensions the President stated the United States' readiness to undertake serious negotiations with the Soviet Union and other countries on unresolved problems. He pointed out as had many of the neutralists, that the world's problems went beyond merely the United States and the Soviet Union, and therefore, could not be solved on a bilateral basis. While willing to meet with anyone if such a meeting promised results, the President did not want to engage in empty gestures.[56]

Although technically leaving the door open for renewing contacts with the Soviet Government, Eisenhower was convinced that Khrushchev was not interested in conducting serious talks with him and, therefore, hoped his letter to the neutralists would close the matter. In some quarters though, hope seemed to spring eternal. Nehru, having received Eisenhower's response prior to addressing the General Assembly, claimed in his speech that the President had not rejected the idea of a meeting.[57] Of even greater concern to Eisenhower was Great Britain's attitude. Macmillan apparently chose to interpret Eisenhower's response to the resolution in the same way as did Nehru. Herter reported British moves to promote the idea that Eisenhower had not shut the door on a meeting with Khrushchev. The Secretary of State said he would work on the British delegation.[58]

After allowing Eisenhower time to reply to the neutralists, Khrushchev sent them his own response. He praised the neutralists motives in introducing the draft resolution. He also accused the United States of treacherous acts and claimed that relations between the Soviet Union and the United States could be improved if the United States Government admitted guilt for the U-2 and RB-47 flights, an admission he knew the President could not make.[59] Eisenhower suffered in silence when learning of Khrushchev's reply. Privately, he told Herter that "He was a long sufferer but one day he was going to call him (Khrushchev) the murderer of Hungary."[50]

Eisenhower remained angry over the neutralists' resolution even when it became evident it would not pass. He wanted to know why these men introduced the resolution. It was largely because of this consideration that Eisenhower invited Indonesian President Sukarno (the only one of the five whom he had not seen in New York) to come to Washington. When the two leaders met on October 6, Eisenhower wasted little time before discussing the resolution. While telling Sukarno he did not quarrel with the neutralists' objectives, Eisenhower said he could see no benefit from simply meeting with Khrushchev. He pointed out Khrushchev's expressed personal hatred for the American President. Sukarno said he still thought the two men should meet. Persisting, Eisenhower related the events of the Paris summit conference and Khrushchev's propaganda campaign against the United States and, again, attempted to draw Sukarno out on this point. But the Indonesian President only fuzzily referred to the need for "somehow breaking the ice."[61] Eisenhower reported his frustrating meeting to his cabinet and disgustedly said ". . . This one [Sukarno] would not tell you anything."[62]

Despite the pleadings of the neutralists and the hopes of Macmillan, the resolution got nowhere. The positions taken by Eisenhower and Khrushchev combined with behind the scenes lobbying by the United States delegation to the United Nations assured its defeat. The Assembly later passed a watered down resolution calling for an easing of world tensions. Eisenhower believed that Khrushchev could have used the resolution to greatly embarrass the United States.[63] Instead, the Soviet ruler chose to denounce the idea of an Eisenhower-Khrushchev meeting as "naive" and continued his attacks on the United States during his October 3 address to the Assembly.[64]

The angry tone of Khrushchev's speeches, his attacks on Secretary General Dag Hammarskjold, and his rude behavior during Assembly sessions hardly appeared conducive to achieving his expressed objective of reaching an agreement on general disarmament, or of easing cold war tensions. This behavior reached its climax during a tumultuous plenary session discussion of colonialism when the Soviet ruler pounded his shoe on the table in front of him and effectively disrupted the meeting.[65] Even Eisenhower who had borne the brunt of the Soviet Premier's blasts at Paris in May, was surprised by the harsh September 23 speech.[66] Khrushchev misread or ignored the desire held by most delegates for a cooling of the cold war rhetoric and did not gauge the strength of support for the United Nations organization by the non-aligned nations. Eisenhower believed that the Soviet leader wanted to bully the small nations into supporting Soviet proposals at the U.N.[67] The US Ambassador to the Soviet Union saw the Sino-Soviet split as a crucial determinant of Khrushchev's behavior as the Soviet leader tried to undercut Chinese accusations of being soft on the United States.[68] Pressures from within the Kremlin and from Communist China probably influenced Khrushchev to maintain a firm anti-United States posture at the U.N.

Khrushchev was probably more effective in his private meetings with various heads of state and in the numerous evening receptions. He remained in New York until October 13 and continued to promote his proposals on the reorganization of the U.N. Secretariat, the abolition of colonialism, and the need for general disarmament through press conferences, interviews, and receptions, as well as in his formal speeches. By doing so, he succeeded in obtaining maximum exposure for his views. To the chagrin of the Eisenhower Administration, Khrushchev was a guest at a luncheon hosted by industrialist Cyrus Eaton and accepted an invitation to appear on the nationally televised program "Open End." He used this occasion to outline his attempts to improve relations with the United States and contrasted Soviet intentions with the actions by the United States in sending the U-2 and RB-47 planes on their missions. He tried to build his image as a peacemaker by urging acceptance of his disarmament proposals and by pleading for everlasting peace and friendship between the Soviet Union and the United States.[69]

Despite the failure of the neutralist's resolution and the continuing chill in US-Soviet relations, hopes for eventual high level East-West talks remained alive. Having told Macmillan privately that he favored a renewed four power meeting, Khrushchev claimed during an October 7 news conference that the British Prime Minister assured him there would be a summit conference on Germany and Berlin after January 20.[70]

At this time of course, the 1960 presidential campaign was in full swing and neither major presidential candidate, Kennedy or Nixon, indicated that he would be available for a summit. Both candidates stated that the Paris summit failure demonstrated the need to avoid summits unless the way was paved by diplomacy at lower levels.[71] Nevertheless, some observers believed that Khrushchev could force a summit by exerting pressure on Berlin. Khrushchev's activities in New York helped revive hopes for an eventual East-West meeting and encouraged the belief that such a meeting would be easier to hold after Eisenhower left office.[72]

Khrushchev indicated his desire to open communications with Eisenhower's successor soon after the presidential election when he implied in a message to President-elect Kennedy that the election had cleared the slate and that United States-Soviet discussions might resume.[73] Khrushchev also warmly congratulated President Kennedy upon his inauguration in January, 1961.[74] The Soviet ruler tempered these positive signs with a hard line speech on January 6, 1961 which, among other things, called for the end of the occupation of Berlin and expressed support for wars of liberation. Despite the mixed signals coming from the Kremlin, President Kennedy, being curious about Khrushchev, decided to arrange a personal meeting. He transmitted this desire to Khrushchev on February 22 with the ultimate result being the Kennedy-Khrushchev meeting in Vienna in June, 1961.[75] The practice of bilateral US-USSR summitry was established and continued in this form under succeeding presidents. No more four power summits involving the United Kingdom and France along with the United States and the Soviet Union were held. Neither has an American president met with a head of the Soviet Government in connection with a session of the United Nations despite the potential reduction of formal planning and protocol inherent in a U.N. summit. The value of the US-USSR summits held during the administrations of Presidents Kennedy, Lyndon Johnson, Richard Nixon, Gerald Ford, and Jimmy Carter cannot yet be fully assessed. It is readily apparent, however, that efforts to repair the shattered relationships between President Eisenhower and Premier Khrushchev by inducing a meeting of the two during the Fifteenth U.N. General Assembly were doomed to failure by the political situation in the United States and the Soviet Union as well as by increasingly personal bitterness on the part of the two men. For the sponsors of the neutralists' resolution one fact was clear — the governments of the United States and the Soviet Union could not be persuaded to resume talks if they did not desire to do so.

This examination of the U.N. "Summit Assembly" of 1960 reveals it is largely a transitory, if turbulent episode which had no lasting significance in US-USSR relations. The proposition that the U.N. might offer a potentially auspicious setting for useful summit talks while avoiding some of the drawbacks associated with more formal conferences remains unproven.

The documentation of President Eisenhower's participation in the Fifteenth U.N. General Assembly illustrates the President's moralistic view of the cold war as a struggle between good and evil, and suggests that he failed to understand differing perceptions of the two super powers held by the neutralist nations. It does show that President Eisenhower was clearly in charge of the conduct of U.S. foreign policy during this period. He made key decisions on participating in the Assembly against the often negative advice from the Department of State, and displayed his "hidden hand" style of leadership in working to defeat the neutralists' resolution.[76]

The lack of any comprehensive analyses of United States policies toward the United Nations during the Eisenhower Administration make any conclusions drawn from this study tentative and limited in scope. Eisenhower's firm opposition to the neutralists' resolution suggest that he saw moral and political significance in U.N. resolutions.

As for Soviet Premier Nikita Khrushchev, the limited evidence available indicates that he never seriously considered a meeting with Eisenhower at the U.N. to be feasible and saw nothing to be gained by appearing conciliatory in his public utterances at the U.N. His harsh rhetoric stemmed partly from his need to assert leadership over international communism at Communist China's expense, domestic pressure from hardliners in the Kremlin, and personal bitterness toward Eisenhower resulting from the U-2 incident. Khrushchev was careful, however, to avoid precipitating any major crises over Berlin or any other international hotspot during the waning days of the Eisenhower Administration. He wanted to leave the door open for resuming talks with a new American administration, and seemed to send the appropriate signals to President-elect Kennedy after the election.

While proponents of summit diplomacy as a means of thawing the cold war between the United States and the Soviet Union were disappointed by developments at the U.N. "Summit" Assembly of 1960, the concept of summitry remained alive. In fact it continues at present to be a topic of wide national and international interest.

# CHAPTER TWELVE

# Kennedy, The Bay of Pigs, and the Limits of Collegial Decision Making

RYAN J. BARILLEAUX

ASSISTANT PROFESSOR OF POLITICAL SCIENCE

UNIVERSITY OF TEXAS AT EL PASO

Students of the presidency have been justly interested in presidential decision making, particularly in the matter of how different decision systems affect policy outcomes. Indeed, two recent books on the presidency, Alexander George's *Presidential Decisonmaking in Foreign Affairs*[1] and Roger Porter's *Presidential Decison Making*,[2] have focused on this subject, and both recommend a type of collegial decision making for the President.

In this Collegial Model for decision making, the President is at the hub of a policymaking wheel, and his advisors and other Executive Branch officials are the spokes of the wheel: information and advice flow to the President from several competing sources, rather than through one bureaucratic process. It eschews a hierarchical decision mechanism for a set of collegially related advisors surrounding the President, and is marked by informal channels of information and access to the President.

Not only has the Collegial Model attracted the attention of scholars, but variations on it have served as the bases for decision making by several modern Presidents: Roosevelt, Truman, Kennedy, Johnson, and Carter. Of these, the most notable use of this model was by President Kennedy, who consciously distinguished his decision style from that of his "bureaucratic" predecessor.[3] His use of the Collegial Model is famous largely because of a significant case in which it was employed: the Cuban Missile Crisis. Kennedy's decision-making system, particularly as employed in that case, has been taken by many, especially scholars such as George and Porter, to be a useful model for effective presidential decision making.

For these reasons, scholarly interest and presidential application, the Collegial Model invites closer examination. Its merits, which include flexibility and a lack of bureaucratic "channels," have been addressed at length by others (e.g., George and Porter), and will only be touched upon here. Rather, it is the purpose of this article to examine the limits of collegial decision making by the President, because the promise of this model is accompanied by several problems that cannot be overlooked. If the Collegial Model is to be recommended and employed in the future, as it is likely to be, then Presidents and their advisors must be aware of the limits of this system.

The exploration of these limits will be undertaken through the study of a crucial case in presidential decision making: the case of the Bay of Pigs. As will soon be clear, this case can be used to provide important empirical evidence of the problems inherent in collegial decision making. While the Cuban Missile Crisis may represent a success for the Collegial Model, the disaster at the Bay of Pigs represents a failure of such significance as to merit special attention.

## A. Summary of the Case and its Importance

The 1961 Bay of Pigs affair is a crucial case for studying decision making for two reasons: 1) it involved a conscious attempt by a President to employ the Collegial Model; and, 2) it was a clear failure. For President Kennedy clearly failed in his attempt to manage an assault by Cuban exiles on Castroist Cuba in defense of American interests and to project American power. Consequently, this case casts a harsh light on Kennedy's decision system, and thus provides an excellent opportunity for examining the problem of the collegial system.

Upon assuming the presidency, Kennedy inherited a plan for an exiles invasion of Cuba, with secret United States support, from the Eisenhower Administration. On the suggestion of Vice-President Richard Nixon, President Eisenhower had authorized the CIA to organize an anti-Castro political movement among Cuban exiles in the United States and to secretly train a military force from those exiles willing to undertake guerrilla warfare against Castro in Cuba. As the 1960 presidential election progressed, the CIA developed plans and began preparation for such an operation.

Kennedy learned of the plan soon after his election. On November 7, 1960, he was briefed on the status of the Eisenhower Administration's plans, which were still somewhat tentative. The plan under consideration called for air strikes on Cuba, followed by an amphibious/airborne assault in the area of Trinidad on Cuba's southern coast. After the assault force established a secure beachhead near the landing point, a provisional government would be flown in.

Kennedy's reaction to the plan was mixed. He had previously endorsed American support for anti-Castro "freedom fighters"[4] and advocated the overthrow of Castro.[5] Upon learning of the plan, he was amazed by the magnitude of the large-scale amphibious invasion which the CIA was preparing to mount. He dismissed such a plan as "too spectacular" and insisted that the only plan acceptable to him would be a "quiet" landing of Cuban exiles in Cuba, with no United States military intervention.[6] In subsequent deliberations on the operation, Kennedy reiterated that insistence.

Over the next two-and-a-half months, Kennedy and a select group of his advisors deliberated on the plan. They discussed it informally and also attended several meetings on the Cuban invasion with CIA Director Allen Dulles, Richard Bissell, the CIA's head of covert operations, and the Joint Chiefs of Staff. At one of these meetings, on April 4, 1961, all of the President's advisors gave their approval to the plan. All were convinced that the invasion would be small and "quiet," as Kennedy had insisted, and that the guerrillas would be able to hide in the supposedly nearby Escambray Mountains if they were unable to establish a beachhead at the Cuban Bay of Pigs. Kennedy shared in this belief, which was later proven erroneous, but reserved final judgment on the operation until later.

By now, the plan had changed significantly from its status in 1960. A new landing site was selected in the Zapata area of Cuba, near the Bay of Pigs. The prior air strikes were eliminated, and the assault was to be carried out in the pre-dawn hours and at first light on "D-Day." On April 14, three days before the operation was to begin, Kennedy ordered Bissell, who was in charge of the plan, to make the assault brigade's air support "minimal."

On April 17, Kennedy decided to give the CIA the go-ahead on the mission. A brigade of about fourteen-hundred exiles, with secret American aid, invaded the Bay of Pigs. It was immediately clear that the plan was a failure. Kennedy cancelled the second wave of air support strikes. Castro's air force stopped the brigade's supply ships, and his soldiers quickly surrounded the invaders. The vast majority of those not killed were captured.

The Administration was astounded by the failure of the mission. It was a more difficult operation than Kennedy had expected, and the brigade was cut off from the Escambray Mountains by huge swamps. Soon, the myth of no American involvement in the operation was debunked, and the United States was denounced by several of its Latin American allies. As a result, the Bay of Pigs was soon marked as a crisis for American foreign policy and a failure for President Kennedy. It was a failure as a military operation, as an attempt to engage in covert operations, and it was a failure in terms of all the Kennedy Administration's objectives.

Many have sought to explain this failure, others, merely to understand what happened. Most memoirs of the Kennedy Administration discuss it, with Arthur Schlesinger's *A Thousand Days* providing the most detailed account of the White House deliberations. The most complete reconstruction of the whole affair is Peter Wyden's *Bay of Pigs*, which is useful for the amount of information the author was able to gather about the case. It fails, however, as do the various memoirs of the period, to provide analysis of the case's implications for presidential policy making. Its treatment is atheoretical. In contrast to this approach, there is the treatment that the Bay of Pigs receives in the well-known analysis of Irving Janis' *Victims of Groupthink*.[7] Janis offers a psychological explanation for the decision to proceed with the plan, arguing that overconsensus of "groupthink" characterized the Kennedy Administration's deliberations. Yet this approach is also flawed, for it pays insufficient attention to the President's role in the Bay of Pigs decision, concentrating instead on Kennedy's advisors. Yet the decision to proceed with the invasion was Kennedy's, not the choice of a committee. Consequently, there exists no direct, theory-sensitive treatment of Kennedy's decision making in this affair nor an analysis of the effect of the collegial decision system on the case.

### B. Organization and Staffing of the Collegial System

Scholars of presidential decision making are fond of the Kennedy organizational system, which was marked by its informal channels of information and access. Alexander George has praised this approach for its flexibility, informality, and non-bureaucratic nature,[8] and, indeed, it had those characteristics. But this system was dependent on proper coordination from the President and his ability to use the loose structure to ensure adequate deliberation on policy questions. Since the system was highly informal in its approach to decision making, there were few routines for mandating such deliberations.

In the Bay of Pigs decision, this structure had an adverse impact on the Kennedy Administration's deliberative process. In the Eisenhower Administration, the Cuban invasion plan had been the concern of the Special Group,[9] a secret high-level committee for examining and approving covert operations.[10] The general matter of Cuba was also discussed in the National Security Council. All this changed under Kennedy, who dismantled what he considered to be the overly bureaucratic Eisenhower national security apparatus. The National Security Council, which hardly met, was not in charge of the Cuban invasion. Neither was the Special Group, which continued to debate details of the operation but which exercised no directive authority over it.[11] Even Allen Dulles, the CIA Director, no longer had direct authority in this matter. Rather, Kennedy relied on an informal, select group of his advisors to deliberate on the plan, and allowed Richard Bissell nearly absolute control over planning.

This informal group was not a committee in the sense of having clear responsibility over the plan or discussions about it, as the ExCom would be during the Cuban Missile Crisis, but was a loose assembly that constituted the Collegial Model in action. This group consisted of the secretaries of State, Defense, and Treasury, the Attorney General, an Assistant Secretary of State, the President's Assistant for National Security, his Special Assistant Arthur Schlesinger, Jr., and those minor officials Schlesinger called "appropriate assistants and bottle-washers,"[12] The President and this group met occasionally with CIA officials Dulles and Bissell and the Joint Chiefs of Staff, and senior members of it met with the President either alone or in small numbers. At one meeting in April, 1961, Senate Foreign Relations Committee Chairman William Fulbright joined the discussion. Over the course of the eighty-odd days during which the plan was considered, the group or sets of its members met with the President several times on this matter.

For all the meetings of all of these officials, the Administration's deliberations were marked by an absence of coordination from President Kennedy. There was no staff work to support plan evaluation by senior officials, nor were any of the members of the ad hoc advisory group assigned to provide independent assessments of the project.[13] Indeed, the Taylor Commission Report, which summarized the Administration's official investigation of the Bay of Pigs affair, stated:[14]

> Top level direction was given through ad hoc meetings of senior officials without consideration of operational plans in writing and with no arrangement for recording conclusions reached.

The absence of central direction in Kennedy's collegial system meant that coherence in policy making could not be achieved. Neither Kennedy nor any of his ad hoc group actually had a clear idea of what had been planned and approved and what had not. All materials related to the plan, from briefing papers to maps, were kept by the CIA. Only one man, Richard Bissell, the CIA officer in charge of the invasion, knew the full extent of the plan.[15] Theodore Sorensen, Kennedy's senior advisor at the time, argues that the Administration was too new to counterbalance the influence of the CIA,[16] but the problem seems less one of newness than of a lack of coordination in the collegial system. Such a system revolves around the President, and is thus dependent on him as the engine of the deliberative process. Kennedy's decision-making apparatus required coordination that it did not receive. Kennedy's newness may have been a broad condition that affected his performance in this case, but the organizational structure he employed had an impact on decision making: it produced a system that could only work effectively under close presidential supervision.

Another factor which falls in closely with organization is that of staffing, i.e., the people who inhabit the organization and their impact on it. Here is an important vehicle, for it helps to explain an influence on Kennedy which may account for some of his lack of coordination of the collegial decision apparatus.

The Kennedy Administration stood in awe of two men of the CIA, and the President and his advisors were thus swayed by their perceptions of these personalities. The CIA Director, Allen Dulles, had been in intelligence for decades and was regarded as a "legend." His chief of covert operations, Richard Bissell, was also highly regarded. Faith in their abilities helped to sway the decision process in an adverse way.

First, Allen Dulles' reputation influenced Kennedy's deliberations, despite the fact that the President had removed the Director from oversight of the invasion plan.[18] In the Eisenhower Administration, as CIA Director and a member of the Special Group, Dulles had been intimately involved with the tentative planning of the Cuban operation. Under Kennedy, he was consulted on the question of whether an invasion was desirable or feasible, but Dulles could no longer know the form it would take: Kennedy and Bissell had altered the plan from its 1960 status. Yet the President and his advisors regarded Dulles' support for an invasion as compelling, because he was a "legend." They were impressed enough by this imposing figure to take his views as a predictor of success for Kennedy's "minimal" plan.

At the same time, Richard Bissell swayed the President and his men. He was known to many of these advisors from his days on the faculty at Yale, and none thought of questioning his planning. Significantly, the President bypassed Dulles and dealt directly with Bissell, who was allowed to operate without supervision.[19]

Indeed, it is the generally uncritical support by the Kennedy Administration for Dulles and Bissell which can provide some insight into how the organizational structure contributed to failure. Whereas the collegial system required competing sources of information and advice in order to be effective, as well as presidential orchestration of those sources, the members of the Kennedy Administration found it difficult to challenge an ongoing plan advocated by such imposing figures as Dulles and Bissell.[20] The President did not properly coordinate his decision apparatus, and in part because of the reputation of Dulles and Bissell among his advisors, he did not feel pressed to mobilize that apparatus to critically study their plans.

### C. Management and Oversight of the Collegial System

In the last section, the implications of Kennedy's decision structure and personnel were considered. In this section, that analysis will be complemented by a consideration of how Kennedy performed according to the managerial requirements of collegial decision making.

Management is affected by structure, but there are issues of management which exist regardless of the organization and staffing a President employs. The first of these is the question of whether the President ensures that his policy design is being followed. In the case of the Bay of Pigs, Kennedy did not undertake to fulfill this responsibility. He and his advisors saw the use of a Cuban exile brigade as a way to topple Castro without actual aggression by the United States,[21] and this was the main thrust of Kennedy's intentions in this affair. On the one hand, Kennedy sorely wanted to "do something" about Castro, as his campaign speeches had made clear. He did not want to be charged as being "soft on Communism." At the same time, however, he insisted that there be no overt American aggression. He was concerned about anti-American reactions in Latin America and at the United Nations if the role of the United States was not well concealed.[22]

In accordance with this course, Kennedy allowed the CIA to continue planning the Cuban invasion, but explicitly prohibited American military intervention.[23] Beyond this prohibition, however, he did little to ensure that his design was followed. Rather, the bulk of planning of the project was left to the CIA's Directorate for Plans. He did ask the Joint Chiefs for a military evaluation of the operation, but made little use of his collegial system for oversight and analysis of the plan. Much faith was placed in Bissell's ability to handle the affair. Moreover, Kennedy failed at crucial points to make his specific objectives clear: when pre-invasion bombing missions were to begin, he ordered the number of bombers reduced to a "minimal" level, leaving Richard Bissell to decide what that meant.[24] Bissell regarded this informal sort of decision making as "rather odd."[25] This episode was part of a larger pattern of imprecise and somewhat casual management.

As for directing the policy process, again, as noted above, Kennedy did not employ his collegial system of administration to check the work of the CIA. The Joint Chiefs were asked to assess the military aspects of the plan, but when they issued a vague and ambiguous report, Kennedy did not press for better analysis.[26] Besides this report, other experts who might have made useful contributions were not consulted. For example, Latin Americanists in the State Department were excluded from the decision process, as was the CIA's Directorate for Intelligence.[27] Kennedy consulted his advisors on the plan, and various aspects of it were debated in their meetings, but the project was essentially left to Bissell to handle. He did not effectively direct the policy process toward the implementation of his policy design.

Nor did Kennedy ensure that the decision process in the case of the Bay of Pigs was complete. First, nearly all of the information and analysis in this case came from the plan's advocates. The only other analysis which Kennedy sought was from the Joint Chiefs, and their report was rather ambiguous.

The President had asked the Chiefs for a military assessment of the invasion plan. With the limited information they were provided by the CIA, the Chiefs had produced an ambiguous report which was generally negative in tone and which suggested that the Bay of Pigs area was an inferior landing site. Kennedy was unsatisfied with the report, but never asked for clarification or more specific conclusions. The Chiefs were essentially peripheral to the planning and conduct of the whole operation.

Surprisingly, Kennedy, who exhibited political shrewdness so many other times, did not press for other evaluations of the plan when the Chiefs delivered their report. Not only did he not enlist other of his senior advisors to provide alternate sources of information and analysis, but he also failed to consult important expert sources of information about the plan. The State Department regional experts have already been mentioned, but there were also the Intelligence branches of the CIA and the State Department.[28] None of these groups were either employed or consulted. Richard Bissell effectively controlled information and analysis of the proposed invasion.

Second, in consideration of values and interests relevant to the case, Kennedy and his advisors paid great attention to the possible political consequences of abandoning the invasion plans, particularly the charge of being "soft" on Castro.[29] This was tied to what Dulles called the "disposal problem," i.e., the matter of how to dispose of a force of highly motivated guerrillas without being charged as "soft." They did not, however, give much weight to the interests and consequences which would be involved if the plan was tried and failed (or even succeeded).[30] Alternative views of the values at stake were not ignored, but neither were they given extensive consideration.

It is at this point, in reference to consideration of alternative

views, that Kennedy's actions and responses must be separated
from those of his advisors. The President did try to remain open
to arguments contrary to those of Bissell, but his advisors did
not help this task. Illustrative is the case of Senator J. William
Fulbright. When Fulbright voiced objections to the invasion plan
at a meeting in April, 1961, on the grounds that either success
or failure of intervention would damage the reputation of the
United States, he was coldly received by the advisory group.
William Bundy, for example, felt the need to "rally" in support
of the President against the Senator's objections.[31] Likewise, none
of Kennedy's other advisors displayed interest in Fulbright's
arguments.

Kennedy's advisors did not help the President in that instance
because they did not give attention to dissenting views. So the
President cannot be assigned complete blame for failure to consider such views. This failure cannot, however, eliminate the
fact, discussed above, that Kennedy did not employ his collegial
system to best advantage in considering interests and values.
Rather than seeking alternative evaluations of interests and
values, he relied on the (misperceived) judgments of Dulles and
Bissell. Those who felt that the CIA's analysis of American interests in the case were wrong, such as Fulbright, Schlesinger,
and Under Secretary of State Chester Bowles, all had to take
the initiative in demonstrating the existence of alternate views.
Kennedy did not seek out such views, as his collegial system
required.

In the same way, little was done regarding another criterion
of effective decision making: search for a wide range of options
and assess the consequences of various options. The search and
evaluation of various options were in the hands of the CIA, specifically, those of Richard Bissell. As deliberations on the plan
progressed, the range of options was defined by Bissell as
proceeding with the invasion or calling it off. Kennedy had determined, on his own convictions, that American military intervention would not be allowed. At the same time, he questioned Bissell about the possibility of infiltration of Cuba rather
than invasion, but the CIA officer unilaterally judged that option unfeasible.[32] Because Kennedy relied on Bissell and his
covert division of the CIA to do both planning and analysis,
and did not seek out other evaluations, criticisms, analyses, or
sources of information, he was left with little choice in the matter.

As Arthur Schlesinger noted, Kennedy accepted Dulles' arguments regarding the "disposal problem" and Bissell's analysis of the invasion plan's feasibility.[33] Having placed his reliance in those experts, without establishing competing sources of information and analysis, Kennedy fell victim to their mistakes and misjudgments.

The President thus operated in the point at which his ineffective management combined with his informal decision structure to create problems for him. Although he was not alone in his Administration, as no President is, he was the man at the center of the policy-making wheel in his collegial system. Not only does an effective decision process require certain steps which Kennedy did not ensure were taken, but he also failed to fulfill the role required of him by his organizational structure. When compounded with the problem of overreliance on Bissell, these factors led to the Bay of Pigs disaster.

But Kennedy's advisors also had a hand in the decision, yet they did not press the President to doubt the efficacy of his own view. There are two reasons for that failure. The first is, as discussed above, Kennedy's own approach to the matter. He had dismantled the Eisenhower NSC machinery, and he had refused to consider a major amphibious operation. The second is, surprisingly, Kennedy's skill in consensus building.

### D. Consensus Building and the Collegial System

In order to accomplish anything, a President needs a certain degree of consensus among his advisors and subordinates who will implement the President's decision. In this case, however, Kennedy's problems arose from the ease with which he achieved consensus, because his collegial system reinforced the adverse consequences of his coalition-building skills.

The President had chosen a small group of advisors to help him in his deliberations on the invasion plan, and in part because of the small size and composition of this group he had little trouble developing a consensus. All members of the group were eager to help the President implement his policies and plans for the country, so none wanted to stand in the way of this bold operation.

This group was won over by Kennedy's skills as a welder of coalitions, skills which are generally regarded in politics as useful and good. The President's ability to draw together and maintain a consensus in the affair made it possible for him to proceed confidently with the plan, and to fail disastrously. Crucial to this consensus building was the President's political skill in inspiring his followers. The conventional wisdom implies that the President ought to possess those qualities which can aid him in welding an enthusiastic consensus in support of his decisions and policies, because such qualities will facilitate the achievement of the President's goals. Yet President Kennedy's inspirational qualities in this regard worked against him, for they helped to foster an easy consensus which ushered in disaster.

For the evidence suggests that Kennedy's inspirational qualities stifled a healthy skepticism about the proposed invasion. What this means is that the "Kennedy charisma" created an atmosphere of assumed success. On Kennedy's part, this involved what Arthur Schlesinger described as Kennedy's[34]

> . . . enormous confidence in his own luck. Everything had broken right for him since 1956. He had won the nomination and the election against all the odds in the book . . . Despite himself, even this dispassionate and skeptical man may have been affected by the soaring euphoria of the new day.

On the part of those around him, it was the sense that "Everyone around him thought he had the Midas touch and could not lose."[35] Admiral Arleigh Burke, Chief of Naval Operations at the time and most active of the military leaders involved in the operation, confessed that he hesitated to speak up about his doubts regarding the plan in the presence of Kennedy, the "charmed young man."[36] In the same way, Adolph Berle of the State Department and Paul Nitze of Defense both swallowed their doubts because they wanted to rally behind the President.[37] Arthur Schlesinger, a Special Assistant to the President, opposed the plan but feared becoming a "nuisance."[38] Because Kennedy did not encourage dissent or doubt about the plan, he heard little.

Indeed, Kennedy's inspirational qualities contributed to the mistaken notion that the invasion as planned would be a success. They possessed him with a heady confidence in his own abilities, and they suppressed doubts among the President's advisors. Combined with the problems discussed above, Kennedy's inspirational qualities helped to make disaster at the Bay of Pigs.[39]

## E. The Limits of Collegial Decision Making

As the preceding analysis has demonstrated, the Bay of Pigs affair points to several significant problems in the Collegial Model. As a clear failure of decision making which was the result of an application of that model, this case serves as a crucial test of the collegial system. Presidents and students of the presidency can profit from the consideration of these problems.

1. *Demands on the President's Time and Attention.* Use of the Collegial Model requires an enormous effort on the part of the President: he must act to drive the decision process from beginning to end. As this case illustrates, collegial decision making involves the active participation of the President in initiating consideration of a problem, overseeing the various deliberations of his subordinates, cross-checking of deliberations and planning, and implementation. The single case of the Bay of Pigs affair involved several months and extensive presidential effort, and at that Kennedy did not even live up to all of his responsibilities under this system. When multiplied by the vast number of issues considered and decisions which a President must make, the presidential effort demanded by the Collegial Model is tremendous. Poor use of this system can be disastrous, and effective use of can be prohibitively demanding.

In this regard, it is probably true that even a highly motivated President who wished to properly employ the Collegial Model would be unable to do so. For he could properly attend to effective management of the collegial system in only a limited number of cases. In order to accommodate some decisions, he would be forced to leave the bulk of his decisions to subordinates, to a routinized process, or to a slipshod version of the collegial process.

The problems with this mixed approach are twofold. First, it means that, for whatever benefits promised by collegial decision making, the majority of presidential decisions will never be exposed to those benefits. Second, and more significantly, the amount of time and attention which the President would have to devote to even the most important issues would probably prohibit him from properly overseeing other matters. He would thus be forced to allow many decisions to slip from his grasp, decisions which might later cause problems.

The consequences of all this is that the Collegial Model is

at best a system for making some decisions, but certainly not all. Even an energetic and highly motivated President would be unable to use it as a general decision mechanism. Moreover, because of this limit, it is clear that all Presidents, even those who seek to employ the Collegial Model, must develop decision mechanisms which do not require such attention and time in order to handle decisions other than the most significant ones. In short, even those Presidents who wish to maximize the effectiveness of collegial decision making must pay careful attention to the development and operation of non-collegial decision systems.

2. *Lack of Routine Oversight.* As the Bay of Pigs demonstrates, a significant flaw of the Collegial Model is its lack of routine procedures for overseeing and cross-checking decision processes, planning, and implementation. The Taylor Commission noted how no records were kept of the deliberations, and the President did not see to it that the Joint Chiefs provided a thorough review of Bissell's plans.

Yet this problem is larger than Kennedy's negligence in this particular case. For, as noted above, the demands on the President's time and attention will make it likely that the lack of routine oversight will not be corrected by presidential initiative. Oversight in the Collegial Model depends on the President, and at some point he will be unable to spare time or attention for it. The result could be disastrous.

As this and other cases of decision making have demonstrated, there is a significant need for routine oversight mechanisms in the President's decision process. Even a highly capable planner such as Richard Bissell could not bring to his own work the detachment of another reviewer. That is the reason President Eisenhower had insisted on oversight of Bay of Pigs planning by the National Security Council's Operations Coordinating Board: to subject decision making to careful scrutiny and oversight.

The Collegial Model, then, neither provides for routine oversight nor makes corrective presidential initiative likely. For the demands of this decision system will at some point overwhelm even the most energetic President.

3. *Susceptibility to Personality and Charisma.* The first two problems of the Collegial Model are important, but this third one is perhaps the most dangerous. For the case of the Bay of Pigs

illustrates the influence of personality and charisma on collegial decision making. Not only did the personalities of Richard Bissell and Allen Dulles discourage skepticism about the plan, but the "Kennedy mystique" encouraged a docility among the President's advisors.

Here is where the Collegial Model presents its greatest problem: that the personality of the President can be the biggest obstacle to effective decision making. In this sense, Kennedy was his own worst enemy, because his charisma inhibited any real deliberation on the merits of the invasion plan. Advisors were afraid of becoming "nuisances," intent on "rallying around" the President, and unwilling to challenge "this charmed young man," so the collegial decision group did not really deliberate at all.

This problem extends beyond the case of the Bay of Pigs, for any President will be vulnerable to it. The Collegial Model does not provide any safeguards against the influence of charisma, and if the President does not make an extraordinary effort to reduce its influence, then collegial decision making will produce not deliberation but docility.

## F. Conclusions

The Collegial Model is significant because of its popularity among students of presidential decision making and Presidents themselves. Indeed, in recent years, most Democrats who have become President have attempted to use some variation on this model. Accordingly, it is likely to be used again in the future.

The model has great appeal because of its several benefits, which George and Porter have considered at length: informality, flexibility, avoidance of over-bureaucratization. Yet, for all these benefits, there are significant costs. It has been the purpose of this article to examine these problems.

The Bay of Pigs provides an important case for studying the limits of collegial decision making, because it was such a significant failure of that system. There are few cases of decision making where the results are so clear, so the ones which do exist offer important lessons for students of the presidency.

One of the most important of these lessons is the need for attention to non-collegial decision systems, even if a President is intent on employing the Collegial Model. The problems engendered by that model indicate the need for scholars and Presidents to devote significant attention to other, more routinized or "bureaucratic" systems for decision making. The limits on presidential time and attention necessitate decision mechanisms to help the President make his way through the vast amount of issues and problems he must confront, rather than counting on a system which only increases his workload.

# President Carter and the Soviet Union: The Influence of American Policy on the Kremlin's Decision to Intervene in Afghanistan

MINTON F. GOLDMAN
ASSOCIATE PROFESSOR OF POLITICAL SCIENCE
NORTHEASTERN UNIVERSITY

When the Soviets intervened in Afghanistan in December, 1979, it was to protect and control the Marxist regime in Kabul threatened by an Islamic inspired conservative revolution that had spread throughout the country.[1] But the Kremlin's decision to intervene in Afghanistan was also a reaction to the sharp deterioriation of Soviet-American relations caused by American policies it considered discriminatory, a challenge to Soviet strategic interests in the Middle East and central Asia, and a threat to Soviet security. Moreover, Soviet leaders apparently believed that the United States under President Carter's leadership — because of perceived American military and diplomatic weaknesses — could not and would not block a Soviet entry into Afghanistan. As one reviews Soviet-American relations in the 1970's from the Kremlin's perspective, it is possible to see how the political and military diplomacy of the Carter Administration paradoxically contributed to a Soviet action it very much wanted to deter.

## Deterioration of Soviet-American Relations

According to a Soviet view recent problems in Soviet-American relations have their origins in an historic American prejudice towards the Soviet State. Soviet writers have argued that ever since the 1917 revolution, Americans have viewed the Soviet state with disdain and condescension, regarding it as "a kind of illegitimate child of history . . . 'an historical misunderstanding' . . . which has to be ended in one way or another, as quickly as possible." For this reason, so the Soviet argument runs, the United States hoped, after 1917, that the new Soviet system would disappear. Hence, successive American Administrations had refused to recognize the Soviet government until 1933, sixteen years after it had come to power and had obtained the recognition of other countries. And even after the recognition and the Grand Alliance of World War II, the United States continued to deny the legitimacy of the Soviet state and to view its policies as a threat to American interests. Soviet experts attributed to the Americans a "vicious" anti-communism which, they said, was responsible for prolonged periods of American hostility to the Soviet state.[2] The legacy of this prejudice, according to the Soviets, was the Carter Administration's hostile and provocative behavior toward the Soviet Union, in particular its policies on trade and human rights, defense and arms control; the resumption of formal diplomatic relations with China; and its efforts to expand American political and military influence in the Middle East and central Asia.

## 1. Trade

At the time of President Carter's election in November, 1976, the Soviets were still smarting from a failure of the U.S. Congress in December, 1974, to approve a draft Soviet-American treaty granting most favored nation treatment to Soviet trade with the United States unless the Soviet government liberalized its emigration policy. The collapse of the treaty originally had caused indignation in Moscow not only because the United States had granted most favored nation treatment to the trade of many other foreign countries, including, incidentally, socialist Poland, without regard to their domestic policy, but also because American linkage of trade concessions to the Soviet Union to its liberalization of emigration policy represented to the Kremlin an unwarranted American interference in Soviet internal affairs. The Kremlin was angry also because trade discrimination by the United States hurt the Soviet Union in an area of vital importance to its economic well-being. The Soviet leadership wanted to expand trade with the United States to obtain advanced industrial technology needed to modernize an aging and inefficient economic plant and to facilitate exploration of the vast oil and natural gas reserves in Siberia. It also wanted American investment capital for the construction of pipelines to market these resources.[3]

## 2. Human Rights

The Kremlin was angered also by the Carter Administration's aggressive human rights campaign,[4] in particular its conspicuous sympathy for individual Soviet political dissidents who had been punished in Soviet courts and therefore were considered criminals. For example, the Soviet leadership was vexed by the hospitable reception both President Carter and Vice President Walter Mondale gave in Washington D.C. to Soviet dissident Vladimir Bukovsky, who had come to the United States early in 1977 after having spent eleven years in and out of Soviet jails and mental institutions.[5] The Soviets referred to Bukovsky as a "jailbird."[6] Brezhnev publicly condemned what he called "American efforts to teach the Soviet Union and other countries how to manage their internal affairs."[7]

The Kremlin also took offense at American charges of Soviet violations of the human rights provisions of the Helsinki agreements. They were enraged by a published report of the Joint Congressional Committee on Security and Cooperation accusing the Soviet Union of ". . . systematic disregard of civil and political rights." In August, Georgi Arbatov, a leading Soviet expert on American affairs and executive head of the Institute for the Study of the United States and Canada, commented that the United States was poisoning the atmosphere of Soviet-American relations by incessant anti-Soviet propaganda campaigns and attempts to interfere in the internal affairs of the Soviet Union under the pretext of "defense of human rights."[8] And in October, in a speech delivered to the Supreme Soviet, Brezhnev called the President's policy on human rights little more than an ill-disguised attempt at subversion of socialist governments and not the principled concern with the human condition Mr. Carter implied it was.[9]

There was another explosion of Soviet wrath in the summer of 1978. The Soviets were furious over critical U.S. commentary on the trial in May of Yuri Orlov, founder of the so-called Helsinki Human Rights Monitoring Group in the Soviet Union,[10] and over President Carter's condemnation of the trial of Anatolyi Shcharansky, another Soviet human rights activist, but one accused by Soviet authorities of having been employed by the C.I.A. and therefore of being a traitor.[11] The President called the Soviet trial of Shcharansky a "blow against liberty" and spoke of retaliation in the form of a curtailment of sales to the Soviet Union of industrial technology.[12] *Pravda* in mid-July accused President Carter of undermining *détente* and said: "The campaign of interference in the internal affairs of socialist countries is becoming an uncontrollable process, a tide that is carrying those who swim it on toward the cliffs of confrontation." It said also that those responsible for the "insincere speeches" defending freedom and human rights really were bent on poisoning the international atmosphere and were the same people who in their opposition to Soviet-American trade, were responsible for a repudiation of *détente*.[13]

President Carter's trade and human rights policies contributed to the development of a hostile environment of Soviet-American relations on the eve of Soviet intervention in Afghanistan. The President may well have encouraged the Soviets to see in a successful military takeover of Afghanistan a means of responding to American prejudice by an act that at once would enhance their international prestige, soothe their injured pride, and gratify their mounting anger.

## 3. American Defense Spending and Arms Control

Soviet leaders believed at the end of 1979, that decisions by President Carter to construct the MX missile system, to station new Pershing 2 intermediate range missiles in western Europe — despite explicit Soviet warnings against such a move — and to have the United States and other NATO governments increase their defense spending by 3% for each of the next five years,[14] were part of an American determination to achieve military superiority. The Kremlin considered this American objective not only a violation of the spirit and intent of the recently concluded SALT II agreements limiting the production of strategic nuclear weapons, but also a denial of the strategic equality between the two Superpowers agreed upon — at least from the Soviet point of view — by Soviet party leader Brezhnev and U.S. President Nixon during their summit meeting in Moscow in May, 1972.

Undoubtedly in the expectation of obtaining a revision of these presidential decisions, Soviet leader Brezhnev announced in Oc-

tober, 1979, that in the next year the Soviet Union would withdraw 20,000 troops and 1,000 tanks from East Germany.[15] When
the Carter Administration did nothing to reciprocate this gesture, the Kremlin became convinced that the Americans indeed
were bent on achieving military superiority over the Soviet
Union. They adopted a belligerent tone toward the Americans.
In November, Leonid Zamyatin, head of the international
department of the Soviet Communist Party Central Committee
warned of "countermeasures" if NATO stationed new missiles
in western Europe.[16] At the same time, Soviet Defense Minister Dmitri Ustinov referred admonishingly to a buildup of the
aggressive NATO bloc in which the U.S. was setting the tone.
He spoke of ". . . stepped-up U.S. military preparations in various parts of the world."[17]

The Soviets were also disappointed and flustered by the Carter
Administration's failure to get Senate approval of the SALT II
agreements which were the most visible and conspicuous product
of *détente*. The achievement of these agreements was important
to those in the Kremlin who had advocated *détente*, notably
Brezhnev and Gromyko, as well as to their advisors in the U.S.A.
Institute, notably Arbatov. Brezhnev told Senate Majority
Leader Byrd during his July, 1979 visit to Moscow that the SALT
II agreements were the greatest contribution so far to the cause
of restraining the nuclear arms race. The Soviet leader also said
that the agreements were "based on the principle of equality and
equal security of both sides and on a complete balance of obligations and interests for both the USSR and the U.S." He said
that SALT II would "clear the way for the working out of new,
more far reaching measures for limiting and reducing strategic
arms during the course of the SALT II negotiations and would
help disarmament in Europe."[18]

The Soviets suspected that the Carter Administration did not
want an arms limitations agreement with the U.S.S.R. They
said they could not understand the President's difficulty in obtaining ratification given his party's control of the Senate,[19] and
believed the U.S. was playing a double game of seeking to limit
strategic weapons while continuing the arms race.[20] Evidence
for the Kremlin of this perceived duplicity were the comments
of Democratic Senator Sam Nunn of Georgia and former Secretary of State Henry Kissinger that ratification of SALT II be
made contingent on an Americans arms build-up to match ex-

isting Soviet deployment.[21] And Democratic Senator Frank Church of Idaho, who was chairman of the Foreign Relations Committee and a supporter of the SALT II agreements, stated publicly that the Senate would not approve them as long as a combat-ready brigade of Soviet troops remained in Cuba.[22] Certainly it came as no surprise to the Kremlin that, on November 2, the Senate adopted a resolution — to which the Carter Administration offered no public objection — that the SALT II treaty should not be ratified until the President had assured the Senate that Soviet troops in Cuba "were not engaged in a combat role."[23]

By the end of 1979, the Soviets had much to support a view that the Carter Administration, despite its negotiation of the SALT II agreements and its brief but extensive, albeit unsuccessful, campaign to win Senate approval of them, was determined to achieve military superiority over the Soviet Union. Arbatov wrote in March, 1980, that Americans still looked with nostalgia on the postwar period of military superiority, which was the result of transient historical circumstances, though the United States continued to assume such circumstances were the natural order of things.[24] The timing of this statement suggests another inspiration of the Kremlin's decision to intervene in Afghanistan, namely a need to demonstrate Soviet military prowess and to assure the U.S.S.R. a strategic equality the Americans seemed determined to deny them.

### 4. China

The Soviets were alarmed by the Carter Administration's efforts in 1978 to resume formal diplomatic ties with China. They saw it as a departure from past American neutrality in the Sino-Soviet dispute. They believed it would embolden the Chinese leadership to work against Soviet interests in Asia, notably in Afghanistan, where there already was some evidence of Chinese collusion with the insurgents.[25] The Soviets also suspected that the Americans would encourage China to strengthen its already friendly ties with Pakistan and induce the Pakistanis to increase their aid to the Afghan insurgents.[26] Soviet anxiety undoubtedly was heightened by the ongoing Sino-Japanese negotiation of a political treaty (ultimately concluded in August, 1978), and the prospect of an American-Chinese-Japanese *entente* in East Asia.[27]

Soviet reactions to the new American initiative toward China were swift and vigorous. On June 25, in a speech in Minsk, Brezhnev accused the U.S. of pursuing a "short-sighted and dangerous policy of trying to play the 'China card' against the Soviet Union." He said, "its architects may bitterly regret it."[28] And in November, Arbatov as well issued a warning to the Carter Administration that an alliance between the United States and China could destroy *détente*. [29] In December the Soviets said that American overtures to China "give (the Chinese) the green light for expansion in whatever direction they choose for themselves."[30] Soviet leaders were convinced that the new Chinese relationship with the United States had an anti-Soviet strategic objective. [31]

The Soviets were furious also over what seemed an excessively cordial American reception of Deng Xiaoping in Washington during January, 1979, to conclude the formal resumption of diplomatic relations between China and the United States. For example, they complained that the Americans were sympathetic listeners to speeches by Deng calling for cooperation between China, the U.S., Europe and Japan to counter a world-wide Soviet threat. [32]

The Kremlin also believed that high American officials in a meeting with Deng had expressed support of China's hostile policy toward Vietnam, with which the Soviet Union recently had concluded a treaty of friendship and cooperation. Soviet Premier Kosygin told American diplomats in Moscow, according to *The New York Times*, that Deng's suggestions of the possibility of a Chinese punitive action against Vietnam for its presence in Cambodia, were "outrageous" and certainly should have been refuted by the Carter Administration. [33]

When the Chinese did invade Vietnam in February shortly after Deng's return from Washington, and the State Department issued a warning to the Soviet government against retaliation, [34] the Soviets became convinced of American complicity. *Pravda* stated: "It was not without coincidence that the Chinese leadership reached the decision to begin the invasion right after Deng's return from the United States." To the Soviets the U.S. reaction to Chinese aggression most nearly resembled, if not approval, then at least indirect encouragement. "Official Washington," they said, "has taken only half-hearted efforts to weaken an impression in most countries of a direct connection between Chinese aggression and Deng's visit to Washington. Washington's ambiguity is a contributory factor in Peking's open embarcation on a path of war."[35]

To the Soviets it also looked as if the Carter Administration in the Summer and Fall of 1979, was moving toward military cooperation with China. A *Pravda* article in October cited a U.S. Defense Department Staff Study that recommended military help to the Chinese to strengthen their defense.[36] Other evidence Moscow had of imminent Sino-American military cooperation was an announcement in October that Secretary of Defense Harold Brown was to go to Peking for discussions with his Chinese counterpart early in 1980.[37]

By the end of 1979 the Soviets were angry and frightened by the Sino-American reconciliation. They saw it as another gesture of American hostility toward them if only because it was inspired — they believed — by President Carter and National Security Advisor Z.K. Brzezinski, whom they considered a militant Russophobe. They also considered the improvement of Sino-American relations during 1979, a threat to their strategic interests in Asia, in particular their territorial security and that of their Vietnamese ally given the deterioration of the political and military situation of their client government in Kabul. Intervention in Afghanistan was from the Soviet vantage point a necessary response to the perceived dangers of the Carter Administration's aggressive diplomacy toward China in 1978 and 1979.

### 5. American Moves in the Eastern Mediterranean, South Arabia, Iran and Afghanistan

The Soviet perception of American expansion in the Middle East and Central Asia in 1978 and 1979, in particular (a) the aggressive and persistent American efforts that led to the signing, in March 1979, of the Egyptian-Israeli Peace Agreement, (b) the dispatch of American military aid to the Yemeni Republic in its war during February and March 1979, with pro-Soviet South Yemen, (c) evidence of an American threat to the new Khomeini regime in Iran, and (d) clandestine support the Carter Administration was allegedly giving throughout 1979 to the Afghan insurgents in their fight against the Marxist government in Kabul; was another determinant of the Kremlin's decision to intervene in Afghanistan. The Soviet leadership quite possibly saw in a takeover of Afghanistan a response to this American advance into areas of political and military importance to the Soviet Union and a way to prevent a shift in the global strategic balance between the U.S.S.R. and the United States against the Soviets.

### a. The Eastern Mediterranean

The Soviets believed the United States had scored a major strategic gain with the conclusion of the Egyptian-Israeli peace agreement in March, 1979.[38] According to *Pravda*, Egypt and Israel would now become "gendarmes of the Pentagon" in the eastern Mediterranean.[39] The Soviets believed also that the Carter Administration viewed Egypt and Israel as replacements for the strategic bases the United States lost in Iran following the collapse of the Shah's government earlier in the year and that the treaty signalled an American drive into South Arabia and the Persian Gulf.[40]

Part of Soviet frustrations over the conclusion of the Egyptian-Israeli peace agreement derived from an inability to prevent it. The Soviet Union had lost most of its influence in Cairo following the expulsion of its advisers by President Sadat in 1973, and had practically no leverage in Jerusalem, having broken off diplomatic relations with the Israeli government after the 1967 war. At the same time, it was clear to the Kremlin that the Americans, conversely, had good relations with both Jews and Arabs, had worked hard for the treaty through several years of so-called "shuttle diplomacy" between the Egyptian and Israeli leadership, and, despite obstacles and setbacks, had achieved it.

### b. South Arabia and the Persian Gulf

A flurry of American political and military activity in South Arabia in 1979 seemed to the Kremlin further evidence of a U.S. challenge to Soviet interests in the Middle East. In March, 1979, the Carter Administration decided to give 400 million dollars worth of emergency aid to the Yemeni Republic,[41] which had been invaded in February by pro-Soviet South Yemen, and to order a task force into the Arabian Sea.[42] The Administration also agreed to sell the Saudi government 5,000 missiles, an arrangement originally concluded by President Ford but never put through because of congressional opposition, to bolster the confidence of the Saudis and ready them for a role in regional defense against future Soviet expansion in South Arabia.[43]

The Soviets considered American help to the Yemen Republic and the projected sale of arms to the Saudis a threat to the strategic balance in the Persian Gulf, where they had been insisting on a parity of influence with the United States to promote their image as a global superpower and to develop a leverage on countries that supply oil to the West.[44] Soviet Ambassador to France Chernenko frankly admitted publicly in Paris in June, 1980, that his country had entered Afghanistan to assure this parity of influence in the Gulf region.[45]

### c. Iran

The Soviets also worried about a possible American military move against Iran not only because of the new Khomeini regime's virulent anti-Americanism that had led to an abrupt end of American influence in Teheran, but also because of the seizure of the American hostages in November, 1979. Indeed, the Soviets believed the Americans as a face saving device or in an explosion of national wrath might use force in Iran to secure the release of the hostages.[46] Hence, following the collapse of the Shah's regime, Brezhnev spoke of a Soviet concern about the security of Iran's territory because of its strategic location on the U.S.S.R.'s southern frontier.[47] During 1979, the Soviets alluded to an American plan to blockade Iran. They called attention to the despatch to Iranian waters in November of an American naval armada armed with atomic weapons.[48] A belief at the end of 1979, that the Carter Administration would interfere militarily in Iran and again threaten Soviet security as in the Shah's time when the Soviets viewed Iran as a U.S. client, undoubtedly helped to move the Kremlin closer to a decision to go into Afghanistan.

### d. Afghanistan

Throughout 1979, and especially after the assassination of President Nur Mohammed Taraki and the succession of Hafizullah Amin in September, 1979, there was a steady weakening of the Marxist government in Kabul as it tried to put down the everwidening insurgency against it. Indeed, Amin was no more able than his predecessor to restore order. He also defied the Kremlin, refusing to accept large scale Soviet military assistance the Kremlin wanted him to use against the insurgents. By the end of the year the Soviets faced the possibility of not only losing Afghanistan to a conservative counter-revolution, which, if successful, would have destroyed the Marxist regime in Kabul and replaced it with an Islamic government hostile to the Soviet Union and Communism, but also of having to work with an arrogant, inept and potentially disloyal client bound to be troublesome to Moscow even if his government should be successful in suppressing the insurgency against it.

The Soviets insisted that the Carter Administration was supporting this anti-Marxist insurgency. The Soviets believed also that the Administration had been opposed to the Marxist regime in Kabul since it had come to power in April, 1978, because of its closeness to the Soviet Union, confirmed by the Soviet-Afghan treaty of friendship and cooperation concluded in December, 1978.[49] In the Soviet view, the Administration had decided, following the collapse of the Shah's government in Teheran and the consequent loss of American spy installations on the Iranian frontier with the Soviet Union, to undermine the new Afghan government in the hope that it would be replaced by one that would allow Afghanistan to become an American client as Iran had been under the Shah.[50]

According to a report in the Indian left-wing weekly *Blitz*, reprinted by the Novosti press agency in Moscow, the United States envisaged Afghanistan part of the new CENTO-like anti-Soviet alignment of countries on the Soviet Union's southern frontier. For this reason the Carter Administration had sent Deputy Secretary of State Warren Christopher in February, 1979, to Ankara to discuss Turkey's role in such an alignment.[51] *Blitz* held also that a critical turning point in American policy toward Afghanistan was the assassination of U.S. Ambassador Dubbs in Kabul, who was "sacrificed" by the U.S. Central Intelligence Agency (CIA) for the sake of providing the American government a pretext for criticizing and opposing the Marxist government, which, incidentally, it blamed for the assassination. Following the assassination, so the argument ran, the Carter Administration cancelled U.S. economic agreements with Afghanistan and delayed appointing a new ambassador to replace Dubbs.[52]

Soviet commentators said also that after the assassination of Ambassador Dubbs, the Carter Administration had stepped up its subversive anti-Afghan activities. CIA agents, they said, acting under cover of the Drug Enforcement Administration, were on the Pakistani frontier with Afghanistan helping to arm and train Afghan anti-government rebels in camps set up for this purpose with the connivance of the Pakistani government, which, the Soviets said, was acting in this business as a client of the United States. The Soviets identified Afghan insurgent camps in Peshawar and other places along Pakistan's frontier with Afghanistan.[53] The Soviets insisted that the CIA, in cooperation with Saudi Arabian intelligence, was using extremist Muslim groups of the "Muslim Brotherhood" type against not only the Marxist government in Kabul, but also the Ayatollah Khomeini's anti-American regime in Teheran.[54]

Whether these allegations of a secret American hand in the Afghan rebellion were valid or merely fabrication elaborately contrived by the KGB as part of an alleged program of promoting misinformation to discredit the United States and other capitalist governments in Third World countries,[55] is less important than the fact that to an over-sensitive, suspicious, and insecure Soviet leadership, American collusion with the Afghan rebels was plausible. The Soviets said they had warned the United States on several occasions to stop helping the Afghan insurgents but that their warnings had been ignored by Washington.[56]

According to its military experts,[57] the Kremlin had no possible alternative to intervention to maintain Communist and Soviet influence in Afghanistan. Hence the only real obstacle to their entry would have been broader foreign policy considerations, such as the willingness of the United States to use force to stop them. Here another large facet of Carter Administration behavior toward the Soviet Union becomes important to an understanding of the Kremlin's decision to intervene in Afghanistan, namely a Soviet perception of its weakness of will as well as of power.

## The Appearance of American Weakness

For some time the Soviets had doubted American resolve to oppose their initiatives in the Third World. They concluded in 1979 that, despite forward American moves in the Eastern Mediterranean and South Arabia, despite the possibility of a sudden American retaliatory act against Iran, and despite a belief the Americans were assisting Afghan insurgents, President Carter would not use military force to block a military takeover of Afghanistan. There are several reasons for this conclusion.

### 1. Past Presidential Restraint

Soviet analysts wrote in the 1970's that, since the Vietnam war, U.S. presidents from both parties were inhibited as strong leaders by pressures from Congress and public opinion for presidential restraint in the use of force in foreign policy. They said that its lack of political and military success and the enormous economic, social and human cost of the Vietnam experience made the American leadership of the 1970's skeptical of traditional foreign policies requiring force.[58] One Soviet expert observed that the Americans were moving away from foreign policies of force after Vietnam because Vietnam "made America recognize that it played a more humble role."[59] The Soviets concluded that as a result of Vietnam American leaders had a "new, realistic, sober, sensible and constructive approach to U.S. foreign policy." They pointed out that conservatives like Nixon and Kissinger were ready to improve U.S.-Soviet relations because they did not have the inferiority complex of many liberals who needed to act tough toward the Soviet Union to prove that they were not "soft on Communism."[60]

### 2. Weakness of President Carter

Soviet views of Presidential restraint were reinforced by the behavior of President Carter, whose hesitant, uncertain, and contradictory style of decision making must have made him look to the Soviets, as he did to his own countrymen, as an indecisive, ambivalent and vascillating leader in foreign policy. They noted his refusal, despite an aroused public opinion, to use force against the Soviet-Cuban involvement in Angola and his failure to give substantial military aid to Somalia against Ethiopia. They dismissed his warning in a speech on June 8, 1978 to the U.S. Naval Academy at Annapolis, that Soviet expansionist activity in Africa could lead to confrontation with the United States, because he undercut the strength of his words by avowing a desire for negotiation. They viewed the President's hard line toward them as an effort to appease and silence hawkish elements in the American military establishment. Indeed, they ridiculed his inconsistency and his complaints about their policies in Angola and Ethiopia in terms that suggested a very low estimate of, perhaps even a contempt for, his foreign policy leadership.[61]

The Soviets saw more evidence of President Carter's inconsistency and weakness in his handling of the flap in the American communications media in August, 1979, over the combat-ready brigade of Soviet troops in Cuba. At first he condemned the brigade's presence in Cuba as, "intolerable"; then he retreated, saying it posed no threat to American security. And, while announcing counter measures to increase military power in the Caribbean, the President ruled out the use of force to evict Soviet troops from Cuba.[62]

Also, the Soviets very likely interpreted the President's passivity on the occasion of the attack on the American embassy in Islamabad in November, 1979, and his conciliatory policy in the hostage crisis with Iran as still more proof of his hesitancy to use force. Indeed, the advocacy of "prudent restraint" by Brzezinski in dealing with the provocative Iranian regime may well have given the Soviets the impression that the American government at least in this instance was paralyzed.

There is another argument that the Soviets considered President Carter weak because of his accommodation of them — which they may have interpreted as a retreat — on a variety of arms control issues. For example, it may have looked to them that, as a result of only mild complaints, the President had cancelled production of the B-1 bomber, vetoed the construction of another attack carrier, and decided not to manufacture the neutron bomb even though he had pressured NATO allies to accept it in the face of adverse public opinion. And they may have interpreted as another sign of the President's weakness his willingness to make concessions to them on the SALT II in regard to the cruise missile, their "backfire" bomber, ICBM ceilings, and verification.[63]

The Soviets concluded that, because of an ambivalence in decision making, a perceived willingness to conciliate, and an evident reluctance to use military force in support of foreign policy, President Carter would not try to block their intervention in Afghanistan. They reasoned that he would get angry, especially since his administration had signalled them, albeit somewhat obliquely, of its opposition to an escalation of their military involvement in Afghanistan; that he would threaten use of force; but ultimately, he would back down from such a threat, settle upon a policy of temporization and, over the long term, return to a "business-as-usual" relationship with them, almost as if a crisis had never occurred in the first place.[64]


## 3. American Military and Diplomatic Unpreparedness

The Soviets accurately surmised American weakness in west central Asia. Whereas NATO had developed elaborate contingency plans for the defense of western Europe from a possible Soviet attack through the Scandinavian north, it had no comparable political and military readiness to counter a Soviet advance through Afghanistan, Iran, or Pakistan to the Persian Gulf. Turkey in late 1979, was an unreliable partner in NATO partly in consequence of its conflict with Greece over Cyprus. Also, Turkey's relations with the United States were strained. The Turks were angry over the Carter Administration's refusal to sell arms to them. They rightly suspected that this policy was inspired by an American sympathy for the Greek side in the Cyprus question.

At the same time the Soviets had been cultivating the Turkish government. They had proposed to Ankara a treaty of mutual friendship and cooperation. Though Turkey would not conclude such a treaty with the Soviet Union, it could not be counted on by the West to play an effective role in blocking the expansion of Soviet power in west central Asia.[65]

Another source of American strategic weakness in west central Asia was Pakistan which was unwilling and unable to do more to block Soviet expansion into its Afghan neighbor than provide a refuge for the anti-Marxist insurgents, despite anxiety over the way in which the government in Kabul had become a Soviet client in 1978 and 1979. The Carter Administration had done little to lessen Pakistan's vulnerability to Soviet retaliation and to a Soviet inspired pressure from India, which in the 1970's had become quite friendly with Moscow. The Administration's policy toward Pakistan was inspired by pique over its decision to build a nuclear weapon in opposition to American efforts to promote nuclear non-proliferation.[66]

Nor could Saudi Arabia help significantly in the defense of

the Persian Gulf against a Soviet thrust south through Afghanistan or north from Aden. The tripartite security arrangement for the Gulf discussed by the governments of Saudi Arabia, Iraq, and Iran in the summer of 1978 had not materialized by the time the Soviets had decided to intervene in Afghanistan. Furthermore, though Saudi Arabia, like Pakistan, was vulnerable to a Soviet military threat, the Carter Administration had remained hesitant to give the Saudis substantial military assistance because of strong pro-Israel sentiment in Congress. By the end of 1979, the Administration still had not executed a previously agreed-upon missiles sale to the Saudis to strengthen their defense capability.

By contrast, the Soviets had a substantial military capability that made them confident about responding successfully to a confrontation with the United States over their intervention in Afghanistan in the unlikely event the Carter Administration did try to block them.[67] Since their retreat in the 1962 Cuban missile crisis, they had built up their conventional and nuclear weaponry. Their military budget is estimated to have grown by 3 or 4 % annually in the 1960's and through the 1970's. By 1979, the Soviet Union had achieved superiority *vis-a-vis* the United States in several weapons categories.[68] Their growing military power had made possible an expansion of influence during the 1970's in Angola, Ethiopia, and South Yemen. The Soviet military intervention in Afghanistan in December, 1979, was the logical climax of a long period of Soviet weapons buildup undertaken in the aftermath of the Cuban missile crisis.

*4. Intervention and* Détente

The Soviets rejected an unenforceable and therefore unrealistic American position that *détente* required mutual restraint worldwide. Rather, the Soviets believed *détente* involved restraint only in western Europe and, indeed, that they could and should intervene in the Third World, especially in countries neighboring the Soviet Union and thus important to its territorial security and internal political stability, to help progressive and Marxist forces fight wars of national liberation or civil wars against conservative and counterrevolutionary antagonists.[69] The Soviet decision to use massive military power in Afghanistan in December 1979, confirmed this application of an equivalent to the

Brezhnev Doctrine, used to justify the 1968 intervention in Czechoslovakia, to Third World countries.[70]

At the same time for the Soviets, the concept of mutual restraint was in a shambles in 1979 because of Carter Administration policies that were dangerous to their security in Europe, the Middle East and central Asia, and therefore productive of the tensions and animosities characteristic of the pre-*détente* "Cold War" era. *Détente*, therefore, could not be and was not the deterrent to a Soviet intervention in Afghanistan President Carter believed it to be. Thus, even if the Soviets had accepted a view that *détente* precluded intervention in the Third World, they still would have intervened in Afghanistan. By the end of 1979 the Soviets had become convinced that the Carter Administration had cheapened *détente*, depriving it of any value to them.

## Conclusions

The state of Soviet-American relations in the late 1970's was a critical determinant of the Soviet decision to intervene in Afghanistan, to look at the internal situation in Kabul in 1979 alone would not do justice to an investigation of Soviet motives. An oversensitive, image-conscious and insecure Soviet leadership decided to intervene in Afghanistan not only to enhance the Soviet Union's image as a global superpower undercut by a perceived American discrimination in the areas of trade, human rights, and arms control, but also to protect Soviet interests in Asia threatened by a Chinese leadership seemingly emboldened by the American reconciliation. The Soviets also saw in a military takeover of Afghanistan an opportunity to adjust to their advantage the strategic balance in the Middle East and central Asia they believed disrupted by not only the American inspired Egyptian-Israeli peace treaty and the Carter Administration's dispatch of American weapons to North Yemen, but also by perceived American pressures on the Khomeini regime in Iran and the Marxist government in Kabul.

The Soviets also minimized the possibility of American resistance. They undoubtedly calculated that the Carter Administration would not use force to block their entry into Afghanistan — despite its known opposition to such a move — partly because of its hesitation to use force to protect American interests in other foreign crises, notably over the American hostages in Iran and the "discovery" of a Soviet brigade in Cuba. The Kremlin's readiness to discount American resistance also was a result of the Carter Administration's failure in the late 1970s to keep America's political fences mended with Turkey and Pakistan and to provide not only those countries but others along the Persian Gulf weapons they needed for a credible defense.

The Soviets went into Afghanistan also because they never had accepted an American view that *détente* required mutual restraint not only in Europe but elsewhere in the world. Indeed, contrary to the American concept of *détente*, they justified interventionist policies in the Third World by an expansive interpretation of the Brezhnev doctrine. Thus *détente*, which the Soviets insisted had been abused by the Americans, was not the deterrent to a Soviet move into Afghanistan President Carter mistakenly believed it to have been.

Finally, the Soviets confidently assumed that even if they had a confrontation with the United States over a military invasion of Afghanistan, they would be able, once a crisis with the Americans had passed, to resume with them a business-as-usual relationship. They seemed to have been led by the Carter Administration — quite inadvertently, of course, and despite its signals to the contrary — to believe that a move into Afghanistan would not cause serious or long term damage to their relationship with the United States, which ostensibly they wanted to keep in good repair. They appreciate the benefits, not the obligations, of *détente*. That their invasion of Afghanistan has proven a disaster, however, is inconsequential to their motivation. That they perceived American weakness should reinforce the wisdom of American negotiations from a position of strength.

# PART THREE

# Organization, Reform, and Strategy

# CHAPTER FOURTEEN

# The Commander in Chief: Constitutional Foundations*

JAMES D. WEAVER
ASSOCIATE PROFESSOR OF POLITICAL SCIENCE
MARYMOUNT COLLEGE
TARRYTOWN, NEW YORK

The formula for American civil-military relations was conceived and arranged in the post-Revolutionary period, and is the first attempt of the new nation-state to integrate the objectives and procedures of democratic, constitutional politics with military power. A synopsis of the Revolutionary leaders' goals and accomplishments reveals: *unanimity* in their concern for the survival of the nation with civilian supremacy as an intact, inviolable and operative principle; *consensus* in their suspicions and fears of standing professional military organizations as "dangerous to liberty" and constitutional politics; but *controversy* in their perceptions of how to meet necessary defense needs and still maintain effective political command and control (ie., what civil authority should be created over military forces and how could it be structured and distributed in the new political system). The Revolutionary leaders' instincts and knowledge of an acceptable civil-military formula in a "liberal democratic construct" meant that military organizations and influence should only function on behalf of autonomous but interdependent political forces that could subordinate military power to civil power. The will to survive and the instruments of violence must be reconciled with the priorities and theories of American constitutionalism.

First concern, then, was providing for appropriate national security arrangements compatible with the principle of civilian supremacy. Clearly, the revolutionary leaders espoused a political ideology that disavowed and opposed any sense of militarism in the nation. It was an ideology promoting limited govern-

* *Editor's note: This essay is part of a larger work presently being written by Professor Weaver on the President as Commander in Chief.*

ment and fundamental rights and liberties that simply could not sustain a militarist system. In addition, the distaste and suspicions of military organizations further meant that the anti-militarist may recognize the infrequent need for military force but such force should be made as impotent and regulated as possible. To support this concept, one can point to the colonists' British anti-militarist tradition originating from the 1628 Petition of Right and the 1689 Bill of Rights that opposed martial law and the quartering of troops; indeed, the colonial experience of a permanently stationed British Army was a perpetual threat to subverting the colonists' civil authority. The following documents preceding the 1787 Constitutional Convention, in fact, illustrate the colonists' anxieties over the political-military dilemma: 1) the Declaration and Resolves of the First Continental Congress (14 October, 1774) that prohibited the maintenance of a standing army in peacetime without the consent of the legislature; 2) the Virginia Bill of Rights (1776) and Massachusetts Bill of Rights (1780) stated that "standing armies in time of peace should be avoided as dangerous to liberty . . . in all cases the military should be kept under strict subordination to and governed by the civil power"; and 3) the Declaration of Independence (1776) which accused King George III of maintaining armies in the colonies without legislative consent, and "affected to render the military independent of and superior to the civil power".[1]

Also, it is interesting to note that even General Washington, as commander in chief of the revolutionary forces, apparently favored the paramountcy of civil power as indicated in correspondence to Henry Laurens, President of the Continental Congress, concerning the jealousy and suspicion of the people about military forces and how one must be aware and cautious of military power. Furthermore, in 1783, Washington's "Sentiments on the Peace Establishment" recommended to Alexander Hamilton's Congressional Committee on Military Establishments that military academies be established and a permanent but limited standing army (2,631 soldiers) is "indispensably necessary" for internal and external security (Indian attacks, foreign invasions, citizens' insurrections, trade protection); *but* that it be a "well regulated and disciplined militia" and "General officers will take their instructions from the Secretary of War".[3] These examples of pre-Constitution ideas on civil-military relations certainly indicate that the Revolutionary leaders were in agreement about their distrust of military forces in the body politic, and the consequent need to ensure the subordination of the military element to civil power.

When the Constitutional Convention was convened in the summer of 1787, the delegates were firmly committed to the principle of civilian supremacy and anxious to structure that interest into an intact and on-going political system. But the conflicting perceptions on the ways and means to achieve those objectives were soon expressed. It appears that the fundamental differences lay, in the first place, in the preferences for citizens' state militias vis-a-vis a standing army to guarantee internal and external security; and, secondly, in the nature and scope of the authority and responsibility delegated to the national executive and legislative branches to effect civilian control over all armed forces — with special concern to check any exploitive control of military forces for political purposes (a "check" later adopted in the purse-and-sword division). *No delegate proposed a concentration of power, military and political, executive or legislative*, but certain delegates did favor selective views of the nature, purpose and organization of a new federal union and articulated their prescriptions for achieving both civilian supremacy and national security. What the delegates finally resolved was a very compromising division and overlapping of authority in national and state governments regarding the military question. As Samuel Huntington has written, the thinking was that liberalism is inherently hostile to military institutions and functions, so "if military organization is necessary, it must be military organization reflecting liberal principles. Civilian control in liberalism means the embodiment of liberal ideas in military institutions".[4] Thus, whatever perspectives, the final provisions for civilian supremacy and national security were quite properly compromised within the liberal code. Attention to the specifics of the military question at the Constitutional Convention (standing national armies and navies, citizens' state militias, limited appropriations, the purse and sword responsibilities, "war making", and, of course, the commander in chief authority) will reinforce and illustrate these interpretations.

The rationale expressed at the Convention to oppose a national standing army not only reiterated the threat to civilian supremacy by establishing a permanent military presence in a democratic republic but, moreover, questioned the requirement for such a force considering the limited defense needs of the new nation. In addition, it was believed that the citizens' state militias could provide the bulk of defense forces and act as a buffer against a national army if necessary; and that the creation of an elitist aristocratic officer corps managing a professionalized army unnecessarily threatened civil authority. Furthermore, limitations on manpower and funds for any national armed force, if created, were demanded, and the quartering of troops and restrictions on the citizens' right to bear arms must be prohibited. In effect, these views implied that a meaningful guarantee of civilian supremacy really required the elimination of any distinct military force.

Reflecting upon these points, one can see some truth in their convictions. Perhaps the state militias could have handled the anticipated threats of Indian attacks, civil insurrections or even foreign invasions at the time. Perhaps a professional army with an elitist officer corps, supported by unlimited funds and manpower, may have unnecessarily overprepared and perhaps over-utilized a national military force to safeguard national interests and possibly determine national policies. The formation in 1783 of the officer corps organization headed by George Washington called the *Society of the Cincinnati*, for example, was viewed by many delegates as the establishment of an aristocratic military caste designed to promote defense priorities in national policies.

The opinions of the chief spokesmen for the "opposition", however, namely, Edmund Randolph, George Mason, Elbridge Gerry and Charles Pinckney best illustrate the argument against the maintenance of a military presence. Randolph stated that every delegate "felt indignation" about the prospect of maintaining a standing army and that the state militias really provided ample national defense.[5] Gerry suggested that manpower limitations could be established for a standing army,[6] and Pinckney proposed restrictions or prohibitions on the quartering of troops, expenditures for armed forces beyond one year, and the existence of a standing army in peacetime (to be subject to legislative consent).[7] George Mason was particularly concerned with the purse and sword separation, and issued his famous dictum — "the purse and the sword ought never to get into the same hands".[8] Regarding appropriations, the decision to empower Congress to "raise and support armies" was eventually accompanied by the two-year limitation provision on funding. Although delegates like Gerry feared any funding beyond one year was "dangerous to liberty", it was pointed out that appropriations were only permitted, not required; and that a biennially-elected legislature might have no time to review and renew one-year appropriations.[9] Finally, on the matter of "war-making", the "opposition" was in agreement that *only Congress can judge if a war ought to be commenced or waged* (a corollary to the purse and sword division theory);[10] and the approved phraseology was to read "to declare war" instead of "to make war", to "raise and support armies" instead of "to raise armies", and to "provide and maintain a navy" instead of "to build and equip fleets".

The consequences of the "opposition's" efforts must *first* be evaluated by acknowledging the rationale developed by the other side: delegates more favorably disposed to a national military establishment. Alexander Hamilton and George Washington were recognized as the most staunch proponents of a national military establishment — a structure that would reflect a strong national government responsible and empowered to maintain law and order and security by military means if necessary. Hamilton's and Washington's views are significant because they realized that the effectiveness of national political authority is inextricably tied to and dependent upon various instruments of national policy making; and that a national armed force is the essential prerequisite to provide for the common defense, even if only as a reserve, emergency force readied to resolve internal or external disorders. The implications of these views should be explored, but it must first be made clear that, essentially, it was Hamilton's and Washington's appeals to "think first of survival" that later persuaded all the delegates (and thereafter the ratifying conventions in the states) at least to concede and support a provision for some form of national military forces, excluding federalized state militias. Perhaps the absence of an organized vocal defense at the Convention, mandating the existence of standing armies, is the best evidence of the tacit consent of the delegates to form national armed forces. Once the Convention was committed to the establishment of a strong federal republic, it would necessarily be obliged to effect whatever ways and means to ensure "the common defence and general welfare". Any controversy, then, would be confined to proposed safety valves regulating military forces.

To reconcile the dilemma of "what would be the nature and quality of national security needs in a constitutional system", the Hamiltonian-Washington nascent strategy concentrated on allaying the fears expressed regarding the composition and behavior of permanent standing armies. *The issue was no longer whether to provide for a standing army in peacetime, but rather of what organization, size and jurisdiction, and how, when and by whom utilized.* Washington's and Hamilton's earlier rejected recommendations (in 1783–84) to the Continental Congress to establish a very limited standing army as a minimum security force were now revised and modified to meet concurrent demands to restrict a national army. The argument that American defense needs were quite limited was affirmed but also interpreted that national security interests may often depend upon a readied national force to safeguard the nation (especially, anticipated frontier, Indian, and citizens' disputes). The proposal that citizens' state militias could undertake defense needs was countered by recognizing the value of militias for local and state emergencies, and as an "armed citizenry" symbolizing the liberal tradition and possibly serving as a counterweight to check a professional military organization.[11] Yet the limited and often inefficient, incompetent nature and performance of the state militias must be subject to the overall authority of the national government (ie., Congress may prescribe the organization and discipline of the militias, and may "call forth the Militia to execute the laws of the Union, suppress insurrections and repel invasions; and the President shall be Commander in Chief of the Militia "when called into the actual Service of the United States . . ."). James Madison, for example, stated the Militia must be maintained "on a good and sure footing" — available to Congress "if resistance is made to execution of laws . . . for insurrections or invasions the people can be employed to suppress and repel, rather than a standing army".[12] In short, the Militia must be supplemented by a more dependable, prepared national army.

On the proposal of a standing army, special concern was given to correct the liabilities existing in the Revolutionary and post-Revolutionary Congresses and colonial forces: namely, the legislature's inability to take actions beyond recommendations, which certainly adversely affected Washington's authority and responsibility to command and regulate an often insubordinate and ill-trained Army. Thus, to "raise and support armies" (jointly with federalized Militias) would *legitimize national conscription*, and, in general, delegate clear responsibility to the new national legislature "to provide for the common defence." This provision to sanction legislative consent in forming and maintaining armies seemed to satisfy Charles Pinckney's and others' earlier objections to raising armies without such consent. By the end of the Convention, consensus was reached on Congressional responsibility to regulate and perhaps call forth the Militia, and to establish separate national forces if necessary. With regard to the earlier Pinckney proposals for limiting military appropriations to one year, prohibiting the quartering of troops and officially declaring the principle of Civilian Supremacy, it was resolved to extend the appropriation restriction to *two years* and delete the other proposals.[13]

In *The Federalist Papers*, Hamilton, Madison and Jay pursued a very astute and convincing defense of national security needs. Jay wrote on the priority to first provide for the safety of the nation (*Federalist #3*), and Hamilton stressed the importance of unity among the states and the need to establish national security structures even if they threatened to destroy or impair civil and political rights (although he speculated that America's *isolated* position would mean "extensive military establishments cannot be necessary to our security") (*Federalist #7, #8*). Hamilton further stated that the federal government is primarily responsible for the common defence, and ought to hold and exercise vast authority "because it is impossible to foresee or define the extent and variety of national exigencies"; yet legislative authorization and appropriations for security needs provide an adequate check on federal power (*Federalist #22-29*). Finally, Madison reiterated that the federal government holds foremost responsibility "in war and danger" and must provide for "security against foreign danger," and that any fears of a standing army may be calmed since the ocean barrier "destroys every pretext for a military establishment which could be dangerous" (*Federalist #41, #45*).

Clearly, the intent of these writers was to illustrate the inherent hegemonial nature of the national government in national security matters—enacted by granting numerous delegated powers to the legislature and, primarily, residual authority to the Chief Executive as Commander in Chief. *The potential dangers of standing armies would be minimized since the new nation's national security conditions mandated an extremely limited, practically non-existent professional army that would be well checked and regulated, in turn, by state militias and shared legislative and executive control.* What this implies is that Civilian Supremacy is well provided in the division and sharing of national authority, and so the issue of subordination of the military to civil power is moot and resolved. Conversely, why worry about how to subordinate a force that really doesn't exist?

In addition, many of the states' ratifying conventions (Pennsylvania and Massachusetts, in particular) did object to the standing army concept and the centralized control of the military; and sufficient influence was exerted to include a quartering of troops prohibition and a citizen's right to bear arms in the later Bill of Rights. In fact, it may well be the promises and provisions for guaranteeing citizens' basic rights and liberties (which, in turn, hold military and political forces accountable to respect such rights and liberties) that persuaded the skeptics of military power to confront and institutionalize an acceptable civil-military relationship. It seems the proponents of a national military force ably dispelled and resolved the issue about standing armies, state militias, and appropriations for them. It was a successful effort, largely because they insisted that appropriate "responsible" attention be paid to the priority of national survival (the primary purpose of the state) that requires provisions for armed forces and then, enumerated the many checks established to discipline and regulate the military element.

The purse-sword division and war-making powers are the remaining issues preceding a look at the commander in chief power. The purse and sword issue is probably the best example of how to provide for an adequate common defense through divided and shared, yet coordinated and operative civilian control. Madison's statement in *Federalist #51* that the dilemma in forming a government of men over men is that "you must first enable the government to control the governed; and, in the next place, oblige it to control itself", is reflected in the Convention's commitment to grant ample military power to the federal government as dispersed power to Congress and the President. The separation and overlapping of powers reinforces the primacy of elected civilian decision makers, yet guards against and inhibits manipulative civilian control of military power for political goals. Mason's early warning that "the purse and the sword ought never to get into the same hands", then, was taken very seriously in that Congress can determine military policy by legislating the creation, organization, equipment, maintenance, regulation, and utilization (in declaring war) of the nation's armed forces. However, it must be remembered that the scope of this authority was envisioned with a preference for federalized citizens' militias as the main defense of the state. The power of the sword essentially is a "Commander in Chief issue", but it may be presently noted that the authority and responsibility *to conduct war*, which implies to command, administer and recommend priorities, policies and strategies, was viewed primarily as an inherent executive prerogative and compatible with democratic civilian control *as long as the legislature held the purse. The power to conduct war with what military power Congress decided to provide* was the enticing and seemingly perfect mixture to sustain both liberty and security.

War-making decisions (ex "war powers") were an inevitable extension of the purse-sword dilemma: ie., whether the preparation for "raise and support" and the administration of war (commander in chief function) can be seen as distinct legislative and executive functions in terms of war-making. *In other words, who decides if the nation should, is, or will be initiating, preparing for or being swept toward a war-footing or state of war? Or does "to make war" simply connote "to wage and conduct war", which then reinforces the Executive role and virtually eliminates legislative interests, functions or prerogatives?*

Certainly, these key questions about authority and jurisdiction regarding war have continued and, indeed, have become the heart of the matter in 20th century Congressional-Executive relations when distinctions of purse and sword powers among the branches are no longer clear or applicable. The point is however, that the Revolutionary leaders were quick to distinguish and to distribute "war-making powers" after resolving peacetime security needs (the nature and scope of war, of course, was more delineated and proscribed in the 18th century). Their simple and probably rather clever solution was to delete the term "to make war" since it did imply a broad, ambiguous area of activity that, in turn, traditionally favored Executive authority, and inserted the term "to declare war" — a power to reside only in the Legislature. This enabled the Legislature to extend its "raise and support — call forth the Militia" powers in deciding whether or not a national conflict employing military forces should be commenced; and at least the President, with the exception of repelling sudden internal and external attacks, should *not* presume "to make war" without legislative consent. It was proposed at the Convention (by General Pinckney) that the Senate alone declare war; but George Mason, in particular, was adamant against the Senate's and certainly the President's privileged position to declare war — he was for "clogging war and facilitating peace".[14] Delegate Oliver Ellsworth's comment that "war should be more easy to get out of than into"[15] reflected the delegate's serious concern that *full Congressional approval* — as the people's branch of equal and proportional representation — *must precede the waging of war.* In certain respects, this becomes a corollary to Clemenceau's warning "war is much too serious a business to be left to the generals"; moreover, it is a signal to delineate and curb the Executive's residual authority in national security decision making.

What all this reveals is that the very important but unclear, unregulated subject of war-making was another political-military problem to be resolved in the tradition of separated and shared powers. War-making falls within the Legislative and Executive domain: it was crucial to distinguish, if possible, implications and applications of this term and, above all, at least to charge the "popular branch" with the responsibility to deliberate on and, perhaps as a collective action, launch the nation into war. It was natural also to empower the branch that creates and regulates military organizations to commit those forces if deemed necessary. The development of Presidential war powers since 1787, on the other hand, has illustrated the overwhelming expansion and exercise of Executive power in war-making vis-a-vis Legislative power — whether in peacetime or in wartime. It seems that whatever piece of the "sword" was intended for Congress has been replaced or appropriated by most of the later Presidents.

All of the preceding views and decisions mark the Revolutionary leaders' interest and commitment to civilian supremacy through divisive and coordinative, sometimes cooperative structuring of national political organs and national-state organs regarding national security policy. Civilianizing military institutions and functions — supplemented by centralized command and control of minimal armed forces (national or state) — was the early strategy developed in American civil-military relations.

In his book, *A Study of War*, Quincy Wright has assessed the constitutional civil-military formula by concluding that "the U.S. (as a democracy) . . . has insisted upon civilian control of the Army and Navy with *parliamentary control* of appropriations, of military organization, and of the major use of force . . ."[16] Since this view could now be rejected and changed to read "executive control of" instead of "parliamentary control of", it is now appropriate to understand the Constitutional Convention's thoughts and decisions on the President's Commander in Chief power, especially as it supports and discharges civilian supremacy in command and control responsibilities.

Most studies of the Revolutionary leaders' intentions toward Executive authority and responsibility regarding the military factor tend to support the view that the President's Commander in Chief title was natural and inevitable, was a considerably less controversial check to military power than the aforementioned legislative checks, and was in accordance with the establishment of a reasonably strong Executive.[17] Although the list of Congressional military powers and some opposition to the President's Commander in Chief power at the Convention indicated concern about Executive military powers, it is nevertheless clear that the Constitutional Framers believed the President, as the highest legitimate, single civilian authority, and foresworn to execute the "common defence", should be the ultimate commander of standing military forces. There was little dispute over the commander in chief clause largely because they were committed to organizing a surviving nation with a strong centralized Executive who would be responsible for safe-guarding national security. Furthermore, the British-European tradition had placed the commander in chief authority in the Executive (the monarch); and several colonies (New York and Massachusetts, for example) had granted this authority to the Governor where it was believed greater command and control of the military was effected than in those colonies which appointed a military commander in chief. Thereafter, Washington's successful leadership in the Revolution as the single commander in chief, and the likelihood of his nomination and election as the first President, supported the notion that a single civilian Executive — the President — could best regulate and discipline national armed forces (a federalized militia and a standing army already anticipated). The options for placing this authority elsewhere, namely in the Legislature or a military chief, would only further debilitate civilian supremacy. A collective, competitive command or a potential rival military command simply would not encourage efficient civilian control.

The Revolutionary leaders' inclinations to appoint the President as commander in chief, however, encountered some opposition that would have to be reconciled. The major objections raised at the Convention centered around anxieties that the President could exercise considerable power on the matters of war and peace, especially since he could assume *personal command* of a national army and the state militias. This could lead, in turn, to opportunities for suppressing constitutional government, particularly over citizens' rights and liberties. After several discussions held in early June 1787 about the composition and tenure of the Executive, it became clear that a single Executive with "confined and defined powers" was preferred; and, on June 15th, it was proposed that command and direction of military forces be entrusted to the federal Executive, provided that the "persons composing the federal Executive never personally command any troops or conduct any military operations".[18] William Patterson moved to amend the proposal to suggest that a *collective executive* (elected by Congress) be responsible for directing military operations and never assume personal command;[19] and even Alexander Hamilton first stated that the Executive "ought to have the direction of war when authorized or begun" and later wrote that the Commander in Chief "shall have the direction of war when commenced, but he shall not take the Actual Command in the field of an Army without the consent of the Senate and Assembly".[20] It is interesting that Hamilton's later writings in *The Federalist Papers* differed from these earlier thoughts on personal command, for in *Federalist #69* he wrote that the President would have only "occasional command" of the Militias, and that the Commander in Chief power means "nothing more than supreme command and direction of army and navy, as first General and Admiral of the Confederacy".[21] Clearly in *The Federalist* Hamilton desirous for the adoption of the Constitution, was seeking to assuage the anxieties of the anti-federalists.

The issue of personal command was raised again by George Mason during the Convention and thereafter at several state ratifying conventions; but it seems the delegates eventually acquiesced to this "unreconcilable dilemma" (Luther Martin's phrase) and, rather, became more concerned about structuring numerous checks on the availability and size of armed forces accountable to the commander in chief. What developed was a movement not only to institutionalize and clarify the legislature's sole authority to declare war and provide for necessary armed forces (militias and/or national forces), *but an attempt to define "what and when" the commander in chief can ever command.* The problem was how to acknowledge and yet "confine and define" the commander in chief's interests and duties in "war-making" (as his presumed obligation to insure national safety, enforce laws and repel sudden invasions) as they would affect the preparation, regulation, and implementation of armed forces which in turn, might jeopardize the constitutional system. In other words, the commander in chief's direction of military forces was intended and recognized as long as such command authority was proscribed to prevent the commander in chief's usurpation or abuse of executive power.

But the results of these efforts to delineate executive power are strikingly meager. They range from early deliberations and proposals that the President be "Commander in Chief of Land and Naval Forces of the Union and of the Militia of the Several States" . . . and "direct all military operations" (perhaps the President should always require additional military forces beyond the militias to enforce the laws), to Sherman's motion on August 27th that "when called into the Actual Service of the United States" be added to the proposed commander in chief clause. Also included is the Committee of Style's September 10th revision to delete Sherman's phrase, and, finally, to the Convention's restoration of Sherman's phrase on September 15th and the ultimate adoption of the final Commander in Chief clause.[22]

The deliberations imply that *at least* the Revolutionary leaders restricted the commander in chief's authority to the command of only those military organizations (militias et al) raised and supported, armed and disciplined by the Congress, and all to be committed probably solely in a major war first declared by Congress (sudden crises excepted). And, *at most*, the Constitutional Framers granted the President an additional "office, not a function" (granting authority over national security affairs) — a title so vague and unrestricted that the clause would later rank among the most important residual or inherent powers of the Presidency. To explain adequately the "meager efforts" and accomplishments of those delegates who were skeptical and fearful of the Commander in Chief power is difficult and highly speculative. Perhaps the division of power between the two branches for exercising civilian control over a military establishment was a satisfactory solution to constrain both military power and influence and excessive Presidential power. Or, as Senator Paul Douglas viewed the Constitutional Convention,

> ". . . it is clear that the Convention did not want to tie our country's hands by requiring Congressional assent for all employment of armed forces. It is obvious, instead, as Madison said, 'they wanted to leave to the President the power to use force' to repel sudden attacks even though not authorized by Congress. This, as the Founding Fathers were quick to distinguish, was not equivalent to a declaration of war."[23]

At least several points became clear about the Convention's decision making. First, most delegates obviously did not take the Commander in Chief power very seriously, considering the needs and expectations of the times. The Hamiltonian concept was heeded in that it was natural and necessary for the Chief Executive to assume the Commander in Chiefship as long as he could *not* become the sole arbiter of peace and war. In addition, the Commander in Chief clause was viewed by some delegates as more of a "function" than a separate "office" — so that the President possessed one more means to execute the laws. Certainly this attitude designated the Executive branch as the appropriate and legitimate sphere responsible for maintaining civilian control.

Secondly, the "unity of command" concept would likely insure and enhance civilian control since it obligates and empowers the executive with ample authority to execute general administration and direction of political-military affairs. Effective direction, coordination and subordination of military power would result from Presidential leadership equipped with clear constitutional authority to command. The objectives and accomplishments of a successful Presidency, of course, would depend heavily on the display of individual executive command and control abilities regarding national security forces. But residual and discretionary authority was entrusted to a single Commander in Chief who could act swiftly and decisively if unforeseen national crises developed. To what extent, then, could the Constitutional Framers responsibly "confine and define" the Commander in Chief?

Thirdly, the military forces available to the Commander in Chief were already well regulated and defined by the Legislature. Specifically, the Commander in Chief's jurisdiction over the Militia must never precede Congressional approval, and his direction of national armies and navies was restricted to command national forces already prescribed and authorized by Congress. Again, this intention to divide and share power was the civil-military formula to obstruct both military and political authoritarianism, and considerably weakened the efforts of the Commander in Chief "opponents".

It is true the Commander in Chief clause provides broad latitude for the President in defense policy making and implementation: but the civil-military powers granted to Congress also are broad and well-defined and operative unless the Legislature elects to be dormant and simply accommodates executive authority. It is mainly in the development of such a distorted executive-legislative relationship that anxieties about personal command and suppression of constitutional values and practices have any validity. In that context, remarks about executive absolutism by Patrick Henry, Richard Henry Lee, Luther Martin, Elbridge Gerry and William Miller at their respective ratifying conventions may well have been unnecessary overreactions. This does not mean that the "opponents" fears were unfounded or mistaken, but neither were they correct in opposing vesting the Commander in Chiefship in the President since, after careful deliberation, they dispersed civilian control powers throughout the political system. The observer of civil-military relations, particularly in a "liberal democracy", well knows the possible threats and philosophical incompatibility of military power to liberty. But the intention to construct a surviving nation-state with tiers of authoritative, competitive civilian control ought to calm even the most anxious critics and pessimists.

In the sense of this study, if command implies executed authoritative rulership, and control implies institutionalized regulatory checks to effect rulership, then placing the Commander in Chief authority in the Presidency was a mandatory and desirable investiture intended to maximize executive supervision of national security. The goal was operative civilian supremacy, and a new means of command and control was found in uniting the two offices of Commander in Chief and President. Walter Millis has written that "the President was made Commander in Chief of military forces and, alone, given the power to make treaties. . . . His power in military and foreign policy, in other words, was complete. This, the authors of the Constitution regarded as unavoidable."[25] The development of the Commander in Chief power and Presidential War Powers since 1787 is the next concern, yet Millis' view is pertinent because it illuminates the motivations and achievements of the Constitutional Framers to delegate and so obligate the President with authority and supreme direction over military forces. The Constitution has deliberately and succinctly emplaced the power of the sword in the Presidency, and indisputably substantiates the legitimacy and paramountcy of Presidential power in the management of civil-military relations in national policy making.

In reflecting upon the Constitutional Framers' objectives and accomplishments in structuring an acceptable and effective civil-military formula, one should be impressed with the very positive results from superimposing constitutionalism (limited government) on civil-military relations. At the least, the legal and ideological organization of political control dispersed among the elected leadership over a citizenry protected by a Bill of Rights assures legitimate foundations for maintaining civil authority at many levels of influence. Subordination of military power, then, is no longer an issue since the Constitution contains many guidelines to safeguard civilian supremacy. Extremely limited available military forces, dependent on and constrained by many tiers of political checks, hardly encourages military usurpation of civilian rule. Yet, subordination as a principle or a goal is not sufficient to sustain meaningful civilian supremacy. A government must build upon the legal-ideological provisions to administer and coordinate civil power over the military, and in a political system of fragmented power this requires the establishment of well-defined command and control machinery, ultimately responsible to executive authority — the President.

It must be made clear that coordinative civil power does not warrant *unification* of political forces or even collusive policy making. Rather, coordinative governing of the military permits the continuation of the separation and sharing of powers among the Executive and Legislative branches as sketched in the Constitution. The frequent proposals for greater coordination in political-military decision making stem from the Constitution's civil-military arrangements where the Constitutional Framers, fearful of any concentration of power, military or especially political, in fact constructed such divided and weakened civilian control provisions. Unfortunately, this dispersion of civilian control authority has also weakened civilian supremacy since the armed forces are accountable to a variety of civil-political chains of command — hence, a "unity of command" over military power may *not* function. Nonetheless, although the dispersion of power in federalism and constitutionalism permits military organizations to enjoy access to many levels of authority (often leading to self-serving exploitations of political power), it also indicates that, what Samuel Huntington terms "subjective control" over the military, is the most effective approach to civilian control in the American system. "Subjective control" means maximization of civilian control through civilianizing or politicizing the military establishment so that it becomes "the mirror of the State" — a preference to "objective control" which maximizes military professionalism and isolates the military establishment, making it "the tool of the State".[26] *To civilianize and politicize the military elements, supplemented by executive-dominated coordinative command and control, therefore, is the key to operative civilian supremacy in the US.* It is too simplistic to criticize the Revolutionary leaders' obsession with their preferred "liberal notions" of political relationships and functions. One may be assured that if divided authority impairs or is detrimental to effective civilian control, then maximized coordinated civilian power is a desirable and possible alternative strategy.

What becomes increasingly clear is that the Constitution's various clauses to guarantee the primacy of civil power provide a multi-tiered superstructure for civilian control. The President's Commander in Chief power, distinctively expansive and congruent to his other executive responsibilities and prerogatives, can motivate and assemble the formation of an integrated command and control apparatus. The Constitutional legitimacy for Presidential initiative and activity to oversee and shape civilian supremacy has always existed. On this foundation, through the Commander in Chief clause, most notably in times of crisis, executive authority has grown. Whether the Congressional checks instituted by the War Powers Resolution of 1973 and the National Emergencies Act of 1976 will survive [see Chapters Sixteen and Twenty] is an issue beyond the scope of this chapter.

# CHAPTER FIFTEEN

# The National Security Council: Organization for Policy Making

**ROBERT C. McFARLANE**
ASSISTANT TO THE PRESIDENT FOR NATIONAL SECURITY AFFAIRS

WITH

**Richard Saunders**
ASSISTANT PROFESSOR OF SOCIAL SCIENCES
UNITED STATES MILITARY ACADEMY

**Thomas C. Shull**
MILITARY ASSISTANT TO THE ASSISTANT TO THE
PRESIDENT FOR NATIONAL SECURITY AFFAIRS

A former Secretary of State was once reported to have said that one of his greatest challenges was finding ways to "establish diplomatic relations with the Department of Defense." In this way he underscored the tremendous problems of interagency communication and coordination facing national policy makers as they work towards a national security policy that is both consistent and responsive to the needs of the country and the views of the President. The requirement for institutional mechanisms to effect this coordination came to a head during World War II and led to the establishment of the National Security Council (NSC) in 1947. This began a continuing process of seeking the organizational and procedural arrangements that would best serve the leadership style of each president as well as manage the interacting interests of departments and agencies as they attempt to deal with an ever more complicated and dangerous world.

This chapter examines the process of national security policy making as it has been developed by the Reagan Administration. The NSC system that has evolved over the past four years is designed to bring together the four pillars of national security — foreign policy, defense policy, economic policy, and intelligence operations — in ways that support the President's ability to make wise and timely decisions. In developing a system that will serve his needs, President Reagan has worked to balance his fundamental commitment to cabinet government with the need for central policy guidance and control. As a result, the current NSC system is not intended to dominate the policy making process. Instead, it must perform the much more difficult task of policy facilitation and coordination, while still exercising enough power and influence to initiate and guide policy as necessary.

### The History of the NSC System

As the United States became more deeply involved in world affairs in the 20th century, it became clear to members of the Executive Branch and the Congress alike that national security issues cut across the traditional conceptual and organizational boundaries of diplomatic, military, economic, and intelligence affairs. Traditional policy making processes were clearly inadequate to meet the foreign affairs crises posed by World Wars I and II, and a series of ad hoc committees were established to place policy planning and execution on an interdepartmental basis.

By the end of World War II, there was general agreement within the government that the United States could not go back to its pre-war security policy making procedures and that some central coordinating body was needed to combine military and foreign policy considerations into a coherent policy making process. The National Security Council was established as a relatively uncontroversial part of the otherwise bitterly contested restructuring of the defense establishment at the end of the war. Congress, the armed services, and the State Department all agreed in principle that a new coordinating body was necessary. The debate that did occur centered on organizational issues, membership, and how to prevent domination of the new organization by the military.

The National Security Act of 1947 gives the following purposes to the NSC:

> The function of the Council shall be to advise the President with respect to the integration of domestic, foreign, and military policies relating to the national security so as to enable the military services and the other departments and agencies of government to cooperate more effectively in matters involving the national security.

The Council consists of the President, the Vice President, the Secretary of State, and the Secretary of Defense. The Chairman of the Joint Chiefs of Staff is the President's principal military advisor and the Director of Central Intelligence is the senior advisor on intelligence matters. Other department and agency heads attend NSC meetings as required, with the Secretary of the Treasury being consulted whenever important economic issues are addressed. The NSC is assisted by the NSC staff and the departmental staffs of the sitting members.

President Eisenhower established the post of Special Assistant to the President for National Security Affairs (later to become the Assistant to the President for National Security Affairs) to coordinate NSC operations and to supervise the NSC staff. In Eisenhower's design, the National Security Advisor (NSA) was to be a policy facilitator, not a policy maker. Subsequent occupants of this position have, of course, vastly expanded the role of the NSA and have often wielded significant power and influence.

The operating styles and personal relationships of each president since Truman have determined the organizational principles governing the NSC system as well as the nature of the system's participation in the policy process. President Truman paid little attention to the NSC until the start of the Korean War, when he began to use the Council as an important source of advice on foreign and military issues. President Eisenhower felt that the NSC system should have much more breadth, depth and policy management capability and so created an elaborate NSC staff structure. President Kennedy judged the Eisenhower system to be overly rigid and replaced it with an informal arrangement that placed greater reliance on close White House advisors. President Johnson's approach was not radically different, although he did try to deemphasize the role of the Kennedy "brain trust" and relied more on department heads. His Tuesday luncheon meetings were a mechanism for Vietnam policy making and were attended by five or six of his closest advisors, at least two of whom were also cabinet members.

President Nixon drew heavily on his experience with the Eisenhower NSC and reestablished a much more formal system. The Nixon NSC was designed to ensure that policy issues were thoroughly studied and that comprehensive alternatives were generated before an issue was brought to the White House for decision. Under this system, Henry Kissinger quickly became the administration's principal spokesman on national security issues. As the Kissinger NSC evolved, he also began to rely on a nucleus of a few key advisors within the NSC staff for policy planning. This further focused policy making in the West Wing of the White House. The Ford NSC continued many of the organizational principles of the Nixon years, although the NSA, Brent Scowcroft, consciously sought a less visible role and concentrated more on policy coordination and advising the president than did his predecessor. President Carter, at least initially, established a more open, multi-channeled advisory structure and relied on a relatively large number of assistants to the president for advice and policy coordination.

Although organizational and procedural modifications have occurred throughout the history of the NSC, the most significant single step in the system's evolution came in 1961 with President Kennedy's politicization of the NSC staff. During the Truman and Eisenhower years, the NSC staff had been a professional organization working to facilitate the decision making process. With the appointment of McGeorge Bundy as Kennedy's NSA, however, the staff became a personal staff which was to serve as an advocate for the president's foreign policy objectives.

The controversy over the proper role for the NSC system was well illustrated in the Carter Administration. President Carter's system was initially designed with multiple channels of access to the president and a relatively weak NSC. As the administration progressed, however, it became apparent that such an arrangement was too open and disjointed for effective policy making. The administration suffered from charges that its policy making apparatus was in disarray and had to face a virtually insoluble foreign crisis. In the face of these problems, the President moved to strengthen his NSC and the role of his NSA. Critics argued that his moves came too late to salvage the process. Nevertheless, they did indicate a recognition that the NSC system must possess a certain amount of centralized strength and authority if it is to have the capacity to coordinate effectively the efforts of the many powerful and contentious components of the policy making community.

## Principles of NSC Organization

Like President Carter, President Reagan rejected the idea that the NSC system should dominate the policy process. Instead, he feels that cabinet departments and agencies concerned with the four principal aspects of security policy — diplomatic, military, economic, and intelligence affairs — should play the lead role in policy development. Although an NSC-centered system can be very responsive to a president's desires, the alternative, a cabinet government, ensures that the President is not isolated from political and institutional realities. The departments are better able to broaden the spectrum of options and to integrate the concerns of diverse organizational and political constituencies than is any White House staff arrangement.

Cabinet government also allows the President to extend his control much more pervasively throughout the policy making process. An NSC-centered system pulls some decisions into the White House but destroys the credibility of departmental decision makers who must act on the majority of issues. By concentrating on coordination and policy guidance, the President of a cabinet government does not undercut the authority of key department heads, thus facilitating their ability to act in the president's name and in line with his policy directions.

President Reagan has shown continuous support for cabinet government throughout his time in office by appointing strong individuals to head the departments and by allowing them to take the lead on important issues. He has also ensured that, once his guidance is provided, the White House staff works to coordinate — not dominate — the departments' efforts. To support this approach to government, the NSC system must allow members of the cabinet to present their views and recommendations directly to the president, who is the final policy maker on national security issues, while still providing an adequate level of central policy control and guidance.

The NSA must play two distinct roles in such a system. He must be an honest broker of advice coming to the President from outside the White House, and he must be an independent advisor and policy manager for the president on national security matters. Cabinet government places special emphasis on the NSA's role as policy broker. He must be able to present the views of each department to the President so that the President appreciates the substantive nature of the debates within his administration and so that the departments will have confidence that their positions are being considered.

At the same time, the NSA must provide central direction

to the policy process. He must be an independent advisor who can present issues to the President from a perspective that transcends individual agency perspectives to encompass the policies and concerns of the administration as a whole. The NSA occasionally must be a policy initiator, placing issues on the agenda when the departments are unwilling or unable to do so. Likewise, he must have the power and influence necessary to spur the development of consensus when it does not arise out of the interagency process. Finally, the NSA must be a policy arbitrator, drawing heavily upon his personal knowledge of the President's values. The position must be strong enough to enable its occupant to make decisions involving relatively minor issues on which the departments cannot reach agreement without having to go to the president. The independent powers of the NSA must be carefully managed by the advisor himself and by the President, however, or the principles of cabinet government will be threatened.

### The NSC and Interagency Coordination: The SIG/IG Process

The NSC system includes specific organizational procedures designed to manage and coordinate the departments' participation in the national security decision making process. The National Security Council itself sits at the top of this structure as the principal forum for consideration of national security policy issues requiring presidential decision. The Council has averaged about two meetings a month since the start of the administration. These meetings are actual policy making sessions at which the President seeks out debate and differences of opinion among the Council members. His decisions are often based on these discussions and the meetings usually culminate with specific implementation directives. The meetings also serve an important consensus building function and support implementation by communicating clear presidential commitment to specified courses of action.

The NSC staff does the preparatory work to support NSC meetings. Agendas and position papers are collected and evaluated to ensure that they respond to the president's guidance. If so, they are circulated in advance. The staff then ensures that meeting minutes and decision papers are distributed to the appropriate officials.

Senior Interagency Groups (SIGs) have been established to assist the NSC and individual departments in specific policy areas. The four principal SIGs reflect the "four pillar" philosophy of national security as groups exist for foreign policy, defense policy, international economic policy, and intelligence policy. These groups work to translate policy goals into objectives, develop options, make recommendations, and consider policy implications. Each SIG is chaired by the head of the department most concerned with the group's particular area of interest. This is a change from past practices when such groups were often headed by the NSA and reflects another aspect of the administration's commitment to cabinet government. The NSA is a member of each SIG, as are representatives of other key departments and agencies.

In a few cases, groups have been created at the SIG level that are not chaired by a department head but by the NSA. These exceptions to the principles of cabinet government occur in issue areas involving particularly complex and sensitive interdepartmental relations. The first such group deals with strategic arms control. Like the SIGs, the group includes the heads of the relevant departments and focuses on the interdepartmental aspects of policy planning. It is likely that more such groups chaired by the NSA will be created as the NSC system evolves and more critical issue areas are identified that fall across the boundaries of the original SIGs.

Interagency Groups (IGs) are subordinate to the SIGs and are generally chaired by assistant secretaries. They are organized along regional and functional lines to conduct more detailed policy planning than is possible at the SIG level. Like the SIGs, the IGs are interdepartmental in their composition and have NSC staff personnel as members. Their decisions and recommendations go to the SIG for consideration and then to the NSC for final disposition by the President.

The basic design of the SIG/IG system is in line with the fundamental concepts of the cabinet system of government. Early in the administration, however, it was realized that greater central coordination was needed to ensure that the system produced coherent and consistent policies that were responsive to the needs of the president. A formal decision directive procedure was added to the SIG/IG process to facilitate the White House's ability to direct the policy making process and to tighten up management. Under this system, a SIG, individual NSC members, or the

NSA and his staff can call for a policy study on significant security issues. If the President concurs in the need for such a decision, he can issue a National Security Study Directive (NSSD) that defines the problem, states his policy goals, poses questions to be answered, and establishes the group that will develop recommendations.

The relevant SIG/IG or other group conducts policy analysis in response to the NSSD. The interagency nature of these groups and the participation of the NSC staff at each level helps ensure that a consensus is reached at as low a level as possible and that unresolved issues are forwarded for decision at a higher level. The NSC staff prepares the overview paper which covers the study before it goes to the President for decision. The actual decision is usually made at an NSC meeting where the President receives the views of his cabinet officers personally. Once the President decides the matter, he issues his judgement in the form of a National Security Decision Directive (NSDD). The NSDD then becomes the explicit statement of administration policy and is used as the basis for implementation and further policy development.

The NSA and the NSC staff, then, are participants at each level of the SIG/IG process. The staff is primarily concerned with ensuring that interdepartmental analyses are developed that support administration policy goals. Often, such analyses are a natural result of the study process, and the NSC staff is able to serve as a facilitator pushing the action through the decision making apparatus. At other times the NSA and his staff take a more aggressive stance as the interpreter of the president's philosophy to the departments. The staff can bring pressure to bear to support particular courses of action that have not originated in the departments or received their support but are favored by the President. The staff must assure that disagreements are brought to the President's attention for resolution promptly.

## The NSC and Consultations with Congress, Allies, and Friends

Although the NSC staff's primary function is to coordinate policy within the Executive Branch, it has implicit and sometimes statutory responsibilities to consult with institutions and organizations outside the Executive Branch. This consultative role has become increasingly important to effective policy development and implementation. In fact one of the key lessons of national security policy formulation learned over the past decade is that close contacts with the Congress must be established and nurtured throughout the policy process. One of the key functions of the NSC staff is to work with the White House office of congressional relations to ensure that these requirements are met. At a broader level, the staff also ensures that congressional concerns are considered in the policy development process, that the Congress is kept informed of policy decisions, and that the Congress has the information and arguments it needs to judge adequately the administration's recommendations on security issues.

Attempts to bring in outside opinion and to build support for administration positions is not limited to relations with the Congress. Public diplomacy has been recognized as a key part of national security and the NSC staff is required to consider the public diplomacy aspects of policy decisions. Also, the administration has relied upon formal bi-partisan mechanisms to generate positions on two of the most pressing and controversial issues it faced — MX basing and Latin America. The Scowcroft and Kissinger Commissions operated outside the normal NSC system but provided reports that became the basis for administration positions.

Consultations with allies and friends are also critical to effective policy development and implementation because of the extensive interdependencies that exist among the Western nations. As the NSC system approaches a decision point or takes up a major issue that could affect an ally or a friend, the NSC staff at both the working and the NSA level will ensure that appropriate consultations occur.

## NSC Staff Organization

The NSC staff itself is organized to support the NSA in both his coordinating and his advisory roles as well as to facilitate staff participation in the interagency processes. The staff contains approximately forty-five professionals who are drawn from the career service, the military, and the private sector. Most are not political appointees in the normal meaning of the term. Nevertheless, they serve at the pleasure of the President and are expected to bring a White House perspective to their policy analysis. The staff is organized along functional and regional lines similar to the State Department to help delineate staff responsibility for participation in the SIG/IG process. A great deal of emphasis has gone into ensuring that the entire staff contributes to the policy process. To avoid over-reliance on a few key staff members, as has occurred in past administrations, access to the NSA, the assignment of actions, and the flow of substantive paperwork is carefully managed to ensure that the entire resources of the staff are exploited.

A significant recent change in the staff structure was the revitalization of the position of the NSC Executive Secretary. This is the only staff position specifically authorized by the 1947 law but has been formally vacant for several administrations. The executive secretary is responsible for internal staff management and operations and for coordinating the internal flow of substantive paperwork. The executive secretary performs qualitative review of policy papers culminating in memoranda to the NSA advising him on final dispositions. Aspects of the secretary's review include checking for completeness of staff work and coordination, gauging performance of the interagency process, and judging the feasibility of policy alternatives and implementation strategies. The executive secretary is also the focal point for all external coordination with the NSC and the NSA. All interdepartmental paperwork flows through the secretary's office for accountability, management, and substantive review.

### Crisis Management

The principal difference between the crisis management system and the SIG/IG system is that the former is controlled more directly by the White House for reasons of policy responsiveness. While the SIG/IG system is able to ensure that policy proposals receive thorough study and analysis before coming to the president for decision, the system is too slow moving to be used for crisis management. Similarly, since the interagency groups are chaired by departmental officials, the SIG/IG process does not allow for the close White House guidance needed to conduct effective planning and execution under severe time pressure.

Two groups assist the NSC in crisis management. The Special Situation Group (SSG) is chaired by the Vice President and meets frequently throughout the crisis period to provide high level advice to the President on policy options and recommendations. The Crisis Pre-Planning Group (CPPG), chaired by the Deputy Assistant to the President for National Security Affairs, provides coordination and support for the SSG. It also meets throughout the crisis to conduct policy planning and to supervise implementation.

The NSC Crisis Management Center provides permanent staff support for crisis decision making. The center conducts pre-crisis collection and analysis of information about likely crisis areas in an effort to anticipate events and to provide extensive background information to decision makers as a crisis preventive. The center also provides analytical capabilities that can be drawn upon during a crisis. Finally, it represents an institutional memory for the policy makers so that past decisions and events can be more comprehensively integrated into consideration of a current crisis.

### The System in Action: International Energy Policy

The workings of the NSC system are illustrated by the analysis and decision making that established US energy policy in response to the threat to Persian Gulf oil shipments growing out of the Iran-Iraq war. The system worked to build a consensus within the government on the appropriate US policy initiatives and to support the US negotiating position with other participants in the International Energy Agency (IEA) system. As a result, the IEA adopted stockpiling policies that were very much in line with US desires and which contributed to reducing the chance that a severe oil shock could disrupt the international economy.

As Iran and Iraq began to threaten shipping in the Persian Gulf in the spring of 1984, fears grew that supply interruptions might create an oil shock similar to the one in 1979. The NSC staff responded to the President's concern on this issue and began to work on policy alternatives that combined two fundamental requirements. First, the policy had to address key Western security interests. These included preventing escalation, meeting our strategic requirements for oil, maintaining a healthy economic and political situation here and among our allies, and preserving economic recovery both in the West and in the Third World. Second, our responses had to follow the President's commitment to rely on market mechanisms wherever possible and to avoid central allocation and control of oil supplies in a crisis.

Representatives from the NSC staff, the Department of Energy, and the Central Intelligence Agency began to work together to develop positions and alternatives. The view soon emerged that absolute reliance on market mechanisms might lead oil importers to turn to the spot market early in a crisis with the result that oil prices could be driven up substantially. To avoid this, a policy was sketched out that would share the burden of any shortage through drawing down previously established national reserves and through lowering of demand. The market would continue to function, but the IEA, it was hoped, would provide a buffer in the form of brokering the adoption of consistent policies for the use of reserves and restraining demand so as to prevent excess demand from having an uncontrolled effect.

As the policy developed, the NSC system began to build consensus among key departments and agencies. Cabinet members were briefed on these proposals and their opinions and suggestions were sought and incorporated. In the meantime, the NSA's daily meetings with the President served as a forum for keeping the President informed of the developing positions and for obtaining his guidance. These efforts, along with discussion of the proposals at NSC meetings, greatly facilitated the concurrent efforts to reach agreements at the working group level. As a result, policy consensus was reached early in the analysis process and recommendations quickly reached the President. The President then signed an NSDD which became the basis for subsequent actions.

There are many benefits to such a multi-level approach to policy formulation with NSC staff participation at each step. Unnecessary interagency battles are avoided as differences are surfaced for early resolution. Similarly, the developing policy is kept closely tied to the President's guidance by almost constant communication between the departmental analysts and the NSC staff. The strong internal consensus that can result from such an approach then lets the administration take a leadership role in subsequent international negotiations. The clarity and obviously broad internal support for the US position at the

IEA meetings in June 1984 strengthened the US hand and was an important contributor to the final result.

## Conclusions

National security policy in the Reagan Administration is made through the cabinet approach to government. The President expects his cabinet members to be his principal policy advisors and fundamental policy planning is the responsibility of the department heads through the interagency mechanisms of the SIG/IG process. Nevertheless, experience has demonstrated that the NSC system must have the capacity to accomplish the critical coordination and advisory functions for which it was created almost thirty-five years ago.

The current system makes some important contributions to the effectiveness of the national security decision making process. The management and coordinating work of the NSC staff ensures that the administration's policy decisions are consistent and follow the policy guidance set forth by the President. At the same time, the important role played by the departments ensures that their invaluable ideas and perspectives receive thorough consideration, thus preventing the President from becoming isolated by the White House staff. The system also permits the effective integration of the four pillars of national security policy. The fundamental structure of the SIG/IG system gives equivalent importance to each aspect of national security, and the interdepartmental nature of each group ensures that coordination among agencies takes place from the initiation of the policy making process. The NSC staff manages this integration at all levels, and the NSC itself considers the proposals from each of the four major policy areas.

The President is the final maker of decisions on national security issues, and the NSA and the NSC staff serve as his agents to represent his interests to the departments. The present system is suited to President Reagan's leadership style and to his views on how his administration should be run. The underlying principles of coordination and thorough policy analysis, however, are applicable to any administration. The challenge is to adapt these principles to the individual desires and objectives of each chief executive.

# Reconsidering the National Emergencies Act: Its Evolution, Implementation, and Deficiencies

## HAROLD C. RELYEA*
CONGRESSIONAL RESEARCH SERVICE
LIBRARY OF CONGRESS

After three years of public hearings, debate, and thoughtful consideration by a trio of congressional committees and a panoply of Executive Branch entities, the National Emergencies Act was signed into law by President Ford on September 14, 1976. Two years later it became fully operational. In the autumn of 1979 it was implemented for the first time. The statute constitutes a first attempt by Congress to regulate the exercise of formal national emergency powers available to the President. A degree of controversy regarding the implications of this law, which was prevalent before its enactment, remains in the aftermath of its adoption and use. The Act marks a momentary point of policy agreement between Congress and the Chief Executive in a contest of basic constitutional power, establishing procedures through which statutorily specified national emergency authority shall be invoked and utilized. This assessment explores the policy background from which this statute derives and analyzes, as well, the letter of the law, its implementation, and certain national emergency matters to which it does not extend.

## The Theoretical Background

In the American governmental experience, arrogance in the exercise of power militates against self-correcting actions to curb its perpetuation. Those authoring the Constitution of the United

---

* *The views expressed in this article are solely those of the author and are not attributable to any other source.*

States recognized this potentiality and, in an attempt to prevent its occurrence, sought the establishment of a tripartite governmental arrangement. In the celebrated words of James Madison found in Federalist Paper No. 47: "The accumulation of all powers, legislative, executive, and judiciary, in the same hands, whether of one, a few, or many, and whether hereditary, self-appointed, or elective, may justly be pronounced the very definition of tyranny."

The idea of a divided governmental power arrangement did not, of course, originate with the Federal Convention of 1787. Plato had explored the concept in his *Laws* and the historian Polybius had utilized this thought to explain the supposed stability of the Roman state. During the 18th Century, the thinking of these men was revitalized at the hands of the philosophs. The benefits of balance and equilibrium suggested by them for governmental arrangements was propounded by Isaac Newton as a law of physics in the realm of nature. But it was Charles de Secondat baron de la Brede Montesquieu who, particularly in his *The Spirit of the Laws*, impressed the founders of the American Republic with his separation of powers doctrine.[1]

And while this concept seemingly has served the citizenry well, its maintenance depends upon the watchfulness of its sovereign subscribers. Indeed, Madison recognized its fragile and rationally contrived nature when, in Federalist Paper No. 48, he wrote:

> It is agreed on all sides, that the powers properly belonging to one of the departments ought not to be directly and completely administered by either of the other departments. It is equally evident, that none of them ought to possess, directly or indirectly, an overruling influence over the others, in the administration of their respective powers. It will not be denied, that power is of an encroaching nature, and that it ought to be effectually restrained from passing the limits assigned to it. After discriminating, therefore, in theory, the several classes of power, as they may in their nature be legislative, executive, or judiciary, the next and most difficult task is to provide some practical security for each, against the invasion of the others. What this security ought to be, is the great problem to be solved.

This great problem remains today. While a variety of crises have confronted the Federal Government, it has endured, but not, perhaps, without some extraction of cost. A price which is of interest here concerns the harm inflicted upon the tripartite governmental arrangement and the concomitant erosion of the rights and liberties of the American public. The concern, of course, is the exercise and effect of national emergency powers.[2]

## Emergency Power

With American armed forces in full retreat, pursued by Chinese Communist troops streaming across the Yalu River into Korea, and with the Soviet Union poised possibly to plunge the world into nuclear holocaust in the event of a formal United States declaration of war on its Asian combatants, President Truman, acting on the advice of his Treasury Secretary, issued a proclamation of national emergency shortly before Christmas, 1950.[5] The occasion marked the third instance in the Nation's history when the Chief Executive had declared a condition of general national emergency to be in existence. At the time, both of the earlier proclamations, one in 1939 and the other in 1941, were still in effect. What did they mean? In one regard, they were an attempt to mobilize public opinion and rally the populace in the face of a crisis. President Truman took the occasion to address the country and explain the grave difficulties at hand.[4]

But such proclamations also served to activate certain statutory provisions of the United States Code, increasing the powers of the Chief Executive and his officers. Presumably, such allocations of extraordinary authority are temporary in nature, lasting only until a short time after the exigency prompting their catalyzation has ceased to exist. But, while the 1939 and 1941 proclamations were terminated in 1952, the 1950 instrument remained operative for 28 years. Indeed, it persisted together with more particularistic emergency proclamations of 1933, 1970, and 1971, which, though specific with regard to policy subject matter, were no less potent in activating the whole canon of statutory emergency powers. Not only was their continued presence historically unwarranted, but they threatened the tripartite power arrangement established by the Constitution, as well, by granting the President a basis for pursuing actions which, under other circumstances or color of law, might have been more readily subject to challenge. The authors of the National Emergencies Act, unable, due to perceived constitutional problems, to rescind directly the Chief Executive's emergency proclamations, chose to blunt their effect by withdrawing the statutory powers activated by their issuance. Further, the Act established procedures whereby Congress might scrutinize, challenge, and even attempt to rescind resort to these laws in the future.

An inherent element in the American concept of self-rule is a belief in the supremacy of the law. Yet, as John Locke, himself a pre-eminent exponent of "a government of laws and not of men," argued, occasions may arise when the Executive must exert a broad discretion in meeting special exigencies or emergencies for which the legislature has provided no relief and/or existing law does not directly remedy. Professor Edward S. Corwin has noted that Locke did not limit this prerogative to war time or to matters of "urgency," but felt the exercise was justified if the "public good" was advanced.[5] It will be recalled that much the same argument was made by Theodore Roosevelt, but with a different justification. While reflecting on his activities as President, he advanced his "theory that the executive power was limited only by specific restrictions and prohibitions appearing in the Constitution or imposed by Congress under its Constitutional powers."[6]

This "stewardship" view of the presidency received expressed opposition from none other than T. R.'s Secretary of War, personal choice for, and actual successor as, Chief Executive. As articulated in his now well known Blumenthal Lectures at Columbia University in 1916, William Howard Taft argued "that the President can exercise no power which cannot be fairly and reasonably traced to some specific grant of power or justly implied and included within such express grant as proper and necessary to its exercise."[7] At a different time, on another occasion, he specifically criticized Roosevelt for actions reflective of the "stewardship" theory of presidential power.[8]

During the initial years of the Republic, a view of the presidency similar to that of Taft's seems to have been held by Thomas Jefferson. While serving in the office, he was confronted with the option to purchase the Louisiana Territory, an undertaking for which he had no specific grant of authority. To the extent that the situation required immediate response and the threat posed to American security by a neighboring imperial and aggressive titan could be eliminated, the matter might be viewed as an exercise of emergency power. In responding to the exigency, Jefferson must have taken succor from the broadest grants of Executive authority implied by the Constitution to justify his action in his own mind. Perhaps he realized then what history subsequently would bear out: that those Presidents holding the "stewardship" view of their high office would be vigorous proponents of the Lockean application of emergency powers. Only after Lincoln's tenure, when the presidential exercise of emergency powers reached a zenith, would Congress and the Judiciary seek to limit the Chief Executive's discretion to utilize such authority. The number and range of statutory emergency powers, however, continued to grow. The diversity, breadth, and easy activation of this canon of law in the 20th Century through a presidential proclamation, as well as congressional frustration over a means to control the President's use of such powers, all contributed to the development of the provisions of the National Emergencies Act.

## The Formative Period

Emergency powers actually came to be realized in American law prior to the founding of the Republic when, between 1775 and 1781, the Continental Congress adopted various ordinances and resolves which, in the view of one authority, should be regarded as being among the first such legal expressions of this type in the life of the new Nation. These instruments, of course, pertained almost exclusively to the prosecution of the war.[9]

During the course of the Constitutional Convention, emergency powers, as such, failed to attract much attention during the course of debate over the charter for the new government. Subsequently, after the Constitution had been accepted by the delegates, Alexander Hamilton addressed the issue of emergency power when, writing Federalist Paper No. 23, he said:

> The authorities essential to the care of the common defence are these: To raise armies; to build and equip fleets; to prescribe rules for the government of both; to direct their operations; to provide for their support. These powers ought to exist without limitation; because it is impossible to foresee or to define the extent and variety of national exigencies, and the correspondent extent and variety of the means which may be necessary to satisfy them. The circumstances that endanger the safety of nations are infinite; and for this reason, no constitutional shackles can wisely be imposed on the power to which the care of it is committed. This power ought to be co-extensive with all the possible combinations of such cir-

cumstances; and ought to be under the direction of the same councils, which are appointed to preside over the common defence.

This is one of those truths, which, to a correct and unprejudiced mind, carries its own evidence along with it; and may be obscured, but cannot be made plainer by argument or reasoning. It rests upon axioms, as simple as they are universal — the means ought to be proportioned to the end; the persons from whose agency the attainment of any end is expected, ought to possess the means by which it is to be attained.

Whether there ought to be a Federal Government entrusted with the care of the common defence, is a question, in the first instance, open to discussion; but the moment it is decided in the affirmative, it will follow, that, that government ought to be clothed with all the powers requisite to the complete execution of its trust. And unless it can be shown, that the circumstances which may affect the public safety, are reducible within certain determinate limits; unless the contrary of this position can be fairly and rationally disputed, it must be admitted as a necessary consequence, that there can be no limitation of that authority, which is to provide for the defence and protection of the community, in any manner essential to the formation, direction, or support of the national forces.

Consequently, among the Constitution's provisions which may be regarded fairly as directly granting emergency discretion are Article I, section 5, the House of Representative's power of impeachment; Article I, section 6, the Senate's authority to try all impeachments; Article I, section 8, Congress's discretion to declare war or call forth the militia to execute the laws, suppress insurrections, and repel invasions; Article I, section 9, Congress's power to suspend the privilege of habeas corpus only in cases of rebellion or invasion when the public safety may require it; Article I, section 10, setting certain restrictions on the States unless actually invaded or in "imminent danger"; Article II, section 3, allowing the President to call special sessions of Congress; Article III, section 3, defining treason against the United States; and Article IV, section 4, guaranteeing every State protection against invasion or domestic violence. The limited debate over emergency powers at the Constitutional Convention perhaps is indicative of the manner in which such authority would be regarded and exercised after the ratification of the Constitution: Presidents came to rely upon implied powers or the stewardship view of office in meeting crisis; justices challenged only those emergency actions presenting the gravest threat to constitutionally guaranteed liberties and democratic practice; and Congress, like the courts, sanctioned most presidential efforts at meeting an exigency, so long as the general welfare of the Nation seemed to be preserved by such endeavors.

One of the first experiences of the Federal Government with the exercise of emergency power occurred during the summer of 1792 when residents of western Pennsylvania, Virginia, and the Carolinas began forcefully opposing a national excise tax on whiskey. Anticipating rebellious reaction, Congress enacted legislation providing for the calling forth of the militia to suppress insurrections and repel invasions. Section 3 of this statute required that a presidential proclamation be issued to warn insurgents to cease their activity: if hostilities continued, the militia would be dispatched. On August 7, 1794, President Washington issued such a proclamation.[10] When its warning was ignored, he then took command of forces organized to put down the rebellion. Subsequently, after the disruptions were put to rest, he pardoned two of the leaders of the insurgents who had been tried, convicted, and sentenced to be hanged.[11]

More sweeping emergency authority was granted to the President in 1798. The Alien Act obligated the Chief Executive to issue a proclamation to the public declaring the existence of a state of war (established by congressional action) or threatened invasion (discerned by the President) and this action entitled the Executive to utilize the extraordinary powers articulated within the statute regarding the control of aliens.[12] Such broad authority, largely still available today, was virtually an open mandate for the Chief Executive, affecting all non-citizens with no distinctions as to enemies or innocents.[13]

Insurrection once again prompted an emergency action on the part of the President in 1799. Efforts at collecting revenues authorized by Federal law during the previous year were greeted in eastern Pennsylvania with organized hostilities instigated by one John Fries. Although Fries had commanded a company of militia during the so-called Whiskey Rebellion, his antics prompted the Chief Executive to issue a proclamation calling forth military force to halt the insurgency. Facing a possible war with France, President Adams, according to the proclamation, regarded the domestic disturbance against the government as occurring

. . . at a time when its sovereignty and liberties are threatened by a powerful, implacable, and insidious nation, who have been accustomed to divide and conquer other nations. It is not doubted, therefore, but that they (the troops) will exhibit a useful example upon this service of military promptitude, spirit, vigilance, discipline, and obedience of orders.[14]

Not only did the President mobilize units of the Pennsylvania militia and two volunteer companies of cavalry from Philadelphia, but he also pressed five and one half companies of the regular army into the campaign. This latter action was without congressional authorization, as a statute sanctioning the use of regular troops in situations of insurrection did not exist until 1807.[15]

Jefferson and Madison also enlarged the scope of presidential discretion with other emergency innovations. In May, 1803, President Jefferson entered into the final phase of negotiations to obtain the Louisiana Territory from the French. While the Constitution provided no explicit authority for this venture, the undertaking appears to have been regarded as something of an emergency action by the Chief Executive. As early as January, 1803, he wrote to Treasury Secretary Albert Gallatin, saying: "There is no constitutional difficulty as to the acquisition of territory, and whether, when acquired, it may be taken into the Union by the Constitution as it now stands, will become a question of expediency." Later, in his third annual message to Congress, Jefferson justified the purchase as a foreign policy accomplishment which enhanced the defense position of the nation while extending the guarantees of liberty and democratic practice to a populace previously under the control of an imperial power.[16]

Similarly, President Madison's efforts toward, and subsequent proclamation regarding, the United States' possession of West Florida could be regarded, for reasons of maintaining national defense and sovereignty, as a justified emergency action. Madison's proclamation, in part, offered this particular argument: "Whereas a crisis has at length arrived subversive of the order of things under the Spanish authorities, whereby a failure of the United States to take said territory into its possession may lead to events ultimately contravening the views of both parties, whilst in the meantime the tranquility and security of our adjoining territories are endangered and new facilities given to violations of our revenue and commercial laws of those prohibiting the introduction of slaves. . . ."[17] With such justifications was West Florida annexed and ultimately incorporated into the Mississippi Territory on May 14, 1812.[18] What was not immediately apparent was that this emergency probably occurred at Madison's instigation. It now seems likely that the President dispatched at least one, and possibly two, *agents provocateurs* to Florida to engender civil unrest among the populace and ultimately create the crisis to which Madison responded with his annexation plan.[19]

During the wars of 1812 and 1847, special emergency powers statutes were enacted, generally conveying broad discretionary authority to the Executive. These laws pertained largely to shipping, trading with the enemy, the regulation of imported goods, control of foreign vessels in American waters, and compensation for property lost and destroyed during military service.[20]

By the middle of the 19th century, the President, through statutory arrangements and historical precedent, exercised a considerable degree of discretion in emergency matters. Tempered by his view of the limitations of the office and guided by general requirements to maintain the security, tranquility, and welfare of the Nation, the President alone identified and, absent legal or resource constraints, acted upon "national emergencies." It may be argued that this exercise of power was often distinct from Commander-in-Chief obligations, far exceeded the constitutional requirement "that the laws be faithfully executed," but had not, to date, contravened expressed legal prohibitions. Because emergency actions are often theoretically self-justifying — occupying a pre-existing policy vacuum with their own precedent — there is little argument which can be offered to check their propriety. This situation is complicated further by the speed with which emergency actions occur and that they usually concern matters of the gravest peril to the Nation. And if the occasion for overturning an illegal emergency action by the Executive is available to countervailing branches of the government, will the President be reversed? On this point, emergency powers developments during the Civil War offer both enlightenment and, perhaps, for the implementation of the National Emergencies Act, an element of disconcertion and consternation.

## National Rebellion

In virtually every regard, President-elect Lincoln was unable to halt the cataclysm of a dissolving Union and open warfare among the States. By the time of his inaugural (March 4, 1861), the Confederate Provisional Government had been established (February 4, 1861), Jefferson Davis had been elected (February 9, 1861) and installed as President of the Confederacy (February 18, 1861), an army had been assembled by the secessionist States, and Federal forts and arsenals within the South had been seized, beginning with the Charleston weapons installation (December 30, 1860).

Lincoln had a little over two months to consider his course of action; his personal role was decisive in shaping the outcome of the situation. While Professor Wilfred Binkley has pondered "what Lincoln conceived to be the limits of his powers," the Great Emancipator, late in the conflict, wrote:[21]

> . . . my oath to preserve the Constitution to the best of my ability, imposed upon me the duty of preserving, by every indispensable means, that government — that nation — of which that Constitution was the organic law. Was it possible to lose the nation, and yet preserve the constitution? By general law life *and* limb must be protected; yet often a limb must be amputated to save a life; but a life is never wisely given to save a limb. I felt that measures, otherwise unconstitutional, might become lawful, by becoming indispensable to the preservation of the constitution through the preservation of the nation. Right or wrong, I assumed this ground, and now avow it. I could not feel that, to the best of my ability, I had ever tried to preserve the constitution, if, to save slavery, or any minor matter, I should permit the wreck of government, country, and Constitution all together.[22]

To paraphrase the more contemporary view of Professor Clinton Rossiter, Lincoln implied that the Federal Government had an absolute power of self-defense (*salus populi, suprema lex*), and that this authority might realize its fullest exercise at the hands of the President, even to the point of breaking the fundamental laws of the Nation if such was unavoidable.[23]

Lincoln's role derived from the popular prestige of his office and the crisis confronting the Nation. After 1862, he could not rely upon support from the Republican Party as it split into two camps, conservatives and moderates generally loyal to the President and radicals who attacked Lincoln for his authoritarian leadership and his failure to prosecute the war with greater vigor. His Cabinet was a pretense, requiring constant manipulation in order that it might remain together to convey the image of a loyal coalition.[24] He often found himself working at cross-purposes with the Legislature and, with the press of rapidly transpiring events demanding action, he supposedly observed: "I conceive I may in an emergency do things on military grounds which cannot constitutionally be done by the Congress."[25]

When Lincoln assumed the presidency and the responsibility for preserving the Union, Congress was not in session. Issuing a proclamation in mid-April, 1861, the Chief Executive declared that the execution of the Federal law was being thwarted in the seven southernmost States, compelling him, therefore, to call forth "the militia of the several States of the Union to the aggregate number of 75,000" to quell the rebellion. Simultaneously, with the same proclamation, he called for a special convening of Congress on July 4 "to consider and determine such measures as, in their wisdom, the public safety and interest may seem to demand."[26]

The President's reasons for delaying a congressional convocation on the impending crisis are not historically clear and, as various motivations for his behavior have been suggested by later scholars, numerous theories have been advanced with regard to his hesitancy. Professor Rossiter, for one, offered that Lincoln very likely thought the rebellion would be over by July 4.[27] The date also is of importance if one considers the President was to be facing a hostile and divided Congress at a time of tumult. The date of the meeting might symbolically have fostered unity. Recognizing the need for immediate action, Lincoln also may have thought congressional deliberations over the crisis a costly democratic extravagance and that, as Commander-in-Chief, he had not only the authority, but the obligation to meet the emergency quickly and decisively.

Whatever his reasons, the President not only delayed calling Congress into immediate session, but entered into its constitutionally designated policy sphere as well. On April 19, Lincoln issued a proclamation establishing a blockade on the ports of the secessionist States,[28] an action, according to Rossiter, which contravened both the Constitution and the law of nations, unless utilized by the government when engaged in a declared foreign war.[29] On this particular occasion, of course, Congress had not as yet had an opportunity to consider a declaration of war.

The next day, the President ordered nineteen vessels added to the Navy "for purposes of public defense."[30] A short time later, the blockade was extended to the ports of Virginia and North Carolina.[31]

In a proclamation of May 3, Lincoln ordered the enlargement of the regular army by 22,714 officers and men, that navy personnel be increased by 18,000 hands, and that 43,032 volunteers be accommodated for three-year terms of service.[32] Such a directive, of course antagonized Congress which, according to Article I, section 8, of the Constitution is empowered specifically "to raise and support Armies."

In his July 4 message to Congress, Lincoln suggested that, while his actions with regard to the expansion of the armed forces were legally questionable,

> . . . (t)hese measures, whether strictly legal or not, were ventured upon under what appeared to be a popular and public necessity, trusting then, as now, that Congress would readily ratify them. It is believed that nothing has been done beyond the constitutional competency of Congress.[33]

The Legislature, of course, subsequently did sanction the President's actions regarding the armed forces, noting in an act of August 6, 1861:

> That all the acts, proclamations, and orders of the President of the United States after the fourth of March, eighteen hundred and sixty-one, respecting the army and navy of the United States, and calling out or relating to the militia or volunteers from the States, are hereby approved and in all respects legalized and made valid, to the same intent and with the same effect as if they had been issued and done under the previous express authority and direction of the Congress of the United States.[34]

What choice did the Legislative Branch have in the matter? Lincoln's actions were a *fait accompli*. The President had invaded the prerogatives of Congress, yet, legislators apparently were willing to justify his actions as a unique occurrence not to be repeated ever again. Few lawmakers called for a careful examination of any proposition approving or legalizing these presidential infringements upon Congress's constitutional role.

The result was a necessary defense policy response — and jealous controversy over powers shared by the President and Congress.

The hostilities between the Union and the Confederacy opened without a declaration of war and terminated without a formal treaty of peace. Thus, when the President, as Commander-in-Chief or as Chief Executive, took action to quell the rebellion and maintain the Union, there was no determination, other than his own, that a condition of war or national emergency actually existed.[35] While Congress seems to have been willing to accept presidential transgressions involving the usurpation of its constitutional prerogatives for emergency purposes, the Judiciary argued against the necessity of a formal declaration of war to justify Lincoln's actions in meeting the crisis. In a 5-4 decision in the *Prize Cases*, the Supreme Court, in the opinion of Justice Grier, observed:

> Insurrection against a government may or may not culminate in an organized rebellion, but a civil war always begins by insurrection against the lawful authority of the Government. A civil war is never solemnly declared; it becomes such by its accidents — the number, power, and organization of the persons who originate and carry it on. When the party in rebellion occupy and hold in a hostile manner a certain portion of territory; have declared their independence; have cast off their allegiance; have organized armies; have commenced hostilities against their former sovereign, the world acknowledges them as belligerents, and the contest a *war. They* claim to be in arms to establish their liberty and independence in order to become a sovereign State, while the sovereign party treats them as insurgents and rebels who owe allegiance, and who should be punished with death for their treason. . . .
>
> As a civil war is never publicly proclaimed, *eo nomine*, against insurgents, its actual existence is a fact in our domestic history which the Court is bound to notice and to know.

With regard to the President and his authority to meet the immediate hostilities, Justice Grier opined:

> Whether the President in fulfilling his duties, as Commander in Chief, in suppressing an insurrection, has met with such armed hostile resistance, and a civil war of such alarming proportions as will compel him to accord to them the character of belligerents, is a question to be decided *by him*, and this Court must be governed by the decisions and acts of the political department of the Government to which this power was entrusted. "He must determine what

degree of force the crisis demands." The proclamation of blockade is itself official and conclusive evidence to the Court that a state of war existed which demanded and authorized a recourse to such a measure, under the circumstances peculiar to the case.[36]

Professor Rossiter, after thoughtful consideration of the President's conduct and the larger implications of the Court's decision, offered the shocked conclusion that, according to this doctrine, insurrectionary citizens may be treated, with "almost unrestrained power" by the Executive, as "enemies of the United States" who are "outside the protection of the Constitution." Such presidential authority was, in his view, "dictatorial power in the extreme."[37] Virtually unrestrained by Congress or the courts, Lincoln would apply his emergency power in a variety of policy areas.

Rising out of the question of whether Congress or the President is to determine the existence of a rebellion or similar such exigency which imperils the public safety is the matter of the legal suspension of the habeas corpus privilege. According to Article I, section 9, of the Constitution: "The privilege of the writ of *habeas corpus* shall not be suspended, unless when in cases of rebellion or invasion the public safety may require it."

On April 27, 1861, Lincoln issued a proclamation authorizing the Commanding General of the United States Army to suspend the writ of habeas corpus "at any point or in the vicinity of any military line which is now or which shall be used between the city of Philadelphia and the city of Washington."[38] Another proclamation of July 2 extended this jurisdiction to the area between New York and the capital.[39] Apparently prevailing opinion at the time was almost unanimous on the point that suspension of the habeas corpus privilege was reserved to Congress, which was not in session at the time of the Chief Executive's proclamations, and was not shared with the President.[40]

At one time it was thought that Lincoln's power to suspend the habeas corpus privilege had been tested in the case of *Ex parte Merryman*. Chief Justice Roger B. Taney, after his writ of habeas corpus for John Merryman was refused on the basis of Lincoln's order suspending the privilege, delivered an opinion holding the President's action void as the matter of suspension was a power which the Constitution assigned to Congress alone.[41] Taney's decision in this case, however, was not particularly significant in resolving the dispute over the legal suspension of habeas corpus. At the time it was issued, of course, it was ignored and Merryman remained under detention. On the larger issue, the Supreme Court has yet to provide a definite and conclusive pronouncement as to where the suspension authority rests. Taney's opinion was rendered while he was on circuit; it was not a decision of the Supreme Court. Further, it was issued from chambers and not in open court.

During the controversy over the habeas corpus suspension, Congress offered no immediate solution to the question, although the subject of the proper suspension of the privilege was debated in all three sessions of the 37th Congress. At least one scholar has suggested that this inaction served as a tacit sanction of the President's right in the matter.[42] However, by the summer of 1862, efforts were underway in the House to legislate on the issue, even if only to once again approve immediate presidential action.[43] It was not until the following year that the Habeas Corpus Act, after tedious and turbulent debate, was adopted and allowed that "during the present rebellion the President of the United States, whenever, in his judgment, the public safety may require it, is authorized to suspend the privilege of the writ of *habeas corpus* in any case throughout the United States or any part thereof."[44]

Under the provisions of the act, officers in charge of the prisons would be required to obey a judge's order for releases and those against whom no violation of Federal law was charged could not be held. Also, lists of those political prisoners arrested in the past, as well as those incarcerated in the future, were required to be kept and furnished to the courts. In general, the mandate of officers for arresting and detaining political prisoners was to come from Congress, not the President. But there is some question as to the statute's practical effect. Professor Randall, an expert on the administrative history of this law, has concluded that it was not sufficiently executed to have any really significant impact upon procedures for the arrest, confinement, and release of political prisoners.[45]

The fourth and final section of the act, according to the author of the provision, "indemnified the President, Cabinet, and all who in pursuance of their authority made arrests during the period of the suspension of the *habeas corpus* privilege by the President."[46] This clause further added to the air of confusion. Those, like the Attorney General, who argued that the Chief Executive was empowered to suspend the writ, saw no necessity for indemnification; others, viewing the statute as a temporary authorization of the suspension power, maintained the indemnity section reflected the lack of a resolve as to the Chief Executive's constitutional exercise of authority in this regard.

Turning to another area of concern, Secretary of State Seward and Secretary of War Stanton both operated somewhat unorthodox domestic intelligence and secret police services.[47] Persons suspected of disloyalty or aiding the enemy cause in any way were seized in their homes, often late at night, taken away to the nearest fort, deprived of valuables, and incarcerated with other civilians who had undergone the same experience. Such prisoners had no visitors, no counsel, no hearing, and no trial. Unsealed letters would be forwarded if they contained no objectionable material. Petitions for release filled departmental files, but failed to receive a response.[48]

Those imprisoned under these conditions received some relief in February, 1862, when the President ordered the release of most political dissidents, excepting only "persons detained as spies in the service of the insurgents, or others whose release at the present moment may be deemed incompatible with the public safety."[49] The discretion permitted by the directive was exercised by a special review panel which, for the most part, opted for releases. Secret agents of the Executive and the military continued their activities, however, and political dissent remained a punishable offense during the rebellion.

Intrigue and injustice also prevailed in government efforts at controlling the press. Journalism in the 1860s was far more sensational and blatantly political than it is in the contemporary era. Nevertheless, the guarantees of the First Amendment were no less then, whether abused or misused, than they are today. During the Civil War both military and civilian authorities within the Federal Government engaged in practices which intimidated, stifled, and suppressed the functioning of the free press. These actions included the seizure and destruction of any offensive, critical, or factually damaging issue of a newspaper; halting press operations for a short time as a punishment practice; denying the use of the mails; restricting the geographic distribution of a newspaper; and the actual arrest of editors, publishers, or other press personnel. While such practices were justified at the time as necessary emergency efforts to assure public safety and the successful prosecution of the war, there is serious doubt that they were actually warranted or legally defensible.[50]

Finally, although Lincoln generally sought authority from Congress after its convening in 1861 to meet the domestic crisis, he issued the Emancipation Proclamation on September 22, 1862, without a clear constitutional or statutory mandate. In his inaugural address of the year before, Lincoln had disclaimed any role of interference with slavery at the sub-national level. In passing the Crittenden resolution on July 22, 1861, Congress had avowed that the war was being pursued not to overthrow or interfere with matters of State jurisdiction, of which the slavery issue was considered to be a part, but "to defend and maintain the supremacy of the Constitution, and to preserve the Union with all the . . . rights of the several States unimpaired."[51] Yet, in making his emancipation declaration, Lincoln could find recent congressional sympathy for his action in section 9 of the Confiscation Act of July 7, 1862, and perhaps in section 12 of the Militia Act of the same date.[52] The Thirteenth Amendment, adopted December 18, 1865, finalized the matter by abolishing slavery within the United States "or in any place subject to their jurisdiction" and by specifying that further regulation of the issue would be left to Congress and "appropriate legislation."

Examination of the record of emergency actions taken by Lincoln has prompted the conclusion "that neither Congress nor the Supreme Court exercised any effective restraint upon the President."[53] The deeds of the Chief Executive either were unchallenged or sanctioned by Congress and either were justified or, because of no opportunity to render judgment, went without verdict by the Supreme Court. The President rapidly made unilateral responses to the emergency at hand by declaring policies which should have been legislated and pursued executing them, responses which Congress or the Court might have rejected in law but, having in fact been made, enjoyed some degree of popular support.

### The Later Years

In the years following the Civil War, until World War I, Presidents sought and were granted emergency powers through specialized statutes. Sometimes this authority was exercised after a proclamation had been issued announcing the existence of an exigency. In 1917, President Wilson promulgated the first proclamation declaring a condition of national emergency, activating certain reserved statutory powers available only after the issuance of such a formal decree. On occasion, some Chief Executives took emergency actions without clear legal authority, but such occurrences were far less frequent than they had been during the Lincoln tenure.

With the collapse of the Confederacy, President Andrew Johnson sought to effect reconstruction in the South through emergency proclamations. In the congressional view, however, the crisis justifying resort to this procedure in the immediate past had ceased to exist. A bitter disagreement between the two branches ensued with the President's approach eventually being rejected and Congress setting policy through statutes. In 1871, the Legislature demonstrated its willingness to allow the Chief Executive some emergency role with regard to reconstruction government when it passed legislation designed to control the rampages of a new conspiratorial organization known as the Ku Klux Klan. The law allowed the President, "when in his judgment the public safety shall require it," to suspend the privilege of the writ of habeas corpus for purposes of repressing unlawful combinations against the United States amounting to rebellion.[54] President Grant issued a proclamation suspending the habeas corpus privilege in nine counties of South Carolina. His announcement specifically cited the 1871 statute as the authority for his action.[55]

Other presidential emergency actions prior to World War I involved the use of the military to exercise Federal police power in acute labor disputes threatening the public welfare. Strikes in the railroad industry were widespread shortly after President Hayes assumed office. Because State authorities could not halt the impulsive and frequent outbursts of violence, various governors prevailed upon the White House for assistance. After deliberating with his Cabinet, the Chief Executive decided to declare martial law in the areas of severest turmoil and to dispatch Federal troops.[56] In fact, military personnel were sent only after a formal request had been received from a State and were used to protect Federal property and to enforce the decisions and orders of United States courts.[57]

In 1893, when Jacob Coxey organized a march of the unemployed to Washington, some contingents located in the far West seized trains to make the long journey. Because many of the western railroads were operated by receivers appointed by the Federal courts, United States marshals were ordered to protect their property. Deputy marshals were required in fourteen States and two territories. Some supplemental military personnel were pressed into service, but the disturbances soon ended when the leaders of the march were arrested in Washington.[58]

While the Coxeyite effort constituted more of a nuisance than an actual threat to the public safety, it prompted emergency policy procedures which were utilized again the following year in the Pullman strike. The dispute in this situation concerned wages. The Pullman Palace Car Company reduced workers pay by twenty-five percent while the salaries of managers remained untouched and dividends actually had been increased. In May, when an employees committee formally requested the restoration of the old wage standard, the company flatly refused the request even though its practice of taking contracts at a price less than the cost of labor and materials had prompted the cut. The following day, three members of the committee were laid off and, after a majority of the organized union membership voted that evening to strike, the entire workforce was laid off and the plant was closed. In reaction to this situation, a general railroad strike occurred. Because this development interfered with the transmittal of the mail, Federal attorneys, in conjunction with railroad lawyers, sought an injunction against the unions. Attorney General Richard Olney supported this strategy in order that the President might use the army to execute the orders of the U. S. courts. Ultimately, the Chief Executive did dispatch troops to break the strike.[59] In sustaining the conviction of labor leader Eugene V. Debs, the Supreme Court supported the President's intervention, saying:

> The entire strength of the Nation may be used to enforce in any part of the land the full and free exercise of national powers and the security of all rights entrusted by the Constitution to its care. The strong arm of the national government may be put forth to brush away all obstructions to the freedom of interstate commerce or the transportation of the mails. If the emergency arises, the army of the Nation, and all its militia, are at the service of the Nation to compel obedience to its laws.[60]

Coincidental with the Pullman strike were disputes between mine operators and laborers in the Coeur d'Alene region of Idaho. Federal troops were dispatched to assist State forces in quelling disturbances in 1892 and 1894.[61] A major outbreak of violence occurred in 1899, prompting the President to order over 500 soldiers into the area which was placed under martial law by the army field commander and the governor. These actions brought President McKinley sharp criticism from Congress.[62] Perhaps as a consequence of this rebuke, President Roosevelt declined three requests from the governor to bring order to a strike situation in Telluride, Colorado, in 1903. When Federal troops were dispatched to Goldfield, Nevada, in 1907, their role was extremely limited and as soon as state forces were authorized for service in the dispute area, the regular army was withdrawn.[63]

Roosevelt, however, had intervened decisively in the anthracite coal strike of 1902. In the spring of the year, a universal strike was effected by the miners in the anthracite coal regions of Pennsylvania. It was marked by increasing violence as the summer months gave away to autumn. State forces appeared to be inadequate for restoring order and the governor declined to appeal for Federal assistance. Concern over the effects of the strike mounted in the nation as the winter months approached. Uncertain of what action he might take on the matter, President Roosevelt first urged the disputants to reconcile their differences by themselves; next, he attempted formal mediation; then, he dispatched an investigating commission. Behind the efforts of the commission, however, was one of T. R.'s "big sticks." He threatened to send the army into the area to act as receivers of the mines, to put down all violence, and, if necessary, to operate the facilities. If the operators sought to enjoin this action, the commanding general was to ignore such a court order and to send the writ on to the President and await instructions. Made aware of this threat, the disputants settled their differences through the President's investigating commission.[64] Certainly Roosevelt's proposed ultimate action was extraordinary. Reviewing this incident a few years later, T. R.'s successor in the White House, William Howard Taft, characterized the scheme as "lawless." The proposal, in Taft's view, was an extreme response to an exigency, a plan which the President never should have entertained had he "listened to those about him, who were better advised as to the constitutional limitations imposed by his oath of office."[65]

Taft's arguments against the "stewardship" view of the presidency did not always impress his successors to the Oval Office. President Wilson exercised dictatorial powers in dealing with the emergency conditions of World War I. Professor Rossiter has observed that the "preponderance of his crisis authority was delegated to him by statutes of Congress."[66] The Chief Executive, however, also engaged in certain actions which involved questionable authority. For example, he armed American merchantmen in February, 1917; he created a propaganda and censorship entity — the Committee on Public Information — which had no statutory authority for its limitations upon the exercise of First Amendment rights; and he established various emergency agencies under the broad authority of the Council of National Defense to do his bidding.[67]

When Franklin Roosevelt assumed the presidency, he told the Nation and other branches of the Federal Government his view of crisis leadership in his inaugural address, saying:

> It is hoped that the normal balance of Executive and legislative authority may be wholly adequate to meet the unprecedented task before us. But it may be that an unprecedented demand and need for undelayed action may call for temporary departure from that normal balance of public procedure.
>
> I am prepared under my constitutional duty to recommend the measures that a stricken Nation in the midst of a stricken world may require. These measures, or such other measures as the Congress may build out of its experience and wisdom, I shall seek, within my constitutional authority, to bring to speedy adoption.
>
> But in the event that the Congress shall fail to take one of these two courses, and in the event that the national emergency is still critical, I shall not evade the clear course of duty that will then confront me. I shall ask the Congress for the one remaining instrument to meet the crisis — broad Executive power to wage a war against the emergency, as great as the power that would be given to me if we were in fact invaded by a foreign foe.[68]

The day after the inauguration, President Roosevelt called a special session of Congress.[69] The purpose of the gathering was not specifically stated in the President's proclamation, but it appears that the objective was to obtain legislation supporting the "bank holiday" declared by the Chief Executive and then to continue the meeting for as long as it suited the mutual purposes of the two branches. In fact, it was the beginning of the famous "Hundred Days" when the New Deal was launched. The measures enacted during the special session constituted emergency policy. While the President had hinted he might take action to meet the exigencies of the moment on his own authority, Congress demonstrated a willingness to support his innovations or, at his request, statutorily grant him the emergency powers he sought.

In the period between the outbreak of war in Europe in 1939 and American involvement in world hostilities in 1941, President Roosevelt took certain emergency actions on his own authority which were consistent with a "stewardship" view of his office. For example, he transferred fifty retired U. S. destroyers to Great Britain in exchange for American defense bases in British territories located in the Caribbean; he negotiated a series of defense agreements whereby U. S. soldiers were stationed in foreign territory or utilized to replace the troops of nations at war in non-belligerent tasks, allowing these countries to commit their own military personnel to combat; he negotiated an agreement with Denmark to the effect that Greenland would be defended by American armed forces; and he unilaterally entered into the Atlantic Charter. By contrast, existing or newly enacted statutes allowed him to regulate foreign assets — those of the Axis powers as well as those of nations occupied by them — in the United States and to enter into the transmittal of war material to countries whose defense he deemed vital to the protection of the United States.[70]

After Congress formally declared American entry into World War II, the President exercised emergency powers tracing their origin to some statutory endowment. The broadest grants of authority came in the First War Powers Act of December 18, 1941, the Second War Powers Act of March 27, 1942, and the Emergency Price Control Act of January 30, 1942.[71] Even the President's most controversial war time action, the internment of Japanese-Americans, which initially was effected by an ex-

ecutive order based upon implied constitutional authority, received congressional support through a statute confirming the
directive.[72]

### Reserved National Emergency Authority

Until the period of the Civil War, Congress had extended few
grants of emergency authority to the President through statutory pronouncements. In responding to the crisis that greeted
him, Lincoln justified his actions in terms of "a popular and
a public necessity, trusting . . . that Congress would readily
ratify them." In the face of world wars and devastating economic
catastrophe, Congress has demonstrated a willingness to delegate emergency powers to the Chief Executive in a variety of
policy areas. In addition to these statutory allocations of authority, some Presidents, consistent with the "stewardship" view
of the office, have relied upon implied constitutional powers to
pursue some emergency action.

Underlying this historical pattern in the evolution of presidential emergency authority is the development of reserved national emergency powers. In this arrangement, Congress granted
certain powers to the Chief Executive which were to be used
only when a major exigency threatened the Nation. The statutes allocating such powers not only contained language
qualifying their use "during a condition of national emergency,"
but seemingly required that the President proclaim the existence
of such an emergency to activate these otherwise dormant provisions. While it is not certain as to when this practice began,
it is evident that such authority was available in 1917 when President Wilson issued the first such activating proclamation of national emergency. Subsequent history, according to a Senate
committee study of the matter,

> . . . reveals a consistent pattern of lawmaking. It is a pattern showing
> that the Congress, through its own actions, transferred awesome
> magnitudes of power to the executive ostensibly to meet the prob-
> lems of governing effectively in times of great crisis. Since 1933,
> Congress has passed or recodified over 470 significant statutes
> delegating to the President powers that had been the prerogative
> and responsibility of the Congress since the beginning of the
> Republic. No charge can be sustained that the Executive branch
> has usurped powers belonging to the Legislative branch; on the

contrary, the transfer of power has been in accord with due process of normal legislative procedures.[73]

The first national emergency proclamation, explicitly issued as such, was made by President Wilson on February 5, 1917.[74] Declared by virtue of the authority conferred upon the Chief Executive by legislation establishing the United States Shipping Board, the proclamation was concerned with matters of water transportation policy.[75] Its effect was terminated, along with a variety of other war time measures, by statute on March 3, 1921.[76]

The next national emergency proclamation was promulgated by President Roosevelt on March 6, 1933, some 48 hours after assuming office.[77] Issued upon the somewhat questionable authority of the Trading With the Enemy Act of 1917, the proclamation declared a "bank holiday" and halted all financial transactions by closing the banks.[78] The Chief Executive's action and proclamation were sanctioned by Congress with the passage of the Emergency Banking Act on March 9.[79] The day this legislation was signed into law, the President issued a second banking proclamation, based upon the authority of the new law, continuing the bank holiday until the various banking institutions established that they were capable of conducting business in accordance with new banking policy.[80]

In fact, the powers possessed by the President as a consequence of this emergency proclamation continued in force until their termination by the National Emergencies Act some four decades later.

On February 28, 1935, President Roosevelt promulgated a proclamation which, while not directly announcing a condition of national emergency, recognized the continuation of an existing national emergency in the agricultural industry.[81] Accordingly, the proclamation established the effective dates of the Cotton Control Act approved April 21, 1934.[82] It was repealed on February 10, 1936.[83]

On September 8, 1939, President Roosevelt issued a proclamation of "limited" national emergency, though the law gave no recognition to the qualifying term.[84] Two years later, on May 27, 1941, the Chief Executive issued a proclamation of "unlimited" national emergency.[85] This action did not add significant new powers to the list of emergency authorities made available to the President by the 1939 proclamation.[86] Instead, the action was a political gesture prompted by the conflict in Europe and by growing tensions in Asia.[87]

These two war-related proclamations of a general condition of national emergency remained in effect until 1947 when certain specific emergency and war statute provisions were terminated by a law approved on July 25 that year.[88] Earlier, on September 29, 1945, President Truman had withdrawn, by proclamation, certain emergency provisions of the Internal Revenue Code as the end of hostilities in both theaters of war made their use no longer warranted.[89]

On October 19, 1951, Congress terminated the declaration of war against Germany.[90] On March 20, 1952, the Senate ratified the treaty of peace with Japan. Because these actions legally established the end of World War II, congressional intervention was required to continue certain emergency provisions of law desired for the post-war conversion effort. By joint resolution, Congress enacted the Emergency Powers Interim Continuation Act to maintain such emergency authority.[91] This law was renewed three times[92] before the successor Emergency Powers Continuation Act was prepared and adopted.[93] This latter statute was continued until August, 1953, when its emergency authorities finally were allowed to elapse.[94] On April 28, 1952, President Truman terminated by proclamation the 1939 and 1941 national emergency declarations, leaving operative only those selective authorities statutorily continued by the special laws cited here.[95]

Truman's 1952 termination action specifically exempted a proclamation of national emergency he had issued on December 16, 1950.[96] This new declaration, promulgated to provide the Chief Executive with additional powers to respond to hostilities in Korea, remained operative until two years after the enactment of the National Emergencies Act.[97] This statute also provided for the effective termination of two emergency proclamations issued by President Nixon, one declared in 1970 in response to a postal service strike[98] and the other made the following year in regard to a national emergency concerning balance of payments in overseas trade.[99]

### Congressional Concerns

As the years passed, concern grew in Congress over the fact

that President Truman's 1950 proclamation of national emergency continued to exist long after the conditions prompting its issuance had disappeared. Some felt that the President was retaining extraordinary powers intended only for time of genuine emergency and that the Chief Executive was thwarting the legislative intent of Congress by his failure to terminate the declared national emergency. Ironically, other proclamations of emergency were not apparent until studies disclosed their existence in 1973. At the same time, concern over the President's exercise of war powers was growing as the United States became deeply embroiled in hostilities in Vietnam. These anxieties subsequently were responsible, at least in part, for the development of the War Powers Resolution enacted in 1973.[100]

To pursue the matter of presidential retention and exercise of national emergency powers, the Senate created a special study panel in 1972. Initially called the Special Committee on the Termination of the National Emergency, the body was renamed the special Committee on National Emergencies and Delegated Emergency Powers in 1974, reflecting the broader mission and subject matter of the panel.[101] Co-chaired by Senator Frank Church (D.-Idaho) and Senator Charles Mathias (R.-Md.), the committee was unique in its bi-partisan leadership and equally balanced party membership.[102] In addition to holding public hearings,[103] the group produced a compilation of emergency statutes,[104] a collection of related executive orders and presidential proclamations,[105] a history of the development of emergency powers in the United States,[106] an interim report on recommended legislation,[107] a compendium of Executive Branch reactions to this proposal,[108] and a comprehensive final report.[109]

The Special Committee's proposed legislation was introduced in the Senate as S. 3957 on August 22, 1974, by Senator Church for himself, seven other members of the panel, and other co-sponsors.[110] Referred to the Committee on Government Operations, the measure was reported on September 30 without public hearings or amendments.[111] The bill was debated on October 7, at which time Senator Mathias offered certain amendments suggested in behalf of the President by the Office of Management and Budget which were accepted and adopted.[112] Summarizing the proposed amendments, Senator Mathias said:

What they do is very simple. They extend the grace period (regarding the repeal of certain emergency power provisions of the U. S. Code) provided in the bill from nine months to a year.

They provide that while Congress can terminate a national emergency at any time by a concurrent resolution, there will be no automatic termination after six months if there is no affirmative action. This has been replaced by a requirement for the Congress to meet every six months to consider whether to terminate an emergency. An expedited privileged procedure would assure consideration and a vote should the Congress so decide.

We have reduced the list of statutes to be repealed. In working with the other body, partially as a result of special committee studies, most of the provisions that have been deleted from our original list are to be taken care of in various deadwood projects by the Codification Committee of the House of Representatives.

There are six statutes which are to be exempted from the provisions of this act. These statutes include Trading With the Enemy Act, a Ready Reserve provision, purchasing contract lease and claims authorities believed by the Executive branch to be absolutely essential for the operation of government. There is a requirement that the committees with jurisdiction over these provisions must make a study and report recommendations within nine months about modifications or other changes to be made.

Finally, the requirement for accounting of expenditures incurred under the authority of emergency powers statutes . . . had been included.[113]

Although a version of the Special Committee's recommended legislation was introduced in the House as H.R. 16668 on September 16, the Committee on the Judiciary, to which the measure was referred, did not have an opportunity to consider either that bill or the Senate-adopted proposal due to the press of other business, chiefly the impeachment of President Nixon and the nomination of Nelson A. Rockefeller to be Vice President of the United States.[114] The National Emergencies Act thus failed to obtain passage in both Houses of Congress before the expiration of the 93rd Congress.

With the convening of the next Congress, the proposal was again introduced in both chambers. The House took the lead with H.R. 3884 being offered on February 27, 1975; the identical bill was introduced in the Senate as S. 977 on March 6.[115]

Hearings were held in the House before the Subcommittee on Administrative Law and Government Relations beginning on March 6.[116] After receiving testimony from various witnesses and marking up the measure, the Subcommittee reported, by a 4-0 vote, an amended version of the bill to the full Committee on the Judiciary. Major changes in the proposal included the addition of further emergency power provisions of the U.S. Code to the exemption from termination section of the legislation and an extension of the one-year grace period on terminated provisions to two years. On May 21, the full Committee, by voice vote, reported the bill with technical amendments.[117]

During the course of debate on the proposal on September 4, the House agreed to the Committee amendments, adopted an amendment providing that national emergencies end automatically one year after the declaration date unless the President transmits a message to Congress and publishes notice in the *Federal Register* that the emergency is still in effect, and accepted the bill on a 388-5 yea-and-nay vote.[118] The measure was then sent to the Senate where it was referred to the Committee on Government Operations.[119]

At this point, the Senate Special Committee on National Emergencies and Delegated Emergency Powers, on May 28, 1976, issued its final report.[120] After summarizing its activities and efforts, the panel urged immediate passage of the National Emergencies Act, close congressional committee scrutiny of the statutes exempted from the rescinding provisions of the Act, careful congressional review of future requests for permanent statutory emergency authority, vigilance in detecting potential efforts to bypass or circumvent the intent of the Act, congressional inquiry into emergency preparedness efforts conducted by the Executive Branch, congressional preparation for dealing with a declared emergency (including continuous review of the canon of emergency law), striving to halt open-ended grants of authority to the Chief Executive, more vigorous investigation and oversight of delegated powers, and improvement of accountability procedures with regard to Executive Branch decision-making.[121] The Special Committee's mandate and operational authority terminated on April 30.

The Senate Committee on Government Operations held hearings on[122] and subsequently reported the National Emergencies Act on August 26 with one substantive and several technical amendments.[123] According to the panel's report:

> With respect to the substantive amendment, following consulta-

tions with several constitutional law experts, the committee concluded that section 201(a) is overly broad, and might be construed to delegate additional authority to the President with respect to declarations of national emergency. In the judgment of the committee, the language of this provision was unclear and ambiguous and might have been construed to confer upon the President statutory authority to declare national emergencies, other than that which he now has through various statutory delegations.

The Committee amendment clarifies and narrows this language. The Committee decided that the definition of when a President is authorized to declare a national emergency should be left to the various statutes which give him extraordinary powers. The National Emergencies Act is not intended to enlarge or add to Executive powers. Rather the statute is an effort by the Congress to establish clear procedures and safeguards upon him by other statutes.

Therefore, the Committee amendment makes no attempt to define when a declaration of national emergency is proper. The amendment simply requires the President to transmit to the Congress and publish in the Federal Register a Presidential declaration of national emergency authorized by other Acts of Congress.[124]

The following day, the Senate adopted the bill with all committee amendments and returned the measure to the House.[125] On August 31, the House agreed to the Senate amendments, clearing the proposal for the President's signature.[126]

President Ford, after expressing reservations regarding the legislative veto contained in the legislation, signed the bill into law on September 14, 1976.[127]

### Controls Established

As enacted, the National Emergencies Act consists of five titles.[128] The first of these effectively terminated, as of September 14, 1978, declared emergencies in effect at the time the Act was signed into law. In fact, the statute did not cancel the 1933, 1950, 1970, and 1971 outstanding proclamations of national emergency, but terminated "(a)ll powers and authorities possessed by the President, any other executive officer or employee of the Federal Government, or any executive agency . . . as a result of the existence of any declaration of national emergency in effect on the date of enactment of this (National Emergencies) Act. . . ." Because the proclamations themselves seemingly were issued pursuant to Article II of the Constitution, they may be cancelled by the President alone, not by statute. Thus, any executive order or presidential directive promulgated pursuant to any of these proclamations remains outstanding.[129] Most of these secondary instruments, however, would appear to have any meaningful effect only as a consequence of statutory emergency powers which have now been returned to dormancy. Nevertheless, no administration has pursued either their removal or the rescinding of any of the outstanding proclamations which no longer have utility.[130]

In fact, Title I encourages the eradication of such deadwood instruments with a savings provision that exempts from the effects of termination "(1) any action taken or proceeding pending not finally concluded or determined on such (termination) date; (2) any action or proceeding based on any act committed prior to such (termination) date; or (3) any rights or duties that matured or penalties that were incurred prior to such (termination) date."

Title II pertains to declarations of future national emergencies. While the Act does not explicitly define a "national emergency," it grants the President power to declare a national emergency only in terms of statutory provisions authorizing the use of extraordinary or special powers during such a condition. The intent of this limitation, in the words of the Senate report on the Act, is *not* "to confer upon the President statutory authority to declare national emergencies, other than that which he now has through various statutory delegations." In other words, the National Emergencies Act "is not intended to enlarge or add to Executive powers."[131] In addition, the title specifies that statutory provisions granting extraordinary powers during a declared national emergency shall be effective only when the President proclaims such a condition and immediately transmits his proclamation to Congress and publishes same in the *Federal Register*.

Title II further provides that "(a)ny provisions of law conferring powers and authorities to be exercised during a national emergency shall be effective and remain in effect (1) only when the President . . . specifically declares a national emergency, and (2) only in accordance with this Act." Two methods are then provided for terminating "(a)ny national emergency declared by the President in accordance with this title"; a concurrent resolution adopted by Congress or a presidential proclamation. Either of these instruments shall specify a date of termination and if both types of instrument should issue, then the earlier date of one or the other shall prevail. Again, a savings provision allows for the conclusion of outstanding business or obligations incurred as a direct result of the terminated national emergency. A national emergency automatically ends on the anniversary date of its proclamation unless the President, within ninety days prior to the anniversary date, publishes a notice in the *Federal Register* to the effect that the declared emergency is to remain in effect beyond the anniversary mark.

Finally, Title II establishes certain obligations and procedures for Congress regarding declared national emergencies. Congress must meet within six months after the declaration of a national emergency, and at six-month intervals thereafter, for purposes of considering the continued need for the application of extraordinary powers. Special procedures are provided for acting on a concurrent resolution terminating the effect of a proclamation of national emergency. Allowances also are made for either House of Congress to modify specified deadlines for acting on a pending concurrent resolution or alter its procedures regarding same.

Title III prohibits the President from exercising any statutory emergency powers unless and until he specifies, "either in the declaration of a national emergency, or by one or more contemporaneous or subsequent Executive orders published in the Federal Register and transmitted to the Congress," the "provisions of law under which he proposes that he, or other officers will act."

Title IV specifies accountability and reporting requirements of the President. Here the President is made responsible, whenever he declares a national emergency *or* Congress declares war, "for maintaining a file and index of all significant orders of the President, including Executive orders and proclamations, and each Executive agency shall maintain a file and index of all rules and regulations, issued during such emergency or war issued pursuant to such declarations." These same instruments are to be "transmitted to the Congress promptly under means to assure confidentiality where appropriate." And, "the President shall transmit to Congress, within ninety days after the end of each six-month period after such declaration, a report on the total expenditures incurred by the United States Government during such six-month period which are directly attributable to the exercise of powers and authorities conferred by such declaration." A final report is required of the President within ninety days after the termination of such declarations.

Title V repealed or amended certain specific statutory provisions of emergency law and exempted others from the effects of the National Emergencies Act until appropriate committees of the House and the Senate had examined them with a view to necessary revisions. Only two committees published findings or recommendations resulting from this review requirement.[132]

During the course of the adoption of the National Emergencies Act, three other significant emergency powers developments occurred. Although efforts were made to continue the authority, a title of the Federal Civil Defense Act of 1950, granting the President or Congress power to declare a "civil defense emergency" whenever an attack on the United States occurred or was anticipated,[133] expired on June 30, 1974, after the House Committee on Rules failed to report on the measure extending the statute.[134] Thus, a means of declaring an emergency was terminated and statutes activated pursuant to this provision were relegated to permanent dormancy.

By proclamation of February 19, 1976, President Ford gave notice that E.O. 9066, providing for the internment of Japanese-Americans during World War II, was cancelled as of the issuance of the proclamation[135] formally establishing the cessation of the hostilities on December 31, 1946.[136] Certain statutory authority relevant to this executive order was repealed by the National Emergencies Act.[137]

Also, legislation was adopted on May 14, 1976, granting the President the authority to order certain selected members of an armed forces Reserve component to active duty other than during a state of war or a condition of national emergency. Previously, this authority[138] had been limited to a "time of national emergency declared by the President" or "when otherwise authorized by law."[139]

After the National Emergencies Act was enacted, Congress completed action on legislation regulating the international economic powers of the President during a declared war or proclaimed national emergency.[140] This measure, signed into law on December 28, 1977, basically did three things.[141] It amended the Trading With the Enemy Act of 1917, an old emergency statute, to limit the use of its international economic authority by the President to times of declared war only. It then granted the Chief Executive new powers, subject to the procedures of the National Emergencies Act, to regulate certain categories of international economic transactions during future national emergencies. This new authority, contained in a title called the International Emergency Economic Powers Act, would be activated by a proclamation of national emergency and subject, as well, to use in accordance with prescribed procedures set forth in the Act. Third, it amended the Export Administration Act of 1969 to confer non-emergency authority to the President to control non-U.S.-origin exports by foreign subsidiaries of United States corporations and business concerns.

## Policy Evolution

When the Senate Special Committee began its work early in 1973, the immediate task was "to conduct a study and investigation with respect to the matter of terminating the national emergency proclaimed by the President of the United States on December 16, 1950."[142] Three other outstanding proclamations of national emergency eventually were included in this mandate, but the mission remained one of cancelling a presidentially created condition of national emergency. Past precedent evidenced two options to this end. In 1921, Congress had nullified the effect of President Wilson's national emergency proclamation of 1917 by withdrawing the statutory powers it had activated.[143] In 1952, President Truman issued a proclamation terminating the 1939 and 1941 national emergencies declared by President Roosevelt.[144] But the Special Committee, in considering these or other possibilities to halt the continued availability of national emergency authority, was also to "consider the problems which may arise as the result of terminating such national emergency; and consider what administrative or legislative actions might be necessary or desirable as the result of terminating such national emergency, including consideration of the desirability and consequences of terminating special legislative powers that were conferred on the President and other officers, boards, and commissions as the result of the President proclaiming a national emergency." In the view of Committee Co-chairman Church, the mission of the panel was not merely one of discontinuing the legal effects of some presidential proclamations.

It is with the recognition that the Executive Branch must have the authority and flexibility to deal with emergencies, that the Special Committee was created. For it is not enough to state, as we believe correctly, that the Great Depression is over and that the state of economic emergency declared in 1933 should be repealed. It is not enough to state that the Korean hostilities are over and that the state of national emergency proclaimed by President Truman on December 16, 1950, is no longer valid. It is not enough to terminate any given declaration of national emergency because, if past precedents are continued, the President can, at any time he sees fit, declare a new state of national emergency.[145]

By the time of its first formal meeting in March of 1973, the Special Committee had a preliminary formula for regulating the exercise of national emergency powers.[146] It had begun to focus, as well, upon five central considerations. The first of these concerned the scope of presidential emergency powers, reflected in the following comments by the panel's staff director and cochairmen:

*William G. Miller*: The main dilemma is how to provide for emergency action within the framework of the Constitution. It is clear that Congress itself since 1933, through its own delegation, has yielded up not only its own power but it has, in many cases, made it possible to abridge the individual rights of citizens. One of the issues is how it is possible to provide for these situations and still maintain a constitutional framework.[147]

*Senator Church*: The mandate for the committee would be to define procedures for terminating the present national emergency and restoring normalcy to the Government by eliminating most of the emergency powers that these various statutes confer. We would not try to go beyond that to define whatever further inherent power the President may have under the Constitution itself.[148]

*Senator Mathias*: It seems to me the fact that Presidents, by and large — and we have to rely on staff to give us the historical background — must have come to Congress and asked them for these 300 odd powers. This certainly creates a presumption that the Presidents, themselves, did not feel that they had inherent constitutional authority to perform these 300 acts. There may be other Acts beyond these that they can perform, on the Canadian border or elsewhere, but not these Acts, and I think that is important.[149]

As reflected in the Special Committee's preliminary formula

and executive session deliberations, there was a desire to determine the nature of or to define a "national emergency."[150]

There was, as well, a concern with procedural safeguards as a means of controlling the invocation and exercise of statutory national emergency powers.[151]

In establishing a process for the declaration of national emergencies in the future, there was interest in how to "cut Congress in for a part of the action."[152]

Finally, there was a desire for improved accounting and reporting procedures relative to the exercise of national emergency powers. Executive orders and presidential directives implementing this authority should be accounted for with great care and immediately made known to Congress upon issuance.[153]

During the course of its hearings, the Special Committee received the support of constitutional law and other legal experts for its proposal that a presidential proclamation of national emergency receive congressional approval before becoming effective,[154] the exercise of vigorous congressional oversight in the emergency powers policy field,[155] the idea of emergency authority being delegated for specific purposes,[156] and the notion that such delegations should be made for specific periods of time.[157]

After its hearings were concluded, the Special Committee issued an interim report on August 22, 1974, containing recommended legislation which eventually became the National Emergencies Act. Unfortunately, by the time the panel issued its final report on May 28, 1976, major attention was focused upon the final adoption of the National Emergencies Act, which was then being expedited in the House.[158] Little attention was given to the Special Committee's final report and the panel ceased operations before the Senate considered its proposal. Had it remained in operation a little longer, it might have prompted a better statute and a more thorough treatment of national emergency powers concerns.

## Policy Problems

While the public record acknowledges and the legislative history demonstrates close cooperation between Congress and the Executive regarding the development of the National Emergencies Act, it must be borne in mind that the issues surrounding the formulation of this statute concerned such fundamental matters as the independence and integrity of each branch of government in the exercise of its duties and responsibilities, the proper exercise of extraordinary powers within the existing constitutional setting, and congressional control over delegated authorities. The legislation was developed during a time (1973–1976) when the President's continued commitment to American involvement in the Vietnam conflict was in serious question with the public and under mounting congressional challenge; indictments of the "imperial presidency" were appearing; revelations about the Watergate incident and surrounding unusual presidential exercises of power resulted in a Chief Executive's resignation and the discrediting of his administration; and excesses by the Federal intelligence community and law enforcement agencies were just coming to congressional and popular attention. Thus, as was noted earlier, the National Emergencies Act marks a momentary point of policy agreement between Congress and the President in a contest of basic constitutional power, establishing procedures through which statutorily specified national emergency authority shall be invoked and utilized.

In spite of its name, the National Emergencies Act contains no explicit definition of what it attempts to regulate — presidentially declared "national emergencies." Instead, the Act permits the Chief Executive to proclaim a "national emergency" whenever he perceives conditions warranting such an action are in existence. Congress may check this deed to the extent that "Acts of Congress authorizing the exercise, during the period of a national emergency, of any special or extraordinary power" are activated *and* cited by the President for use during the period of exigency. Although an attempt was made in the House to establish factors or conditions constituting a "national emergency," the amendment was defeated on the grounds it would have limited severely the situations in which the President could effect a "national emergency" and otherwise restrict his flexibility in responding spontaneously to crisis conditions.[159] Thus, the Act provides no specific standards by which Congress may judge the propriety of an emergency declaration. Each "national emergency" is assessed *de novo* by each Member, perhaps in terms of the threatening situation or the powers sought or both.

This omission of a definition or criteria regarding a condition of "national emergency," together with the President's discretion to declare or not to declare such, suggests that a Chief

Executive might circumvent the National Emergencies Act by using some statutorily delegated "special or extraordinary powers" which he determines are available to him without activation by a proclamation.[160] In addition, an examination of the Senate Special Committee's published compendium of emergency powers statutes suggests a semantic question: are laws authorizing certain executive actions "in the national interest,"[161] during "unusual economic stress,"[162] or "in the interest of national security"[163] to be considered within the ambit of the National Emergencies Act? The third of these referents is particularly intriguing in terms of attempts to regulate presidential discretion in the exercise of special powers.

The term appears about 390 times in the 1970 edition of the United States Code, with additional inclusions in the uncodified statutes. Of the 390 entries, a little more than 100 pertain to Government institutions, such as the National Security Agency or the National Security Council. Another two score are section headings or cross-references, and another two score refer to the National Security Act. However, slightly more than 240 of the remaining citations are descriptions of a policy condition granting the President extensive discretionary powers. They include such phrases as: "for reasons of national security," "for purposes of national security," "in the interest of national security" or "detrimental to the national security."

While the precise origins of the national security concept are uncertain, its adaptive value was well appreciated by 1949 when, writing in the pages of the *American Political Science Review*, Sidney W. Souers, then Executive secretary of the National Security Council, called it "a point of view rather than a distinct area of governmental responsibility."

At best, national security is a policy phrase of convenience, yet rarely is it defined or meaningfully explained. At worst, it is a term of art with little precise denotation but subject to broad interpretation by executive branch officials. It has been both the justification and apology for the Nation's clandestine adventures overseas, for broad claims of official secrecy, for domestic covert intrusions by the state into private dwellings and for surreptitious Government electronic eavesdropping everywhere in the world. Indeed, the danger underlying the use of the concept national security is that it could become the cause for excusing actions contrary to law. These considerations should be kept in mind when contemplating the concept of an emergency.[164]

Unfortunately, in its failure to define or demarcate what constitutes a "national emergency," Congress has neglected to indicate, as well, the extent to which delegated "national security" authority falls within the scope of the National Emergencies Act.

Finally, the Act's lack of a definition of "national emergency" conditions or criteria, together with its applicability only to "Acts of Congress authorizing the exercise, during the period of a national emergency, of any special or extraordinary power," negates the use of its provisions to cancel a proclamation of national emergency relative to the exercise of authorities other than delegated statutory powers. Former Solicitor General Erwin N. Griswold did not regard this as a problem when, in testifying before the Senate Special Committee, he observed:

> That in the absence of a statute passed by Congress giving the President some kind of special authority in the event an emergency is declared, I don't see that the declaration of an emergency by the President has any significance except psychological and public relations. It only gives him new powers if there is some statute which says that in the event an emergency is declared, you have those new powers.[165]

Former Attorney General Elliot L. Richardson agreed, saying:

> His declaration of the emergency on that basis would not give him any power he did not otherwise have in the absence of the declaration. The issue here is one of the legitimacy of the exercise of power. A statute providing for the declaration of a national emergency, and with the other provisions that have been discussed here today, could spell out specific delegations to the President that he would not otherwise have had once he had declared the emergency. And only after this had been done, pursuant to the provisions of the statute, would he be lawfully able to exercise those powers. That is the kind of thing a statute can and should deal with.[166]

But the National Emergencies Act does not fully address this matter, and for constitutional reasons, perhaps it cannot do so. Certainly the Senate report on the legislation makes it clear that the Act "is not intended to enlarge or add to Executive power."[167] In brief, the authors of the statute did not want it to be used as authority for the issuance of proclamations of national emergency. According to the Senate report, "the definition of when a President is authorized to declare a national emergency should be left to the various statutes which give him extraordinary powers."[168] But what may Congress do if the Chief Executive proclaims a national emergency for "psychological and public relations" reasons, which apparently was one of the purposes behind the Truman proclamation in 1950[169] and why President Reagan contemplated declaring a national economic emergency at the outset of his administration, and then exercised only implied constitutional powers or statutory exigency authority available to him apart from the procedures of the National Emergencies Act? Should the proponents of the National Emergencies Act regard this as a legitimate exercise of power?

At present, this type of situation cannot be addressed by Congress through the Act. It could be addressed, however, if Congress had made the use of any statutory powers for national emergency purposes subject to its direct approval. Executive implementation of statutory powers for national emergency purposes not so approved might be checked by some form of congressional veto or court injunction, as well as judicial negation of the particular actions taken. In addition, Congress might have given closer attention to statutory authorities for dealing with exigencies which are available to the President without activation by a proclamation of national emergency, and might have placed them in dormancy, to be activated in the future through the procedures established by the National Emergencies Act.

During the course of its proceedings, the Senate Special Committee discovered that certain presidential directives concerning major steps in United States military involvement in Vietnam were missing from the *Federal Register* system.[170] When the panel issued its final report, direct attention was given to improving the accountability of Executive decision-making, including *Federal Register* reforms.[171] Yet, although the existing problem of vague definition as to what official instruments are to be published in the *Federal Register* was known,[172] the National Emergencies Act relies upon this system of public reporting.[173] No attempt was made to improve the prevailing *Federal Register* arrangements relative to national emergency policy instruments, to establish penalties when directives or regulations are withheld improperly from publication in the *Federal Register*, or to modify law allowing the suspension of the production of the *Register* during a given crisis.[174]

In a related matter, Title IV of the National Emergencies

Act requires that, during a declared war or national emergency, the Chief Executive "shall be responsible for maintaining a file and index of all significant orders of the President, including Executive orders and proclamations, and each Executive agency shall maintain a file and index of all rules and regulations issued during such emergency or war issued pursuant to such declarations." While these instruments must be transmitted promptly to Congress, as specified in the Act, there is no reinforcement of the obligation to publish them in the *Federal Register*. Also, there is no definition or explanation of the phrase "significant orders of the President." The House report on the statute differs somewhat on this point, saying "the President shall maintain a file and index of *all* Presidential orders and each executive agency shall maintain a file of *all* rules and regulations issued during the emergency or war."[175] (Emphasis added) This discrepancy in language remains to be resolved.

As the National Emergencies Act progressed in its legislative development, enthusiasm for the elimination and restriction of delegated emergency powers seemed to have waned. In its interim report of August, 1974, the Senate Special Committee sought the outright repeal of 49 emergency authority provisions.[176] Before the proposed statute became effective, the Executive Branch might seek the restoration of any of these powers in their original or amended form. These repeal targets remained in the proposal (S. 3975) until it came on the Senate floor in October when the title was modified to include three provisions designated for amendment, five provisions designated for repeal, and six provisions reserved for further study by congressional committees.[177] Two years later, the Senate altered this formula to three provisions for amendment, four provisions for repeal, and over eight provisions reserved for further study.[178]

The Special Committee had been encouraged by former Associate Justice Tom Clark, former Attorney General Nicholas Katzenbach,[179] and former Solicitor General Erwin Griswold to reduce significantly the canon of existing national emergency statutes.[180] The legislative committees developing the National Emergencies Act did not pursue this challenge. In addition, the Act required that only selected committees further review particular provisions of emergency law. The entire body of emergency statutes escaped such critical scrutiny. Relevant Executive Branch contingency arrangements, such as the assignment of emergency preparedness functions,[181] the Executive Reserve Roster,[182] the stand-by censor,[183] were never placed on a committee agenda and remain outside of the legislative history and provisions of the National Emergencies Act.

It also would appear that the Act suffers from weak control mechanisms. Unlike the War Powers Resolution enacted before it[185] or the International Emergency Economic Powers Act adopted after it,[186] the National Emergencies Act contains no requirement that the President consult with Congress prior to activating its provisions. President Truman did so consult with congressional leaders before issuing his proclamation of national emergency in December, 1950, and made much of this fact in his memoirs.[187] The Senate Special Committee was aware of this,[188] but seemed to be unfavorably disposed to the idea.[189] An amendment to this effect was offered in the House, but was rejected.[190] Thus, the Act is devoid of this feature.

The principal mechanism offered by the National Emergencies Act for canceling an unwanted presidential proclamation of national emergency is an over-riding concurrent resolution adopted by a majority in each House of Congress. Former Solicitor General Erwin Griswold expressed his doubts as to the constitutionality of this procedure when testifying before the Senate Special Committee.[191] Assitant Attorney General Antonin Scalia did the same during hearings on the legislation before a subcommittee of the House Committee on the Judiciary.[192] And President Ford indicated his reservations on this point when he signed the measure into law.[193] As the legislative history of the Act indicates, no presidential proclamation of national emergency, issued in whole or in part pursuant to Article II of the Constutition, can be rescinded by statute. If, indeed, the concurrent resolution veto only would return activated statutory emergency powers once more to a state of dormancy, is this procedure not significantly different from the one followed to produce the return-to-dormancy effect contained in Title I of the National Emergencies Act? Although the ultimate test of the constitutionality of this congressional veto provision admittedly will have to be decided by the courts, its questionable legal status is itself a weakness in the Act.

Another shortcoming in the statute may be found in Title II where either House of Congress is allowed to modify specified action deadlines pertaining to a concurrent resolution of veto effect, or to alter its procedures regarding same. These arrangements open the way for a controlling faction in one chamber to delay a vote on terminating the effects of a proclamation of national emergency. To eliminate this potential mischief, mandatory deadlines and fixed procedures for acting on a veto resolution seemingly would be preferable.

And how much of a check is the congressional veto, even if it is found to be constitutional? If the President disagreed with a congressional termination of a national emergency, the Chief Executive could issue a second proclamation and Congress would be obligated to cancel the effect of the declaration once again. Commenting on this potentiality, Senator Church said:

> We did consider that possibility and saw no way around it. But we thought in the future, if we reached a point where the Congress and the President were in serious disagreement with respect to the need to continue a national emergency, the majority of both Houses of Congress voted to terminate an existing emergency, it would be very unlikely for the President to turn around and reinstate it through a new declaration.[194]

Senator Mathias added his own observation, remarking: "If a President couldn't summon up this much support in the Congress for the existing emergency condition, it would be unlikely that he could mobilize the country itself to respond to the emergency."[195] Nevertheless, the potential remains for Congress to be harassed with repeated proclamations of national emergency in a contest of wills where the stakes are very high.

Finally, there appears to be some uncertainty over congressional oversight responsibility for the National Emergencies Act. The committees responsible for the legislative development of the statute are neither the recipients of official presidential communiques regarding actions taken pursuant to the Act nor do they exercise any review of those actions under the law. Instead, the principal foreign policy committees of Congress appear to be the primary overseers of the moment.[196] At a minimum, this situation indicates that oversight responsibility for the National Emergencies Act is allocated differentially among four committees; in a larger sense, if oversight responsibility is shared broadly within Congress along committee jurisdiction lines, then it suggests that even more panels may be involved, depending upon the particular emergency powers that are activated. These arrangements would seem to suggest that no one congressional committee necessarily has the full view of how statutory emergency authority is exercised during any particular national emergency or, through time, during various national emergencies. They may result in the chairman of the subcommittee of the House Committee on the Judiciary which originally reported the National Emergencies Act not knowing that the six-month congressional review of President Carter's proclamation of national emergency of 1979 had been performed, as required by the Act, by another House panel.[197] They may contribute, as well, to the failure of any congressional committee to protest publicly the violation of the six-month reporting requirement by the Carter Administration.[198] And they seem to suggest that a recommendation of a few years ago for a special emergency powers oversight committee, raised again during the hearings of the Senate Special Committee, be re-examined.[199]

### Unfinished Business

President Carter's proclamation of a national emergency in 1979 prompted the first general implementation of the National Emergencies Act since its enactment.[200] This particular action by the Chief Executive, together with related policy developments, provide both an opportunity and a vehicle for general oversight hearings by the congressional committees directly responsible for the legislative development of the statute. Such proceedings by these particular panels could review the administration and operation of the National Emergencies Act, examine the recommendations contained in the final report of the Senate Special Committee, and pursue such amendments to the Act as seem appropriate.

In the course of scrutinizing the implementation of the National Emergencies Act and related policy developments, congressional overseers might explore the apparent failure of the Carter Administration to meet the six-month reporting requirement of the statute as well as obtain and analyze the expenditures data which should have been included in the delinquent reports. In addition, the adequacy of the files and indexes required in Title IV of the Act might be assessed. Finally, because the principal emergency power exercised pursuant to the 1979 proclamation of national emergency pertained to the freezing of Iranian government assets held by American banking institutions and their subsidiaries, consideration might be given to the allegation that the Carter Administration did not properly retain control of the assets[201] and to the complaint that better arrangements are needed for the Federal Government to keep account of such blocked foreign assets.[202]

Various suggestions for oversight evaluation arise from the final report of the Senate Special Committee on National Emergencies and Delegated Emergency Powers. A poll might be taken among the committees of both Houses of Congress with a view to identifying provisions of emergency law which were exempted from the coverage of the National Emergencies Act or otherwise returned to a dormant status and are now in need of modification or repeal.[203] An example of such outstanding emergency authority presently warranting cancellation seemingly is the President's power to establish defense areas and zones. Deriving from a congressional enactment sanctioning President Roosevelt's order for the internment of Japanese-Americans in 1942,[204] this authority, as it pertained to the army,[205] was condemned at various junctures by the Special Committee.[206] Parallel authority pertaining to the navy,[207] however, appears to have escaped the panel's notice.[208] Nevertheless, when the provision was brought to the attention of the Senate Committee on Government Operations during hearings on the legislation which became the National Emergencies Act,[209] the omission seemingly was ignored.[210] Only the army provision was repealed in Title V of the Act. The navy provision awaits cancellation.

The Special Committee warned against "efforts to thwart (the) intent of (the) law—Congress must be wary of potential efforts to bypass or circumvent the intent of the new legislation" governing national emergency declarations by the President.[211] The panel suggested that such deviousness might be evidenced in legislation

> . . . by dropping the wording "national emergency" and introducing different terminology. Committees must insure that all emergency legislation, however denominated, has the same accountability and reporting requirements and termination procedures. No claim can in the future be advanced that a particular type or class of emergency can arise in which the President's powers are not subject to Congressional review.[212]

This warning raises a consideration addressed earlier: the National Emergencies Act might be well served by a definition or statement of conditions which constitute a "national emergency." It suggests, as well, that congressional overseers might reexamine the canon of emergency powers to determine if there have been statutes enacted of late which delegate emergency authority in a manner which is either inconsistent with or contrary to the procedures of the National Emergencies Act.[213] As noted previously, perhaps there are statutory delegations of "national security" authority which should be exercised in accordance with the procedures of the Act. Congressional grants of power to combat "terrorism" are still another consideration.[214]

The Special Committee also recommended "that emergency preparedness efforts in the United States be investigated" and appended a staff analysis on this subject to its final report.[215] Considering the panel's suggestion in more contemporary terms, congressional overseers might review the organization and operation of the Federal Emergency Management Agency,[216] the adequacy of the national civil defense program, and the usefulness of such contingency arrangements as the assignment of emergency preparedness functions,[217] the Executive Reserve Roster,[218] the stand-by censor,[219] and emergency relocation facilities.[220] Underlying considerations pertaining to these matters include the nature of the authority mandating the various preparedness activities and the extent to which the National Emergencies Act should apply, in any way, to them.

Another area of concern to the Special Committee and in need of review is the extent to which Congress "will be able to act quickly and effectively in time of emergency."[221] In the words of the panel's final report:

> The Committee believes that more thought should be given to emergency preparedness. Congress must anticipate diverse scenarios and insure its ability to survive a crisis and to act effectively in its aftermath. There must be an intelligent definition of the role Congress should assume in emergency preparedness efforts and other emergency activities.[222]

To this end, the Special Committee suggested three options. Congress might wish "to appoint personnel or to establish an administrative mechanism to assume responsibility for coordinating emergency preparations."[223] Another possibility, not necessarily mutually exclusive from the first suggestion, would be a new subcommittee which "could, on an ongoing basis, review Congressional activities, oversee Executive efforts, and coordinate the work of the two branches of government" as well as "work out administrative details of the National Emergencies Act and insure that its provisions are followed in time of emergency."[224] A third alternative might be to "establish, on a reserve basis, a panel which would come into existence as soon as a national emergency has been proclaimed." Such a unit — perhaps functioning as a special or select committee or as a temporary subcommittee — "would provide a coordinating center to bring concentrated attention to the emergency."[225] The Special Committee concluded on this subject, saying:

> Regardless of whether any Congressional structures are established, regular examination of the canon of emergency statutes, Executive orders and related administrative rules, regulations and instruments — operative, dormant, limited — is imperative to keep the Congress apprised of developments and advised as to corrective actions which should be undertaken. The potential threat posed by national emergency law to the political well-being of a democracy makes essential regular examination of policy developments by a Senate committee.[226]

The Special Committee next urged "that Congress end its dangerous practice of extending open-ended authority to the President."[227] In this regard, the report criticized the routine manner in which Congress periodically had renewed the authority of the Defense Production Act "giving the President wide-ranging powers to control the production of materials needed for national defense efforts connected with the Korean War."[228] The panel offered the following recommendation for congressional overseers: "Future legislation should include a terminal date for authorities granted to the Executive and provide for Congressional review."[229]

Continuing on the theme just discussed, the Special Committee urged better congressional investigation of and stricter controls over delegated powers, saying "there must be a reexamination of the whole issue of Congressional delegations of power to the Executive."[230] There are strong implications here for the application of so-called "sunset" controls,[231] legislative veto authority,[232] or similar alternatives.[233] Although recent debate over these techniques indicates there is considerable concern about their practicality and constitutionality,[234] the Special Committee, nevertheless, appears to be convinced of the need for some such controls:

> In the future, when Congress delegates power to the Executive, it should be more specific in defining the conditions in which the authority may be used. Beyond that, the challenge is to devise means by which Congress can monitor the exercise of delegated powers and control those actions deemed to be unnecessary or undesirable. Serious consideration should be given to legislation which would give Congress some type of veto over Executive branch rules and regulations judged to be inconsistent with the legislative intent of the authorizing statute. The law might also cover Executive directives, rules, and regulations which only come into effect during a condition of national emergency. These instruments, though effective only at some future time, should be subject to Congressional scrutiny prior to issuance or activation so that, when they are needed, they will truly reflect the intent of the legislative branch and will not require adjustment in the midst of a crisis.[235]

Finally, the Special Committee urged improvements in the accountability of Executive Branch decisionmaking. This might be accomplished, in part, "by regularizing the procedures surrounding the issuance of Executive orders."[236] The panel's final report justified this course of action, saying:

> Title 3 of the Code of Federal Regulations indicates that in issuing decisions and commands, Presidents have used such diverse forms as letters, memorandums, directives, notice, reorganization plans, administrative designation, and military orders. The decision whether to publish an Executive decision is clearly a result of the President's own discretion rather than any prescription of law. In recent years, the National Security Action Memorandums of Presidents Kennedy and Johnson and the National Security Action Directives of President Nixon represent a new method of promulgating decisions, in areas of the gravest importance. Such decisions are not specifically required by law to be published in any register, even in a classified form; none have prescribed formats or procedures; none of these vital Executive decisions are revealed to Congress or the public except under irregular arbitrary or accidental circumstances. For instance, the 1969–1970 secret bombing of Cambodia has recently come before Congressional and public notice. The public record reveals very little about how the commands for such far reaching actions were issued. What is most disturbing is lack of access to any authoritative records in these matters. In short, there is no formal accountability for the most crucial Executive de-

cisions affecting the lives of citizens and the freedom of individuals and institutions.[237]

The solution to this dilemma, according to the Special Committee, "would seem to be amendment of the Federal Register Act of 1935, which provides the present statutory guidelines for the issuance of Executive decisions and orders."[238]

But this was not the only aspect of the accountability problem troubling the Special Committee. The situation

> . . . is exacerbated by the classification of sensitive or important Executive decisions, classification which in most cases prevents even Congress from having access to these documents. While no one would wish to prevent sensitive documents from being classified for reasonable cause, the absolute discretion given to the Executive in this area has led to abuse. It has permitted and encouraged inclusion in this category of many documents in no way connected with essential national security. Moreover, not only are their contents kept secret, but even the extent of such documents is unascertainable.[239]

The Special Committee further observed that:

> Congress has not specified substantive standards for the recording of Presidential directives. In addition, Congress has not yet enacted laws to prevent the Executive branch from abusing its power to classify documents where its purpose is to withhold information from Congress and the public.[240]

Thus, the panel reached the following conclusion.

> Amendment could be made to insure the publication of all significant Executive directives, however denominated, in the Federal Register. At the same time some thought should be given to establishing a system whereby classified rules and orders, by whatever name called, would be registered.[241]

This policy prospect remains to be explored by congressional overseers.

Overlapping with these various considerations from the final report of the Senate Special Committee are the policy options identified earlier in this assessment of the National Emergencies Act. In the course of a congressional review of the statute with a view to amendment, attention might be given to a definition of or criteria denoting a condition of national emergency, the feasibility of extending the coverage of the Act to all statutes delegating emergency powers to the President, the possibility of requiring prior consultation by the Chief Executive with Congress before proclaiming a national emergency, the desirability of mandatory congressional action deadlines for acting upon a resolution disapproving an emergency declaration, the development of alternatives to the constitutionally suspect legislative veto contained in the Act, and the usefulness of some special congressional oversight panel to monitor national emergency policy and practice.

## Overview

The National Emergencies Act constitutes a first attempt by Congress to regulate the exercise of delegated national emergency powers available to the President. Developed and enacted during a period of widespread mistrust of an "imperial presidency," the law marks a momentary point of policy agreement between Congress and the Chief Executive, establishing procedures through which statutorily specified national emergency authority shall be invoked and utilized. The historical record, from the earliest days of the Republic to modern times, reflects a willingness on the part of Congress and, to some extent, by the Federal courts as well, to sanction almost any emergency action of the President, sometimes after the fact and in the face of serious legal question, and, subsequently, to delegate broad open-ended grants of emergency powers with little or no congressional check on their activation and implementation. The Senate Special Committee on National Emergencies and Delegated Emergency Powers and the National Emergencies Act sought to curb this trend, but to do so in a manner which would not breach constitutional prerogatives or inappropriately limit the President's flexibility or spontaneity to respond to an exigency. This assessment of the Act and the final report of the Special Committee suggest that further refinements in the regulation of congressionally delegated emergency authority might be pursued. The realization of these reforms, however, also must be balanced with constitutional standards and the need for presidential volition in crisis resolution.

These principles are underscored in the Supreme Court's recent decision in *Immigration and Naturalization Service* v *Chadha* (S.C. No. 80-1832 June 23, 1983). The ruling declared a provision of the Immigration and Nationality Act, authorizing one House of Congress, by resolution, to invalidate a decision of the Executive Branch, to be unconstitutional because this procedure was not in accord with the prescription for legislative action found in Article I. By implication, any legislative veto that does not meet this constitutional standard would seem to be invalid (see editorial published in the Fall 1983, *Presidential Studies Quarterly*). The National Emergencies Act would have allowed Congress, through the adoption of a concurrent resolution, to rescind effectively a presidentially proclaimed national emergency.

Assuming the legislative veto procedure of the National Emergencies Act is invalid, the Court's ruling raises a question as to whether or not this provision can be severed from the other provisions of the statute. In *Chadha*, the Court held the veto provision separable from the remainder of the law. The Immigration and Nationality Act contained a separability provision which, in the Court's view, raised a presumption that Congress did not intend the entire statute to fall if one provision was invalid. The National Emergencies Act contains no separability provision. However, courts favor separability and, to the extent that the legislative history indicates that Congress would have enacted the valid provisions independently of the invalid provision, then the remainder of the Act will survive. The record indicates that those responsible for the development of the National Emergencies Act were publicly apprised by legal scholars, Executive Branch officials, and congressional colleagues that the legislative veto provision was constitutionally suspect. In the face of these warnings, the legislation was enacted into law. Thus, Congress gave its approval to this measure with the knowledge that the legislative veto provision might not endure, strongly suggesting that it was willing, in the words of the *Chadha* court, to enact "those provisions which are within its power, independently of that which is not." It appears that the remaining provisions of the National Emergencies Act shall prevail in the aftermath of the *Chadha* decision and that the demise of its legislative veto provision poses one more additional consideration for Congress when it again returns to national emergency policy matters.

# Toward Coherence in Foreign Policy: Greater Presidential Control of the Foreign Policymaking Machinery

**RICHARD BROWN**
DEPARTMENT OF POLITICS
NEW YORK UNIVERSITY

### *Introduction*

A recurring criticism of American foreign policy since the resignation of President Richard Nixon is that it lacks coherence. The problem of incoherence in foreign policy is of particular urgency because incoherence creates the impression that policy is unpurposive, thereby depreciating its credibility. As a result our ability to shape global events is diminished. If we as a nation are to master our destiny, we must have the ability to shape global events.

Coherence in foreign policy can be defined as the systematic uniting of specific, often seemingly divergent, policies to one another through their relationship to a broad conceptual design, combined with an unambiguous public perception of that relationship. From this definition it becomes clear that coherence in foreign policy is not a function of Presidents or policies per se, but of process. Therefore, in order to uncover the sources of incoherence one must look to the foreign policymaking process.

The American foreign policymaking process is an amorphous collection of institutions, functional responsibilities, and channels of communication; as such it cannot be modeled with precision. Major participants and subprocesses can, however, be generalized and modeled in such a way as to illustrate the essence of the process (see model). Three sources of incoherence emerge from this model:

1. A President may fail to develop a broad conceptual design, fail to adequately articulate a design, or change designs in mid-term. In the first two cases policies are not traceable to

## THE AMERICAN FOREIGN POLICY PROCESS

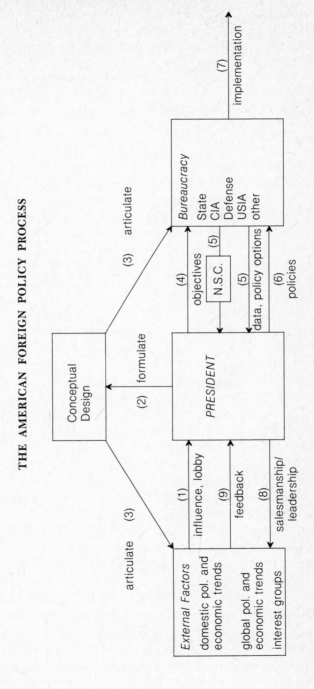

a common purpose, while in the third case new policies will conflict with those already set in motion.

2.   The bureaucracy may fail to develop sound policy options.[1] In this case a President will either create an informal organization to serve this purpose or he will simply allow policy to flounder until a crisis brooks no further delay.

3.   The bureaucracy may delay or subvert policy through failure to effectively implement policy, thereby creating uncertainty and cynicsm.

By process of elimination I have chosen to focus this paper on the second of these three sources. Regarding the first source, a President must simply develop a conceptual design, articulate it well, and then stick to it. Regarding the third source, bureaucratic obstinacy in policy implementation is a fact of life that transcends political ideology and government structure, and which can at best be reduced to tolerable levels. Thus there is not much fertile ground in these two areas for the political scientist to explore. The area of policymaking, on the other hand, is a fluid process, susceptible to modification, and characterized by competing centers of power whose responsibilities can be redefined. For this paper I have focused on the State Department's role in this area since it is the State Department (hereafter State) that is primarily responsible for foreign policymaking.

A survey of the literature on foreign policymaking shows that most scholars and ex-State officials who have addressed the subject use as their point of departure the belief that foreign policymaking should be centered at State. They then proceed to recommend organizational and procedural changes such as building lines of confidence down through the bureaucracy (Destler 1971), increased Presidential involvement to mitigate subordinate infighting (Gelb 1980), decreased Presidential involvement through greater delegation of power (Jackson subcommittee 1962), reduction in the size of State (Hoover Commission 1949 and Holbrooke 1971), downgrading the position of the National Security Adviser (Destler 1981), and improving management (Herter 1962). All of these arguments, while logically presented, fail to reconcile the general pattern in which recent Presidents have entered the White House affirming the belief that foreign policymaking should be centered at State; while the locus of foreign policymaking has consistently gravitated to the White House.[2] In light of this pattern I chose as my point of departure the thesis that State is beset with institutional weaknesses that render it incapable of effectively supporting the President's responsibility to conduct a coherent foreign policy, and that a new structure must be forged; one based on an unambiguous separation of functions—policymaking to be centered in the White House and policy implementation to be the responsibility of the various executive departments and agencies concerned with foreign affairs. This same proposition, in essence, was presented by Nelson Rockefeller at the Jackson subcommittee hearings on foreign policy machinery in 1960. Thus I am not breaking new ground, but merely resurrecting an old idea.

Two approaches were utilized in gathering data for this analysis. These approaches were undertaken in parallel. One is therefore not intended to build on the other, but rather they are intended to reinforce each other.

One approach was to analyze State in terms of its ability to formulate sound policy options. This analysis was designed to test the validity of the thesis statement that State is incapable of supporting the President's responsibility to conduct a coherent foreign policy. This analysis was subdivided into what I have termed a general institution analysis and a specific institution analysis. The former being a functional analysis of the general nature of bureaucracy, focusing on the ability of a bureaucracy to function efficiently and creatively. The latter is a functional analysis of State, focusing on its ability to formulate sound policy options. A thorough analysis in both of these areas was beyond the time and resource limitations of this paper.[3] Alternatively, I drew from the general conclusions and observations of those who in the one case have studied the nature of bureaucracy extensively, and in the other case have had first hand experience at State.

The other approach utilized was a historical/comparative analysis of how Presidents since Kennedy have delegated the responsibility for foreign policymaking.[4] This analysis was designed to either affirm or refute the generalization that in recent Administrations the locus of foreign policymaking has gravitated from State to the White House. Affirmation of the generalization would then support the recommendation that foreign policymaking be centered in the White House. The preferred method in this analysis would have been to identify the major foreign policy initiatives of each Administration and the individuals around whom the initiative evolved. Those initiatives centered in the White House could then be quantitatively and chronologically compared with those centered at State. Time and resource limitations, however, precluded using this method. Alternatively I analyzed each Administration in the broader sense of where the locus of foreign policymaking started and where it ultimately ended up. Alternative policymaking groups that Presidents have improvised in lieu of State, along with selected observations on the policymaking process by key personnel in each administration are identified.

Based on the conclusions drawn from this two-track approach, recommendations for restructuring the foreign policymaking machinery are made in the final part of the paper.

### The Bureaucracy

The economist/socialist Max Weber, writing in the late 19th and early 20th centuries, described the future societies of the industrial nations as being dominated by large organizations, or bureaucracies.[5] Weber attempted to develop a structural and behavioral paradigm that would maximize the efficiency of the bureaucracies. Weber's paradigm consisted of a hierarchically organized administrative structure based on functional specialization and written guidelines, and a group ethos based on professionalism and impersonality of attitude and procedure. Reared in the disciplined Prussian culture of the late 19th century, Weber believed that individuals were capable of devoting their full attention to their assigned role in the bureaucracy, devoid of any interest in encroaching on others. This behavior would enable the bureaucracies as a whole to function in a completely rational fashion.

The weakness in the Weberian paradigm is that individuals have never acted wholly rational on a sustained basis, nor is there any indication that they will be capable of doing so in the future. People are vulnerable to self-interest, jealousy, envy, thirst for power, and other such militants against rational behavior. Herbert Simon has observed,

The limits of rationality have been seen to derive from the inability of the human mind to bring to bear on a single decision all the aspects of values, knowledge, and behavior that would be relevant. Human rationality operates within the limits of a psychological environment. . . . Moreover, if loyalty to an organization's goals is lacking, personal motives may interfere with administrative efficiency.[6]

Michael Crozier adds,

> By and large, the common underlying pattern of all the vicious circles that characterize bureaucratic systems is this: the rigidity of task definition, task arrangements, and the human relations network results in a lack of communication with the environment and a lack of communication among the groups. The resulting difficulties are utilized by individuals and groups for improving their position in the power struggle. This is based on the active tendency of the human agent to take advantage in any circumstances of all available means to further his own privileges.[7]

Bureaucratic rationality, therefore, can never be fully realized, only strived for. The corollary is that bureaucratic irrationality cannot be eliminated, only controlled. It seems that there exists a wide range of behavior between Weber's paradigm and dilettantism.

Private sector bureaucracies have demonstrated a greater capacity to control bureaucratic irrationality than public sector bureaucracies. This is because private sector bureaucracies operate in the market system which stresses competition and a consumer orientation, and which provides feedback in the form of tangible losses and gains. Public sector bureaucracies, on the other hand, operate in a service oriented, monopolistic environment. Rules, not profit, are the guiding forces. Devoid of a commercial outlook public sector bureaucracies inevitably lapse into a state of inertia. The incentives for creativity, boldness, and exploration posed by competition are substituted for by a quest for security, certainty, and familiarity posed by rules. Individual success is determined not by innovation and aggressiveness, but by avoidance of disruption. Institutional success is determined not by profits or lack thereof, but by sheer physical and budgetary size.

Economist Ludwig von Mises has observed,

> Private management produces what consumers want, guided by the standard of profit and loss. Men are judged by their competence because profit provides an objective standard by which to evaluate men, products, and methods. Bureaucratic (government)

management, in contrast, is concerned only to comply with rules, regulations. Lack of a profit standard kills initiative and the incentive to do a really good job. Guided by rules rather than profit, public administration is necessarily inefficient.[8]

Bureaucratic irrationality manifests itself in various forms which can be described in operational terms. These manifestations exhibit themselves in all bureaucracies, but tend to be more frequently found and more fully developed in public sector bureaucracies.[9] Marshall Dimock has identified twenty-six such manifestations of bureaucratic irrationality, or pathologies as he calls them.[10] They include:

- impersonality stemming from the lack of sales motivation.
- delay in decisionmaking when channels of communication are over extended through many echelons of authority.
- routinism imposed by tradition.
- timidity due to an urge to play it safe.
- mediocrity resulting from a belief that leveling is the best policy.
- conformity for fear of being considered ambitious and a threat to the group norm.
- group resistance due to a desire to keep to the old ways of doing things.

Obviously such behavior militates against the ability of an organization to function creatively and efficiently.

At another level of analysis, Alexander George attributes the problems in foreign policymaking to the expansion of the number of agencies and departments within the executive branch that are involved in foreign policy. According to George, in addition to the obvious difficulties in communication between "subunits,"

> The difficulties of achieving coordination and intellectual interaction are further compounded by virtue of the fact that subunits within an organization typically develop interests and goals of their own; often these are in sharp variance with the organizational goals and value priorities as seen from the perspective of the top executive. The executive's task of policy control, policy analysis, coordination and implementation is jeopardized, moreover, by competition and conflict among the various subunits.[11]

George goes on to describe the ill-effects of "bureaucratic politics" in four areas: (1) information processing tasks; (2) the content and quality of the decisions taken; (3) diplomatic negotiations and communications; and (4) implementation of presidential policy.

From the foregoing analysis it can be inferred that the very nature of a large bureaucracy, particularly a large public sector bureaucracy, is not conducive to the formulation of sound policy options.

## Policymaking at State

Policymaking at State is an amorphous process, one that does not lend itself to generic modeling. There are, however, certain identifiable characteristics which inhere State's policymaking process, and which militate against the formulation of sound policy options.

The myriad of groups, offices, bureaus, and agencies at State creates excessive overlap of functional responsibilities.[12] Intradepartmental committees must be formed, usually on an ad hoc basis, to bring together various inputs and to reconcile conflicting interests. Once a consensus is achieved the policy option(s) is then subjected to modification as it is processed through the various layers of authority in the vertical chain of command. Even after reaching the Secretary's level, policies are subjected to further modification at the interdepartmental level and at the National Security Council level.

Policy by committee, as broadly described here, has a pernicious effect on the formulation of sound policy options. Nelson Rockefeller, testifying before the Jackson Subcommittee on National Policy Machinery in 1960, stated,

> Excessive government by committee can be anything but constructive. In the field of executive action it can reduce government action to the least bold or imaginative–to the lowest common denominator among varying positions. Policy is determined not for the sake of its rightness, but for the sake of agreement . . . the committees of a democratic government cannot hope to meet or master problems simply by outnumbering them.[13]

Henry Kissinger, writing in 1968, observed,

> What is considered policy is usually the embodiment of a consensus within a committee . . . the ideal committee man does not make his associates uncomfortable by operating too far out of what is generally accepted. The thrust of the committees is toward a stan-

dard of average performance. They provide great pressure in favor of the status quo. Committees are consumers and sterilizers of ideas, rarely creators of them. The committee system stresses avoidance of risk rather than boldness of conception . . . This explains to a considerable extent why American policy has demonstrated such a combination of abstraction and rigidity.[14]

And finally, the Jackson Subcommittee staff report concluded,

Committees have a built in drive toward lowest common denominator solutions. They are not good instruments for innovation. The main source of innovation is the contribution of the individual . . . (committees) are not creative instruments for bringing forth imaginative and sharply defined choices, particularly in uncharted areas of policy.[15]

A second critical factor that renders State incapable of formulating sound policy options is its physical detachment from the external factors that impinge on a President's foreign policy decisions (see model). Policies emanating from State, tend to reflect the needs and interests of elements within the department, and of the department as a whole, rather than those of the President. This is why State's policies are consistently oriented toward "maintaining good relations" with the country or countries involved. This phenomenon cannot be attributed exclusively to conscious bureaucratic parochialism. That State officials, with the exception of the Secretary, are detached from the White House milieu precludes their having a full appreciation for the "external factors" and for the diplomatic nuance that only a President and his closest advisers can have. As Leslie Gelb points out, "I have generally found that staffers from the Department of State behave very differently when they are moved to the White House . . . . They become more conscious of Presidential stakes and interests."[16] Even when a Secretary of State views policymaking from a Presidential perspective, he must still defend the work and interests of his department lest it, and he, lose all credibility and power.

A consequence of these institutional and structural barriers confronting State is that a President's confidence in State's ability to serve him diminishes. In the realm of Presidential politics, and especially in foreign affairs, an individual's or an institution's power is directly proportional to the level of confidence that he or it holds in the eyes of the President. Using this theory, some scholars have suggested that a President should work at building lines of confidence down through the bureaucracy.[17] But such suggestions ignore the reality that confidence is a function of demonstrated loyalty and competence, which normally can be realized only through day to day interaction. This criteria is usually met by a President's White House advisers and his cabinet Secretaries, never by a sprawling bureaucracy.

Based on the analyses in sections II and III of this paper it can be concluded that the thesis statement, that State is beset by weaknesses that render it incapable of supporting the President's responsibility to conduct a coherent foreign policy, is valid. The upshot of this is that Presidents are confronted with a policymaking vacuum. To the extent that the vacuum is not filled by another policymaking apparatus, incoherence in foreign policy will prevail.

The acid test of State's ability to formulate sound policy options is the extent to which Presidents have entrusted State with that responsibility. This section of the paper includes brief accounts of how each President since Kennedy has delegated the authority for foreign policymaking.

John F. Kennedy entered the White House with the belief that foreign policymaking should be centered at State. Although he never retreated from this belief as a matter of principle, circumstance forced him to do so as a matter of practical necessity.

The Bay of Pigs invasion was Kennedy's first exposure to State's inability to serve Presidential needs.* State's failure to provide alternative policy options to balance the C.I.A. and Defense plans impelled him to relocate policymaking to the White House. The new policymaking structure evolved around National Security Adviser McGeorge Bundy. Bundy assembled a staff of experts that were both loyal to Kennedy and sensitive to his needs.[18] Bundy also arranged to have raw intelligence flowing into the bureaucracy channeled directly into the White House; thus providing him and his staff with an unbiased source of information on which they could base their recommendations. The staff met regularly, inviting representatives from the bureaucracy on an as required basis. A regular participant in

---

* *Editor's Note: For differing interpretation of the Bay of Pigs fiasco see Chapter Twelve, "Kennedy, the Bay of Pigs, and the Limits of Collegial Decision Making", by Ryan J. Barilleaux.*

the staff meetings was Kennedy's domestic adviser and chief confidant Theodore Sorenson.

Subsequent failures by State to satisfy Kennedy (e.g. Berlin, Laos, and South America) cemented the power shift. As Arthur Schlesinger described it, "It was a constant puzzle to Kennedy that the State Department remained so formless and impenetrable. He would say, "'Damn it! Bundy and I get more done in one day than they do in six months . . . they never have any ideas over there, never come up with anything new . . . The State Department is a bowl of jelly.'"[19]

In addition to the "Bundy staff," Kennedy initiated a series of task forces consisting of representatives from the bureaucracy and members of Bundy's staff. The task forces, which were responsible to Bundy, were designed to formulate long term planning. Kennedy's purpose, as described by Schlesinger, was "to stay ahead of events, to avoid being surprised by unexpected events, and to shape events." He wanted to "end the faceless system of indecision and inaction which diffused foreign policy among State, Defense, and the C.I.A." He wanted "quick and personal replies to significant questions to replace the ambiguity and lack of specific guidance coming from the bureaucracy."[20]

Lyndon Johnson, having been elected to a full term as President in 1964, was determined to make his own imprint on that office. One of Johnson's first acts in this regard was to demonstrate that he did not need another "Bundy" to conduct foreign policy. He did so by reinvesting policymaking authority with State through a number of interdepartmental committees designed to strengthen the Secretary of State's hand in foreign policy. But Johnson never gave his full support to the committees, thus precluding any potential influence that they might have had. This was partly the consequence of the Viet Nam War which, by its nature, required direct White House control. It was also attributable to the fact that Johnson did not vest the committees with the same confidence that he did with his senior White House advisers. Eventually, foreign policymaking became the purview of the "Tuesday lunch group" which consisted of White House advisers and representatives from the bureaucracy and which, according to Johnson's National Security Adviser Walt Rostow, "had an agenda that reached far beyond Viet Nam."

Gradually, Rostow's role came to resemble the role that Bundy had played for Kennedy. That the National Security Council staff did not attain the same prominence under Rostow as it did under Bundy was because Rostow was less inclined toward building a machinery than toward acting as a personal adviser, and because Johnson's interest in foreign affairs was far less than was Kennedy's. Nonetheless, the locus of foreign policymaking had perceptibly gravitated from State to the White House.

White House domination of foreign policymaking reached its apex in the Administration of Richard Nixon. Determined to secure his place in history through boldness in foreign affairs, Nixon was not going to entrust his grand design to an institution that he felt was incurably beset with functional weaknesses, and one that he felt would not be loyal to him. "From the outset of my Administration I planned to direct foreign policy from the White House; therefore I regarded my choice of National Security Adviser as crucial."[21] Henry Kissinger was equally disdainful of the bureaucracy. His exegeses on bureaucracy provided Nixon's raw pragmatic rationalizations with an intellectual underpinning.[22]

Upon his appointment as National Security Adviser, Kissinger assembled what came to be the largest National Security Council staff in the history of that institution. All of the key policy initiatives in the Nixon Administration (Berlin, Europe, China, SALT, the Soviet Union, and Viet Nam) were delegated to Kissinger and his staff. "Backchannels" were employed to an unprecedented degree to exclude the normally responsible officials at State. Unbeknownst to State, its negotiations in some of the aforementioned areas were strictly for public posturing as the substantive negotiations were conducted by Kissinger and his staff in private.

The de facto institutionalization of foreign policymaking in the White House during the Nixon years led many academicians and political commentators to express fears over Nixon's concentration of power. The extraordinary success of Nixon's policies, however, stultified these challenges. Based on the analysis presented here, I would add that it was not coincidental that this period of diplomacy, perhaps America's finest, was also the period in which bureaucratic involvement reached its nadir.

The pattern of White House dominance in foreign policymaking changed somewhat with Kissinger's appointment as Secretary of State and with the ascension of Gerald Ford.

Kissinger continued to personally dominate policymaking as he acted more in the role of an independent agent than the Secretary of State. Brent Scowcroft, Ford's National Security Adviser, played that role as the consensus description says it should be. This was due, in part, to Scowcroft's professional convictions that supported this role concept and, in part, to Kissinger's dominance. As R. Gordon Hoxie has stated, ". . . . How else could one occupy the position with the irrepressible Kissinger shuttling back and forth between the Oval Office and Foggy Bottom?"[23] In the context of this analysis, then, the Ford Administration was a holding pattern with neither State (in its entirety) nor the White House having clear dominance.

Candidate Jimmy Carter campaigned on a pledge to end Henry Kissinger's "Lone Ranger" diplomacy and to restore policymaking to State (in its entirety). As President he set broad policy objectives based on human rights, limiting nuclear proliferation, and withdrawal of American global presence. Roughly eighteen months into his term Carter became convinced that the Soviet Union had not responded, nor were they going to respond, favorably to his conciliatory initiatives. The Iranian Revolution in early 1978 and the Soviet invasion of Afghanistan in December 1979 finally impelled Carter to shift to more assertive objectives.

The inertia that had set in at State, however, resisted the shift as conciliatory policies continued to be pursued. Carter was forced to turn inward to his White House advisers, particularly National Security Adviser Brzezinski and his staff, for policies that would be consistent with the new objectives. Hence the widespread criticism of disarray in foreign affairs and the much publicized Vance-Brzezinski struggle. Ultimately, Vance resigned as power in foreign policymaking became centered in the White House. Although Brzezinski was portrayed as power-hungry and egotistical throughout the struggle, he never had any ambitions of becoming another Kissinger. He assumed his post committed to a collegial approach to foreign policymaking, acting more as an adviser than as a formulator. His ascension was attributable more to the gradual shift in the control of policymaking from State to the White House than to any personal grab for power.

The resignation of Alexander Haig in the summer of 1982 was, in retrospect, the logical outcome of a situation in which a determined, egotistical Secretary of State attempted to center foreign policymaking at State. Haig's desire to be the "vicar" of foreign policy exacerbated the inherent tension between State and the White House over the control of foreign policy. Haig, it should be remembered, was not Ronald Reagan's personal choice for Secretary of State (George Shultz was). Rather than reacting to the tenuousness of his position in a cautionary fashion, Haig tried to establish his authority through public pronouncements designed to aggrandize his own status and that of his department. In the early months of the administration Haig's posturing did not pose any serious policymaking problems, as the President was preoccupied with getting his budget and tax proposals through Congress. Once the President turned his attention to foreign policy, however, tension between State and the White House mounted; with Haig publicly accusing White House personnel of engaging in political sabotage against him. Haig's critics in the White House did not relish his vicarage presumptions. He did not work well with the Reagan close advisers that included Chief of Staff James Baker, III, Deputy Chief of Staff Michael Deaver, Counsellor Edwin Meese III, National Security Adviser, Richard Allen, and Secretary of Defense Caspar Weinberger. In an attempt to alleviate the tension, Reagan replaced Richard Allen, who resigned ostensibly for receiving gifts from a Japanese journal, with his long time friend, William Clark. Clark's reputation as a conflict manager, along with his holding of Reagan's confidence, were the primary qualifications he brought to this key position. But Clark, too, soon became embroiled in the policymaking struggle as he and Weinberger, who was Reagan's most trusted National Security Policy Adviser, pursued policies that were at variance with those of Haig (e.g. the Israeli invasion of Lebanon, the Soviet pipeline, and the Falkland's war).

The struggle over control of foreign policy during the first eighteen months of the Reagan administration is a vivid illustration of the inherent tension between State and the White House in this area, and of the tendency for the locus of foreign policymaking to drift to the White House. In his resignation statement Haig acknowledged that the foreign policy course that he and Reagan had originally charted was being abandoned. Haig was keenly aware that it was Reagan's White House advisers who had the President's ear and who were becoming the driving force behind foreign policymaking. George Shultz, Haig's replacement, has thus far demonstrated none of the maverick behavior that proved so debilitating to his predecessor. Shultz's low-keyed approach and quiet confidence has won him widespread respect. It is simply very difficult to dislike or not respect George Shultz. The question that surrounds Shultz is, therefore, not one of character, but one of performance. The first eight months of Shultz's tenure has been devoted to restoring stability in American foreign policy. Although stability in foreign policy is desirable, it should be a means to an end and not an end in itself. Stability merely preserves the status quo unless it is used to help effect positive change. Whether Shultz can infuse dynamism, creativity, and coherence into foreign policy remains to be seen.

A second question that surrounds the performance of Shultz is his professional relationship with the President. Shultz has always been considered a "team player," and has thus far lived up to that standard as Secretary of State. This disposition has been sustained, thus far, by the conformance of views between Shultz and State on the one hand, and the President and his White House advisers on the other. If history is a reliable guide, however, these views will at some point diverge. The likelihood of this occurring will increase proportionally as policy becomes more substantive and as the President becomes more involved. At that point Shultz will have to either remain a team player at the risk of alienating himself from his department, or defend his department at the risk of alienating himself from the President.

The foregoing analysis clearly affirms the generalization that in recent Administrations the locus of foreign policy has gravitated from State to the White House (thereby supporting the recommendation that policymaking be centered in the White House). Former State official Leslie Gelb has made the following observation which corroborates this conclusion:

> Every newly elected President in the last twenty years has expressed the belief that he must vest the authority for making the nation's foreign policy clearly and firmly in the Department of State. In this sense Presidents have echoed the recommendations of most public commissions, organizational experts, and foreign policy commentators who have addressed the problem of how to organize the foreign policy apparatus in the executive branch. But none of these Presidents have followed through.[24]

*Epilogue*

The last President to clearly place the leadership in foreign policy at State was Eisenhower, with John Foster Dulles; albeit Ford did it for a shorter period with Kissinger. Now in the fourth year of the Reagan administration, Reagan is making a clear effort in the same direction. Like Scowcroft who trained him, Robert C. McFarlane is a low-key White House national security adviser. Shultz has earned the respect both of State and the White House. Still this writer believes after Reagan, after Shultz, almost inevitably the balance, the leadership of foreign policy will shift back from Shultz to the White House.

The overarching objective of this paper was to uncover sources of incoherence in foreign policy by looking at the foreign policy process itself, and particularly at that aspect of the process which involves policymaking. The general pattern of foreign policymaking gravitating from State to the White House in recent Administrations underlies the thesis of the paper. If the evidence presented in the following analyses has validated the thesis, as I believe it has, then the solution to the problem is reduced to institutionalizing that which has existed in a de facto sense. To wit, designate a special White House staff to be responsible for policymaking on major foreign policy issues.

There is nothing inherently radical about this proposal, as White House personnel have traditionally controlled domestic policy. Moreover, it is the President who is responsible for conducting foreign policy and, therefore, his prerogative to construct whatever machinery best serves him in this capacity. To be sure, there would likely be significant opposition not only from the bureaucrats at State, but also from those who would fear the concentration of power in the White House and from those wedded to tradition. These are real political problems that a President or Presidential candidate would have to address skillfully.

Notwithstanding the political obstacles, the advantages of centering foreign policymaking in the White House are compelling. First, policymaking would be freed from the bureaucratic constraints that militate against creativity and boldness. Second, the incessant struggle between the White House and State over policymaking authority would be ended. Third, policy would be enunciated with a "single voice," thus putting to rest the specter of confusion and disarray that prevails when policy is enunciated from competing centers of power.

It is beyond the scope of this paper to describe in detail how the new White House staff would be organized, or to delineate its responsibilities. This is a task for a commission of foreign policy "wisemen." I would be amiss, however, if I did not address even briefly some of the glaring problems that are posed by this protocol.

1. Public support is essential for a restructuring of this sort. It is important, therefore, that a sitting President have confidence in the level of public support before acting. Better yet, a Presidential candidate who is favorably disposed to the proposal should campaign on it and then, if victorious, use his election as a mandate for the change.

2. The responsibilities of the new White House staff, of State, and of the National Security Council should be defined as unambiguously as is practical.

3. Personnel appointments are critical to the success of the proposal. The new staff head must possess the rare combination of geopolitical acumen, prescience, political pragmatism, and the restraint to not overshadow the President. Experienced, "idea oriented" personnel should comprise the staff. The Secretary of State should be a skilled administrator, experienced in foreign affairs, and disinterested in power or self-aggrandizement.

# CHAPTER EIGHTEEN

# National Security Policy: New Problems and Proposals

**R.D. McLAURIN**
ABBOTT ASSOCIATES, INC.
ALEXANDRIA, VIRGINIA

Over the past quarter century, but particularly in the last 15 years, the process of planning, formulating, administering, and implementing U.S. national security policy has become significantly more troublesome and the results of that process have with increasing frequency (but with one instructive exception) carried observers to question the coherence of policy and the very existence of integrated objectives. The present discussion considers some of the substantive changes in the external environment which U.S. policy must address. Following this brief review of "new realities," we will survey some of the major organizational problems. The essay concludes with a far-reaching proposal designed to overcome the organizational impediments and thereby facilitate better responses to substantive challenges.

## New Realities

Why has policy planning fallen on such hard times? What prevents the United States from pursuing clear-cut interests with equally clear-cut policies as the country is said to have done during the Eisenhower-Dulles period? A number of fundamental international and domestic changes have taken place since the 1950s which significantly alter the capabilities of the United States to identify and analyze its interests, articulate objectives that will support those interests, design policies to mediate between and optimize the realization of its objectives, and to carry out actions in accordance with prescribed policies.

First, the United States is more active in the world of today than it was many decades ago. Its virginal image is tarnished with the problems its leaders (and all countries) face in real-life interactions — real conflicts of interests with other peoples as well as commonalities of interests. In the 1950s, active American participation in world politics was still new; the American President, Dwight D. Eisenhower was recognized world-wide as a hero; and many regions—to a great extent coterminous with what came to be called the "Third World"—were left to our European allies who had major continuing or post-colonial residual interests there. Despite our best intentions and aid programs, masses and elites around the world no longer see the United States in such positive light.*

Second, the United States is relatively less powerful than it was in the 1950s. This is a reality to which Americans and foreign nationals alike have had an extremely difficult time adjusting. Power is an expression of a relationship between two or among several parties; it is "relative" by definition. That the United States possesses greater destructive military capability than ever before in its history is clear. But, then, so do France, Britain, and Italy. Yet, no one would argue that France is more powerful than it was in the Napoleonic era, Britain more powerful than it was during the 19th century, or Italy more powerful than in Roman days. The United States has greater military force than ever before, but has experienced a decline in power as a result of

• the sudden emergence of the Soviet Union and Soviet state system;

• behaviorally narrower boundaries for the application of military force outside superpower relationships;

• the proliferation of independent states and growth of alternative power centers (Western Europe, China, Japan, the Middle East); and

• a growing disjunction between military and other elements of national power.

The post World War II dominance of the United States receded in the mid-1950s as the Soviet Union's strategic military strength grew and its political control of Eastern Europe solidified. At the time of the Cuban missile crisis in 1962, the United States still enjoyed clear superiority. Only in the 1970s did Soviet military power really develop to a level where it could be considered essentially equal to that of the United States. After

---

* *Editor's Note: A somewhat more optimistic view is given by M. Peter McPherson in Chapter Six.*

the 1962 imbroglio the Soviets enormously increased their military build-up. Since the mid-1970s it can be said that there *are* in fact two superpowers.

Yet, Soviet power is in fact also in decline. The United States recent military build-up is a factor. Even as the Soviets own military capabilities have increased, the extent of Soviet control exerted over Eastern Europe has diminished. Since 1948, when Yugoslavia broke with the Comintern, this renegade communist state has been joined by Albania, Cambodia, China, Czechoslovakia, Hungary, Poland, and Romania — at different times, to different degrees, and in different domains. Few today would argue that the communist world is monolithic. The institutionalization of the Sino-Soviet conflict, one of the most important developments since World War II, in forcing the U.S.S.R. to consider China as well as the United States, in and of itself has greatly diminished Soviet power in world and even in U.S.-Soviet terms.

The second factor reducing U.S. power is greater limitation on the political use and impact of military force. "Gunboat diplomacy" is not a relic of the past, but it is clearly less credible than ever before. The United States dispatched a carrier task force to the Indian Ocean to influence Iran (while the latter held 52 U.S. diplomats against their will) in 1979–1980, and U.S. and Soviet ship and troop movements usually attend crises around the world. Nevertheless, the *use* of such force has been extremely rare in the last decade, partly due to offsetting force of the other superpower and partly due to the political costs of this kind of behavior in the Third World.

Third World views, and the views of U.S. and Soviet allies for that matter, are much more important than they were in the past, as the interdependence of the United States and the rest of the world has grown. Economically, militarily, politically — in all these ways United States interests are much more dependent on factors beyond our shores today. Only in the past decade have U.S. imports and exports become significant commercial and financial considerations in the economy. Only in the past two decades have our two oceans been overcome as natural defenses by potential adversary capabilities. Only recently has our political future become so dependent for these reasons on Europe, Middle East, and Asian developments. When the views of others outside a two-party conflict must be considered, the boundaries of the acceptable use of force narrow appreciably.

Interdependence, then, has increased the "power" of the weaker states whose resources (whether intangible, such as political support, or tangible, such as strategic minerals) are otherwise limited. So too has the very proliferation of these states, as the larger world community dilutes the power and capabilities of those trying to manage it, notably the superpowers. Moreover, the growth in the number of states, each acting independently on its own perceived interests, complicates regional political realities, increases the number of actual and potential conflicts that may arise, thereby providing new vehicles for outside penetration by the superpowers. On the one hand, then, it becomes less and less feasible to exclude or extrude the Soviet Union from *any* region — to "contain" Russia; on the other hand, external intervention is less and less able to control (even if it significantly influences or alters the course of events).

States may be juridically equal (the doctrine of sovereign equality), but they are not equal in capabilities or resources. Still, the number of alternative power centers — i.e., apart from the superpowers — has clearly increased and the nature of effective power has broadened. Today, countries like Saudi Arabia, with negligible military forces, are actors of great consequence globally as well as regionally, based upon resources and finance factors. Historically there are discrepancies between military and other types of power, but the degree of disjunction today is unprecedented.

These considerations suggest strongly that the relative decline of U.S. and Soviet power may be an enduring phenomenon, not one caused by ineffective policy formulation, inconstant will, or isolationist thinking. Another phenomenon related to the decline of bipolar power is political fluidity. American leaders generally react negatively to significant political change, especially in areas still largely under U.S. or other Western influence (e.g., Latin America). The same reaction is characteristic of any great power in history in similar circumstances. Yet, major changes can be anticipated in the decade of the 1980s. Fluid political alignments are likely as a result of many of the developments already discussed. Moreover, growing pressures toward political disintegration of existing non-national states all over the world — in North America (Canada and the Caribbean), Europe (Belgium and Cyprus), Asia (especially in the Middle East and Oceania)—even if they do not result in the redrawing of boundaries are certain to threaten *regional* as well as internal stability. These pressures, which will provide a fertile ground for troublemakers, will challenge both the creativity of U.S. policy and the resilience of the world community.

In addition to the new international realities discussed above, there are a number of developments *within* the United States that have been inadequately considered heretofore. Two of the most important of these phenomena are the impact of communications and thinking along the lines of Henry Prince of Wales. Together these changes have paralyzed U.S. national security policy formulation.

Modern communications has wholly altered the relationship between government and the public, particularly in open societies where the fourth estate can and does penetrate the innermost circles of the decision elite.

• The constant awareness that private communication among executive, legislative, and even judicial branch elites may be "revealed," that is to say spectacularly exposed in the public media, outside the unique private context in which it took place, has had an increasingly chilling effect on the willingness of those involved in the policy process to express their ideas openly when they believe those policies to be opprobrious.

• Ubiquitous mass media demand an instant response to new developments, frequently forcing decisions before adequate intelligence is available to support the decision.

• The focus of media attention tends to give out-sized and enduring significance to marginal and ephemeral events only because they are likely to interest—for a brief period—a broad audience. The omnipresence of communications media in virtually all major sectors of the articulate public tends to pervert perspective.

• Highly developed communications techniques and facilities have significantly strengthened interest groups of all types, enabling them to mobilize their often small constituency forcefully around the few issues that deeply concern them. Because the *formation* of interest groups has also been facilitated by the availability of communications, virtually *every* action of government now affects some interest groups that can mobilize against it. Consequently, government is paralyzed not by the wishes of the majority but increasingly by the mobilization of a multitude of minorities, often minute minorities at that.

In Shakespeare's King Henry IV, Part II, the king said to Henry Prince of Wales, "Thy wish was father . . . to that thought." Yet, wishful thinking is not merely a positive orientation towards an unrealistically favorable approach or policy; it consists as well of the refusal to recognize unfavorable realities. True, real leadership needs to shape the environment rather than merely respond to it. However, it is the positive duty of leadership to recognize and adapt to unalterable realities. American leaders have been unwilling to face many of the new realities we have discussed in this paper. In addressing the public they shy from the unpopular truths which must guide any amelioration of U.S. national security policymaking. They are afraid they will be labeled negativists if they point to the decline and future decline of U.S. power. The same spirit guides their pronouncements on military, economic, and political aspects of national policy: they seek and promise output with no input, profit with no risk, progress without resource allocation.

As our international relations directly affect a larger and larger segment of the American population for reasons discussed earlier, the growing paralysis of government ever more seriously imperils the ability of the United States to identify, assess, and choose from the full range of options truly available.

### Planning National Security Policy

We turn now to the process of planning policy. Until recently, the decisionmaking system or model used for national security planning was largely ignored. Observers, analysts, and even decisionmakers paid scant attention to *process* factors in their discussions of national security planning, relegating these considerations to the descriptive background. It is hardly reasonable to suppose the first 30-odd presidents and their secretaries of state were ignorant or stupid. Rather, we suggest that organizational issues have become *objectively* more important in the policy process: the decision-making elite is larger, the federal bureaucracy is enormous, the United States is much more actively involved in the world, that "world" is composed of far more actors, and so forth.

Until relatively recently — let us say, some time after the Second

World War—the foreign policy of the United States could be formulated, administered, and executed within the Department of State. Only in times of military crisis or in terms of a very few issues were inputs required from the War and Navy Departments, or after 1947, the Department of Defense, or other cabinet departments. Until the same date, 1947, there was no Central Intelligence Agency to organize the information relevant to policy making, although centralized intelligence functions really date to World War II's Office of Strategic Services (OSS). If "war is much too important to be left to generals," then surely it is clear that foreign policy is far too broad, in view of the contemporary role of the United States in the world, to be left to the Department of State.

National security policy involves critical decisions—and, admittedly, many more less-than-critical ones—involving the resources of the Departments of Defense and State and the information and analysis of the CIA, primarily, and, secondarily, the more intermittent contributions and perspectives of other elements of the executive branch.

The growth of the requirement for defense and intelligence communities' participation in foreign policy is one of the most important developments in modern U.S. government. It has also proved one of the most difficult problems, because interdepartmental policy coordination has always been characterized by conflict between divergent interests, perceptions, objectives, and decisionmaking styles.

As a result of the inability of ad hoc interdepartmental cooperation to meet the challenges of the 1960s, Henry Kissinger, then the designee for the position of special assistant to the president for national security affairs, developed a system that resuscitated the moribund National Security Council. The NSC, operating as a part of the White House, was given a more formal role and broader powers in policy review and coordination as well as in the articulation of policy options for presidential decision. Even after Kissinger became secretary of state, he retained substantial influence over the NSC apparatus both through personal loyalty and through the clear-cut dominance of channels of communication with an increasingly embattled presidency. Under President Jimmy Carter the NSC retained its central role in the policy process, but absent Kissinger competition arose between the new secretary of state and the new national security affairs chief. Consequently, the political opposition stated it would, if elected, return the state department to its foreign policy primacy, subordinating the NSC to the cabinet departments.

Any student of government decisionmaking patterns or anyone who has been intimately familiar with or a part of the national security apparatus over the past decade, should have recognized the problems facing President Reagan in re-arranging decision roles in the national security system. Foreign and defense policies are so interwoven today that myriad issues cannot be resolved in interdepartmental councils without the superimposition of the president's authority. The problem is complicated by bureaucratic styles that are virtually opposite as between the two departments. This essay in no way denigrates the efforts of the Reagan administration to effectively utilize the cabinet. For this President the cabinet councils are an effective device. For this President the National Security Council with its Senior Interagency Groups is functioning reasonably well.* Ultimately, and except for periods when one of the two secretaries has a distinctly predominant influence that allows him to impose his will on both departments, the United States will be forced toward an approach returning more integrating and coordinating power to the White House staff.

A major national security planning problem facing the United States is the *absence* of coherent planning. What commands attention within the bureaucracy is work on *existing* problems, so this is what the aspiring bureaucrat seeks to be involved in. In his terms, he wants "to make a difference"; "to make a contribution." Since, as Parkinson's Law stipulates, "work expands so as to fill the time available for its completion," planners inevitably devote their time to putting out today's fires. Every study of policy planning in the U.S. Department of Defense and State shows immediate erosion of the policy *planning* function in favor of policy *action*. In the halcyon days of Kissinger's NSC, however, the ability of the "White House" to command and direct the planning guaranteed greater attention to this function. (It did not, of course, guarantee the *quality* of planning.) Without super-departmental direction, the national security team tends

---

* *Editor's Note: See Chapter Fifteen on the Reagan National Security Council.*

to exhibit greater diversity and to allocate inadequate resources to planning. The inattention to linkages between issue-areas and developments often strikes outside observers as appalling, but it is a natural result of incoherent planning.

Similarly, the central purpose of planning is to establish priorities. Without a clear-cut set of priorities, consistent and effective policy becomes impossible. Yet, overall national security priorities cannot be established within the federal government, and the mechanics of interdepartmental prioritization are at best clumsy. Here, too, the orchestration of multidepartmental inputs to facilitate presidential priority determination has probably dictated accretion of authority around the White House staff. It remains to identify a means to institutionalize and legitimize this role.

What can be done to resolve this seemingly insurmountable bureaucratic hurdle in the formulation of effective national security policy? It is my belief that there is no side-effect-free answer to the problem, any more than there are clear-cut and cost-free resolutions to other complex problems. We can strengthen one cabinet secretary or the other, we can strengthen or weaken the NSC advisor. Each approach has its advocates, each its advantages, each its pitfalls. To a large extent, the "best" alignment must be determined on the basis of the personalities of the president and his national security advisors at any specific moment. Thus, there is no single answer, but there *may* be a set of options that optimizes decisionmaking potential.

## A Proposal

Since its first cabinet, the United States has had a secretary of state. The secretary of defense, of course, is a much newer position established by the National Security Act of 1947, but cabinet-level secretaries of the army (called secretary of war until 1947) and navy also dated from early years of the republic. Distinct functions clearly inhere to those two primary national security departments, state and defense. However, it is widely forgotten today that the proposal to create a department of defense was considered a major change in U.S. defense organization. Indeed, it is arguable that the results of that change have far exceeded what many anticipated. Reorganizations are endemic to the defense department (as they would be to any organization of equal size), but few seriously propose a return to the pre-1947 era.

I believe serious consideration should be given to the creation of a department of national security. Make no mistake — I do not believe serious consideration *will* be given to the idea, only that it should be. As I indicated, there is no single solution to the problems of reorganizing the national security structure, and I do not except this idea from that general caveat. However, the idea of a unified department of national security, while it would attract little support and much opposition at this time, does appear to address some of the most important problems we have encountered heretofore. There are at least two alternative forms such an approach might take; following a brief discussion of these I shall discuss the advantages and the general approach offers.

The first, most desirable, most controversial, and least likely alternative is a truly unified cabinet department of national security composed of at least two elements — a department of defense and a department of foreign affairs (or state). (I shall not address the incorporation of foreign intelligence responsibilities into the proposed creation at this time because it raises many additional questions.) Under this proposal the secretary of national security would be the president's principal advisor on matters of national security, including both foreign and defense affairs. In the case of national security questions, the secretaries of defense and foreign affairs (or state) would be subordinate to the secretary of national security. However, the two principal components of the department would otherwise continue to operate with the degree of independence they do now. The foreign service would remain separate from the civil service, and on matters internal to the departments of foreign affairs and defense the respective secretaries would be the principal decision-makers as at present.

An alternative to the creation of a unified department of national security affairs is the creation of a super-cabinet within the present cabinet with the national security affairs advisor given informal but effective control over defense and state departments. Such a supercabinet might include advisors on national security (defense, state, and the intelligence community), economics (commerce, treasury, transportation, energy), and society (interior, justice, health and human resources). This essay will focus on the first alternative because it is believed to be both constitutionally and administratively superior as well as a greater break with the past.

On the one hand, the vast majority of actions and decisions in both defense and state departments are internal and do not require any outside consultation; on the other, a disproportionate number of the major national security decisions and actions *do* require the consideration and different perspectives of both departments. The major advantage of this proposal in either form is that it recognizes and meets both sets of needs.

## Consideration

Another advantage of this proposal relates to a problem that has troubled observers for at least two decades. The dramatic growth in the symbolic or representational role of the secretary of state, first, and more recently of the secretary of defense as well, has placed unprecedented time demands on these leaders. It is simply impossible for them to give adequate attention to substantive decision responsibilities and still host and visit foreign dignitaries. A variety of suggestions has been advanced that would separate decision-making and representational functions. However, foreign leaders want to meet with the *secretary*, not a subordinate, and they want to interact with the constitutionally sanctioned foreign policy advisor to the president. Again, a completely acceptable resolution is elusive, but the proposal I have advanced assumes that the secretary of foreign affairs (state) remains the principal foreign policy advisor to the president, though he is subordinate to the overall national security secretary. The latter would *not* normally host foreign visitors. He would not administer the foreign policy of the United States. Nor would he have the responsibility for administering the department of defense. Thus, foreign visitors would deal with the secretaries of defense and foreign affairs (state), as they do at present. These two officers would retain cabinet rank.

A precedent for the coincident cabinet rank of the three secretaries is not altogether hoary. Under the National Security Act of 1947 which created the Department of Defense, the newly created secretary of defense joined the service secretaries in the cabinet. This arrangement did not work out well for a number of reasons, and the service secretaries left the cabinet under a

1949 reorganization. The possibility that some of the same problems might arise under the proposed arrangement cannot be excluded, and similar steps might have to be taken, although the clear-cut divisional superordination of the secretary of national security on those policy matters affecting both defense and state departments may go some distance toward precluding jurisdictional squabbles and authority disputes.

As the principal advisor to the president on broad questions of national security, the secretary of national security would have that intangible but far-reaching power to say, in dealing with subordinates, "the president wants." This phrase has been employed by ambitious national security advisors in the past to direct bureaucratic assets otherwise outside their control.

Perhaps the greatest problem in the past has been interdepartmental conflict resolution. When neither cabinet secretary enjoys greater confidence of the president than the other conflict resolution is difficult. Relatively unimportant issues tend to be pushed to unreasonably high levels for decision, and in order to brake this tendency decisions are "waffled" rather than made. The existence of a policy arbiter below the president yet above the current secretarial level and in the interstices of overlapping departmental responsibilities should facilitate decisionmaking, although no organizational framework can overcome individual incompetence. The purpose of the proposal is to better support competent decisionmakers, allowing them to act effectively, rather than to overcome incompetent ones, which is not possible.

The trilateral competition between the advisor to the president for national security affairs and the secretaries of state and defense has resulted in part from the coequal relationship of the latter two. I would not propose to subordinate defense to state or vice versa. However, subordination of both departments to a secretary of national security should dramatically affect the relationships. Certainly, the defense-state bureaucratic rivalry will continue. However, with both secretaries and their bureaucracies *subordinate* to a national security secretary the incentive structure to support the latter is altered, for his views about the support he receives from each subordinate department must affect how the subordinate secretaries look in his — and the president's — eyes. The entire staff structure supporting each secretary is traditionally influenced by sensitivity to the need to protect and advance the image and credibility of its chief officer. In effect, then, defense and state department employees are likely to provide powerful support to the secretary of national security *through* their respective secretaries.

Another problem encountered in the rise of the advisor to the president for national security affairs has been the demoralization of the professional staffs in the departments of defense and state, most notably the Foreign Service of the United States. That this morale problem has arisen should hardly have been a surprise. In effect, the foreign affairs professionals give voice to their views through the secretary of state who may accept their recommendations or reject them. Manifestly, the secretary, who serves at the pleasure of the president, must be sensitive to a much broader range of variables (often, political variables) than his state department subordinates, but he at least is accessible to them and to a certain extent dependent upon them. By contrast, the national security affairs advisor is outside their "loop." He has his own staff, however small, and may never see or consider the professionals' views. The price is in the effectiveness of foreign policy and the relationship with the secretary of state — both important but indirect and unsatisfying considerations to foreign affairs and defense professionals. Under the proposal advanced here, however, the national security secretary would be part of the same bureaucracy as both staffs, and his decisions would necessarily appear to reflect at least consideration of staff views, as do the decisions of the departmental secretaries today.

One objection to the creation of a unified national security department would certainly be that it is too dangerous to create such an "all powerful" position. Let us briefly consider this criticism. Drafted in the aftermath of both the American Revolution and the ill-fated Articles of Confederation, the Constitution of the United States reflects the fears of both an all-powerful *and* an overly weak executive. In order to prevent the emergence of a monarchical presidency, the Constitution divides decision-making authority among the three principal branches of government (the so-called "checks and balances") and provides that residual authority lies in the states ("federalism," much of which is now a disused concept). Executive authority is vested in a president, but the president must look to Congress for both budgetary support and some legislative action for his programs and, traditionally, to the Senate for its (advice and) consent to his appointments. *Custom* has mandated a cabinet system, and American history shows numerous reorganizations of that cabinet. There is certainly no constitutional bar to the proposal made here, and intra-executive branch "checks and balances" were never seen by the drafters of the Constitution as a means to restrain the executive branch.

Historically, we have had some experience with national security affairs advisors whose power extended to the virtual policy direction of both departments of defense and state over a range of issues. That is to say, whether or not the present proposal should be adopted, the national security advisor to the president can be granted virtually the same power *with* the substantial disadvantages I have already discussed and *without* the consent of the Senate.

Moreover, practically speaking, no cabinet department has very much *political* power without the support of the Congress to which it must look for budgetary appropriations and authorizations. As far as *physical* power — the power to stage a *coup d'état* or otherwise use military force, the quasi-addition of a foreign affairs staff to the defense department certainly does not increase its military capabilities. Indeed, it could be argued that a marriage of the two departments might further reduce the probability of such an eventuality.

We have had ample evidence that uncoordinated decision processes and internal conflicts lead to ineffective national security policy. I believe ineffective policy is a proximate threat to vital U.S. interests, and therefore to the overall national security of the United States. A national reallocation of responsibilities in accordance with the nature of contemporary U.S. national security requirements is long overdue.

# No First Use and Conventional Deterrence: The Politics of Defense Policymaking*

**WALLACE EARL WALKER**
ASSOCIATE PROFESSOR OF SOCIAL SCIENCES
UNITED STATES MILITARY ACADEMY

**ANDREW F. KREPINEVICH**
ASSISTANT PROFESSOR OF SOCIAL SCIENCES
UNITED STATES MILITARY ACADEMY

> Military policy can only be understood as the responses of the government to conflicting pressures from its foreign and domestic environments. Decisions on strategic programs, in particular, must be viewed in the broader context of American politics and government. . . . The process of consensus building and consensus changing (innovation) in military policy do not differ significantly from those in other policy areas.[1]

These words ring as true today as when they were written over a generation ago by Samuel Huntington. Indeed, anyone seeking to understand the ongoing debate over the role of U.S. forces in Europe and the corresponding issue of No First Use of nuclear weapons by NATO cannot help but examine the strong currents in American domestic politics which stand to have a major impact on the prospects for change in the Alliance's defense posture. In fact, the current furor over the relative burden to be borne by NATO's nuclear and conventional forces in providing a deterrent to Soviet aggression in Europe has strong domestic political implications which can only be ignored at the Administration's peril.

---

*\* The views contained in this article are those of the authors and should not be considered as those of the Department of Defense, the Department of the Army or the United States Military Academy. Adopted from the forthcoming* Conventional Deterrence in NATO: Alternatives for European Defense, *edited by COL James R. Golden, LTC Asa A. Clark, IV, and CPT Bruce E. Arlinghaus (Lexington, Mass.: Lexington Books, D.C. Heath and Co., copyright 1984, D.C. Heath & Co.)*

At issue is the Alliance's declared policy of shifting the primary burden of deterrence from its nuclear forces to NATO's general purpose, or conventional, forces. The principal benefit to be derived from such a shift, we are told, would be the enhancement of NATO's ability to blunt a Warsaw Pact conventional attack without resorting to nuclear weapons — a defense posture of No First Use of these weapons. As NATO conventional forces are currently considered substantially inferior to those of the Pact, the buildup would be substantial in size and expense.** Yet the benefits of increased flexibility in responding to Soviet aggression and of raising the nuclear "threshold" have been sufficient to place the issue on the Alliance's agenda.

This paper will focus on the American domestic political environment and its role in the defense policy process. That environment imposes substantial constraints on any administration's freedom of action in defense policymaking. However, in order to understand the prospects for an enhanced conventional deterrent in NATO, we must first examine America's perception of the Alliance and the implications involved in adopting such a policy.

Almost from the birth of the post-war era, Americans have seen their security interests inextricably entwined with the democracies of Western Europe. Possessing a common heritage, the United States and the other nations of the North Atlantic Community joined together in the NATO Alliance to preserve common values against a hostile and aggressive Soviet state. Since its formation in 1949, American political leaders have consistently voiced their support for a strong NATO. The American public, with scant exception, has backed its leaders in their efforts to strengthen U.S. ties in what Robert Osgood has called the "Entangling Alliance".[2] Indeed, the bonds of cultural affinity and common acknowledgement of the Soviet threat have made NATO the most stable and enduring alliance in history.

Although America's continued participation in NATO has never seriously been questioned by its political leadership, and only rarely among the American people, the share of the NATO defense burden assumed by the United States has become an

---

** *Editor's Note: For a somewhat differing view of NATO's conventional forces see: Chapter Two of* The Presidency and National Security Policy *and the Editor's Note therein.*

increasingly salient feature in Alliance politics. Thus, while U.S. participation in the Alliance is not a source of friction on the domestic political front, the "fairness" issue (or burden sharing problem) has become a source of intra-Alliance *angst*. The question of how much the proposed shift towards greater reliance on the conventional deterrent will increase the U.S. defense burden for NATO is, therefore, an important one, particularly as it relates to the necessity for creating a domestic consensus in support of such a policy move.

Recently General Rogers, the Supreme Allied Commander in Europe (SACEUR) and a former Army Chief of Staff, contended that Alliance conventional capabilities were "clearly inadequate" to meet the growing Warsaw Pact conventional threat.[3] Moving toward a conventional deterrence posture, according to Rogers, would require NATO members to increase their defense budgets by four percent in real terms annually until 1989, an increase of only one percent over the level agreed upon by the allies in 1977 and reaffirmed by the heads of NATO in June 1982.[4] Thus General Rogers' "Four Percent Solution" would seem to represent the American taxpayer's bill for this shift to an enhanced conventional deterrent, and a possible strategy involving No First Use of nuclear weapons.

However, when the Four Percent Solution is compared to other studies examining the requirements for a shift toward a conventional deterrent, it appears General Rogers may have minimized the actual expense involved. Former Secretary of State Haig, for example, has contended that if the United States and its allies were to rely solely on conventional forces to defeat a non-nuclear Pact assault, America would have to "reintroduce the draft, triple the size of its armed forces and put its economy on a wartime footing."[5] While this may be putting the worst face possible on such a reorientation of Alliance strategy, other studies indicated the Four Percent Solution would provide only a marginal shift in deterrence burden from the nuclear to the general purpose forces. One study by over fifty European and American defense experts sponsored by the American Academy of Arts and Sciences concluded that the Four Percent Solution would allow NATO to fight for only a month, at most, before having to resort to nuclear weapons, and only in the case where the Alliance had two to three weeks advanced warning to mobilize its forces.

The conclusions reached by the American Academy study are reinforced in studies done for the *Economist* and by the Congressional Budget Office (CBO). The *Economist* study concluded that a month's respite was all NATO could hope for from such a policy, and that extending the period of "denuclearization" past that point would require the United States to initiate draft registration, engage in the construction of numerous training facilities, and create additional "surge" capability in the defense industry.[6] The CBO report reached the conclusion that to adopt a credible conventional defense posture, the United States would have to add two fully-supported armored divisions (roughly 100,000 troops) to its NATO contingent and its allies would be required to effect proportionate increases in the size of their forces.[7]

Given the past history of U.S. and allied defense buildups, the prospects for meeting even the minimalist Four Percent Solution do not appear promising. The large U.S. defense buildups of 1950–53 and 1960–63 were undertaken during a period of real economic growth on the order of 16.6% and 12.9% respectively, far in excess of what most experts forecast for the 1980s. The situation becomes even more bleak when one realizes that our NATO allies increased their defense budgets by only two percent per annum in the 1970s, and by less than that in their 1982 expenditures. Secretary of Defense Weinberger has already admitted that ". . . some force goals are only partially implemented or with full implementation delayed beyond 1988."[8] Having said this, and given the scope of the discussion, this paper will limit its analysis to a consideration of whether or not the American domestic political environment is likely to provide fertile ground for acceptance of the "best case" criterion, General Rogers' Four Percent Solution, allowing it to take root as an element of the nation's defense policy.

### Coalitions and Defense Spending

Three primary factions on the issue of national defense spending can be identified. The Defense Advocates favor a large defense buildup in both strategic and conventional forces. The Freezers are preoccupied with stopping production of nuclear weapons, reducing them or making declarations about weapons use. The Priority Shifters want to redesign the defense agenda of the

Reagan Administration by altering the allocation of resources. Clearly some individuals and groups may be classified in two of these categories, but in nearly every case their primary concerns are limited to one faction.

## Defense Advocates

The most significant U.S. political development of the middle and late 1970's was the ascendancy of conservatives in both parties. Growing out of the 1964 Goldwater candidacy, the conservative wing of the Republican party achieved a new salience in that party's affairs. Frequently allied with elements in the Democratic party on national security issues, conservatives continued to support increases in the military budget throughout the 1970's. Perceiving that the Great Society programs had failed, a new group of neoconservative intellectuals coalesced around opposition to increased federal involvement in social and economic affairs and around a growing concern over the nation's defenses in the face of a large and sustained Soviet arms buildup. These concerns were manifested in a nearly successful challenge by then Governor Ronald Reagan to President Gerald Ford in the Republican primaries in 1976. The resulting split between moderates and conservatives in the general election and the national distaste over the Watergate affair cost the Republicans a presidential victory. In place of a conservative to moderate Republican president, the nation chose a fiscally conservative Democratic president in Jimmy Carter.

The Carter Administration's stewardship over defense and foreign policy was not widely acclaimed. Carter's cancellation of the B-1 bomber early in his term upset conservatives who charged that U.S. strategic forces had been seriously impaired by the decision. The SALT II Treaty negotiated by the Administration was viewed by conservatives and by many moderates as unverifiable and too generous to the Soviets in its allocation of strategic weapons systems. Soviet activism in Africa in the 1970's, the invasion of Afghanistan, and political intervention in Poland to quell the Solidarity movement reinforced elite and subsequently mass concern over the Soviet military buildup. The capture of American diplomats by Iranian radicals and the failure of the U.S. rescue mission convinced many in the United States that American military and political influence abroad was waning and that this loss could only be restored by increased military strength.

These shifts in mass opinion were reflected in election results and a new political agenda. Mass support for increased defense spending was manifested in 1976, 1978 and 1980 as conservative candidates were particularly successful in congressional elections.[9] With the election of Ronald Reagan to the presidency in 1980 and with conservative Republicans assuming control of the Senate, the new agenda for American politics became the restoration of U.S. military might, the revival of the American economy through reduced taxes, and a retrenchment in the Welfare State.

The efforts of conservatives in the government were buttressed by neoconservative intellectuals, think tanks and partisan groups, all devoted to enhancing U.S. defense capabilities. Representative of the intellectuals was Norman Podhoretz, whose 1980 book *The Present Danger* called for large increases in the defense budget.[10] Think tanks supporting the Defense Advocates included the American Enterprise Institute, the Georgetown University Center for Strategic and International Studies and the Hoover Institution on War, Revolution and Peace. While some of these research institutes eschewed the conservative label, they provided numerous experts for the foreign and defense policy transition teams established by President-elect Reagan, as well as appointees in that Administration's Defense and State Departments.

Partisan groups professing to be conservative public interest groups also sprung up to support defense increases. The Heritage Foundation and the Committee on the Present Danger organized their activities around the premise that the U.S. had to increase defense spending and modernize its weapons systems to meet growing Soviet military strength. The American Security Council and its arm, The Coalition for Peace Through Strength, designed a voting index that assessed the support of individual congressmen on defense issues, opposed the SALT II Treaty, and resisted the nuclear freeze movement through lobbying and grass root activities.[11]

Of course the leading proponent of the Defense Advocates was President Reagan himself. Reagan campaign aides shaped the 1980 Republican Party platform which argued for military and technological superiority over the Soviet Union. During the campaign Reagan charged that the U.S. military "margin of safety" which had maintained world peace since World War II had diminished as a result of Carter policies. Reagan's campaign called for "the restoration of American military strength as the centerpiece for a new foreign policy".[12]

Once in office the Reagan Administration vigorously pursued this goal. Public statements by President Reagan seemed designed to build public support for increased defense spending. In testimony before Congress, his Defense Secretary argued that the defense budget must respond to the Soviet threat, not to domestic exigencies. The result was that during the first part of Reagan's term, real budget increases were achieved, although they were far below his original proposals.

The Administration's proposals were attacked by defense and foreign policy analysts as well as by the Freezers and Priority Shifters. Some critics argued that Reagan's military policies sought to substitute military power for diplomacy.[13] Others contended that Reagan's statements damaged the Administration's credibility and promoted public anxiety. Still others observed that the 1980 and 1981 consensus for rearming America was frittered away by loose talk and a poor articulation of national strategy.

### The Freezers

The early 1980's witnessed the re-emergence of the semi-dormant Anti-nuclear Peace Movement in the United States, this time focusing its energies on the Nuclear Freeze issue. The movement has a long heritage that is loosely tied to the American tradition of isolationism.

Pacifist traits in the American national character have shown their colors in bold relief within the anti-nuclear forces, which argue that nuclear weapons and the U.S. Defense Establishment have joined the Soviet Union as the source of evil in the world. The same idealism and sense of moral superiority witnessed in isolationist, pre-war America finds its expression today in the Freeze Movement. Unable to influence decisionmakers in the Kremlin, the Freeze advocates focused most of their energies against the Reagan Administration as the stumbling block to progress on their agenda. Thus, for better or ill, the Reagan Administration found itself in the midst of yet another peak in the cyclical phenomenon that is the Peace Movement.

It seems self-evident that the latest resurgence of the Peace Movement had its roots in the election of Ronald Reagan and his efforts to dramatically increase the nation's nuclear forces to close what he perceived to be a "window of vulnerability" to Soviet nuclear attack. Not only did the nuclear buildup serve to catalyze the Freezers, but early rhetoric on the part of the Administration on the subject of nuclear war and the strategic balance expanded their ranks and provided them with not a little ammunition in the war of words.[14]

Significantly, the Freezers reached out beyond the traditional ranks of the anti-nuclear protesters to produce a broad, albeit thin, coalition in support of their platform. Added to the core of pacifists, intellectuals, clergy and students were large segments of the environmentalist lobby along with a number of women's, labor, and minority groups. They were drawn to the movement not only out of anxiety over the prospects of a global nuclear holocaust, but because the Freezers, besides being against nuclear weapons in particular, were *against defense spending in general*. That is to say, while the movement supported a reduction in emphasis on NATO nuclear deterrence, they did not support the increases in general purpose forces to enhance conventional deterrence. As Leon Wieseltier so aptly states it,

> What began as a campaign against bombs has become a campaign against tanks. . . . The problem is not pacifism. . . . [but] a much more serious proposition, which is that the use of force is not a legitimate instrument of national policy in the nuclear age.[15]

Initially the Freeze Movement showed impressive strength. Perhaps its greatest appeal was in its simplicity, advocating a mutual and verifiable Soviet-American halt to the testing, production, and deployment of nuclear weapons coupled with a U.S. declaration of No First Use. The resolution was short and easy for the average American to understand. It offered up an outcome that appeared to be at once both moral and extremely desirable. The effectiveness of the freeze resolution was borne out by its early success on local and state referenda. Through the end of 1982, eight of nine states that had freeze referenda presented for a vote saw the measure passed. Similar results were achieved in nearly three dozen cases on the local level. National public opinion polls taken by a variety of firms showed the vast majority of Americans support the idea of a nuclear freeze. Indeed, over 750,000 people under the combined banner of over 100 organizations participated in a rally in New York's Central Park in June 1982, the largest demonstration of its kind in the City's history.

Of greater concern to the Administration, the Freezers picked up substantial support in the Congress. Following in the footsteps of similar groups, the Nuclear Freeze Political Action Committee distributed funds to the campaigns of congressional candidates supporting the freeze during the fall election campaign of 1982. In the wake of the Democratic gains in the House of Representatives, the Freezers continued to exhibit impressive strength in the months following the congressional elections. The House blocked, albeit temporarily, funds for the production and deployment of the MX missile and then later passed a nuclear freeze resolution. The Freezers received further support when the country's Catholic bishops approved a pastoral letter supporting both the concept of a freeze and a policy of No First Use.

Nor were the leading candidates for the 1984 Democratic presidential nomination hesitant to climb aboard the Freezer bandwagon. Senators Cranston, Glenn, and Hart all came out in support of the freeze proposal, as did former Vice President Mondale. Significantly, Cranston was able to produce straw poll victories in Massachusetts, Wisconsin, and Alabama by portraying himself as the Peace Candidate, much to the delight of the freeze activists.

While the Freezers demonstrated surprising strength, they possessed significant, and perhaps fatal, weaknesses as well. While their resolution held considerable appeal as a moralistic slogan, it was not able to make the transition to workable policy. Although many Americans found it easy to voice support for a mutual, verifiable freeze in *principal*, they voiced equally strong suspicions concerning the *practicality* of a freeze. Most felt that the Russians would cheat on an agreement and gain an advantage over the United States if one were agreed to. Thus while the Freeze won support as a desideratum, the American public saw little hope for its application in a world of realpolitik.

By 1983 there were signs that the movement was running out of steam as the self-proclaimed *zeitgeist* of the eighties. The Freezers record on referenda, so impressive in 1982, slipped dramatically in the early months of 1983 when only thirteen of 39 local and municipal resolutions passed. Furthermore, the Congress eventually traded funding of the MX for increased presidential flexibility on arms control at the START talks. Perhaps the best description of the Freeze Movement by late 1983 was that offered by Roger Mollander, the head of the peace-oriented, educational organization Ground Zero, when he stated "the freeze campaign as a vehicle for raising consciousness on the nuclear war issue probably peaked in the fall of 1982."[16]

### Priority Shifters

The final coalition is an amalgam of three splinter groups generally opposed to increased defense spending. Members of these groups frequently have voted together on defense issues, but their rationales have differed significantly.

*Reformers*. Reformers have traditionally played a role in realigning American military policies. Heretofore men such as Alfred Thayer Mahan, Emory Upton and Elihu Root have transformed military thought from inside the military establishment. A new breed of Reformers has, however, appeared. They have sought promotion of their cause from the legislative branch. Primarily they consist of former DOD employees and whistleblowers. Their conviction is that as much or more defense can be achieved with less spending.

In early 1981 Senator Gary Hart (D, Colo) and Representative G. William Whitehurst (R, Va) agreed to form a Military Reform Caucus on Capitol Hill. The Caucus was to consider changes in military strategy to put more emphasis on maneuver and deception. Eventually, they signed up over 50 members of Congress to include conservatives, moderates and liberals in both parties and in both chambers.[17]

The Caucus loosely allied itself with several groups outside the government. The Center for Defense Information, staffed principally by retired senior military officers, opposed the Reagan defense spending increases and called for more intensive congressional oversight and improved DOD planning. Several DOD critics created the Project on Military Procurement which served reporters as a source for leaked DOD documents about expensive weapons programs.

Defense consultants and analysts played a major conceptual role for the Reformers. Perhaps the father of the movement was retired Air Force Colonel John Boyd, who argued that a maneuver-based fighting doctrine dependent on faster tempos was more effective in destroying the enemy's will to fight than attrition warfare practiced by the United States. Others contended that instead of technologically sophisticated weapons systems, simple and abundant ones were needed to achieve maneuver warfare.[18] James Fallows, whose book *National Defense* was widely read, argued that the Pentagon, dominated by a culture of procurement, inflated the threat to insure Congress would approve its weapons proposals.[19]

The Congressional Military Reform Caucus, like its fellow critics outside the government, had no single, coherent position on reform. Rather it sought to serve as a clearinghouse of information on defense issues, a development of concern to the Pentagon because nearly one-third of the Caucus sat on one of the DOD authorization or appropriation committees. There was widespread agreement among the Reformers that the cost of purchasing weapons systems could be significantly lowered by reduced reliance on advanced technology while at the same time still providing more than adequate combat capability. Furthermore, many indicated that U.S. forces should be more reliant on the reserves and National Guard, a position that both the House and Senate Armed Services Committees adopted in 1983.

Senator Gary Hart used the Reform movement as a platform in his bid for the presidency. He provided a detailed package for defense reform which included a new set of strategic guidelines, budget proposals and weapons procurement decisions. Specifically his proposals called for elimination for Army and Air Force plans for deep interdiction missions against Soviet second echelon forces and an end to Navy preoccupation with aircraft carriers as a form of force projection.

*Domestic Spenders.* Tracing their roots back to the New Deal and profoundly disturbed by the Reagan Administration's cuts in social programs, the Domestic Spenders sought to reduce defense spending in favor of social programs. This group was composed of liberals in Congress as well as liberal organizations in the health, welfare, education, and urban development communities.

Perhaps the most visible Domestic Spender in Congress was Senator Edward Kennedy (D, Mass) who, throughout his 20-year tenure, had championed government programs for the poor. In the debate over the 1983 defense authorization he commented that, "It is clear that Congress must trim the defense budget if we are to insure social and economic health for this nation."[20]

Kennedy's concerns were shared by Senate Minority Leader Robert Byrd (D, W. Va), Speaker of the House Thomas O'Neill (D, Mass), and former Vice President and 1984 presidential candidate Walter Mondale. During the 1983 debate, Byrd introduced an amendment to the defense authorization bill that sought to protect social security entitlements, implying that the Reagan Administration was increasing defense spending and then trying to balance the budget by reducing old-age benefits. In the House, Speaker O'Neill condemned Reagan's budget proposals for cutting too deeply into domestic programs while at the same time increasing defense spending. Mondale called for the reestablishment of social programs allegedly cut back by the Reagan Administration and for "scaling the defense budget [back] to reality."[21]

Supporting these House and Senate liberals were a number of outside groups. The Council on Economic Priorities was critical of both poor cost controls in defense spending and the impact of such spending on the economy, contending that defense spending did not create jobs as fast as public works projects, and that in the longer term, it robbed the high technology sector of engineering talent, thereby impeding that sector's international competitiveness. Similar views were expressed by the National Urban League and People United to Save Humanity (PUSH).[22]

*Deficit Worriers.* The last splinter group among the Priority Shifters included conservatives and moderates who generally favored increased defense spending but not at the growth rates proposed by the Reagan Administration. This group preferred balanced, or less unbalanced, budgets even at the cost of reduced defense expenditures.

The intellectual component of this group consisted of defense, foreign policy and economic analysts located at a variety of research organizations such as Brookings and the Congressional Budget Office. In the Brookings series on *Setting National Priorities*, editor Joseph Pechman observed that unprecedented budget deficits would result from the Reagan defense program. In the same study, noted defense analyst William W. Kaufmann remarked that in the $1.8 trillion Reagan defense plan, specific threats, objectives and programs had to be related and justified;

without such an effort, "a certain doubt about the need for a program of this magnitude is bound to linger."[23] The Congressional Budget Office concluded that although the defense buildup was not likely to rekindle inflation nor stunt employment growth, the deficits occasioned by the buildup would "pose a serious risk" to the economy by choking off interest-rate sensitive spending and thereby stalling the recovery achieved in the early 1980's.[24]

The Deficit Worriers also included business groups, governors and former Executive Branch officials. The National Association of Manufacturers, the Business Roundtable, the U.S. Chamber of Commerce, and the National Governors Conference also worried that the deficits would frustrate the recovery. In a letter to the president's national security advisor, six former Treasury and Commerce Department Secretaries complained that "excessive short-term military spending can actually be harmful by undermining the political consensus required for a sustained defense buildup and smothering economic growth beneath huge out-year deficits."[25]

On the 1984 campaign trail, the Deficit Worriers included presidential candidates (and Senators) John Glenn and Ernest Hollings. Glenn promised that he would "stand up to the military" on defense spending. With an even more conservative record in the Senate than Glenn, Hollings proposed freezing DOD spending at FY 1982 levels. Within the Congress the principal Deficit Worriers were to be found on the House and Senate Budget Committees. The Chairmen of these committees and a number of members sought to slow the growth rate of military spending.[26]

Behind the concerns voiced by the Deficit Worriers lay both U.S. historical experience as well as skepticism. Most Deficit Worriers felt that the deficits incurred during the defense and social program increases of the Vietnam War era increased inflation and results in recession as U.S. leaders sought to stabilize the economy. Furthermore many from this group expressed outright skepticism that Reagan's supply side economics would promote recovery, improve productivity and increase savings. This anxiety created a reluctance to gamble that large defense spending increases would be displaced by increased revenues from a more vibrant economy.

Thus the Priority Shifters represented a disparate coalition generally opposed to defense increases proposed by the Reagan

Administration. The success of this coalition was modest. Initially it was not successful in reducing defense spending but was able to slow down weapons purchases. Later it succeeded in holding DOD spending below the Reagan proposals by again stretching out weapons purchases. Although many members of the coalition were opposed to more controversial weapons purchases such as the MX missile, the B-1 Bomber and more Navy aircraft carriers, they were not able to cancel them.

The Priority Shifters were successful in emphasizing the issue of NATO burden sharing and keeping it on the agenda. Arguing that NATO allies were reducing defense expenditure increases and manpower as the U.S. sought increases, coalition members in Congress froze U.S. troop strength in Europe. Furthermore, Congress refused to increase U.S. equipment stockpiles in Europe and to fund construction projects for U.S. forces, projects that many felt U.S. allies should have undertaken.

The problem, of course, for the Priority Shifters was that they could not agree on an alternative to the Reagan Administration proposals. Increasing taxes to reduce the deficit was not popular with the conservatives in the Reformer or Deficit Worrier groups, for they were convinced that more revenues would be applied to strengthening social programs, a course of action which they firmly opposed. The solution proposed by the Reformers was generally not accepted by the more sophisticated elements in the Domestic Spender and Deficit Worrier groups. They were skeptical that significant increases in defense capability could be coaxed from current expenditures. All in all the Priority Shifters were a fragmented, but vocal opposition.

### Strategic Outcomes

Given this dicey mix of contending groups and coalitions, four strategic alternatives appear possible. Alternative I would witness a move by the United States towards adoption of a Maritime Strategy to replace the Coalition Strategy now in effect. Alternative II would see cuts in real defense spending as part of a strategy focused on minimum deterrence. A third outcome, Alternative III, would involve a serious attempt by the United States to enhance its conventional deterrent in NATO as part of a strategy involving No Early First Use of nuclear weapons. Finally, Alternative IV would see the adoption of the strategy advocated in Alternative III without the corresponding application of resources necessary for its actual implementation.

Alternative I, the shift to a Maritime Strategy, would witness a drastic revision in defense priorities to accommodate domestic needs.[27] By withdrawing the bulk of its ground and air forces from Western Europe, Korea and, perhaps, Japan, the United States could substantially reduce its share of the Alliance defense burden as called for by the Domestic Spenders and Deficit Worriers, who have long chafed at the unwillingness of these allies to carry their "fair share." The buildup of the U.S. Navy to a 600-ship fleet capable of keeping open the sea lines of communication to Europe and the Persian Gulf would represent a defeat for the Defense Advocates save those whose orientation focuses exclusively on naval interests. Residual U.S. ground forces in Europe and the Far East would serve as a "tripwire" in the event of Soviet aggression; thus the burden of deterrence would fall even more heavily on America's nuclear forces than is currently the case. Given this outcome, the Freezers emerge as losers in the struggle to affect defense policy. Sharp cutbacks in U.S. forces in Europe would also have the effect of pre-empting any enhancement of the conventional deterrent through organization and doctrinal changes prescribed by the Reformers.

Alternative II can be called the strategy of "Minimum Deterrence." This outcome posits zero or negative real growth in defense spending. It is, for all practical purposes, an absolute victory for the Freezers and Domestic Spenders as well as elements of the Deficit Worriers. Alternative II would see a substantial decrease in both U.S. strategic and theater nuclear forces, most likely under the guise of "arms control," combined with a commitment to an enhanced conventional deterrent, but without any significant increase in funding for such forces. The victorious coalition would argue here that savings gained through reduction in nuclear forces could be applied to social programs or towards balancing the budget, while contending that the conventional forces would be made significantly more potent through the application of organizational and doctrinal changes as prescribed by the Reformers. Thus the strategy of Minimum Deterrence would represent an unmitigated defeat for the Defense Advocates.

Alternative III represents a victory for the Defense Advocates and Reformers through the adoption of the Four Percent Solution called for by General Rogers. Through a defense buildup which allocates, at a minimum, a real increase of four percent per year to U.S. general purpose forces, the United States can move towards an increased reliance on its conventional deterrent for NATO and the adoption of a No Early First Use posture regarding nuclear weapons. Such a strategy of No Early First Use would represent a successful outcome for both the Defense Advocates and the Reformers. As for the Freezers, the result is a mixed bag. Decreased reliance on nuclear weapons would be applauded; however, the Freezers would oppose the increase in defense spending accompanying such a change and the concomitant upgrading of U.S. intermediate range nuclear forces to maintain deterrence across the spectrum of conflict. As is obvious, the backbone of the Priority Shifter coalition, the Deficit Worriers and the Domestic Spenders, emerge as the big losers in Alternative III.

Alternative IV can most appropriately be termed as Symbolic Response. Here no coalition is able to generate sufficient strength to prevail — impasse being the result. In the face of such a deadlock, the Administration would likely posture that, in principal, U.S. reliance on nuclear weapons is decreasing and the Alliance is moving toward a strategy of No Early First Use, while in fact the United States and its allies fail to take the steps necessary to implement the declared strategy, as has been the case with Flexible Response. Such posturing would serve to somewhat allay the fears of the Freezers, cap defense spending at a low rate of real growth (roughly two-to-three percent per year), and allow for needed "reforms" in military doctrine and organization, if not in weapons and equipment. Furthermore, verbal support for the posture of No Early First Use would reduce intra-Alliance *angst* over the modernization of American theater nuclear forces.

Which of these alternative strategies will emerge from the current domestic political conflict is, of course, dependent upon the endurance of the three coalitions identified here, along with domestic and international developments — probably in that order. Prospects for the Defense Advocates and Alternative III revolve around continued conservative control of the government. With such control, the growth in NATO oriented defense outlays might well achieve something approaching the Four

Percent Proposal over the time frame called for by General Rogers.

While the Freezers are likely to endure in some form or another in the coming years, the realization of their objectives as reflected in Alternative II must be considered remote. Barring a Democratic landslide authored by the left wing of that party, the Freezers will have to be content to influence defense policy at the margins, that is by providing leverage to those congressmen seeking to restrain the growth in defense spending and to induce a degree of presidential "flexibility" in arms negotiations.

The inchoate nature of the Priority Shifter coalition would seem to guarantee opposition to *any* substantial increase in defense expenditures. Each group has its own axe to grind and each seeks to exact its cuts in a different way. Domestic Spenders, for the most part, appear willing to make deep cuts in defense spending such as those called for in the strategy of Minimum Deterrence. However, it is just such a strategic alternative that the Budget Worriers and Reformers are most likely to view as a radical attempt to "gut" national defense.

The Maritime Strategy (Alternative I) offers little in the way of overall budget savings to attract any of these groups. Save for those most ardently committed to increased burden sharing on the part of America's NATO allies, the risks entailed in such a major shift in United States strategic posture are likely to deter most Priority Shifters from supporting this Alternative.

The best hope for Priority Shifter ascendance would be the election of a moderate or liberal Democrat to the presidency or, perhaps, the recapturing of Democratic control in the Senate. This would place the Priority Shifters in a strong position to effect Alternative IV — a verbal commitment to reduce dependency on nuclear weapons to satisfy the Freezers, coupled with a reduction in the rate of defense expenditures to accommodate the Deficit Worriers. The Reformers, a diverse group of liberals, moderates, and conservatives who have yet to fashion an overall manifesto for military reform, would likely be allowed to do some doctrinal and organizational tinkering of small consequence to support the new administration's claims for an enhanced conventional deterrent.

Domestic and international developments will also shape the outcome of the defense budget debate. The state of the economy will not only heavily influence forthcoming elections, but will also provide limitations on budget increases. If the Deficit Worriers concerns are realized — that is the economy stagnates as capital markets dry up from heavy Treasury borrowing and unemployment stabilizes at nine percent and then increases — pressures on defense outlays will grow as social groups clamor for relief. In such a case, real growth beyond at most one or two percent would appear unlikely.

On the other hand, some scholars are arguing that a significant policy realignment has occurred in American politics. That is, the New Deal agenda has been replaced by another more conservative one which provides for less reliance on the federal government to resolve social and economic inequalities.[28] If such a shift has occurred, prospects for defense budget increases would be enhanced as federal dollars are redirected away from social programs.

Pulling in another direction, adverse developments abroad will enhance the prospects for budget increases. Continued barbaric behavior as displayed by the Soviets in shooting down an unarmed South Korean airliner will reinforce calls for improved U.S. and NATO military readiness. On the heels of Soviet intervention in Afghanistan, meddling in Polish affairs, and the airliner incident, further Soviet misbehavior would significantly strengthen the case made by the Defense Advocates. Misbehavior impedes the prospects for arms control, thereby disarming the Freezers. Furthermore such behavior suggests that NATO cannot rely predominantly on conventional deterrence, for it may be argued the Soviets seem capable of no restraint regardless of the number of lives involved.

The United States government is, therefore, likely to find itself heavily cross-pressured from contending defense coalitions and from domestic and international developments. For the remainder of the 1980's, Symbolic Response (Alternative IV) would thus appear the most likely outcome. While our NATO allies have historically experienced waves of anxiety about Soviet force buildups and international Russian meddling, they have been unwilling to make significant weapons or manpower increases. Their reluctance has impeded U.S. defense budget growth. Without Allies support, the U.S. Congress has fussed over NATO burden sharing and resisted budget increases.

The state of European economies does not provide much optimism for sustained four percent budget growth in NATO. Furthermore, regardless of the results of upcoming elections, the mobilized resistance of the Freezers and Priority Shifters to budget increases will impede a Four Percent Solution and is also likely to restrain even modest increases. Both the Maritime Strategy and Minimum Deterrence are improbable outcomes because of recent Soviet behavior, domestic elite and mass concerns over U.S. security, and the volatile condition of the Freezer and Priority Shifter Coalitions.

## The Changing Shape of Defense Policymaking

This analysis of the prospects for defense budget increases suggests a great deal about the prospects for defense policymaking and the institutions which make those policies. Clearly defense policy is shaped as much or more by domestic considerations as foreign developments. Heretofore foreign developments provided the threat and the "opportunities" to meet that threat, but seldom have mass protests permeated U.S. defense policymaking in peacetime. That is, Soviet behavior and military process have since World War II provided the rationale for much of our defense structure, and NATO and other alliances have been the opportunities we seized upon to deal with that threat. Nothing new here.

What is new are public referendums on weapons systems, a form of protest which have dramatically shifted the debate over NATO strategy. The conventional option is now in vogue, whereas before these developments the nuclear deterrence strategy was widely accepted. The promoters of freeze referendums clearly possess a policy sophistication in national security affairs not experienced outside the executive branch a generation ago. In fact it appears that much of this sophistication in effect came from the executive branch, for many of the organizers served there at some point. So people experienced in government now work outside government to change government. Or if not to change government, then at least to get back inside government.

Protests alone have not altered the defense debate. Public opinion shifts, the proliferation of defense public interest groups and conservative think tanks, a transformed Congress and a savvy president also bear responsibility. The shift in Gallup Poll results on defense spending portrays dramatic changes in mass support between 1977 and 1980.[29] These changes were manifested in the election of a more conservative president and Congress, both of which have been intent on enhancing U.S. military preparedness. Opinion shifts and protests portend an increased mass involvement in defense affairs, a policy area which has heretofore primarily been dominated by elites.

Another new development in defense affairs is the proliferation of public interest groups and ideological think tanks. Although public interest groups have existed in arms control and peace issues for decades, the numerical growth of such groups in the last decade is impressive. The Committee on the Present Danger, Ground Zero, and the Project on Military Procurement all represent a new force on the military scene which will question both defense policy and weapon selections. Interestingly these defense-oriented public interest groups appear just as similar interest groups in the social reform sector are struggling to sustain their accomplishments and to maintain their memberships and budgets.[30] Having observed the success of social public interest groups, defense groups were formed to influence decisions made by an Administration committed to a significant growth in defense expenditures. Thus activism in government promotes activism in the quasi-public world of interest representation.

Still another new force on the national scene is composed of conservative think tanks. Liberal think tanks which promoted the welfare-environmental state, such as the Urban Institute and the Environmental Policy Institute, have been on the scene for several decades. Other even-more-established research institutes such as Brookings and the American Enterprise Institute, while avowedly nonpartisan and nonideological, in practice have tended to support one of the parties. The organization though not the detachment of these research institutes has been adopted by a new breed of institute which consciously supported and promoted candidate Ronald Reagan as well as conservative candidates in the Congress. Perhaps the archtype of this breed is the Heritage Foundation whose 20-volume *Mandate for Leadership* provided the incoming Administration with 1,270 recommendations for reforming government in the conservative image and has since sought to provide a conservative position to the

Administration and to members of Congress just as policy issues are being discussed.[31]

In 1960 Samuel Huntington observed that the involvement of private interests in national security policymaking was still "uncertain and fragmentary. . . . Individual outside experts experienced considerable frustration in attempting to play a positive role in the bureaucratic process."[32] These interests now seem not only fully formed but also effective in influencing strategic and structural decisions. Where defense lobbyists before sought contracts or support for the National Guard or war veterans, public interest groups and think tanks now seek to design and promote national strategies, to rescind existing strategies, and to eliminate or alter proposed weapon systems. If the accomplishments of the social public interest groups and liberal think tanks are any indicator, the road ahead is likely to be a rugged one as these defense groups assail the expertise and confident judgment of the Pentagon and national security policymakers.

Another pronounced shift in the last decade is a new role for Congress in defense policymaking. Again relying on Huntington's book as the baseline, Congress in 1960 was more lobbyist than policymaker. With the explosion of outside groups possessing defense expertise and inside staff resources, the Legislature is now more a partner in policymaking. As the discussion above indicates, factions in Congress have allied themselves with and are sustained by defense public interest groups and think tanks. The growth of personal and committee staffs in the 1970s as well as congressional support agencies such as the Congressional Research Service, the Congressional Budget Office and the General Accounting Office also provide Members the expertise they heretofore lacked in seriously questioning executive proposals and generating alternatives.

Furthermore, the growth of subcommittee government in Congress and member independence and interest in defense policymaking have further complicated the defense policy process. Indeed as former Secretary of Defense Harold Brown has observed,

Senior policymakers in the executive branch—in the Department of Defense and other agencies—now spend much more time testifying before Congressional committees and answering detailed questions prepared by individual legislators. . . . Congress not only examines but also legislates foreign and defense policy and programs at a much more detailed level.[33]

Thus uniformed military and DOD influence on defense policymaking has waned and that of factions and groups outside the Executive Branch has been enhanced. This may be a positive development. In the past Executive-made decisions were fragile, subject to the vagaries of international circumstances and shifting public mood.[34] With Congress more involved, decisions may become more legitimate and more enduring.

A further complication for defense policymaking has been the entrenchment of the Welfare State in the United States, coincident in the past decade with a period of economic stagnation. The result has been the creation of an increasingly large and vocal constituency dependent in part or in whole on the expansion of various entitlement programs in a slow-or-no-growth economy. Competition between this constituency and defense needs became inevitable when one realizes that, in this economic environment, any increases in military spending imply a loosening of the social "safety net" or an acceptance of increased taxes or swollen budget deficits. The question of whose ox is to be gored has, not surprisingly, resulted in an enhanced awareness on the part of many interest groups of the threat posed to their agenda from U.S. military expenditures.

Given this new intervention by outside groups and by Congress, the President's problem is not a simple one. To counter a large Soviet military buildup, U.S. forces need more modern weapons systems; this is the only feasible response in a political system which will not support larger standing forces. But to modernize forces is to shift resources on a massive scale. Historically the principal techniques in the American elite repertoire to promote such a shift are to energetically market (Theodore Lowi uses the term "oversell"[35]) both the threat and the remedy. Marketing a threat is creating a crisis.[36] While such tactics can achieve consensus on a need for action, the backlash may be considerable once the public perceives the Administration's rhetoric does not mirror real-world conditions. One thinks of Nixon and Kissinger "overselling" the SALT I agreements, Carter "overselling" the SALT II treaty, and the accompanying backlash from conservatives as a case in point.

To address its "crisis", the Reagan Administration promoted a new technique which was to undersell the remedy. Traditionally, political elites have tended to "oversell" the remedy to achieve domestic consensus on divisive foreign policy questions. By claiming that its proposals would just barely meet the Soviet threat and by resisting compromise on defense expenditures, the Administration applied a tourniquet to its legislative opponents. In essence the Administration argued that "If the U.S. doesn't do at least this little bit on defense, our international situation will be much, much worse", thereby leaving the Congress to take the rap if international events continued to sour. This was not a comfortable position for legislators who instinctively search for cover, not for the limelight.

President Reagan's success with these tactics in increasing defense expenditures flew in the face of many who said it couldn't be done. Thus in the face of all the centrifugal forces discussed above, an adroit, clever president can still achieve his goals by carefully husbanding his bargaining power. The difference is that the task is just much harder in defense policymaking than it was a generation ago.

It is, alas, too early to decide whether these shifts in public opinion, group pressure, congressional criticism and presidential bargaining tactics will augur a new consensus. Defense policymaking in the Cold War, now newly revived, has always been fickle with support for a defense buildup withering as the public and policymaking elites have realized that the opportunity costs of a heavier military budget impacts adversely on domestic needs. In such past debates, numbers have taken on a symbolic and almost magic quality — 1,000 Minuteman missiles, three separate nuclear delivery systems known as the triad, a 500 or 600-ship Navy, three active Marine and 16 active Army divisions. The same may be said of the Four Percent Solution. Unlike an antibiotic with a prescribed percentage of some drug in solution, the Four Percent Solution will not cure our defense ills. What is needed is not a fixed percentge, but sustained support for a given defense program which elites and mass publics can agree will ensure American security. Given the debate on the Four Percent Solution, one cannot be sanguine about such a consensus being established in the near future.

# CHAPTER TWENTY

# The War Powers Resolution:
# An Infringement on The President's
# Constitutional and Prerogative Powers*

KENNETH M. HOLLAND
ASSISTANT PROFESSOR OF POLITICAL SCIENCE
UNIVERSITY OF VERMONT

## Introduction

By a vote of 75 to 18 in the Senate and 284–135 in the House of Representatives, overriding President Nixon's veto, the War Powers Resolution became law on November 7, 1973. Mr. Nixon justified his veto on the ground that the joint resolution was repugnant to the Constitution. Consistent with his belief in the act's lack of validity, President Nixon declined to file a report with Congress as required by the resolution when in July 1974 he ordered two Navy helicopters and five surface ships to evacuate 500 U.S. citizens and foreign nationals during the Turkish invasion of Cyprus. Although subsequent presidents have filed reports (although not in every case where they may have been required), none has acknowledged the constitutionality of the War Powers Resolution. In each instance President Ford, Carter and Reagan cited either the president's executive powers, his constitutional authority with respect to foreign relations or his authority as commander in chief as grounds for his decision to deploy U.S. armed forces into a hostile situation. They all denied the authority of Congress through the War Powers Resolution to infringe upon the office's constitutional powers.

The one apparent exception was President Reagan's signing into law the Multinational Force in Lebanon Resolution on October 12, 1983. This resolution states that the sixty-day period during which the Marines could be deployed in Lebanon without congressional authorization according to Section 5(b) of the War

---

* *This essay is based upon a paper prepared for delivery at the 1984 meeting of the Southwestern Political Science Association, Ft. Worth, Texas, March 21–24, 1984*

Powers Resolution began on August 29, 1983. The resolution, also consistent with a provision of the War Powers Resolution, gave the president specific authorization to keep the Marines in the Beirut area for eighteen months. When he signed the Multinational Force Resolution, however, President Reagan refused to concede the War Powers Resolution's constitutionality, arguing that he did not need congressional permission to keep U.S. forces in Lebanon and warning that his signing should not "be viewed as any acknowledgement that the President's Constitutional authority can be impermissibly infringed by statute."[1]

Are Presidents Nixon, Ford, Carter and Reagan correct? Is the War Powers Resolution an unconstitutional infringement on the chief executive's power to commit troops to armed hostilities and to maintain them until in his opinion they should be removed? In order to answer this question it will be necessary to identify the meaning of the relevant constitutional provisions, the intent of the Constitution's framers and the philosophical understanding that underlies that intent. Before turning there, it will be useful to describe the War Power Resolution's key features and the instances where presidents have ordered U.S. armed forces into dangerous overseas situations since October 1973.

## The War Powers Resolution

The first point to be made about the joint resolution is its purpose: "to fulfill the intent of the framers of the Constitution of the United States," viz., "that the collective judgment of both the Congress and the President will apply to the introduction of United States Armed Forces into hostilities . . . and to the continued use of such forces in hostilities" [Section 2(a)]. The fact that the resolution is an effort at constitutional exegesis is evident from the number of times the founding document is mentioned: Section 2(b), in which congressional authority to enact the resolution is traced to Article I, Section 8's "necessary and proper" clause; Section 2(c), interpreting "the constitutional powers of the President as Commander-in-Chief to introduce United States Armed Forces into hostilities" as limited to situations where there exists "(1) a declaration of war, (2) specific statutory authorization, or (3) a national emergency created by attack upon the United States, its territories or possessions, or its armed forces"; and Section 8, which states that nothing in the resolution is intended to alter the constitutional authority of the Congress or of the President.

The question that Congress' language invites is whether its reading of the framers' intent with regard to the president's power to use military force in the conduct of foreign policy is warranted. The key provisions of the resolution are Section 3 which requires that "the President in every possible instance shall *consult* with Congress before introducing United States Armed Forces into hostilities"; Section 4(a), which requires that the President shall submit within forty-eight hours of the introduction of armed forces into a foreign nation a *report* to Congress "setting forth (A) the circumstances necessitating the introduction of United States Armed Forces; (B) the constitutional and legislative authority under which such introduction took place; and (C) the estimated scope and duration of the hostilities or involvement"; Section 5(b), which states that whenever the president introduces armed forces "into hostilities or into situations where imminent involvement in hostilities is clearly indicated by the circumstances" the president *shall withdraw such forces within sixty days* "unless the Congress (1) has declared war or has enacted a specific authorization for such use of United States Armed Forces, (2) has extended by law such sixty-day period, or (3) is physically unable to meet as a result of an armed attack upon the United States"; and Section 5(c), authorizing the Congress by *concurrent resolution* to direct the president to remove any armed forces he has introduced [emphasis added].

## Military Operations, 1973–1984

How many instances have occurred since October 1973 where the president introduced armed forces arguably triggering either the consultation and report requirements, i.e., where armed forces were introduced "into the territory, airspace or waters of a foreign nation, *while equipped for combat*" [Section 4(a)(2)] or where they are introduced "in numbers which *substantially enlarge* United States Armed Forces equipped for combat already located in a foreign nation" [Section 4(a)(3)], or the consultation, report and sixty-day time limit stipulations, i.e., when they are introduced "into hostilities or into situations where *imminent involvement in hostilities* is clearly indicated by the circumstances"

[Section 4(a)(1)] [emphasis added]? Six instances occurred when the president used armed forces abroad and did not file a report. The president has submitted reports on ten occasions.

(1) President Nixon did not file a report after he ordered the evacuation during the July 1974 hostilities in Cyprus.

(2) President Ford submitted the first report under the act on April 4, 1975, following an order to use Navy vessels, helicopters and Marine forces to transport refugees in South Vietnam.

(3) After ordering Marines, Navy helicopters and Air Force tactical elements to assist with the evacuation of Americans in Cambodia, President Ford submitted a second report on April 12, 1975.

(4) Navy helicopters, Marines and Air Force fighters evacuated U.S. citizens and foreign nationals trapped in South Vietnam. President Ford made his third report on April 30, 1975.

(5) President Ford submitted a fourth report on May 12, 1975, after ordering U.S. military forces to rescue the crew of the U.S. *Mayagüez* which had been seized by Cambodian communists in disputed waters. Marines assaulted the island of Kon Tang, sustaining several casualties, and retook the ship.

(6) On June 20, 1976, a Navy landing craft evacuated 263 Americans and Europeans from Lebanon during an eruption in its civil war. President Ford did not report his order to introduce the landing craft to Congress.

(7) After two U.S. Army servicemen were killed by North Korean soldiers in the demilitarized zone in August 1976, President Ford ordered additional military forces, a squadron of twenty F-111's and eighteen F-4's, to Korea. Representative Elizabeth Holtzman (D-N.Y.) in the House Committee on Foreign Affairs asked why the president had not complied with the War Powers Resolution by submitting a report. The Ford Administration responded by saying Section 4(a)(3), the "substantial enlargement" provision, did not apply to the addition of a "relative handful" of personnel. There were already 41,000 U.S. troops in South Korea before the fighter aircraft arrived.

(8) President Carter did not submit a War Powers Resolution report when he ordered U.S. military transport aircraft to assist the French and Belgians rescue foreign nationals endangered by a civil war in Zaire. Flights occurred in May and June 1978. During compliance hearings in August 1978, Represen-

tative Paul Findley (R-Ill.) contended that President Carter had triggered Section 4(a)(1) by introducing U.S. armed forces into a situation "where imminent involvement in hostilities is clearly indicated by the circumstances." No action was taken on Representative Findley's motion to request the President to submit a report.

(9) President Carter filed his first and only report under the War Powers Resolution on April 26, 1980, after ordering U.S. armed forces, including eight Air Force helicopters and six fixed-wing aircraft, on April 24 to rescue the American hostages in Iran.

(10) During the month of March 1981, the Reagan Administration dispatched twenty additional military "advisers" to El Salvador to assist the nineteen sent earlier by the Carter Administration. No report was filed. Representative Richard Ottinger (D-N.Y.) introduced a concurrent resolution declaring that a war powers report was necessary. The Reagan Administration responded by saying that because U.S. personnel were not being introduced into hostilities and were not equipped for combat (they were armed only with "personal sidearms") neither Section 4(a)(1), 4(a)(2) nor 4(a)(3) applied.

(11) In August 1981 the Reagan Administration ordered U.S. jet fighters to fly into airspace over the Gulf of Sidra, claimed by Libya as internal waters but regarded by the United States as international waters. On August 19 two U.S. Navy F-14's were fired upon by a Libyan Su-220. The U.S. fighters returned fire in self-defense, destroying both Libyan aircraft that had intercepted them. President Reagan did not report the introduction of the jets into the Gulf of Sidra apparently on the ground that "imminent involvement in hostilities [was not] clearly indicated by the circumstances" [Section 4(a)(1)].

(12) President Reagan submitted his first report on March 19, 1982, after ordering U.S. military personnel to the Sinai to carry out the peace treaty between Egypt and Israel. Mr. Reagan stated that his report was "consistent with" Section 4(a)(2), relating to the introduction of armed forces "equipped for combat."

(13) President Reagan's second report was submitted on August 21, 1982, after he ordered 800 Marines to assist with the withdrawal of Palestinian armed forces from Lebanon.

(14) The third report occurred on September 29, 1982, after

the introduction of 1,200 Marines to Lebanon as part of a temporary multinational peacekeeping force designed to assist the Lebanese government restore control over its territory. Mr. Reagan mentioned no specific section of the War Powers Resolution. The President submitted a supplemental report on August 30, 1983, after the Marines had been fired upon and two had been killed.

(15) On August 8, 1983, President Reagan reported for the fourth time after deploying several AWACS and F-15 fighters to assist the government in Chad in its struggle against rebel and invading Libyan forces. The president mentioned Section 4 but no subsection of the War Powers Resolution.

(16) On October 25, 1983, President Reagan for the fifth time reported the deployment of U.S. armed forces overseas. On that date Mr. Reagan had ordered 5,000 Marines, Army Rangers and paratroopers to invade the Caribbean island of Grenada in order to protect the lives of 1,000 Americans who were endangered by lack of order on the island. Eleven U.S. soldiers were killed and thirty-five wounded in the attack.

A number of things can be said about these incidents. First, although presidents submitted reports, they stated clearly that such submissions in no way indicated their belief in the constitutionality of the War Powers Resolution. They all avoided saying the reports were "pursuant to the requirements" of the resolution. President Ford used the language "taking note" of the resolution; Presidents Carter and Reagan have preferred the phrase "consistent with the provisions of the War Powers Resolution." In these reports, considered by the presidents as optional rather than mandatory, the introduction of armed forces is always justified by reference to the president's powers under the Constitution as chief executive, conductor of foreign relations or commander in chief. Presidents occasionally cite *in addition* specific statutory authorization, such as the Multinational Force and Observers Participation Resolution mentioned by President Reagan in his 1982 report regarding the Sinai force.

Second, although Section 3 requires "in every possible instance" consultation with Congress before introducing armed forces "into hostilities or into situation where imminent involvement in hostilities is clearly indicated by the circumstances," no president sought the advice of Congress before any of the sixteen introductions. Only President Ford approached Congress prior to com-

mencing a military operation and with very illuminating consequences. On April 10, 1975, the president addressed a joint
session of the House and Senate and asked the Congress to "clarify
immediately its restrictions on the use of U.S. military forces
in Southeast Asia for the limited purposes of protecting American lives by ensuring their evacuation, if this should become
necessary."[2] Because of the urgency of the situation in South
Vietnam, the president asked Congress to respond by April 19.
The Senate finally passed a bill, after extensive debate, on April
25. On April 28, however, before the House took any action,
President Ford ordered the evacuation to begin, relying on "the
President's constitutional executive power and his authority as
Commander-in-Chief of U.S. Armed Forces."[3] The House fi-
nally acted on May 1, rejecting the bill.

Occasionally the administration *informed* congressional *leaders*
of its intention to introduce armed forces. For example, House
Speaker O'Neill, Majority Leader Wright, Minority Leader
Michel, Senate Majority Leader Baker and Minority Leader
Byrd were called to the White House the night before and told
an invasion of Grenada was in the works. The congressional
leaders were not given a chance to offer their advice.[4]

Third, Congress has developed a definite pattern in its response to presidential employment of the armed forces for foreign policy purposes. If the introduction is successful, Congress
does not object; if it fails, Congress objects vehemently that the
president has not complied with the War Power Resolution. For
example, the recapture of the *Mayagüez* and the invasion of
Grenada, although both resulted in numerous U.S. casualties,
were highly popular with the American people and received almost no criticism from the Congress. On the other land, the
ill-fated attempt to rescue the hostages in Iran and the ineffective and costly second deployment of Marines in Lebanon by
President Reagan (the initial deployment to assist PLO withdrawal was successful and applauded) were unpopular and received widespread congressional criticism, resulting in calls for
President Carter's impeachment for violating the consultation
requirements of the resolution[5] and to the imposition on President Reagan of an eighteen-month time limit for the presence
of Marines in Lebanon and to their withdrawal by presidential
directive in February 1984, twelve months before the congressional deadline, a withdrawal at least in part brought about by
constant congressional pressure.

The lesson of this history is that hardly any congressman will challenge a military operation that is swift and successful. Some will rebuke a president, such as Mr. Carter, for engaging in an operation that is swift but unsuccessful. A protracted military operation that does not have widespread popular support, such as the second Lebanon deployment, will produce a sustained congressional challenge. The reason for this criticism is not lack of consultation (it is not even clear that congressmen really want to be consulted, for consultation implies responsibility for the consequences) but lack of success. The truth is that "public opinion tends to support the president in times of military crisis whatever its views beforehand about the merits of becoming involved in the crisis."[6] Congress will not ignore the existence of public support for the president, regardless of what the law says.

The War Power Resolution, therefore, has made no difference in the pattern of congressional reaction to presidential uses of the armed forces. Public opinion is decisive and it is negatively affected not by non-compliance with legal procedures but (with the exception of World War II) by lack of early success. Protracted and indecisive military operations still require the support of congressional appropriations. The power of the purse remains, as it was before 1973, the real source of congressional limits on the president's use of the armed forces to secure foreign policy goals. Two examples of the effectiveness of this power are the Eagleton amendment calling for an end to the bombing of Cambodia in 1973 through termination of funding and the Senate's vote to cut off funds in 1972 for base agreements with Portugal and Bahrein unless the administration submitted them to the Senate for ratification as treaties.[7]

Secretary of State George Shultz believes, however, that the War Powers Resolution has made a difference, and he has called on Congress to review the law. He told the Senate Appropriations Subcommittee on Foreign Operations that the act made it impossible to conduct a "sensible" policy in Lebanon. Mr. Shultz said:

> Our own debate here totally took the rug out from under our diplomatic effort. . . . I think there is a question as to whether [the War Powers Resolution] is the most desirable way to structure the interaction between the legislative and executive branches for dealing with issues involving force. . . . [The debate] was an exercise in getting the executive branch so tied up that it was hard to do sen-

sible things that probably everyone supported, because the process of consultation you have to go through, which is *public* no matter which room you hold it in, makes it impossible to execute the policy. I think it was absolutely astonishing to the Soviet Union and Syria that we did not exact a price for moving the marines offshore.[8]

During the hearing Senator Arlen Specter (R-Pa.) asked Mr. Shultz whether, in order to avoid the kind of debate that was touched off by the president's intervention in Lebanon, he would support a congressional resolution that would set *in advance* the limits of presidential involvement should Iran try to close the Strait of Hormuz at the exit from the Persian Gulf, through which much of the world's oil passes. The Secretary of State agreed that another War Powers Resolution debate should be avoided but said he did not favor such a resolution. It would require an undesirably close consultation with the Congress and might restrict the administration's flexibility to respond appropriately.[9] One of the lessons of the past eleven years, however, is that should the president respond militarily to an attempt to close the vital straits and should the operation be, as is likely, swift and successful, Congress will follow public opinion and applaud the measure, even in the absence of prior consultation.

President Nixon believed that both Sections 5(b) and 5(c) were unconstitutional. In his veto message he said that the War Powers Resolution

> would attempt to take away, by a mere legislative act, authorities which the President has properly exercised under the Constitution for almost 200 years. One of its provisions [Section 5(b)] would automatically cut off certain authorities after sixty days unless the Congress extended them. Another [Section 5(c)] would allow the Congress to eliminate certain authorities merely by the passage of a concurrent resolution — an action which does not normally have the force of law, since it denies the President his constitutional role in approving legislation.[10]

The Supreme Court on June 23, 1983, agreed with Mr. Nixon that the "legislative veto" is repugnant to the Constitution. In *Immigration and Naturalization Service* v. *Chadha*, the Court, by a margin of 7–2, held that the legislative veto permits the Congress to legislate without following the procedures set out in Article I of the Constitution requiring that all laws be passed by a majority of both houses and presented to the president. This procedure, explained the Court, is an integral part of the constitutional design for the separation of powers. Chief Justice Burger concluded his opinion for the Court with these words: "With all the obvious flaws of delay, untidiness, and potential for abuse, we have not yet found a better way to preserve freedom than by making the exercise of power subject to the carefully crafted restraints spelled out in the Constitution."[11] Congress may no longer legislate by concurrent resolution.

What is the effect on the efficacy of the War Powers Resolution of depriving Congress of the ability to order withdrawal of forces by concurrent resolution? The answer is that *INS* v. *Chadha* has rendered the resolution unenforceable. If a president fails to make a report and Congress deems that one should have been made, or if the president reports an introduction of armed forces into hostilities and Congress declines to authorize their presence within sixty days, there is now no way within the terms of the resolution that Congress can force presidential compliance. Its only recourse would be to enact a joint resolution to cut off funds for the operation. The resolution would have to be presented to the president for his signature and could be passed over a veto by a 2/3 vote in each house. This option, however, was available to Congress before enactment of the War Power Resolution. Congress could not enact a resolution (passed presumably over the president's veto) ordering the president to withdraw the forces. It seems clear that, once armed forces are committed, the president as their commander in chief can keep them committed as long as he thinks necessary or prudent. He might very well argue that an immediate withdrawal would endanger the troops and if he were to comply with Congress' wishes he would be remiss in his constitutional duties. Congress cannot by mere legislation infringe upon the president's *constitutional* powers.

Staff members of the Senate Foreign Relations Committee said in the wake of *INS* v. *Chadha* that it is the committee's view that the War Powers Resolution's basic requirement of seeking permission within sixty days does not constitute a legislative veto and survives the Supreme Court's ruling. The staff members added, however, "that the means Congress might have for forcing the president to comply are unclear."[12]

*The Constitutional Text*

Is the Congress correct that the limitations of the War Powers Resolution "fulfill the intent of the framers of the Constitution" or is President Nixon correct that "the restrictions which the resolution would impose upon the authority of the President are . . . unconstitutional"? In order to answer this question it is necessary to look at what the framers said about the presidential power to use force to achieve foreign policy goals. Since the framers relied upon certain theoretical understandings of the nature of government, it will also be helpful to look at the views on executive power of the philosopher who most influenced the framers.

Article I, Section 1 states "All legislative Powers *herein granted* shall be vested in a Congress of the United States" [emphasis added]. By contrast Article II, Section 1 says "The executive Power shall be vested in a President of the United States of America." This difference in wording is significant because it means the list of specific legislative powers in Article I, Section 8 is *exhaustive* whereas the enumeration of executive powers in Article II, Section 2 is *illustrative*. The Constitution expressly divides the war powers. It gives Congress the power "to declare War," "to raise and support Armies," and "to provide and maintain a Navy." Very few wars in the eighteenth century, however, were "declared." Of the early United States wars, those against the Indians (1789), the Barbary states (1802) and France (1798) were undeclared; only the war against Britain (1812) was declared by Congress.

In fact, at the time of the constitutional convention of 1787 neither international law nor international custom required a declaration of war. According to a leading scholar of the period, "The 17th century saw the entire disappearance of declarations of war in spite of contemporary assurances by Grotius of their necessity. Between 1700 and 1870, declarations of war prior to hostilities only occurred in one case out of ten, and such declarations were also very rare after operations of war had been commenced."[13] The convention debate is also illuminating. The August 1787 draft of the Committee of Detail would have granted Congress the power "to *make* war." Elbridge Gerry and James Madison moved to change this to the power "to *declare* war." During the ensuing debate on the motion, the delegates expressed a desire to preserve for the executive the power to repel sudden attacks and the power to *conduct* war, which some might believe was included in the power to *make* war. The motion carried unanimously.[14]

Congress' power to declare war, therefore, is a rather limited one and is certainly not co-extensive with the power to introduce armed forces into hostilities, which we shall see is part of the executive power. One of the listed illustrations of the executive power is the president's role as "Commander in Chief of the Army and Navy of the United States, and of the Militia of the several States, when called into the actual Service of the United States." Congress can *authorize* the initiation of hostilities, but it cannot *require* the president to obtain its permission before initiating hostilities. This is clear from the fact that under Article I, Section 8 the president may call "forth the Militia to execute the Laws of the Union, suppress Insurrections and repel Invasions." If the president may use the militia to "repel Invasions" he of course can also use the army and navy. For this reason the constitutional convention deliberately gave to Congress the power "to declare" war, leaving to the president the power "to make" war. It is also worth noting that the states, according to Article I, Section 10 are authorized to "engage in War [if] actually invaded, or in such imminent Danger as will not admit of delay." If the states can engage in hostilities to *prevent* an attack without congressional authorization, it would seem obvious that the Constitution grants to the president similar authority.

The difficult question is not whether the president can defend the country and its armed forces without consulting Congress but whether he can on his own authority launch an attack on a potential enemy or rescue Americans or foreign nationals or protect Americans when they are on international waters or in foreign countries. The War Powers Resolution says no, because its premise is that the initiation of hostilities is essentially a legislative power. The Eighteenth Century documents, however, suggest that this assumption is incorrect.

### Intention of the Framers

In April 1793, President Washington, who had presided at the constitutional convention, proclaimed that the United States was neutral in the war between France and Britain. Although the

United States and France had entered into a treaty in 1778, President Washington interpreted it as not requiring U.S. intervention on behalf of France. Alexander Hamilton, one of the chief architects of the Constitution, in a series of newspaper essays written under the pseudonym "Pacificus," justified the president's actions on constitutional grounds and examined the nature of the decision to use military force as a tool of foreign policy.

Hamilton points out that the power to declare war by its nature is an executive power. The framers excepted that rather limited portion of executive power and gave it to Congress. Legislative exercise of certain executive powers, e.g., the Senate's power to consent to treaties and appointments, is part of the system of "checks and balances." Other than these exceptions, the grant of the executive power to the president is complete. The specific clauses of Article II are either restrictions on the executive power or illustrations. Because the power to declare war is an exception to a general grant to the president of the executive power, it should, said Hamilton, be construed strictly. Thus while only Congress can "declare war," the president can "do whatever else *the laws of nations* . . . enjoin in the intercourse of the United States with foreign powers."[15] What are the limits on the president's powers in war and foreign affairs? According to Hamilton, they are found not in the Constitution but in "the principles of free government." Hamilton thus refers us to the great expositor of those principles for the founding generation, including himself, John Locke.[16]

*Locke On Executive Power*

According to Locke there are three powers of government: the legislative, executive and federative. Judicial is part of the executive power. "The Power of making Laws [is] a Power to set down, what punishment shall belong to the several transgressions which [the Commonwealth] think worthy of it, committed amongst the Members of that Society" [Section 88].[17] Executive power comprehends "the Execution of the Municipal Laws of the Society within itself, upon all that are parts of it" [Section 147]. The third, or federative, power is "the power of war and peace, leagues and alliances" [Section 146]. It comprehends "the management of the security and interest of the publick without, with all those that it may receive benefit or damage from" [Section 147]. The executive power, therefore, concerns itself with municipal, or positive, law, while the federative power concerns itself with the law of nations, or unwritten natural, law. Although the two powers are conceptually distinct, Locke says they must nevertheless be placed in the same hands, "both of them requiring the *force of the society* for their exercise," which force cannot wisely or safely be placed "under different commands" [Section 148, emphasis added]. And, as if he were speaking to the proponents of the War Powers Resolution, he declares:

> And though this federative Power in the well or ill management of it be of great moment to the commonwealth, yet it is much less capable to be directed by antecedent, standing, positive Laws, than the Executive; and so must necessarily be left to the Prudence and Wisdom of those whose hands it is in, to be managed for the publick good. For the Laws that concern Subjects one amongst another, being to direct their actions, may well enough precede them. But what is to be done in reference to Foreigners, depending much upon their actions, and the variation of designs and interests, must be left in great part to the Prudence of those who have this Power committed to them, to be managed by the best of their Skill, for the advantage of the Commonwealth [Section 147].

Municipal, or internal, law cannot extend to relations with foreign nations, because, although the citizens have a common sovereign to judge disputes between them, sovereign nations have no such common superior and are in a state of nature with respect to each other. Men in the state of nature are bound only by the unwritten law of nature [Section 6]. The conduct of foreign policy and the decision to use military force to protect the interests of the polity necessarily are the province of whoever *commands* the force of the community.

Thus the Constitution's comprehensive grant of the executive power to the president includes what Locke calls the federative power, i.e., the power over war and foreign affairs. This means that there are really two presidencies — a domestic one, limited by the Constitution and laws he is sworn to execute, and one concerned with defense and foreign policy, who is limited only by natural law, or morality.[18]

The Constitution's grant of the federative power is not complete. Only Congress can "declare" war, and the Senate can refuse to ratify treaties made by the president. Congress, moreover, possesses one legislative and one judicial power that serve as

checks on presidential warmaking — the power over appropriations and the power of impeachment. This reading of the extent
of the president's war powers is consistent with what was said
at the constitutional convention.[19]

But what happens when there is a conflict between a law or
a constitutional provision and an action the president deems
necessary to protect national interests? Can a president initiate
hostilities in violation of law *and* the Constitution? Did Presi-
dent Truman have authority to commit American forces to the
Korean War without congressional consent? Did President
Kennedy have authority to order a blockade or invasion of Cuba?
Did President Johnson have authority to conduct hostilities in
Vietnam if Congress had refused to pass the Gulf of Tonkin
Resolution?

### Prerogative Power

One of the standard maxims describing the American political
system is that all exercises of governmental power must be justified by reference to a specific clause of the Constitution. In the
words of Chief Justice Roger B. Taney in *Ex parte Merryman*,
Fed. Case 9487, 149 (C.C.D.Md., 1861):

> The government of the United States is one of delegated and limited
> powers; it derives its existence and authority altogether from the
> Constitution, and neither of its branches, executive, legislative or
> judicial, can exercise any of the powers of government beyond those
> specified and granted; for the tenth article of the amendments to
> the Constitution, in express terms, provides that "the powers not
> delegated to the United States by the Constitution, nor prohibited
> by it to the states, are reserved to the states, respectively, or to the
> people.

Some presidents, however, have claimed powers for which there
appears to be no legislative or constitutional basis. Examples
of such powers are impoundment of appropriated funds, use
of the executive order to alter legislation, drafting men into the
army without congressional authorization, expenditure of un-
appropriated public funds and initiation of hostilities in the absence of a declaration of war. Were these actions usurpations
of power, or does the president of the United States, like many
other executives past and present, possess prerogative — according
to Locke, the "power to act according to discretion, for the public

good, without the prescription of the law, and sometimes even against it" [Section 160]? This question will be addressed in three parts: (1) what precisely is prerogative power, (2) is there a prerogative power in the United States government and (3) if so, does the president enjoy it. Finally, what are the implications for the War Powers Resolution if the president does enjoy prerogative power?

In chapter 14 of the *Second Treatise*, Locke describes three categories of prerogative power. The first is akin to what we think of today as emergency situations: "For the Legislators not being able to foresee, and provide, by Laws, for all, that may be useful to the Community, the Executor of the Laws, having the power in his hands, has by the Common Law of Nature, a right to make use of it, for the good of the Society, in many Cases, where the municipal Law has given no direction, till the Legislative can conveniently be assembled to provide for it." Note that prerogative, at least according to this example, is a domestic power. The central thought is that the executive must be able to act when the legislature is not in session. Prerogative, however, is not confined to executive measures pending legislative action: "Many things there are, which the Law can by no means provide for, and those must necessarily be left to the discretion of him, that has the Executive Power in his hands, to be ordered by him, as the publick good and advantage shall require." The second category of prerogative originates in the inherent defectiveness of law — its generality. Certain things must be left to the discretion of the man on the scene, of him who has the power. The law can only set the general bounds within which the executive may exercise his judgment. Law as specific prescription cannot exhaust the discretion of the people responsible for administering government.

The third category is founded on the premise that the execution of the law would effect positive harm: "'Tis fit that the Laws themselves should in some Cases give way to the Executive Power, or rather to this Fundamental Law of Nature and Government, *viz*. That as much as may be, *all* the Members of the Society are to be *preserved*." Locke cites two examples, one of which is the pardoning power, a power explicitly conferred on the president by the Constitution's framers: "For since many accidents may happen, wherein a strict and rigid observation of the Laws may do harm; (as not to pull down an innocent Man's House to stop the Fire, when the next to it is burning) and a Man may come sometimes within the reach of the Law, which makes no distinction of Persons, by an action that may deserve reward and pardon; 'tis fit, the Ruler should have a Power, in many Cases, to mitigate the severity of the Law, and pardon some Offenders." Action according to the established rule, thus, may produce positive harm. The executive must then, says Locke, act outside or against the rule.

What, according to Locke, are the checks against executive abuse of prerogative? The legislature can obviate the need for much executive discretion by making legislative provision for as many matters as possible or, when the executive has in fact acted in the absence of or against the law, the legislature may later supersede such exercises of discretion. The legislature cannot, says Locke, displace prerogative on the whole, but it may override it in any particular case. When the executive refuses to acquiesce in the legislative will, who is to judge the issue? "I answer: Between an Executive Power in being, with such a Prerogative, and a Legislative that depends upon his will for their convening, there can be no *Judge on Earth*: As there can be none, between the Legislative, and the People, should either the Executive, or the Legislative, when they have got the Power in their hands, design, or go about to enslave, or destroy them. The People have no other remedy in this, as in all other cases where they have no Judge on Earth, but to appeal to *Heaven*," i.e., revolution.

The Civil War made unprecedented demands upon the office of president. Lincoln was forced to take several measures which had doubtful statutory and constitutional authority. Chief Justice Taney declared the president's suspension of the writ of habeas corpus unconstitutional. Lincoln replied that the Constitution does not say which branch has the power to suspend and that even if his action were illegal it was necessary to preserve the Union. Taney responded by asking how an officer charged with taking care that the laws be faithfully executed could disobey the law. Lincoln argued that he could break one law in order to ensure that the rest are faithfully executed. President Nixon made a form of this argument in justifying impoundment of appropriated funds to control inflation as did President Truman when he seized the steel mills during the Korean War to prevent a strike that would hamper prosecution of the war.

Because all three presidents defended breaking the law for the sake of law, their actions are not prerogative in Locke's strict sense. Congress approved Lincoln's suspension but narrowed the purposes of preventive detention to the situation where the arresting officer intends that the arrestee eventually be brought to trial. The Supreme Court, however, in *Youngstown Sheet and Tube Co.* v. *Sawyer* held that, because Congress had considered whether to authorize seizure in this type of situation and had rejected the idea, Truman had to return the mills to their owners. Truman, however, had regarded his duty to protect American servicemen in battle as more important than this particular legislative determination in the area of labor disputes.

The Supreme Court, however, did defend a presidential arms embargo in 1936 against the charge that the authorizing legislation was an unconstitutional delegation of legislative power. In the course of the Court's opinion, Justice Sutherland made this sweeping claim for governmental prerogative: "the broad statement that the Federal government can exercise no powers except those specifically enumerated in the Constitution, and such implied powers as are necessary and proper to carry into effect the enumerated powers, is categorically true only in respect of our internal affairs,"[20] suggesting Locke's distinction between legislative and executive power on the one hand and federative power on the other. Foreign policy powers are intrinsic, Sutherland is saying, to the nature of sovereignty. The government possesses them independently of a constitutional grant. Congress can delegate these powers to the president, and the Constitution gives him power to preserve the sovereignty of the United States. Sutherland's opinion is not, however, a source for executive prerogative, because he says the president's foreign policy powers derive from the Constitution. The president per se has no extra-constitutional power to deal with foreign affairs. Only the federal *government* has such power outside the Constitution. The Constitution gives him a power that does not itself have a constitutional basis.

There are those, however, who have argued in behalf of a true prerogative power in the war and foreign policy fields. Arthur Schlesinger, for example, concedes at the outset of the *Imperial Presidency* that the president cannot be restrained by law in his ability to act during emergencies.[21] He regards this concession of extra-constitutional presidential power as preparation for a stricter view of the office's *constitutional* powers. This is a typical tactic of strict constructionists. Patrick Henry and Thomas Jefferson, both strict constructionists, for example, acknowledged the need for executive power outside and against the law. The intent of this line of argument is to preserve constitutional limitations by saying necessity, not the instrument, authorizes purchase of the Louisiana Territory, for example. The constitutional language, therefore, does not need to be stretched to cover such a doubtful measure. Justice Jackson, in his dissent in *Korematsu* v. *United States*, made a similar argument. At issue was the constitutionality of the forced relocation of Japanese-Americans away from the coastal areas of the West. He said:

> But if we cannot confine military expedients by the Constitution, neither would I distort the Constitution to approve all that the military may deem expedient. . . . But even if [the relocation orders] were permissible military procedures, I deny that it follows that they are constitutional. . . . Once a judicial opinion rationalizes such an order to show that it conforms to the Constitution, or rather rationalizes the Constitution to show that the Constitution sanctions such an order, the Court for all time has validated the principle of racial discrimination in criminal procedure and of transplanting American citizens. The principle then lies about like a loaded weapon ready for the hand of any authority that can bring forward a plausible claim of an urgent need.[22]

Strict constructionists, moreover, seek to limit the opportunities for the exercise of emergency prerogative by reducing America's involvement in foreign affairs. Patrick Henry, Jefferson and Schlesinger exhibit this tendency:

> Some minds are agitated by foreign alarms. Happily for us, there is no real danger from Europe; that country is engaged in more arduous business: from that quarter there is no cause of fear: you may sleep in safety forever for them.[23]

An isolationist foreign policy is a natural outgrowth of a strict constitutional interpretation of the president's powers to use force to advance national interests overseas.

Locke says that prerogative is as necessary as it is dangerous. How does one deal with the need for prerogative and yet preserve constitutionalism? *The Federalist Papers* speak to this all-important question. James Madison, in #41, for example, warns of the dangers to constitutionalism of limiting government power: "It is in vain to oppose constitutional barriers to the impulse of self-preservation. It is worse than in vain; because it plants in the Constitution itself necessary usurpations of power, every precedent of which is a germ of unnecessary and multiplied repetitions."[23] The exigency which forced Massachusetts to raise troops in peacetime to quell Shay's Rebellion in 1786, in violation of the Articles of Confederation, "teaches us," says Hamilton in #25, "how unequal parchment provisions are to a struggle with public necessity."[24] Hamilton reminds us that constitutions are not natural, but conventional instruments. A constitution, to survive, must be agreeable to the natural operation of things, for "nations pay little regard to rules and maxims calculated in their very nature to run counter to the necessities of society."[25]

Schlesinger contends that the original meaning of the commander in chief clause was narrow and encompassed only direction of troops in the field, subject to the policy making function of Congress. Yet it is patent from a careful reading of the *Federalist Papers* that the clause is designed to open up the presidency to the requirements of necessity. The direction of war, says Hamilton, means, in the final analysis, direction of the common strength of the nation and not merely command of the military forces. Moreover, "it is of the nature of war to increase the executive at the expense of the legislative authority."[26] The lesson of these papers is that a constitution must be open to the necessity of awesome executive power to handle war. If one wishes to avoid monarchy, one must try to steer clear of war. But as the severe demands of foreign policy, defense and war increase, there will be an inexorable growth in presidential power. Not only do we have two presidencies, but we also have two constitutions — a republican, or democratic, constitution for domestic affairs and monarchical constitution for defense and foreign affairs. Hamilton is fond of quoting Montesquieu in the *Federalist Papers*, and in *Federalist* #9 we find this quotation from the French philosopher:

> It is very probable that mankind would have been obliged at length to live constantly under the government of a SINGLE PERSON, had they not contrived a kind of constitution that has all the internal advantages of a republican, together with the external force of a monarchical, government. I mean a CONFEDERATE REPUBLIC.

The purpose of monarchical power in the chief executive is to preserve the republic. That such unlimited power is necessary is one of the paradoxes of republican government.

Lincoln argued that the "take care" clause enjoined him to disregard one law if it were necessary in order to preserve the whole fabric of laws. Similarly, the presidential oath, unique in the Constitution, obliges the chief executive "to preserve, protect and defend the Constitution." The president might sometimes have to roam outside the Constitution, to act on the basis of power unauthorized by it, even to disregard certain portions of it, in order to achieve that higher purpose of preserving it and the nation it establishes. The Constitution, moreover, like all law, is itself a means, an instrument to a superior object — security of those unalienable rights for the sake of which governments are instituted among men. The highest exercise of prerogative would be the taking of measures, by him who holds the power in his hands and who has knowledge of the purpose of government, against the Constitution itself as a whole, when the lives or liberties of the American people could be preserved in no other, less drastic, way.

## Conclusion

The War Powers Resolution is both unconstitutional and is based on a naive understanding of the nature of executive power with respect to defense and foreign affairs. In Section 2(c) it unconstitutionally restricts the instances in which the president may introduce U.S. armed forces into hostilities. It does not recognize the president's authority to use the armed forces to protect American property and lives overseas, to launch preemptive strikes, to rescue American citizens or foreign nationals, to deploy military, air and naval power to advance in subtle ways to goals of diplomacy, or to take whatever actions an emergency situation might require. The picture of the scope of the executive power that emerges from the debates at the constitutional convention, the *Federalist Papers* and the practices of the early administrations is much broader than the portrait painted by the framers of the War Powers Resolution. Section 3's requirement of consultation is an attempt by statute to limit the president's constitutional powers as chief executive. Congress, for example, could not require the president to consult it before exercising his power to pardon, part of "the executive power" granted by Article II. As the Supreme Court indicated in *INS* v. *Chadha*, the only way to restrict the president's constitutional powers is by constitutional amendment. Similarly, Section 4's reporting requirement is an attempt to convert the Congress' right to request information from the president into a presidential duty to provide such information. The doctrine of executive privilege recognized in case law invalidates Section 4.

Section 5(b)'s requirement that the president terminate American involvement in hostilities within sixty days in the absence of congressional authorization is a usurpation of the executive power of command over the armed forces. In fact, is not this sixty-day provision a "silent veto" over presidential deployment of troops? By inaction the Congress can veto the president's use of the armed forces. A strong case could be made that the reasoning of *INS* v. *Chadha* invalidates Section 5(b) as well as the concurrent resolution provision of Section 5(c). If the president has the constitutional authority to deploy force in the first instance, it seems incongruous that the Congress by inaction could nullify this authority after sixty days.

Even if the War Powers Resolution were constitutional, presidents would be forced by necessity to violate it. This is because he who has the power to command the force of the community has the duty to employ that force when the public good requires such employment. The Constitution does not grant to the president prerogative or emergency power. The framers could not, even if they had wanted, have granted such powers to the president, because they are extralegal and antilegal in their nature. Emergency power, by its nature, cannot be limited by law or by constitutional provisions. Emergency power is not, strictly speaking, part of the executive power. The power of war and peace, in Locke's terminology the federative power, is not subject to positive law but is a discretionary power in the hands of whomever the society entrusts command of the armed forces to. Prerogative, federative or emergency power cannot be contained by the Constitution. The history under the War Powers Resolution vindicates Locke's conclusion that the only limitation on the executive's exercise of prerogative and federative power is public opinion. When military operations are successful, regardless of how dubious the authority cited by the president for his decision to employ force, the popular majority supports the president and Congress hardly objects. When the operation fails, public opinion insures a termination of it.

The real danger of the War Powers Resolution is that it impairs the ability of the president to maintain the salutary hypocrisy that the use of force to achieve foreign policy objectives is always authorized by the constitution. We have seen that presidents typically cite their constitutional power as chief executive or commander in chief. By giving a very narrow construction to these powers, the War Powers Resolution makes more likely a confession by the president that although there is no authority in the Constitution for what he has done public necessity required it. If the president is allowed an expansive reading of his constitutional authorities, on the other hand, he must make two arguments to the American people: (1) this action had to be taken, and (2) the Constitution grants me the power to take it. The people can argue the latter point and deny his reading of the instrument. The raw prerogative issue then gets debated as a constitutional question and can draw upon the conservative tradition of constitutional law. This procedure certainly obscures the central issue — was the deployment of armed force in fact necessary to promote the public good — but it does bring our Constitution to bear on the question. Not least among its virtues is that it renders the executive action judicially cognizable.

The Supreme Court cannot review exercises of pure prerogative or emergency power, but it can, and has, reviewed exercises of what is presented as constitutional power. Another merit of keeping the constitutional argument primary is that the president occupies ground on which the Congress can debate his actions. If he says he is exercising emergency power, the president transcends this ground and stills the debate. A president who believes the Constitution permits him to do whatever exigency may require is much more likely to return "dictatorial" power to the people after its exercise than one who believes there is an irresolvable conflict between the Constitution and his responsibility to protect the interests of the United States. The War Powers Resolution, ironically, is more calculated to nurture an "imperial presidency" than an expansive reading of the commander in chief clause.

# Notes

## NOTES FOR PREFACE

1. Daniel Yankelovich and John Doble, "The Public Mood: Nuclear Weapons and the U.S.S.R.," *Foreign Affairs*, 63, 1, Fall 1984, p. 33.
2. Robert W. Tucker, "The Nuclear Debate," *Foreign Affairs*, 63, 1, Fall 1984, 1.
3. Peter W. Bernstein, "Ronald Reagan's Second Term Agenda," *Fortune*, October 1, 1984, p. 29.
4. Kurt Andersen, "America's Upbeat Mood," *Time*, September 24, 1984, p. 16.
5. Richard Pipes, "Can the Soviet Union Reform?" *Foreign Affairs*, 63, 1, Fall 1984, p. 49.
6. John Kohan, "East-West Echoes Across the Gap," *Time*, September 3, 1984, p. 48.
7. R. Gordon Hoxie, *Command Decision and the Presidency: A Study in National Security Policy and Organization* (New York: Reader's Digest Press, 1977), p. 70.
8. *Ibid.*, p. 409.
9. Pipes, *op. cit.*, p. 51.
10. *U. S. News & World Report*, July 9, 1984, p. 29, also Michael Skinner, "Inside the Mountain," *Raytheon Magazine*, Spring, 1984, pp. 14, 17.
11. *U.S.A. Today*, August 31, 1984, p. 10A.
12. "Editors Postscript, June 18, 1984" (in Chapter Four).
13. *The New York Times*, September 19, 1984, p. A5. President Carter had met with Gromyko in September 1977 and 1978; also at the Vienna summit with Brezhnev in 1979. However, after the Afghanistan invasion of December 1979 Carter declined such meetings.
14. Richard Burt, "The Yearlong Shadow of KAL Flight 7," *The New York Times*, August 31, 1984, p. A.23.
15. Kohan, *op. cit*, *Time*, September 3, 1984, p. 49.
16. *Presidential Studies Quarterly*, *XIV*, 4, Fall, 1984, p. 649.
17. I. M. Destler, Leslie H. Gelb and Anthony Lake, *Our Own Worst Enemy: The Unmaking of American Foreign Policy* (New York: Simon and Schuster, 1984), p. 272.
18. *Presidential Studies Quarterly* XIV, 4, Fall, 1984, p. 619.
19. Destler, Gelb, and Lake, *op. cit.*, p. 273.
20. R. Gordon Hoxie, "The Nixon Resignation and the Watergate

Era Reforms Viewed Ten years Later," *Presidential Studies Quarterly*, XIV, 4, Fall 1984, p. 659.

21. *Ibid.*
22. Richard Halloran, "U.S. Troops Termed Able to Fight For 30 Days in Conventional War," *The New York Times*, August 25, 1984, pp. 1, 11.
23. *Presidential Studies Quarterly*, XIV, 4 Fall 1984, p. 649.
24. *U. S. News & World Report*, September 3, 1984, p. 74.
25. R. Gordon Hoxie, ed., *Frontiers for Freedom* (Denver: University of Denver Press, 1952), p. 163.
26. George P. Shultz, "Power and Diplomacy in the 1980s," in R. Gordon Hoxie, ed., *The Presidency and National Security Policy* (New York: Center for the Study of the Presidency, 1984) Ch. 1.

## NOTES FOR FOREWORD

1. Gerald R. Ford, "Foreword", in R. Gordon Hoxie, *Command Decision and the Presidency* (New York: Reader's Digest Press, 1977), pp. xvii–xviii.
2. I. M. Destler, "National Security Management: What Presidents Have Wrought," *Political Science Quarterly*, 95, 4, Winter 1980–81, pp. 573–588.
3. Milton S. Eisenhower, "Organizing the Presidency," in Bradley D. Nash, Milton S. Eisenhower, R. Gordon Hoxie, and William C. Spragens, *Organizing and Staffing the Presidency* (New York: Center for the Study of the Presidency, 1980), pp. 174–180.
4. For example, Norman Podhoretz, *The Present Danger* (New York: Simon and Schuster, 1980).

## CHAPTER FIVE NOTES

1. The Ford Executive Order (#11905) may be found in the *Weekly Compilation of Presidential Documents*, Volume 12, pp. 234–243.
2. The Carter Executive Order (#12036) may be found in the *Weekly Compilation of Presidential Documents*, Volume 14, pp. 194–216. The Reagan Executive Order (#12333) may be found in Volume 17, pp. 1336–1348.
3. *Facts on File*, July 3, 1976, p. 477.
4. Ray Cline, *The CIA Under Reagan, Bush, and Casey* (Washington, D.C.: Acropolis Books, 1981), p. 275.
5. *Public Papers of the Presidents: Jimmy Carter: 1980–1981* (Washington, D.C.: G.P.O., 1981), p. 198.
6. *Congressional Quarterly*, August 16, 1980, p. 2413.

7. *Congressional Quarterly*, July 19, 1980, p. 2051.

8. *Newsweek*, October 10, 1983, p. 38.

9. Emphasis added. Harry Ransom, *The Intelligence Establishment* (Cambridge: Harvard University Press, 1970), p. 85.

10. Cited in *Ibid.*, p. 7.

11. Carter Executive Order #12036, p. 213.

12. Sherman Kent, *Strategic Intelligence for American World Policy* (Princeton: Princeton University Press, 1966).

13. Ransom, *The Intelligence Establishment*.

14. Roy Godson and Richard Shultz, "Intelligence — The Evaluation of a New Teaching Subject," *International Studies Notes* 8 (1981–82).

15. Kent, *Strategic Intelligence for American World Policy*, p. viii.

16. Richard Betts, "American Strategic Intelligence: Politics, Priorities, and Direction," in Robert Pfaltzgraff, Uri Raanan, and Warren Milberg (eds.), *Intelligence Policy and National Security* (Hamden, Conn.: Archon Books, 1981).

17. For a discussion of Carter's changes see Betts, "American Strategic Intelligence," and Cline, *The CIA Under Reagan, Bush, and Casey*.

18. Anthony Downs, *Inside Bureaucracy* (Boston: Little, Brown & Co., 1966), p. 88.

19. *The New York Times*, December 10, 1977.

20. Cline, *The CIA Under Reagan, Bush, and Casey*, p. 278.

21. Theodore Sorensen, *Kennedy* (New York: Harper & Row, 1965).

22. Quoted by Betts, "American Strategic Intelligence," p. 253.

23. For a dissenting view on the invulnerability of technical systems to planned deception see William Harris, "Counterintelligence Jurisdiction and the Double-Cross System by National Technical Means," in Roy Godson (ed.), *Intelligence Requirements for the 1980's: Counterintelligence* (New York: NSIC and Transaction Books, 1980).

24. Robert Dudney and Orr Kelly, "Inside CIA: What's Really Going On," in *U.S. News and World Report*, June 25, 1984, p. 27.

25. Kent, *Strategic Intelligence for American World Policy*.

26. Willmoore Kendall, "The Functions of Intelligence," *World Politics* 2 (1949).

27. An account of the Colby-Helms exchange can be found in the *Washington Post*, October 23, 1979.

28. *Newsweek*, October 10, 1983, p. 43.

29. *U.S. News & World Report*, June 25, 1984, pp. 28–29.

30. *Newsweek*, October 10, 1983, p. 44.

31. *U.S. News & World Report*, June 25, 1984, p. 29.

32. *Newsweek*, October 10, 1983, pp. 38, 43.

33. Roy Godson, "Covert Action: An Introduction," in Roy Godson (ed.), *Intelligence Requirements for the 1980's: Covert Action* (New York: NSIC and Transaction Books, 1981), p. 2.
34. *Wall Street Journal*, March 5, 1982. Cline estimates the real cut in spending at 33–50%.
35. *Newsweek*, October 10, 1983, p. 39.
36. Theodore Shackley, *The Third Option* (New York: Reader's Digest Press, 1981), p. 163.
37. *The Economist*, August 1, 1981.
38. *U.S. News & World Report*, June 25, 1984, p. 28.
39. From the title of David Martin's book on James Angleton and William Harvey, *The Wilderness of Mirrors* (New York: Ballantine Books, 1981).
40. *Newsweek*, October 10, 1983, p. 44.
41. *U.S. News & World Report*, June 25, 1984, p. 30.
42. Martin Tolchin, "Brevity Serves to Soothe the CIA and Senate," *The New York Times*, June 21, 1984, p. 138.
43. *Ibid.*
44. *Ibid.*
45. *U.S. News & World Report*, June 25, 1984, pp. 27, 30.

## CHAPTER SEVEN NOTES

1. A.E. Campbell, *Great Britain and the United States: 1895–1903* (London: Longmans, Green & Co., 1960), p. 22.
2. Samuel F. Bemis, ed., *The American Secretaries of State and Their Diplomacy* (New York: Alfred A. Knopf, 1928), VIII, 292.
3. Charles C. Tansill, *The Foreign Policy of Thomas F. Bayard: 1885–1897* (New York: Fordham Press, 1940), p. 623.
4. Bemis, VIII, 294.
5. Thomas A. Bailey, *A Diplomatic History of the American People*, 10th ed. (Englewood Cliffs, N.J.: Prentice-Hall, 1980), p. 438.
6. Tansill, p. 624.
7. Bailey, p. 439.
8. Dexter Perkins, *The Monroe Doctrine: 1867–1907* (Gloucester, Mass.: Johns Hopkins Press, 1966), pp. 139–141.
9. Fred L. Israel, ed., *The State of the Union Messages of the Presidents: 1790–1966* (New York: Chelsea House, 1966), II, 1765.
10. Nelson M. Blake, "The Background of Cleveland's Venezuela Policy," *American Historical Review*, XLVII (1942), 259.
11. Perkins, p. 143.
12. Blake, pp. 263–265.
13. May 9, 1895. Quoted in Blake, pp. 265–266.

14. *North American Review*, CLX (June 1985), 651–658. Quoted in Perkins, p. 149.

15. Grover Cleveland, *The Venezuelan Boundary Controversy* (Princeton, N.J.: Princeton University Press, 1913), p. 93.

16. Perkins, p. 147.

17. Henry James, *Richard Olney and His Public Service* (Cambridge, Mass.: Riverside Press, 1923), p. 46.

18. Cleveland, p. 94.

19. *Papers Relating to the Foreign Relations of the United States* (Washington: Government Printing Office, 1896), 1895, I, 545–562.

20. *Ibid*, p. 546.

21. *Ibid*, p. 552.

22. *Ibid*, p. 553.

23. Allan Nevins, *Grover Cleveland: A Study in Courage* (New York: Dodd, Mead & Co., 1933), p. 631.

24. Perkins, p. 155.

25. *Foreign Relations*, 1895, I, 554.

26. *Ibid*, p. 555.

27. Perkins, p. 157.

28. *Foreign Relations*, 1895, I, 558.

29. *Ibid*.

30. Perkins, p. 163.

31. *Foreign Relations*, 1895, I, 557–558.

32. Perkins, p. 161.

33. *Foreign Relations*, 1895, I, 559.

34. *Ibid*, p. 558.

35. *Ibid*, p. 560.

36. *Ibid*, p. 562.

37. Tansill, p. 701.

38. Bemis, VIII, 275.

39. Cleveland, p. 96.

40. Bailey, p. 441.

41. Tansill, p. 709.

42. Perkins, p. 173.

43. *Foreign Relations*, 1895, I, 563–576.

44. Bailey, p. 442.

45. *Foreign Relations*, 1895, I, 564–565.

46. *Ibid*, pp. 565–566.

47. *Ibid*, p. 566.

48. *Ibid*, p. 567.

49. Perkins, p. 177.

50. James D. Richardson, *A Compilation of the Messages and Papers of the Presidents: 1789–1897* (Washington: Government Printing Office, 1898), IX, 655–658.

51. *Ibid*, p. 658.
52. Perkins, pp. 193–194.
53. Richardson, p. 658.
54. Perkins, p. 200.
55. Campbell, pp. 29–30.
56. Cleveland, pp. 90–91.
57. Walter La Feber, "The Background of Cleveland's Venezuelan Policy: A Reinterpretation," *American Historical Review*, LXVI (1961), 947–967.
58. *Ibid*, pp. 949–953.
59. Perkins, pp. 196–197.
60. Blake, p. 275.
61. Campbell, p. 22.
62. *Ibid*, pp. 21–22.
63. Cleveland, p. 1.
64. *Ibid*, p. 37.
65. Campbell, p. 23.
66. *Ibid*, p. 30.
67. Tansill, p. 737.
68. Campbell, p. 34.
69. Tansill, p. 741.
70. *Ibid*, p. 776.
71. Bailey, p. 442.
72. *Ibid*, p. 448.
73. Julius W. Pratt, *A History of United States Foreign Policy* (Englewood Cliffs, N.J.: Prentice-Hall, Inc., 1955), pp. 351–352.

## CHAPTER EIGHT NOTES

1. Indispensable for evaluating the Hull-Nomura exchange is a careful reading of previous talks between Grew and Nomura (1939), Sayre and Arita (1940), Grew and Arita (1940).
2. Hull Memorandum, 8 March 1941, U.S. Department of State, *Foreign Relations of the United States: Japan, 1931–1941*, 2 vols. (Washington, D.C.: U.S. Government Printing Office, 1943), II, 389 — hereafter cited as FR (Japan); Memorandum handed to FDR by Bishop Walsh, 23 January 1941, U.S. Department of State, *Papers Relating to the Foreign Relations of the United States 1933–1941* (Washington, D.C.: U.S. Government Printing Office, 1950–1969), 1941, IV, 14–16 (hereafter cited as FR).
3. Wikawa to Drought, 23 January 1941; Drought Memorandum, 10 March 1941; Wikawa to Henderson, 1 October 1945, box 1, James M. Drought Papers, Maryknoll, New York. Wikawa's daughter was a student at Columbia University where he had

earlier delivered a series of lectures; *Japan Times*, 20 April 1939 (clipping contained in Grew Diary, vol. 95 (1939), Joseph Grew Papers, Harvard University (hereafter cited as GP); Donald W. Smith (U.S. Assistant Commercial Attaché) to Hull, 25 February 1941; Grew to Hull, 27 February 1941; Walker to FDR, 28 February 1941; Walker to Hull (11 March 1941?); Ballentine Memorandum, 28 March 1941, FR (1941), IV, 51, 53–54, 69–70, 115. For Chinese interest in involving the Catholic Church as early as 1939, see Hamilton Memorandum, 25 October 1939, FR (1939), III, 302.

4. Cordell Hull, *The Memoirs of Cordell Hull*, 2 vols. (New York: Macmillan, 1948), II, 995; "Proposal Presented to the Department of State through the Medium of Private American and Japanese Individuals on 9 April 1941"; Hull Memorandum, 16 April 1941, FR (Japan), II, 398–402, 407.

5. See Drought Papers, box 1.

6. Walsh Memorandum on the 1940–41 Negotiations, 15 September 1971; Walsh Confidential Memorandum, 11 December 1945, Walsh to Drought, 25 September 1941; Walsh Memorandum, 15 December 1941; Walsh Visitation Diary, 28 September 1941, James E. Walsh Papers, Maryknoll.

7. British Embassy in Washington to the Foreign Office (hereafter cited as FO), undated, FO 371/27910, Public Record Office, Kew, England (hereafter cited as PRO). Hull was saying that if the United States could reach a satisfactory China settlement, "they would not quarrel about Manchukuo," although he would deny the latter if made public. See also, Eugene Ott to Foreign Ministry, 5 May 1941 (on the U.S. position), U.S. Department of State, *Documents on German Foreign Policy, 1918–1945* (series C, 1933–1937, Washington, D.C.: U.S. Government Printing Office, 1959–66; series D, 1937–1941, Washington, D.C.: U.S. Government Printing Office, 1959–64), ser. D, XII, 715; Hull Memorandum, 16 April 1941, FR (Japan), II, 409.

8. Minutes, 13 September 1941, FO 371/27910, PRO; Joachim von Ribbentrop, *The Ribbentrop Memoirs* (London: Weidenfeld and Nicolson, 1954), p. 153; Ernst von Weizsäcker, *Memoirs of Ernst von Weizsäcker* (London: Victor Gollancz, 1951), p. 261; Drought Memorandum, undated (1941 or 1942?), box 1, Drought Papers, Maryknoll; Walker to Hull, 7 March 1941, FR (1941), IV, 63. See also Johanna M. Meskill, *Hitler and Japan: The Hollow Alliance* (New York: Atherton, 1966). For a dissenting opinion, see R. J. C. Butow, *The John Doe Associates: Backdoor Diplomacy for Peace, 1941* (Stanford: Stanford University Press, 1974), p. 143.

9. James E. Walsh Memorandum, 18 October 1941, FR (1941),

IV, 536–37; Drought to Walker, 4 June 1941, box 1, Drought Papers, Maryknoll; Ballantine Memoranda, 21 and 30 May 1941; Toyoda to Nomura, 13 September 1941, FR (Japan), II, 437–38, 444, 454, 623.

10. Shigenori Tōgō, *The Cause of Japan* (New York: Simon and Schuster, 1956), pp. 71, 174–77; Nobutaka Ike, trans, and ed., *Japan's Decision for War: Records of the 1941 Policy Conferences* (Stanford: Stanford University Press, 1967), p. 263; Paul Schroeder's article in Robert Dallek, ed., *The Roosevelt Diplomacy and World War II* (New York: Holt, Rinehart, 1970); Hull Memoranda, 16 April, 2, 11, and 16 May 1941, FR (Japan), II, 406–11, 417–18, 431–32.

11. Drought to Walker, 4 June and 7 July 1941, Drought to Walsh, 18 June 1941, box 1, Drought Papers, Maryknoll; "Informal and Unofficial Oral Statement Handed by the Secretary of State to the Japanese Ambassador," 16 May 1941, FR (Japan), II, 433. See also, for Wakasugi's indication of Japanese willingness to pull *all* of its troops out of China, Welles Memorandum, 13 October 1941, FR (Japan), II, 685.

12. James MacGregor Burns, for example, insists that Roosevelt did not want war and that he tried to avoid a showdown; the basic problem was that both Japan and the United States misunderstood each other; Burns, *Soldier of Freedom* (New York: Harcourt Brace Jovanovich, 1970), pp. 145–46, 149–51.

13. Drought to Walker, 7 July 1941, box 1, Drought Papers, Maryknoll; Ballantine Memorandum, 1 September 1941; Grew Memoranda, 3 and 4 September 1941; Hull Memoranda, 28 August and 3 September 1941; FDR to Konoye, 3 September 1941, FR (Japan), II, 571–72, 584–94; Tōgō, *The Cause of Japan*, pp. 90–92; R. J. C. Butow, "Backdoor Diplomacy in the Pacific: The Proposal for a Konoye-Roosevelt Meeting, 1941," *Journal of American History* 59 (June 1972), pp. 48–72; Hull, *Memoirs*, II, 1019–27; Ike, *Japan's Decision*, p. 146; Konoye Memoir in U.S. Congress, 79th Congress, 1st Session, *Pearl Harbor Attack*, Hearings Before the Joint Committee on the Investigation of the Pearl Harbor Attack, 39 parts, pt. XX, pp. 4001–4002 (hereafter cited as *Pearl Harbor Attack*).

14. Nomura to Hull, 20 November 1941; Ballantine Memorandum, 22 November 1941; Grew to Hull, 24 November 1941, FR (Japan), II, 755–62.

15. Irvine H. Anderson, Jr., "The 1941 *De Facto* Embargo on Oil to Japan: A Bureaucratic Reflex," *Pacific Historical Review* 44 (May 1975), pp. 230–31.

16. For the use of the term Indochina, see Hull Memorandum, 27

November 1941; Ballantine Memorandum, 1 December 1941, FR (Japan), II, 770, 775.

17. For an example of Hull's vagueness, see his *Memoirs*, II, 1034 ff. See also, Grew Memoranda, 7 and 8 October 1941, FR (Japan), II, 446, 665–68; FDR to Hull, 28 September 1941; Walsh Memorandum for Hull, 15 November 1941, FR (1941), IV, 483, 527–28.

18. Hull, *Memoirs*, II, 984, 1015, 1033; Butow, *John Doe*, p. 156; Memorandum by Far East Division for Hull, 10 April 1941; Hornbeck Memorandum, 11 April 1941, FR (1941), IV, 136–37, 142–44.

19. See, for example, Hull Memoranda for 14 April 1941, 2, 11, and 16 May 1941, FR (Japan), II, 402–406, 411, 417–18, 431–32.

20. See, for example, Hull Memorandum, 14 March 1941, FR (Japan), II, 397.

21. Butow, *John Doe*, pp. 212–13; Wikawa to Drought, 18 June 1941, box 1, Drought Papers, Maryknoll; Ballantine Memorandum, 14 July 1941; Turner to Stark, 21 July 1941, FR (Japan), II, 505, 516.

22. Walsh to Drought, 25 September 1941, Walsh Papers, Maryknoll; Welles Memorandum, 24 October 1941; Ballantine Memoranda, 7 and 15 November 1941, FR (Japan), II, 693, 708, 731.

23. Welles Memorandum, 9 August 1941, FR (1941), I, 348; James A. Farley, *Jim Farley's Story, the Roosevelt Years* (New York: McGraw-Hill, 1948), p. 345. See also: Minutes of British War Cabinet Meeting, 19 August 1941, Confidential Annex B, CAB 65/23, PRO; Drought Memorandum for the Acting Secretary of State, 1 November 1934, Official File 197, Franklin D. Roosevelt Library, Hyde Park; Drought to Buell, 28 August 1934, box 2, Drought Papers, Maryknoll.

24. Waldo H. Heinrichs, *American Ambassador: Joseph C. Grew and the Development of the United States Diplomatic Tradition* (Boston: Little, Brown, 1966), p. 348. Hiranuma was shot on 16 August 1941.

25. R. J. C. Butow, "The Hull-Nomura Conversations: A Fundamental Misconception," *American Historical Review* 65 (July 1960), p. 835; Hull, *Memoirs*, II, 996; Lewis L. Strauss, *Men and Decisions* (New York: Doubleday, 1962), pp. 124–25. On the other hand, compare Butow, "Hull-Nomura Conversations," with Butow, "Backdoor Diplomacy," written twelve years later, in which the author continues to criticize the Maryknoll priests, but drops his attack on Nomura.

26. Hull, *Memoirs*, II, 994–95; Butow, "Backdoor Diplomacy," p. 56; Strauss, *Men and Decisions*, p. 125. This is a fair sampling of interpretation.
27. Drought Memorandum, 28 February 1941, box 1, Drought Papers, Maryknoll; Walker to FDR, 28 February 1941, FR (1941), IV, 54. For evidence of Drought's prior consultation with Hull, see Walker to Hull, 17 March 1941 (containing Drought's "Preliminary Draft of an 'Agreement in Principle'"), *ibid.*, IV, 98–102. Hull was not, in other words, faced with any kind of *fait-accompli* on 9 April.
28. Ballantine Memorandum, 7 April 1941, FR (1941), IV, 127.
29. Walker to Hull, 17 March 1941, FR (1941), IV, 97. Drought's memoranda for 17 and 18 March record the danger of assassination as perceived by Japanese envoys and statesmen. Wikawa and Iwakuro were fully aware of the risk to their lives, and Wikawa's mother had expressed herself ready for any eventuality; box 1, Drought Papers, Maryknoll.
30. Walker to Hull, 18 March 1941; to Hull, undated, FR (1941), IV, 112, 119; Hull Memorandum, 16 April 1941, FR (Japan), II, 407.
31. Hull, *Memoirs*, II, 996; Drought, "Private Explanation," 12 May 1941, box 1, Drought Papers, Maryknoll; Togo, *The Cause of Japan*, p. 67; Walker to Hull, 12 May 1941, FR (1941), IV, 184, 186; Konoye Memoir in *Pearl Harbor Attack*, pt. XX, p. 3985.
32. Hornbeck to Hull, 7 March 1941, Memorandum by Far East Division for Hull, 10 April 1941; Memorandum Prepared for the Secretary of State, 15 April 1941; Hornbeck to Hull, 10 June 1941, FR (1941), IV, 62–63, 136–37, 153, 263; Wikawa to Drought, 18 June 1941; Drought to Walker, 20 June 1941, box 1, Drought Papers, Maryknoll.
33. Julius W. Pratt, *Cordell Hull, 1933–44*, 2 vols. (New York: Cooper Square, 1964), II, 480; John H. Boyle, "The Drought-Walsh Mission to Japan," *Pacific Historical Review* 34 (May 1965), pp. 141–61; Ike, *Japan's Decision*, p. xxi; Butow, *John Doe*, p. 140. Compare Walker to Hull, 17 March 1941 (containing Drought's "Preliminary Draft of an 'Agreement in Principle'") with the Draft Understanding submitted by Drought 9 April 1941, FR (1941), IV, 98–102, FR (Japan), II, 398–402.
34. Walsh to Drought, 17 May 1941; Walsh Confidential Memorandum, 11 December 1945; Walsh Visitation Diary, 26–27 and 30 November, 3, 5, 10, 17, 23, 27, 28 December 1940, Walsh Papers, Maryknoll; Drought to Walsh, 3 June 1941; Drought Memorandum, undated, box 1; Drought to Walker, 27 January 1941, box 2, Drought Papers, Maryknoll; Hamilton Memoran-

dum, 25 October 1939, FR (1939), III, 302; Boyle, "Drought-Walsh Mission," p. 154.

35. The same scholar who speaks of Drought's innocence and naiveté attributes his failure in 1941 to the fact that he was highly emotional and vindictive, still suffering from moods of shyness, melancholy, and high scruple which attended his induction into the priesthood. For this and other negative commentary on Drought, see Butow, *John Doe*, pp. 49, 103, 110, 150, 315, 341, 343; Strauss, *Men and Decisions*, pp. 123–25. Butow implies that Drought's reasons for entering the priesthood led to disillusionment, frustration, and a Messiah complex.

36. Drought to Horinouchi, 7 March 1938, box 2, Drought Papers, Maryknoll.

37. Walsh Visitation Diary, 16 and 24 August, 3 September 1940; Paul Le Veness, "Bishop Walsh's China: The Life and Thought of an American Missionary in China," Walsh Papers, Maryknoll.

38. Drought Memorandum, 17 March 1941, box 1, Drought Papers, Maryknoll; Walsh Memorandum, 18 October 1941, FR (1941), IV, 531.

39. Le Veness, "Bishop Walsh's China," Walsh Papers, Maryknoll; Drought to Buell, 28 August 1934, box 2; Drought, "Preliminary Draft of an 'Agreement in Principle' between the United States and Japan," undated, box 5; Drought Memorandum, January 1941, box 1, Drought Papers, Maryknoll.

40. Drought, "Working Analysis of Our [Japan's] Position and Policy in the Far East with Particular Reference to the United States," box 5, Drought Papers, Maryknoll.

41. Boyle, "Drought-Walsh Mission," pp. 147–48; Drought, "Working Analysis of Our Position and Policy in the Far East with Particular Reference to the United States," box 5, Drought Papers; Drought Memorandum "Exclusively From the Japanese Viewpoint," 29 March 1941, box 1, Drought Papers, Maryknoll.

42. Drought, "Preliminary Draft of an 'Agreement in Principle' between the United States and Japan," box 5, Drought Papers, Maryknoll; Butow, *John Doe*, p. 150.

43. Hull Oral Statement to Nomura, 21 June 1941; Ballantine Memorandum, 14 July 1941; Turner to Stark, 21 July 1941, FR (Japan), II, 485, 505, 516; Ike, *Japan's Decision*, pp. 96–97, 263, 282.

44. Craigie to FO, 1 November 1941; Cadogan to Craigie, 8 November 1941 (draft), FO 371/27911, PRO; Lothian to Halifax, 1 February 1940, FO 800/324, PRO; Winston Churchill, *The Grand Alliance* (Boston: Houghton Mifflin, 1950), p. 595.

45. Minute by C. E. Scott, 7 October 1941; Halifax to the British Embassy in Washington, 17 October 1941, FO 371/27910, PRO; Craigie to FO, 1 November 1941, FO 371/27911, PRO; Hull Memorandum, 6 May 1941, (re: Lothian), FR (1941), IV, 198; FO to Washington Embassy, 18 October 1941, CAB 65/23, PRO ("we should prefer, if possible, to keep Japan out of the world conflict and to detach her from the Axis" though we have been content thus far to follow the United States in their policy of "maximum economic pressure").

46. Drought to Walker, 13 August 1941, box 1, Drought Papers, Maryknoll; Tōgō, *The Cause of Japan*, p. 187; Halifax to Eden, 3 June 1942, in Thomas E. Hachey, ed., *Confidential Dispatches: Analyses of America by the British Ambassador, 1939–1945* (Evanston: New University Press, 1973), p. 33.

## CHAPTER NINE NOTES

1. Frances Perkins, *The Roosevelt I Knew* (New York: Viking, 1946), pp. 72–73.

2. Robert E. Sherwood, *Roosevelt and Hopkins: An Intimate History* (New York: Harper, 1948), pp. 42–43.

3. Waldo W. Braden and Earnest Brandenburg, "Roosevelt's Fireside Chats," *Speech Monographs*, 22 (November, 1955), pp. 290–302.

4. *The Public Papers and Addresses of Franklin D. Roosevelt* (New York: Random House, 1938), Vol. III, pp. 59–65.

5. Earnest Brandenburg and Waldo W. Braden, "Franklin Delano Roosevelt," in *A History and Criticism of American Public Address* edited by Marie K. Hockmuth (New York: Longmans, Green, 1955) III, pp. 464–482.

6. Samuel I. Rosenman, *Working with Roosevelt* (New York: Harper, 1952), p. 6.

7. Sherwood, p. 297.

8. *Autobiography of Sol Bloom* (New York: Putnams, 1948), pp. 246.

9. Henry Stimson and McGeorge Bundy, *On Active Service in Peace and War* (New York: Harper, 1947), pp. 374–375.

10. Rosenman, pp. 166–167.

11. Conference with the Senate Military Affairs Committee January 31, 1939 in Donald B. Schewe (ed.), *Franklin D. Roosevelt and Foreign Affairs* (New York: Garland, 1979), Vol. III, No. 1565, p. 3.

12. Rosenman, p. 329.

13. Sherwood, p. 503.

14. Rosenman, pp. 340–341.

15. Rosenman, p. 361.
16. Sherwood, p. 633.
17. Rosenman, p. 361.
18. Rosenman, p. 412.
19. The last four Fireside Chats (Sept. 8, 1943; June 12, 1944; January 11, 1944 and January 6, 1945 were comparatively minor efforts. The first two were used to open War Loan Drives and the last two were just shortened versions of the State of the Union messages.
20. Robert A. Divine, *Roosevelt and World War II* (Baltimore: Johns Hopkins, 1969), p. 5.

## CHAPTER TEN NOTES

1. Paul Y. Hammond summarizes the arguments of critics in his article "The National Security Council: An Interpretation and Appraisal," *The American Political Science Review* December 1960, Reprinted in Alan A. Altshuler, *The Politics of the Federal Bureaucracy* (New York: Dodd, Mead & Co., 1975), p. 147.
2. Stanley L. Falk, "The National Security Council Under Truman, Eisenhower and Kennedy," *Political Science Quarterly*, September 1964, Vol. LXXIX, No. 3, p. 424.
3. *Ibid.*
4. Richard E. Neustadt, *Presidential Power: The Politics of Leadership* (New York: John Wiley & Sons, 1976 edition), p. 229.
5. Richard Tanner Johnson, *Managing the White House* (New York: Harper & Row, 1974), p. 96.
6. *Ibid.*, p. 81.
7. *Ibid.*, p. 92.
8. Quoted in James David Barber, *The Presidential Character: Predicting Performance in the White House*, Second Edition (Englewood Cliffs, N.J.: Prentice-Hall, 1977), p. 163.
9. R. Gordon Hoxie, "The National Security Council," *Presidential Studies Quarterly*, Volume 12, Winter 1982, p. 109.
10. *Ibid.*
11. *Ibid.*
12. Dwight David Eisenhower, *The White House Years: Mandate for Change* (Garden City, New York: Doubleday & Company, Inc., 1963), p. 87.
13. James Lay, Jr., "An Organizational History of the NSC," p. 33, Folder: NSC (1), Papers of Dwight D. Eisenhower as President of the United States, Ann Whitman File, Administration Series, Box 30, Eisenhower Library.
14. R. Gordon Hoxie, *Command Decision and the Presidency: A Study*

*of National Security Policy and Organization* (New York: Reader's Digest Press, 1977), p. 254.

15. S. Everett Gleason, Draft of Speech on NSC presented at the National War College, August 31, 1954, p. 13. Folder: National Security Council (1), Papers of S. Everett Gleason, Box 2, Harry S Truman Library.
16. *Ibid.*
17. *Ibid.*, pp. 14–15.
18. *Ibid.*, p. 8.
19. Robert Bowie, Columbia Oral History Interview, P. 16, Eisenhower Library.
20. *Ibid.*
21. Gleason, Draft of speech on NSC, p. 9.
22. James Lay, Jr., "An Organizational History of the NSC," p. 34.
23. Keith C. Clark and Laurence J. Legere, eds., *The President and the Management of National Security* (New York: Praeger, 1969) p. 64.
24. Memorandum: George Marshall to Dwight D. Eisenhower, February 19, 1953, Folder: NSC Organization and Functions (5), White House Office, Office of the Special Assistant for National Security Affairs, NSC Series, Administrative Subseries, Box 6, Eisenhower Library.
25. Notes of Study Group Conference, February 17, 1953, p. 2, Folder: NSC Organization & Function (5), White House Office, Office of Special Assistant for National Security, NSC Series, Administration Subseries, Box 6, Eisenhower Library.
26. Robert Cutler, Report to the President, April 1, 1955, Folder: April 1955 (1), White House Office, Office of the Special Assistant for National Security Affairs, Special Assistant Series, Chronological Subseries, Box 1, Eisenhower Library.
27. Dillon Anderson, Columbia Oral History Interview #1, p. 18, Eisenhower Library.
28. Dick Kirschten, "Beyond the Vance-Brzezinski Clash Lurks an NSC Under Fire," *National Journal*, May 17, 1980, p. 816.
29. Dwight D. Eisenhower to Gordon Gray, Press Release, January 13, 1961, Folder: Final Reports (2), Papers of Dwight D. Eisenhower as President of the United States, Ann Whitman File, Transition Series, Box 3, Eisenhower Library.
30. Kirschten, "Beyond the Vance-Brzezinski Clash . . .," p. 816.
31. Dwight D. Eisenhower, Columbia Oral History Interview, Interviewed by Ed Edwin, July 20, 1967, p. 103, Eisenhower Library.
32. *Ibid.*, pp. 104–105.
33. Memorandum on Discussion at the 295th Meeting of the National Security Council on August 30, 1956, Dated August 31,

1956, Folder: 295th Meeting of NSC, Papers of Dwight D. Eisenhower as President of the United States, Ann Whitman File, NSC Series, Box 8, Eisenhower Library.

34. *Ibid.*, p. 10.
35. *Ibid.*
36. *Ibid.*
37. *Ibid.*, p. 13.
38. *Ibid.*
39. *Ibid.*
40. *Ibid.*, p. 14.
41. *Ibid.*
42. *Ibid.*
43. *Ibid.*
44. *Ibid.*, p. 15.
45. *Ibid.*, p. 11.
46. *Ibid.*, p. 12.
47. *Ibid.*, p. 11.
48. Memorandum on Discussion at the 363rd Meeting of the National Security Council on April 24, 1958, dated April 25, 1958, Folder: 363rd Meeting of NSC, Papers of Dwight D. Eisenhower as President of the United States, Ann Whitman File, NSC Series, Box 10, Eisenhower Library.
49. *Ibid.*, p. 2.
50. *Ibid.*, p. 4.
51. *Ibid.*, p. 5.
52. *Ibid.*
53. *Ibid.*
54. Robert Bowie, Columbia Oral History Interview, p. 13, Eisenhower Library.
55. Notes of Meeting in President's Office, March 29, 1956, Folder: March 1956 Diary (1), Papers of Dwight D. Eisenhower as President of the United States, Ann Whitman File, Ann Whitman Diary Series, Box 8, Eisenhower Library.
56. *Ibid.*
57. Memorandum of Conference with the President on March 30, 1956, Dated April 2, 1956, Folder: April 1956–Goodpaster, Papers of Dwight D. Eisenhower as President of the United States, Ann Whitman File, Dwight D. Eisenhower Diaries, Box 15, Eisenhower Library.
58. Memorandum: Lt. General F. W. Farrell to Robert Cutler, June 21, 1957, Folder: General Robert Cutler, Vol. I-1, White House Office, Office of the Staff Secretary, White House Subseries, Box 2, Eisenhower Library.
59. Memorandum: Robert Cutler to General Francis Farrell, June

25, 1957, Folder: General Robert Cutler, Vol. I-1, White House Office, Office of the Staff Secretary, White House Subseries, Box 2, Eisenhower Library.

60. List of Meetings with the President, Folder: Meetings with the President 1959 (1), White House Office, Office of the Special Assistant for National Security Affairs, Presidential Subseries, Box 4, Eisenhower Library.

61. Dillon Anderson, Columbia Oral History Interview, pp. 19–20, Eisenhower Library.

62. Robert Cutler, Comments on Speech by Senator Jackson, June 5, 1959, p. 7, Folder: NSC Investigation (Jackson Resolution), Staff Files, Bryce Harlow, Box 17, Eisenhower Library.

63. William Bragg Ewald, Jr., *Eisenhower the President: Crucial Days, 1951–1960* (Englewood Cliffs, N.J.: Prentice Hall, 1981), p. 250.

64. Robert J. Donovan, *Eisenhower: The Inside Story* (New York: Harper, 1956), p. 345.

65. Gleason, Draft of Speech on NSC, p. 1.

66. Sherman Adams, Columbia Oral History Interview, Part 3, p. 154, Eisenhower Library.

67. Clark and Legere, eds., *The President and the Management of National Security*, p. 65.

68. James Lay, Jr., "An Organizational History of the NSC," p. 54.

69. *Ibid.*, p. 56.

70. *Ibid.*, p. 57

71. Robert Cutler, "The Development of the National Security Council," *Foreign Affairs*, Vol. 34 (1956), p. 450.

72. William Jackson to Sherman Adams, Memorandum of April 2, 1956 on "The Role of the OCB," Folder: William Jackson (1) October 1954–March 1961, White House Office: Office of the Staff Secretary: White House Subseries, Box 3, Eisenhower Library.

73. *Ibid.*, p. 3.

74. James Lay, Jr., "An Organizational History of the NSC," p. 53.

75. *Ibid.*, p. 59.

76. *Ibid.*, p. 54.

77. Christian Herter to Gordon Gray, Letter of January 19, 1960, Folder: OCB (1) April 1958–April 1960, White House Office: Office of the Special Assistant for National Security Affairs, Records 1952–1961, OCB Series, Administrative Subseries, Eisenhower Library.

78. Gordon Gray to Christian Herter, Letter of January 22, 1960, Folder: OCB (1) April 1958–April 1960, White House Office: Office of the Special Assistant for National Security Affairs, Records 1952–1961, OCB Series, Administrative Subseries, Eisenhower Library.

79. Memorandum for the Record, January 11, 1961, p. 4. Folder: Memos Staff RE: Change of Administration (3), Papers of Dwight D. Eisenhower as President of the United States, Ann Whitman File, Transition Series, Box 7, Eisenhower Library.

80. *Ibid.*

81. Gordon Gray to Dwight D. Eisenhower, Letter of January 13, 1961, Folder: Final Reports (2), Papers of Dwight D. Eisenhower as President of the United States, Ann Whitman File, Transition Series, Box 7, Eisenhower Library.

82. Theodore G. Sorensen, *Kennedy* (New York: Harper and Row, 1965), p. 281.

83. *Ibid.*

84. Gordon Gray, Memorandum for the Record, January 11, 1961, p. 11, Folder: Memos Staff RE: Change Administration (3), Dwight D. Eisenhower Paper as President of the United States, 1953–1961, Ann Whitman File: Transition Series, Box 7, Eisenhower Library.

85. Sorensen, *Kennedy*, pp. 284–285.

86. Robert Cutler, *No Time for Rest* (Boston: Little, Brown, and Co., 1966), pp. 295–296.

87. Sorensen, *Kennedy*, p. 304.

88. *Ibid.*, p. 305.

89. Gary Wills, "The Kennedy Imprisonment, Part II," *The Atlantic Monthly*, February 1982, p. 54.

90. Bernard Shanley, Oral History Interview #2, Interview by Dave Horracks, May 16, 1975, Eisenhower Library.

91. Hoxie, *Command Decision and the Presidency*, p. 330.

92. Quoted in Charles W. Kegley, Jr. and Eugene R. Wittkopf, *American Foreign Policy: Pattern and Process* (New York: St. Martin's Press, 1979) p. 253.

93. I. M. Destler, *Presidents, Bureaucrats and Foreign Policy: The Politics of Organizational Reform* (Princeton, N.J.: Princeton University Press, 1972), pp. 84–85.

94. Cutler, *No Time for Rest*, p. 294.

95. *Ibid.*, pp. 295–296.

96. Cutler, "The Development of the National Security Council," p. 457.

97. Dillon Anderson, Columbia Oral History Interview, Part 2, pp. 69–70, Eisenhower Library.

98. Destler, *Presidents, Bureaucrats, and Foreign Policy*, p. 2.

99. Henry Kissinger, *White House Years* (Boston: Little, Brown and Co., 1979), p. 887.

100. Zbigniew Brzezinski, *Power and Principle* (New York: Farrar, Straus, Giroux, 1983) reviewed by Kenneth W. Thompson, *Presidential Studies Quarterly*, Vol. XIII, Fall 1983, pp. 666–668.

101. *Ibid.*
102. *Ibid.*
103. *Ibid.*
104. *Ibid.*
105. Kissinger, *White House Years*, p. 30.


## CHAPTER ELEVEN NOTES

1. Keith Eubank, *The Summit Conferences 1919–1960* (Norman: University of Oklahoma Press, 1966) Eubank critically assessed the results of summit meetings and saw the summit as no substitute for quiet, unpublicized diplomacy at the ministerial level. See also Theodore Wilson, "Summit Conferences" in *Encyclopedia of American Foreign Policy* Vol. III, ed. Alexander DeConde (New York: Charles Scribner's Sons, 1978), pp. 936–944.

2. Memorandum of Conversation, President Eisenhower and Korean Prime Minister Hun Chung, June 20, 1960, File Folder: "Staff Notes June 1960," Box 50, DDE Diary Series, Dwight D. Eisenhower's Papers as President (Ann Whitman File), Dwight D. Eisenhower Library (hereafter noted as Ann Whitman File, DDEL).

3. Letter, Platon D. Morozov to U.N. Disarmament Commission, August 1, 1960, published in *New York Times*, August 2, 1960.

4. The President's News Conference of August 10, 1960, *Public Papers of the Presidents of the United States: Dwight D. Eisenhower 1960–61*, (Office of the Federal Register, National Archives and Records Service, General Services Administration: Washington, D.C.), pp. 620, 624.

5. Memorandum of telephone conversation, Dwight D. Eisenhower (DDE) and Christian A. Herter (CAH), August 8, 1960, File Folder: "Presidential Telephone Calls 1–6/60," Box 10, Papers of Christian A. Herter, DDEL.

6. Memorandum of telephone conversation, H. C. Lodge and CAH, August 9, 1960, File Folder: "CAH Telephone Calls 7/1/60 to 8/31/60 (1)" Box 13, Herter Papers, DDEL.

7. Memorandum of telephone conversation, DDE and CAH, August 9, 1960, File Folder: "Presidential Telephone Calls 1–6/60," Box 10, Herter Papers, DDEL.

8. *The New York Times*, September 2, 1960.

9. *Ibid.*, September 3, 1960.

10. Minutes of Cabinet Meeting, May 26, 1960, Box 16, Cabinet Series, Ann Whitman File, DDEL.

11. Michael Tatu, *Power in the Kremlin* (New York: The Viking Press,

1969), p. 41–68. Carl Linden, *Khrushchev and the Soviet Leadership 1957–1964* (Baltimore: Johns Hopkins Press, 1966), pp. 90–116.

12. Telegram, Llewellen Thompson to Secretary of State, September 12, 1960, File Folder: "Herter, Christian—September 1960," Box 11, Dulles-Herter Series, Ann Whitman File, DDEL. See also Memorandum of Conference with the President, July 19, 1960 (Memo dated July 21, 1960), File Folder: "Staff Notes July 1960," Box 51, DDE Diary Series, Ann Whitman File, DDEL.

13. Robert Divine, *Foreign Policy and U.S. Presidential Elections, 1952–1960* (New York: New Viewpoints, 1974), p. 257.

14. Harold Macmillan, *Pointing the Way, 1959–1961* (New York: Harper and Row, Publishers, 1972), pp. 269–270.

15. Statement by Khrushchev, May 20, 1960, *New York Times*, May 21, 1960; Khrushchev address before UNGA, September 23, 1960, text published in Michael H. Prosser ed., *Sow the Wind, Reap the Whirlwind*, Vol. I (New York: William Morrow and Company, Inc., 1970), pp. 237–277; Khrushchev remarks at meeting with members of United Nations Journalists Association, October 7, 1960, text printed in *Khrushchev in New York* (New York: Crosscurrents Press, Inc. 1960), pp. 144–160.

16. See for example Alezander Dallin, *The Soviet Union and the United Nations* (New York: Frederick A. Praeger, 1962), pp. 152–179; Louis J. Halle, *The Cold War as History* (New York: Evanston, 1967), pp. 388–390; Richard B. Stebbins, ed., *The United States in World Affairs 1960* (New York: Council on Foreign Relations, 1960), pp. 48–49; Adam Ulam, *The Rivals* (New York: The Viking Press, 1971), p. 313; Brian Urquehart, *Hammarskjold* (New York: Alfred Knopf, 1972), pp. 459–472.

17. Pre-Press Conference Notes, September 7, 1960, File Folder: "Staff Notes—September 1960" (4), Box 53, DDE Diary Series, Ann Whitman File, DDEL.

18. *Ibid.*, and Memorandum, CAH to DDE, September 2, 1960, File Folder: "United Nations General Assembly September 1960," Box 15, International Series, Records of White House Staff Secretary, DDEL.

19. Letter, C. D. Jackson to DDE, September 2, 1960, File Folder: "Eisenhower, Pres. Corresp. 1960–61," Box 41, Papers of C. D. Jackson, DDEL.

20. Letter, DDE to Jackson, September 5, 1960, *Ibid.*.

21. Memorandum, CAH to DDE, September 2, 1960, File Folder: "United Nations General Assembly, September 1960," Box 15, International Series, Records of White House Staff Secretary, DDEL.

22. Memorandum of telephone conversation, Ambassador Harold

Caccia and CAH, September 14, 1960, File Folder: "Presidential Telephone Calls 7/1960–1/20/61," Box 10, Herter Papers, DDEL.

23. *The New York Times*, September 1, 2, 3, 5, 7, 9, 11, and 13, 1960.
24. *The New York Times*, September 14, 1960. Brian Urquehart, *Hammarskjold*, p. 452.
25. President's News Conference of September 7, 1960, *Public Papers of Dwight D. Eisenhower, 1960*, pp. 681–682.
26. See for example, address by Secretary Herter before American Bar Association, Washington, D.C., September 1, 1960, *Department of State Bulletin*, September 19, 1960; Address by Francis O. Wilcox, Assistant Secretary for International Organization Affairs, before American Association for the United Nations, New York, September 18, 1960, *Department of State Bulletin*, October 3, 1960; and address by Andrew H. Berding, Assistant Secretary for Public Affairs, before National Exchange Club, Birmingham, Alabama, September 11, 1960, *Department of State Bulletin*, September 26, 1960.
27. Dwight D. Eisenhower, *The White House Years: Waging Peace* (New York: Doubleday, 1965), p. 577.
28. Memorandum of telephone conversation, Andrew Goodpaster and CAH, September 1, 1960, File Folder: "Presidential Telephone Calls 7/1960–1/20/61," Box 10, Herter Papers, DDEL.
29. Memorandum of telephone conversation, Goodpaster and CAH, September 8, 1960, *Ibid.*
30. Memorandum of telephone conversation, Goodpaster and CAH, September 14, 1960, *Ibid.*
31. Paper, "The Future of Summitry," dated September 15, 1960, prepared in Department of State, File Folder: "Herter, Christian A. October 1960," Box 11, Dulles-Herter Series, Ann Whitman File, DDEL.
32. Aides Memoire to Hungarian and Soviet Missions, September 10, 1960, and US–Soviet exchange of communications, September 13, 1960, *Department of State Bulletin*, October 3, 1960.
33. *The New York Times*, September 11, 1960.
34. Address by President Eisenhower before UNGA, September 22, 1960, *Public Papers of President Dwight D. Eisenhower, 1960–61*, pp. 707–720.
35. *The New York Times*, September 23, 1960.
36. *Ibid.*
37. Speech by Nikita Khrushchev before UNGA, September 23, 1960, Prosser, ed., *Sow the Wind, Reap the Whirlwind*, pp. 237–277.
38. Memorandum of Conference, DDE and President Tito, September 22, 1960 (Two memcons prepared for this meeting with the second half summarized in a memo dated October 5, 1960),

File Folder: "Staff Notes September 1960," Box 53, DDE Diary Series, Ann Whitman File, DDEL.

39. Memorandum of Conference, DDE and Prime Minister Jawaharal Nehru, September 26, 1960, File Folder: "Staff Notes September 1960 Box 53, DDE Diary Series, Ann Whitman File, DDEL.

40. Letter, Presidents of Ghana, Indonesia, the United Arab Republic, Yugoslavia, and the Prime Minister of India, to the President of the United States, September 29, 1960, File Folder: "Ghana" (2), Box 15, International Series, Ann Whitman File, DDEL.

41. Address by Gamel Abdel Nasser before UNGA, September 27, 1960, printed in Prosser, ed., *Sow the Wind, Reap the Whirlwind*, pp. 395–413.

42. *New York Times*, September 30, 1960.

43. Telegram No. 686, Llewellen Thompson to Secretary of State, September 7, 1960 and Telegram No. 692, Thompson to Secretary of State, September 8, 1960, File Folder: "Herter, Christian September, 1960," Box 11, Dulles-Herter Series, Ann Whitman File, DDEL.

44. The texts of these men's addresses before the UNGA are printed in Prosser, ed., *Sow the Wind, Reap the Whirlwind*. See also Memorandum of Conversation, DDE and Nehru, September 26, 1960 and DDE and Tito, September 22, 1960, both in File Folder: "Staff Notes — September, 1960," Box 53, DDE Diary Series, Ann Whitman File, DDEL.

45. John G. Campbell, *Tito's Separate Road* (New York: Harper and Row, 1967), p. 93.

46. Memorandum of Conference with the President, Herter, Hagerty, et al, October 1, 1960, File Folder: "Staff Notes, October 1960," Box 53, DDE Diary Series, Ann Whitman File, DDEL.

47. *Ibid.*

48. Memorandum of Conference with the President and King Hussein, October 8, 1960, File Folder: "Staff Notes October 1960," Box 53, DDE Diary Series, Ann Whitman File, DDEL.

49. Memorandum of Conference with the President, Herter, Hagerty, et al, October 1, 1960 in *Ibid.*

50. *Ibid.*

51. *Ibid.*

52. *Ibid.*

53. *Ibid.*

54. Memorandum of Conference with the President, Herter, et al, October 2, 1960 in *Ibid.*

55. Memorandum of Conference, DDE, Macmillan, Menzies, et

al, October 2, 1960, File Folder: "Staff Memos, October 1960," Box 53, DDE Diary Series, Ann Whitman File, DDEL.

56. Letter, DDE to Presidents of Ghana, Indonesia, United Arab Republic, Yugoslavia, and the Prime Minister of India, October 2, 1960, *Public Papers of Dwight D. Eisenhower, 1960–61*, pp. 742–744.

57. Address by Jawaharlal Nehru before UNGA, October 3, 1960, Prosser, ed., *Sow the Wind, Reap the Whirlwind* Vol. I, pp. 557–570.

58. Memorandum of telephone conversation, DDE and CAH, October 4, 1960, File Folder: "Telephone Calls, October 1960," Box 54, DDE Diary Series, Ann Whitman File, DDEL.

59. Letter, Nikita Khrushchev to Presidents of Ghana, Indonesia, United Arab Republic, Yugoslavia, and the Prime Minister of India, October 3, 1960, U.S. Department of State, *American Foreign Policy: Current Documents, 1960* (Washington, D.C.: Government Printing Office, 1964), pp. 471–472.

60. Memorandum of telephone conversation, DDE and CAH, October 4, 1960, File Folder: "Telephone Calls, October 1960," Box 54, DDE Diary Series, Ann Whitman File, DDEL.

61. Memorandum of Conference, DDE and President Sukarno, October 6, 1960, File Folder: "Staff Notes, October 1960," Box 53, DDE Diary Series, Ann Whitman File, DDEL.

62. Minutes of Cabinet Meeting, October 7, 1960, Box 16, Cabinet Series, Ann Whitman File, DDEL.

63. Eisenhower, *Waging Peace*, p. 588.

64. Address by Nikita Khrushchev before UNGA, October 3, 1960, Prosser, ed., *Sow the Wind, Reap the Whirlwind*, pp. 537–548.

65. *New York Times*, October 13, 1960; Letter, Francis O. Wilcox to author, March 29, 1982.

66. Memorandum of Conference, DDE and Nehru, September 26, 1960, File Folder: "Staff Notes September 1960, Box 53, DDE Diary Series, Ann Whitman File, DDEL.

67. Memorandum of Conference, DDE, Philippine Vice President Diosdado Macapagal, et al, October 13, 1960, File Folder: "Philippine Islands" (1), Box 40, International Series, Ann Whitman File, DDEL.

68. Telegram, Llewellen Thompson to Secretary of State, October 14, 1960, File Folder: "Herter, Christian A. October 1960," Box 11, Dulles-Herter Series, Ann Whitman File, DDEL.

69. Television interview, Khrushchev with David Susskind, October 9, 1960, *Khrushchev in New York*, pp. 161–184.

70. Remarks by Khrushchev at meeting with members of United Nations Journalist Association, October 7, 1960, *Khrushchev in New York*, pp. 144–160.

71. Telecast remarks of Senator John F. Kennedy, Indianapolis, Indiana, October 4, 1960, *The Speeches of Senator John F. Kennedy in the Presidential Campaign of 1960*. Final Report of Committee on Commerce, U.S. Senate, prepared by subcommittee on Commerce, Part I, (Washington, D.C.: Government Printing Office), pp. 478–487. Press Conference of Vice President Nixon in *The Speeches of Vice President Nixon in Presidential Campaign of 1960*, Ibid., part III, pp. 102–116.

72. Richard B. Stebbins, ed., *The United States in World Affairs, 1960*, pp. 103–104.

73. Arthur M. Schlesinger, Jr., *A Thousand Days* (Boston: Houghton Mifflin Company, 1965), p. 150.

74. *Ibid.*, p. 301.

75. *Ibid.*

76. Fred I. Greenstein, *The Hidden Hand Presidency* (New York: Basic Books, Inc., 1982) This is a study of President Eisenhower's leadership style.

## CHAPTER TWELVE NOTES

1. Alexander L. George, *Presidential Decisionmaking in Foreign Policy: The Effective Use of Information and Advice* (Boulder, CO: Westview Press, 1980).

2. Roger B. Porter, *Presidential Decision Making* (New York: Cambridge University Press, 1980).

3. Recent research has revealed that President Eisenhower's decision style was far from being rigidly bureaucratic. The essential point here is Kennedy's view of it.

4. Peter Wyden, *Bay of Pigs* (New York: Simon and Schuster, 1979), p. 325.

5. Thomas Halper, *Foreign Policy Crises* (Columbus, OH: Charles E. Merrill Publishing Co., 1971), pp. 25–27, and Arthur M. Schlesinger, *A Thousand Days, John F. Kennedy in the White House* (Greenwich, CN: Fawcett Publications, Inc., 1965), pp. 212–213.

6. Schlesinger, p. 228.

7. Irving Janis, *Victims of Groupthink* (Boston: Houghton Mifflin, 1972).

8. George, op. cit.

9. The Special Group consisted of a Deputy Under Secretary of State, the Deputy Secretary of Defense, the Director of the CIA, and the Special Assistant to the President for National Security Affairs.

10. Wyden, pp. 24–25.

11. *Ibid.*, p. 135.
12. Schlesinger, p. 225.
13. Wyden, p. 317.
14. Quoted in ibid., p. 317. The Taylor Commission, officially known as the Cuban Study Group, was chaired by General Maxwell Taylor, former Army Chief of Staff. It was commissioned by President Kennedy to find out what went wrong in the Bay of Pigs affair. Parts of its report have been declassified.
15. *Ibid.*, p. 317.
16. Theodore Sorensen, *Kennedy* (New York: Harper and Row, 1965), p. 305.
17. For an excellent discussion of Bissell's role in this affair, and his effect on the Kennedy Administration, see Garry Wills, *The Kennedy Imprisonment* (Boston: Little, Brown and Co., 1981), Ch. 18.
18. It is clear that Kennedy began bypassing Dulles soon after taking office in 1961. He preferred working with Bissell, whom he intended to name as CIA Director in the very near future. See Wyden, p. 96.
19. This point is seldom noted in analyses of the Bay of Pigs affair. Allen Dulles is routinely assigned responsibility for the failure of the invasion, albeit his limited authority in the matter. Kennedy and Bissell worked together closely, and without dependence on Dulles. Dulles' intimate involvement with the Cuban operation ended in early 1961, after that the plans changed significantly. Indeed, some of the most dramatic changes, as in modifying air cover for the assault force, were made by the President at the last minute.
20. This is an issue of staffing, because it was the fact of these figures and their relationships with Kennedy and his aides which helped to stifle any skepticism about the invasion plan. See ibid., pp. 235–239.
21. Janis, p. 15.
22. Schlesinger, p. 228.
23. Wyden, p. 318.
24. *Ibid.*, p. 170.
25. *Ibid.*, p. 170.
26. Schlesinger, pp. 224–225. See also Wyden, p. 319.
27. Janis, p. 34.
28. Roger Hilsman, *To Move a Nation* (Garden City, NY: Doubleday and Co., 1967), p. 31.
29. Wyden, p. 100; Schlesinger, p. 227; and Hilsman, p. 32.
30. Hilsman, *loc. cit.*
31. Wyden, p. 149.

32. *Ibid.*, p. 316.
33. Schlesinger, pp. 241–242 and 276–277.
34. *Ibid.*, p. 242.
35. *Loc. cit.*
36. Wyden, p. 316.
37. *Ibid.*, pp. 148–149.
38. *Ibid.*, p. 316.
39. In this regard, Wills refers to Kennedy as the "prisoner of charisma." See Wills, Ch. 19.

## CHAPTER THIRTEEN NOTES

1. Circumstances which led to the Soviet Intervention in Afghanistan are discussed at length in Fred Halliday, "War and Revolution in Afghanistan," *New Left Review* (January–February, 1980); pp. 20–41; Anthony Arnold, *Afghanistan: The Soviet Invasion in Perspective* (Stanford, California: Hoover Institution, 1981), pp. 1–67; Alfred L. Monks, *The Soviet Intervention in Afghanistan* (Washington, D.C.: American Enterprise Institute, 1981), pp. 2–17.
2. Morton Schwartz, *Soviet Perceptions of the United States* (Berkeley, California: University of California Press, 1978), pp. 116–119, 123.
3. "Kosygin in Supreme Soviet Assails U.S. Trade Curbs," *N.Y.T.* (July 6, 1977).
4. Georgi Arbatov, "Soviet-American Relations Today," *Pravda* (August 3, 1977) in *Current Digest of the Soviet Press*, Vol. 29, No. 31, 1977), p. 1, hereafter cited as CDOSP etc. See also John M. Howell, "The Carter Human Rights Policy as Applied to the Soviet Union" and Karl Helicher, "The Response of the Soviet Government and Press to Carter's Human Rights Policies," *Presidential Studies Quarterly*, Vol. 13, No. 3 (Spring, 1983), pp. 283–295 and 296–304, respectively; The Administration's position on human rights is set forth in Zbigniew Brzezinski, *Power and Principle: Memoirs of the National Security Adviser 1977–1981* (New York: Farrar, Strauss, and Giroux, 1983), pp. 124–129.
5. "Reception in the White House," *Pravda* (March 3, 1977) in *CDOSP* Vol. 29, No. 9 (March 30, 1977), p. 5; Vladimir Bolshakov, "International Week," a survey, *Pravda* (March 13, 1977), *ibid.*, Vol. 29, No. 10 (April 6, 1977), p. 1.
6. Bernard Gwertzman, "From Soviet Jail to White House: Vladimir Bukovsky," *N.Y.T.* (March 2, 1977).
7. Leonid Brezhnev, "Soviet Trade Unions are an Influential Force

in our Society," *Pravda* (March 2, 1977) in *CDOSP*, Vol. 29, No. 12, (April 20, 1977), p. 5.

8. Arbatov, "Soviet-American Relations Today."

9. Leonid Brezhnev, "On the Draft Constitution . . ." *Pravda* (October 5, 1977), in *CDOSP*, Vol. 29, No. 39, (October 26, 1977), pp. 6–7.

10. "U.S. Government Denounces Moscow Sentence as Gross Distortion," *N.Y.T.* (May 19, 1978).

11. Vladimir Bolshakov, "Concerning a Furor," *Pravda* (July 19, 1978) in *CDOSP* Vol. 30, No. 28 (August 9, 1978), p. 3.

12. Martin Tolchin, "President Deplores the Russian Trials as Blow to Liberty," *N.Y.T.* (July 13, 1978); see also Brzezinski, *Power and Principle*, p. 322.

13. G. Vasileyev, "Behind a Smokescreen of Anti-Sovietism," *Pravda* (July 15, 1978) in *CDOSP*, Vol. 30, No. 28 (August 9, 1978), p. 5.

14. Marshall N. Ogarkov, "The Myth of the Soviet Military Threat and Reality," *Pravda* (August 2, 1979) in *CDOSP*, Vol. 31, No. 31 (August 29, 1979), p. 3; Nicclai Kurdyumov, "To Please the Militarists," *Pravda* (January 5, 1980), Ibid., Vol. 32, No. 1 (February 6, 1980), p. 5; Yuri Gudkov, "Zig-Zags and Throwbacks," *New Times*, No. 2 (Moscow, 1980), pp. 10–11.

15. "Speech by Comrade L. I. Brezhnev," *Pravda* (October 7, 1979) in *CDOSP*, Vol. 31, No. 4, (October 31, 1979), p. 2.

16. *Yearbook of International Communist Affairs 1980* (Stanford: Hoover Institution Press, 1980), p. 84, hereafter cited as *YICA* etc.

17. Marshall D. Ustinov, "*Detente* is a Command of the Times," *Pravda* (October 25, 1979) in *CDOSP*, Vol. 31, No. 42 (November 14, 1979), p. 1.

18. "Brezhnev Receives Byrd," *Pravda* (July 5, 1979) in *CDOSP*, Vol. 31, No. 27 (August 17, 1979), p. 19.

19. Genrich A. Trofimenko, "Too Many Negotiators," *N.Y.T.* (July 13, 1979).

20. R. G. Tumkovsky, "The Soviet-American Strategic Arms Limitation Talks," *Voprosy Istorii* No. 3 (March, 1979) in *CDOSP*. Vol. 31, No. 29 (August 15, 1979), p. 9; Ustinov, "*Detente* is a Command of the Times."

21. Richard Burt, "Are the Russians Outspending the U.S. on Weapons?" *N.Y.T.* (September 23, 1979).

22. Strobe Talbott, "U.S.–Soviet Relations: From Bad to Worse," *Foreign Affairs*, Vol. 88, No. 3 (1979), p. 531; Brzezinski, *Power and Principle*, pp. 347–348.

23. Charles Mohr, "Senate Panel Links Past and Cuba," *N.Y.T.* (November 3, 1979).

24. Georgi Arbatov, "On the Threshold of a New Decade," *Pravda* (March 3, 1980) in *CDOSP*, Vol. 32, No. 9 (April 2, 1980) pp. 1–2.

25. Petrov, "Rebuff to Forces of Reaction and Imperialism," *Pravda* (March 21, 1979) in *CDOSP*, Vol. 31, No. 11 (April 11, 1979), p. 6.

26. "Washington Is Opposed," *Pravda* (July 28, 1978), p. 5 in *CDOSP*, Vol. 30, No. 30 (August 23, 1978), p. 21; I. Aleksandrov, "Reaction's Schemes Against Democratic Afghanistan," *Pravda* (March 19, 1979), ibid., Vol. 31, No. 11 (April 11, 1979) p. 5.

27. M. Demchenko, "In Defiance of the Interests of Peace and *Detente*," *Pravda* (August 13, 1978) in *CDOSP* Vol. 31, No. 32 (September 6, 1978), p. 4; Colonel A. Leonteyev, "A NATO for Asia?" *Krasnya Zvesda* (December 17, 1978), ibid., Vol. 30, No. 51 (January 17, 1979), pp. 3–4.

28. L. I. Brezhnev, "Your Exploit is Immortal, Minsk," *Pravda* (July 27, 1978), p. 3.

29. "Soviet Cautions U.S. on Pact with China," *N.Y.T.* (November 13, 1978).

30. David K. Shipler, "2 Soviet Officials See Danger in U.S.-China Relations," *N.Y.T.* (December 17, 1978).

31. M. Georgiev, "Concerning Normalization," *Pravda* (February 1, 1979) in *CDOSP*, Vol. 30, No. 51 (January 15, 1979), p. 1.

32. A. Petrov, "Concerning Teng Hsiao Ping's Interview," *Pravda* (February 1, 1979) in *CDOSP*, Vol. 31, No. 5 (February 28, 1979), pp. 1–2; "On the American-Chinese Meeting," *Pravda* (February 4, 1979) ibid., pp. 3–4.

33. Craig R. Whitney, "Kosygin Complains to Americans on Teng's Remarks," *N.Y.T.* (February 10, 1979).

34. Talbot, "U.S.-Soviet Relations: From Bad to Worse," p. 525; see also Brzezinski, *Power and Principle*, pp. 413–414.

35. I. Aleksandrov, "Giving Peking's Aggression a Resolute Rebuff," *Pravda*, (February 28, 1979) in *CDOSP*, Vol. 31, No. 9, (March 28, 1979), p. 7.

36. V. Korionov, "Researcher/Provocateur," *Pravda* (October 5, 1979) in *CDOSP*, Vol. 31, No. 4 (October 31, 1979), 13.

37. Talbott, "U.S.-Soviet Relations: From Bad to Worse," p. 525.

38. A. Bovin, "Anatomy of a Betrayal," *Izvestia* (March 29, 1979) in *CDOSP*, Vol. 31, No. 13 (April 25, 1979), pp. 1–2.

39. P. Demchenko, "Risky Game in the Middle East," *Pravda* (March 15, 1979) in *CDOSP*, Vol. 31, No. 11 (April 11, 1979), pp. 1–2.

40. *Ibid.*, p. 2, A. Petrov, "For the Benefit of Imperialism and Against the Will of the Peoples," *Pravda* (March 18, 1979) in *CDOSP*,

Vol. 31, No. 11 (April 11, 1979), p. 4; "Collusion Against the Arabs," *Pravda* (March 27, 1979) *ibid.*, Vol. 31, No. 13 (April 25, 1979), p. 5.

41. Christopher S. Wren, "In Yemen the East and West Do Meet," *N. Y. T.* (May 1, 1980); Brzezinski, *Power and Principle*, p. 447.

42. Richard Burt, "U.S. Sends Ships to Arabian Sea in Yemen Crisis," *N. Y. T.* (March 7, 1979); William Beecher, "U.S. Draws the Line in Yemen," *Boston Globe* (March 10, 1979); Brzezinski, *Power and Principle*, p. 447.

43. Wren, "In Yemen the East and West Do Meet."

44. Yohanan Ramati, "The Gambit in Afghanistan," *Midstream* (April, 1980), p. 5; "Saudi Charges Soviet Acted in Afghanistan From Fears About Oil," *N. Y. T.* (February 8, 1980); Dennis Ross, "Considering Soviet Threats to the Persian Gulf," *International Security*, Vol. 6, No. 2 (Fall, 1981), p. 177.

45. Flora Lewis, "Kremlin's European Policy," *N. Y. T.* (June 22, 1980).

46. Brzezinski, *Power and Principle*, pp. 368–369; see also Schwartz, *Soviet Perceptions of the United States*, pp. 99–100, 105.

47. *Soviet World Outlook*, Vol. 5, No. 1 (January 15, 1980), hereafter cited S.W.O. etc.

48. *Ibid.*

49. Y. Volkov et al. (eds.), *The Truth About Afghanistan: Documents, Facts, Eyewitness Reports* (Moscow: Novosti Press Agency Publishing House, 1980), p. 33.

50. Dimitry Volsky, "The Roots of the Tension," *New Times* (Moscow), No. 4, (January, 1980), pp. 12–13; Victor Sidenko, "Two Years of Afghan Revolution," *New Times* (Moscow), No. 17 (May, 1980), p. 20.

51. Volkov et al. (eds.), *The Truth About Afghanistan*, p. 43.

52. *Ibid.*, pp. 42–43.

53. Igor Alganov, "Dangerous Role," *New Times* (Moscow), No. 6 (February, 1980), pp. 10–11.

54. Volkov et al. (eds.), *The Truth About Afghanistan*, pp. 44–45.

55. Harry Rositzke, "KGB Disinformation," *N. Y. T.* (July 21, 1981).

56. *S. W. O.*, Vol. 5, No. 1 (January 15, 1980).

57. Halliday, "War and Revolution in Afghanistan," p. 27, 34–36.

58. Schwartz, *Soviet Perceptions of the United States*, pp. 96–97.

59. *Ibid.*, p. 110.

60. *Ibid.*, p. 108.

61. "On the U.S. Government's Present Policy," *Pravda* (June 17, 1978) in *CDOSP*, Vol. 30, No. 24 (July 12, 1978), pp. 1–6.

62. Talbott, "U.S.–Soviet Relations: From Bad to Worse," pp. 531–532; Brzezinski, *Power and Principle*, pp. 346–352.

63. Vernon Aspaturian, "Soviet Global Power and the Correlation of Forces," *Problems of Communism* (May-June, 1980), p. 7.

64. *S.W.O.*, Vol. 5, No. 2 (February 15, 1980).

65. See Alvin Z. Rubinstein, *Soviet Policy Toward Turkey, Iran, and Afghanistan: The Dynamics of Influence* (New York: Praeger, 1980), pp. 25-56.

66. For a comprehensive study of United States relations with Pakistan in the late 1970's, in particular Pakistan's difficulties in obtaining a continuous flow of American aid see Shirin Tahir-Kheli, *The United States and Pakistan: The Evolution of an Influence Relationship* (New York: Praeger, 1982); see also William E. Griffith, "The U.S.S.R. and Pakistan," *Problems of Communism* (January-February, 1982), pp. 38-44.

67. *S.W.O.*, Vol. 5, No. 1 (January 15, 1980).

68. Richard Burt, "Soviet Military Buildup a Major Issue for Reagan," *N.Y.T.* (December 7, 1980); Brzezinski, *Power and Principle*, p. 146.

69. At the 25th Congress of the Soviet Communist Party in Moscow in February, 1976, Brezhnev said: "*Detente* does not in the slightest abolish and cannot abolish or alter the laws of class struggle. We make no secret of the fact that we see *detente* as a way to create more favorable conditions for peaceful socialist and communist construction."

70. Zalmy Khalilzad, "Afghanistan and the Crisis in American Foreign Policy," *Survival* (July-August, 1980), pp. 151-152; Monks, *The Soviet Intervention in Afghanistan*, p. 42.

## CHAPTER FOURTEEN NOTES

1. See Henry S. Commager, ed., *Documents of American History*, 4th Edition, (New York: Appleton-Century-Crofts, Inc., 1948), pp. 83, 101, 104, 109.

2. Letter dated December 15, 1777; in William R. Tansill, *The Concept of Civilian Supremacy over the Military in the United States*, (Public Affairs Bulletin 94, 1951), p. 3.

3. See Walter Millis, *American Military Thought*, (Indianapolis: Bobbs-Merrill, 1966), Part I, Document 3, p. 16; and C. J. Bernardo and E. Bacon, *American Military Policy: Its Development Since 1775*, (Harrisburg, 1958), p. 28.

4. Samuel P. Huntington, *The Soldier and the State*, (Cambridge: Random House, 1964), p. 91. This represents Huntington's thesis on "subjective control" of the military in the United States.

5. Max Farrand, *The Records of the Federal Convention of 1787*, (New

Haven: Yale University Press, 1937), Appendix A, CCXI, v. 3, p. 319.

6. *Ibid.*, v. 2, pp. 329–335.

7. *Ibid.*, v. 2, p. 334.

8. *Ibid.*, v. 1, p. 139. Mason also proposed limits on the amount of manpower and appropriations for a standing army (v. 2, p. 326).

9. *Ibid.*, v. 2, pp. 506–509.

10. *Ibid.*, v. 2, p. 318.

11. See Walter Millis, *The Constitution and the Common Defense*, (New York: Fund for the Republic, 1959), p. 14. Millis states that Madison and even Hamilton were outspoken defenders of the Militias' functions and capabilities. Also, in Farrand's *Records*, v. 2, pp. 616–617, Madison's *Notes of the Convention* record that Colonel Mason moved to preface Congress' power to "organizing, arming and disciplining the Militia etc." with "And that the liberties of the people may be better secured against the danger of standing armies in time of peace." The intent to provide for a competent citizens' army, readied to check a professional army, was even supported by Madison since there was no restriction on Congress to raise an Army in peacetime if necessary. Gov. Morris, however, declared that Mason's wording sets a "dishonorable mark of distinction on the military class of citizens," and the motion was defeated 9–2.

12. Farrand, *op. cit.*, v. 3, pp. 318–319. Certainly Shay's Rebellion in 1786 made all the delegates aware of providing for a readied military force. These Constitutional clauses on the Militias and the Commander in Chief role were further strengthened in the 1792 Militia Act that provided the statutory authority to federalize the state militias.

13. According to Farrand, *op. cit.*, neither the Convention's *Journal* nor Madison's *Notes* refer to reasons for deletion of these clauses from the Pinckney Plan presented August 20, 1787 (v. 2, p. 334). Many state-ratifying conventions did propose amendments to the Constitution to guarantee no quartering of troops and citizens' rights to bear arms; perhaps Civilian Supremacy was so well assumed and structured that a statement on it was redundant and unnecessary.

14. Farrand, *op. cit.*, v. 2, p. 318.

15. *Ibid.*, v. 2, p. 318.

16. Quincy Wright, *A Study of War*, (Chicago: University of Chicago Press, 1942), v. 1, p. 264.

17. In particular, the writings of Corwin, Koenig, Neustadt, Rossiter, Berdahl, Binkley, Smith, May, and Hoxie. See R. Gordon

Hoxie, *Command Decision and the Presidency* (New York: Reader's Digest Press, 1977).

18. Farrand, *op. cit.*, v. 1, pp. 244, 247. On June 15th it was resolved that a Federal Executive "ought to appoint all federal officers not otherwise provided for, and to direct all military operations; provided that none of the persons composing the Federal Executive should on any occasion take command of any troops, so as personally to conduct any enterprise as General, or in any other capacity."

19. *The Journal of the Federal Convention,* (Boston, 1819), p. 165. Patterson's proposal was rejected on June 19th.

20. Hamilton's speech on June 18th in Farrand, *op. cit.*, v. 1, p. 292; and Hamilton's "unpresented plan" distributed to selected delegates following the June 18th speech.

21. In *Federalist #69* Hamilton also stressed that the President as Commander in Chief could *not* resemble a monarch since the declaration of war, raising and support of troops powers were granted to Congress. In *Federalist #74,* Hamilton again defended the necessity and desirability of a single Commander in Chief vested in the Presidency. He wrote: "of all the cares or concerns of government the direction of war most peculiarly demands those qualities which distinguish the exercise of power by a single hand. The direction of war implies the direction of the common strength; and forms a usual and essential part in the definition of executive authority."

22. See Farrand, *op. cit.*, v. 1, p. 145, 157; v. 2, pp. 61, 185, 575.

23. Senator Douglas' speech to the Senate on July 5th, 1950, in defense of President Truman's decision to dispatch troops to Korea.

24. E. R. May, ed., *The Ultimate Decision: The President as Commander in Chief,* (New York: George Braziller, 1960), p. 5. In addition to fears of absolutist rule by the Commander in Chief, there seemed to be a general dissatisfaction with the civil-military formula (no limits to the size of a standing army, Congress' unlimited powers to raise and support military forces) among these delegates that may, in fact, have prompted the Bill of Rights' provisions on quartering troops and bearing arms.

25. Millis, *The Constitution and the Common Defense*, p. 8.

26. Huntington, *op. cit.*, pp. 80–83.

## CHAPTER SIXTEEN NOTES

1. Capsulizing a prevailing intellectual view in America at the time of the drafting of the Constitution, Max Farrand has written:

"Montesquieu, whose writings were taken as political gospel, had shown the absolute necessity of separating the legislative, executive, and judicial powers." Max Farrand. *The Framing of the Constitution of the United States*. New Haven and London, Yale University Press, 1913, pp. 51–52.

Montesquieu, however, was also a favorite of those opposing the Constitution, particularly on the point of a centralized government in a large republic being destructive of the civil liberties of the citizens and the principles of local government. See Benjamin Fletcher Wright, comp. *The Federalist*. Cambridge, The Belknap Press of Harvard University Press, 1961, pp. 4–5.

2.  "Emergency is defined as 'an unforseen combination of circumstances which calls for immediate action.' *Webster's New International Dictionary of the English Language* (unabridged 2d ed., Springfield, 1939). It is characterized by urgency and relative infrequency of occurrence and is equivalent to a public calamity resulting from fire, flood, or like disaster not reasonably subject to anticipation. *Home Building and Loan Association* v. *Blaisdell*, 290 U.S. 398, 440 (1934). Professor Edward S. Corwin explains emergency conditions as those 'which have not attained enough stability or recurrency to admit of their being dealt with according to rule.' *The President: Office and Powers* (New York, 1940), p. 1." From Albert L. Sturm. Emergencies and the President. *Journal of Politics*, v. 11, February, 1949: 121.

    In testimony before the Senate Special Committee on the Termination of the National Emergency, Professor Cornelius P. Cotter characterized an "emergency" condition, saying: "It denotes the existence of conditions of varying nature, intensity and duration, which are perceived to threaten life or well-being beyond tolerable limits." Further, he said it "connotes the existence of conditions suddenly intensifying the degree of existing danger to life or well-being beyond that which is accepted as normal." U.S. Congress. Senate. Special Committee on the Termination of the National Emergency. *National Emergency*. Hearings, 93rd Congress, 1st session. Washington, U.S. Govt. Print. Off., 1973, pp. 277, 279.

3.  See Harry S Truman. *Memoirs: Years of Trial and Hope*. New York, Doubleday and Company, 1956, p. 419; the proclamation appears at 64 Stat. A454.

4.  See *Public Papers of the Presidents of the United States: Harry S Truman (1950)*. Washington, U.S. Govt. Print. Off., 1961, pp. 741–746.

5.  Edward S. Corwin. *The President: Office and Powers, 1787–1957. Fourth Revised Edition*. New York, New York University Press, 1957, pp. 147–148.

6. Theodore Roosevelt. *An Autobiography*. New York, Charles Scribner's Sons, 1926, pp. 388–389.

7. William Howard Taft. *Our Chief Magistrate and His Powers*. New York, Columbia University Press, 1916, pp. 139–140; Taft would later evidence a shift in his views on this matter when, as Chief Justice, writing the opinion of the Court in the *Myers* case, he appealed to the appointment clause of Article II of the Constitution in arguing that a statute restricting the President's authority to remove subordinates was unconstitutional. See *Myers* v. *United States*, 272 U.S. 52, 106–177 (1926).

8. See William Howard Taft. *The Presidency*. New York, Charles Scribner's Sons, 1916, pp. 125–130.

9. See J. Reuben Clark, Jr., comp. *Emergency Legislation Passed Prior to December, 1917 Dealing with the Control and Taking of Private Property for the Public Use, Benefit, or Welfare; Presidential Proclamations and Executive Orders of Analogous Legislation Since 1775*. Washington, U.S. Govt. Print. Off., 1918, pp. 201–228.

10. See 1 Stat. 264–265; for the President's directives see James D. Richardson, comp. *A Compilation of the Messages and Papers of the Presidents*. 20 vols. New York, Bureau of National Literature, 1897, pp. 149–154.

11. See Richardson, *op. cit.*, p. 181.

12. See 1 Stat. 577–578.

13. See 8 U.S.C. 1185 (1970).

14. See Richardson, *op. cit.*, pp. 276–277.

15. 2 Stat. 443; also, generally, see Bennett M. Rich. *The Presidents and Civil Disorder*. Washington, The Brookings Institution, 1941, pp. 21–24.

16. See Adrienne Koch and William Peden, eds. *The Life and Selected Writings of Thomas Jefferson*. New York, The Modern Library, 1944, pp. 334–336.

17. See Richardson, *op. cit.*, pp. 465–466.

18. See 2 Stat. 734.

19. See Harold C. Relyea. The Evolution and Organization of the Federal Intelligence Function: A Brief Overview (1776–1975), in U.S. Congress. Senate. Select Committee to Study Governmental Operations With Respect to Intelligence Activities. *Final Report: Supplementary Reports on Intelligence Activities*. Book VI. Washington, U.S. Govt. Print. Off., 1976. (94th Congress, 2d session. Senate. Report No. 94-755), pp. 18–20; also see Richard Wilmer Rowan with Robert G. Deindorfer. *Secret Service: Thirty-three Centuries of Espionage*. London, William Kimber, 1969, pp. 241–242, 705n.

20. See Clark, *op. cit.*, pp. 990–1026.

21. Wilfred E. Binkley. *President and Congress*. New York, Alfred A. Knopf, 1947, p. 126.
22. Letter to Albert G. Hodges (April 4, 1864); see Roy P. Basler, ed. *The Collected Works of Abraham Lincoln*. Vol. VIII. New Brunswick, Rutgers University Press, 1953, p. 281.
23. Clinton Rossiter. *Constitutional Dictatorship: Crisis Government in the Modern Democracies*. Princeton, Princeton University Press, 1948, p. 229.
24. See Binkley, *op. cit.*, pp. 121–122.
25. See George Fort Milton. *The Use of Presidential Power, 1789–1943*. Boston, Little, Brown and Company, 1944, p. 111.
26. See Richardson, *op. cit.*, pp. 3214–3215.
27. Rossiter, *op. cit.*, p. 226.
28. See Richardson, *op. cit.*, pp. 3215–3216.
29. Rossiter, *op. cit.*, p. 226.
30. *Ibid.*
31. See Richardson, *op. cit.*, p. 3216.
32. See *Ibid.*, pp. 3216–3217.
33. See *Ibid.*, p. 3225.
34. 12 Stat. 326.
35. See *Phillips* v *Hatch*, 1 Dillion 571 (1870); *United States* v. *Anderson*, 9 Wallace 56, 71 (1870); *The Protector*, 12 Wallace 700 (1871); James G. Randall. *Constitutional Problems Under Lincoln. Revised Edition*. Urbana, University of Illinois Press, 1951, pp. 49–50.
36. *The Prize Cases*, 2 Black 635, 666-667, 670 (1862).
37. Rossiter, *op. cit.*, p. 230; half a century before Rossiter's observation, the eminent historian W. A. Dunning had concluded: "In the interval between April 12 and July 4, 1861 a new principle thus appeared in the constitutional system of the United States, namely, that of a temporary dictatorship." W. A. Dunning. *Essays on the Civil War and Reconstruction*. New York, Macmillan, 1898, p. 20.
38. See Richardson, *op. cit.*, p. 3219.
39. See *Ibid.*, p. 3220.
40. Rossiter, *op. cit.*, p. 227.
41. See *Ex parte Merryman*, 17 Fed. Cases 144 (1861), No. 9487.
42. See George C. Sellery. Lincoln's Suspension of Habeas Corpus as Viewed by Congress. *Bulletin of the University of Wisconsin*, v. 1, 1907: 213–286.
43. See *Congressional Globe*, July 3, 1862: 3106ff.
44. See 12 Stat. 755–758.
45. Randall, *op. cit.*, p. 166.

46. See *Congressional Globe*, December 8, 1862: 22; the author of the provision was Rep. Thaddeus Stevens (R.-Pa.).

47. See Relyea, *op. cit.*, pp. 24–45.

48. See Frederic Bancroft. *The Life of William H. Seward*. Vol. II. New York, Harper and Brothers, 1900, p. 260.

49. See Richardson, *op. cit.*, pp. 3303–3305.

50. See Randall, *op. cit.*, pp. 492–505.

51. See *Congressional Globe*, July 22, 1861: 222.

52. See 12 Stat. 591, 599.

53. Randall, op. cit., p. 517; for concurrences with this view see Binkley, *op. cit.*, pp. 124–127; Rossiter, *op. cit.*, pp. 233–234; and Woodrow Wilson. *Constitutional Government in the United States*. New York, Columbia University Press, 1907, p. 58.

54. See 17 Stat. 13–15.

55. See Richardson, *op. cit.*, pp. 4090–4092.

56. See Rich, *op. cit.*, pp. 72–82; on earlier policing actions see *Ibid.*, pp. 21–72.

57. See *Ibid.*, p. 83.

58. See *Ibid.*, p. 88.

59. See *Ibid.*, pp. 91–96; Henry James. *Richard Olney and His Public Service*. Boston and New York, Houghton Mifflin, 1923, p. 203; Grover Cleveland. *Presidential Problems*. New York, The Century Company, 1904, pp. 79–121; also, generally, see Almont Lindsey. *The Pullman Strike*. Chicago, University of Chicago Press, 1942.

60. *In re Debs*, 158 U.S. 564, 582 (1895).

61. See Rich, *op. cit.*, pp. 110–113.

62. See *Ibid.*, pp. 118–120.

63. See *Ibid.*, pp. 122–135.

64. See Joseph B. Bishop. *Theodore Roosevelt and His Time*. Vol. I. New York, Charles Scribner's Sons, 1920, pp. 198–212.

65. William Howard Taft. *The Presidency: Its Duties, Its Powers, Its Opportunities and Its Limitations*. New York, Charles Scribner's Sons, 1916, pp. 129–130.

66. Rossiter, *op. cit.*, p. 241.

67. See Seward W. Livermore. *Politics Is Adjourned: Woodrow Wilson and the War Congress, 1916–1918*. Middletown, Wesleyan University Press, 1966, pp. 12–13, 32–37, 42–45; also, generally, see: Franklin H. Martin. *Digest of Proceedings of the Council of National Defense During the World War*. Washington, U.S. Govt. Print. Off., 1934. (73rd Congress, 2d session. Senate. Document No. 193); James R. Mock. *Censorship 1917*. Princeton, Princeton University Press, 1941; Stephen L. Vaughn. *Holding Fast the*

*Inner Lines: Democracy, Nationalism, and the Committee on Public Information.* Chapel Hill, University of North Carolina Press, 1980; Paul L. Murphy. *World War I and the Origin of Civil Liberties in the United States.* New York, W. W. Norton, 1979.

68. *The Public Papers and Addresses of Franklin D. Roosevelt.* Vol. II. New York, Random House, 1938, p. 15.

69. *Ibid.*, p. 17.

70. Foreign assets were protected through the Trading With the Enemy Act of 1917 (40 Stat. 411), as amended, and war material was allocated to selected foreign powers through the Lend Lease Act (55 Stat. 31). With regard to the latter program, see Warren F. Kimball. *The Most Unsordid Act: Lend Lease, 1939–1941.* Baltimore, The Johns Hopkins Press, 1969.

71. See 55 Stat. 838; 56 Stat. 176; and 56 Stat. 23.

72. 56 Stat. 173; continued as 18 U.S.C. 1383 and 2152 until the former of these was cancelled by the National Emergencies Act.

73. U.S. Congress. Senate. Special Committee on the Termination of the National Emergency. *Emergency Powers Statutes: Provisions of Federal Law Now in Effect Delegating to the Executive Extraordinary Authority in Time of National Emergency.* Washington, U.S. Govt. Print. Off., 1973. (93rd Congress, 1st session. Senate. Report No. 93-549), pp. 6–7.

74. 39 Stat. 1814.

75. See 39 Stat. 728.

76. 41 Stat. 1359.

77. 48 Stat. 1689.

78. See 40 Stat. 411, as amended.

79. 48 Stat. 1.

80. 48 Stat. 1691.

81. 49 Stat. 3438.

82. 48 Stat. 598.

83. 49 Stat. 1106.

84. 54 Stat. 2643.

85. 55 Stat. 1647.

86. See Frank Murphy. *Executive Powers Under National Emergency.* Washington, U.S. Govt. Print. Off., 1939. (76th Congress, 2d session. Senate. Document No. 133); Cf. U.S. Library of Congress. Legislative Reference Service. *Acts of Congress Applicable in Time of Emergency.* Washington, Legislative Reference Service, 1945. (Public Affairs Bulletin No. 35).

87. Apparently a proclamation of national emergency had been contemplated in late 1937 at the time Japanese aircraft bombed the American gunboat *Panay* on the Yangtze River in China. The desire was to seize Japanese assets and investments in the United States and to extract payment for damages. The idea for a na-

tional emergency proclamation on the matter was outlined by
Herman Oliphant, a Treasury Department legal expert and close
personal assistant to Treasury Secretary Henry Morgenthau who
also was involved in developing the plan. Although a memorandum on the scheme reached President Roosevelt's desk, he did
not implement it and there is no evidence to indicate it was consulted on the occasion of preparing the 1939 proclamation.
Oliphant died in January, 1939. See John Morton Blum. *Roosevelt
and Morgenthau*. Boston, Houghton Mifflin, 1970, pp. 225–230.

88. 61 Stat. 449.
89. 59 Stat. 886.
90. 65 Stat. 451.
91. 66 Stat. 54.
92. See 66 Stat. 96, 137, and 296.
93. 66 Stat. 330.
94. See 67 Stat. 18, 131.
95. 66 Stat. c31.
96. 64 Stat. A454.
97. 90 Stat. 1255.
98. 84 Stat. 2222.
99. 85 Stat. 926.
100. See 87 Stat. 555.
101. The charter of the Special Committee initially was established
by S. Res. 304, 92nd Congress, 2d session. It was continued
by S. Res. 9, 93rd Congress, 1st session, and S. Res. 242, 93rd
Congress, 2d session. The third resolution changed the name
of the panel to the Special Committee on National Emergencies
and Delegated Emergency Powers to reflect its focus upon matters
apart from the 1950 emergency proclamation.
102. Members of the Special Committee were Senators Philip A. Hart
(D.-Mich.), Clifford P. Case (R.-N.J.), Claiborne Pell (D.-R.I.),
James B. Pearson (R.-Kan.), Adlai E. Stevenson III (D.-Ill.),
and Clifford P. Hansen (R.-Wyo.).
103. See U.S. Congress. Senate. Special Committee on the Termination of the National Emergency. *National Emergency*. Hearings,
93rd Congress, 1st session. Washington, U.S. Govt. Print. Off.,
1973.
104. See Note 73, *supra.*; this compilation was issued in an abridged
form as well.
105. See U.S. Congress. Senate. Special Committee on National
Emergencies and Delegated Emergency Powers. *Executive Orders
in Times of War and National Emergency*. Committee print, 93rd
Congress, 2d session. Washington, U.S. Govt. Print. Off., 1974;
this compilation was issued in an abridged form as well.
106. See U.S. Congress. Senate. Special Committee on National

Emergencies and Delegated Emergency Powers. *A Brief History of Emergency Powers in the United States* by Harold C. Relyea. Committee print, 93rd Congress, 2d session. Washington, U.S. Govt. Print. Off., 1974.

107. See U.S. Congress. Senate. Special Committee on National Emergencies and Delegated Emergency Powers. *A Recommended National Emergencies Act: Interim Report.* Washington, U.S. Govt. Print. Off., 1974. (93rd Congress, 2d session. Senate. Report No. 93-1170).

108. See U.S. Congress. Senate. Special Committee on National Emergencies and Delegated Emergency Powers. *Executive Replies.* Committee print, 93rd Congress, 2d session. Washington, U.S. Govt. Print. Off., 1974.

109. See U.S. Congress. Senate. Special Committee on National Emergencies and Delegated Emergency Powers. *National Emergencies and Delegated Emergency Powers.* Washington, U.S. Govt. Print. Off., 1976. (94th Congress, 2d session. Senate. Report No. 94-922).

110. See *Congressional Record*, v. 120, August 22, 1974: S15784–S15794.

111. See U.S. Congress. Senate. Committee on Government Operations. *National Emergencies Act.* Washington, U.S. Govt. Print. Off., 1974. (93rd Congress, 2d session. Senate. Report No. 93-1193).

112. See *Congressional Record*, v. 120, October 7, 1974: S18356–S18367.

113. See *Ibid.*, p. 18357.

114. See *Ibid.*, September 16, 1974: H9266.

115. See *Ibid.*, v. 121, February 27, 1975: H1260; *Ibid.*, March 6, 1975: S3202.

116. See U.S. Congress. House. Committee on the Judiciary. *National Emergencies Act.* Hearings, 94th Congress, 1st session. Washington, U.S. Govt. Print. Off., 1975.

117. See U.S. Congress. House. Committee on the Judiciary. *National Emergencies.* Washington, U.S. Govt. Print. Off., 1975. (94th Congress, 1st session. House. Report No. 94-238).

118. See *Congressional Record*, v. 121, September 4, 1975: H8327–H8341.

119. *Ibid.*, September 5, 1975: S15373.

120. See Note 109, *supra.*

121. These recommendations largely have gone unnoticed in Congress and are explored in the final section of this article.

122. See U.S. Congress. Senate. Committee on Government Operations. *National Emergencies Act.* Hearings, 94th Congress, 2d session. Washington, U.S. Govt. Print. Off., 1976.

123. See U.S. Congress. Senate. Committee on Government Oper-

ations. *National Emergencies Act*. Washington, U.S. Govt. Print. Off., 1976. (94th Congress, 2d session. Senate. Report No. 94-1168).

124. *Ibid.*, p. 3.

125. See *Congressional Record*, v. 122, August 27, 1976: S14840–S14844.

126. See *Ibid.*, August 31, 1976: H9253.

127. See *Weekly Compilation of Presidential Documents*, v. 12, September 20, 1976: 1340.

128. For other assessments of the National Emergencies Act see: Glenn E. Fuller. The National Emergency Dilemma: Balancing the Executive's Crisis Powers with the Need for Accountability. *Southern California Law Review*, v. 52, July, 1979: 1453-1511; A. S. Klieman. Preparing for the Hour of Need: Emergency Powers in the United States. *Review of Politics*, v. 41, April, 1979: 235–255; _____. Preparing for the Hour of Need: The National Emergencies Act. *Presidential Studies Quarterly*, v. 9, Winter, 1979: 47–65; also see Arthur S. Miller. Constitutional Law: Crisis Government Becomes the Norm. *Ohio State Law Journal*, v. 39, Number 4, 1978: 736–751.

129. See Note 105, *supra*.

130. The 1933 proclamation of national emergency (48 Stat. 1689) seemingly would no longer have utility, but the proclamations of 1950 (64 Stat. A454), 1970 (84 Stat. 2222), and 1971 (85 Stat. 926) apparently maintain the provisions exempted from the effects of the National Emergencies Act by section 502 of Title V (50 U.S.C. 1651) of the statute.

131. See Note 124, *supra*.

132. See: U.S. Congress. House. Committee on International Relations. *Trading With The Enemy: Legislative and Executive Documents Concerning Regulation of International Transactions in Time of Declared National Emergency*. Committee print, 94th Congress, 2d session. Washington, U.S. Govt. Print. Off., 1976; U.S. Congress. Senate. Committee on Banking, Housing, and Urban Affairs. *Assignment of Claims Act*. Washington, U.S. Govt. Print. Off., 1978. (95th Congress, 2d session. Senate. Report No. 95-1086).

133. 50 U.S.C. App. 2297.

134. See: U.S. Congress. House. Committee on Armed Services. *Full Committee Consideration of . . . H.R. 13329*. Hearings, 93rd Congress, 2d session. Washington, U.S. Govt. Print. Off., 1974; U.S. Congress. House. Committee on Armed Services. *Extending Civil Defense Emergency Authorities*. Washington, U.S. Govt. Print. Off., 1974. (93rd Congress, 2d session. House. Report No. 93-1243); Washington *Post*, September 19, 1974.

135. See *Federal Register*, v. 12, December 31, 1946: 1.

136. See *Federal Register*, v. 41, February 20, 1976: 7741.
137. The National Emergencies Act repealed 18 U.S.C. 1383 but, as discussed in the text of this article, left parallel authority pertaining to the navy, 18 U.S.C. 2152, intact.
138. 10 U.S.C. 673, as amended by 90 Stat. 517.
139. See U.S. Congress. Senate. Committee on Armed Services. Subcommittee on Manpower and Personnel. *Military Manpower Issues of the Past and Future*. Hearings, 93rd Congress, 2d session. Washington, U.S. Govt. Print. Off., 1974, pp. 7–9, 17, 32–36, 38–40; U.S. Congress. Senate. Committee on Armed Services. Subcommittee on Manpower and Personnel. *Reserve Call-Up*. Hearings, 94th Congress, 1st session. Washington, U.S. Govt. Print. Off., 1975; U.S. Congress. Senate. Committee on Armed Services. *Enabling the President to Authorize the Involuntary Order to Active Duty of Selected Reservists for a Limited Period Without a Declaration of War or National Emergency*. Washington, U.S. Govt. Print. Off., 1975. (94th Congress, 1st session. Senate. Report No. 94-562); U.S. Congress. House. Committee on Armed Services. *Full Committee Consideration of S. 2115*. Hearings, 94th Congress, 2d session. Washington, U.S. Govt. Print. Off., 1976; U.S. Congress. House. Committee on Armed Services. *Authority for Limited Reserve Mobilization*. Washington, U.S. Govt. Print. Off., 1976. (94th Congress, 2d session. House. Report No. 94-1069); Robert K. Musil. Troops for a Five-Star President. *The Nation*, v. 222, February 28, 1976: 238–241.
140. 91 Stat. 1625.
141. See U.S. Congress. House. Committee on International Relations. *Trading With the Enemy: Legislative and Executive Documents Concerning Regulation of International Transactions in Time of Declared National Emergency*. Committee print, 94th Congress, 2d session. Washington, U.S. Govt. Print. Off., 1976; U.S. Congress. House. Committee on International Relations. Subcommittee on International Economic Policy and Trade. *Emergency Controls on International Economic Transactions*. Hearings, 95th Congress, 1st session. Washington, U.S. Govt. Print. Off., 1977; U.S. Congress. House. Committee on International Relations. *Revision of Trading With the Enemy Act*. Markup, 95th Congress, 1st session. Washington, U.S. Govt. Print. Off., 1977; U.S. Congress. House. Committee on International Relations. *Trading With the Enemy Act Reform Legislation*. Washington, U.S. Govt. Print. Off., 1977. (95th Congress, 1st session. House. Report No. 95-459); U.S. Congress. Senate. Committee on Banking, Housing, and Urban Affairs. Subcommittee on International Finance. *Amending the Trading With the Enemy Act*. Hearings, 95th

Congress, 1st session. Washington, U.S. Govt. Print. Off., 1977; U.S. Congress. Senate. Committee on Banking, Housing, and Urban Affairs. *International Emergency Economic Powers Legislation.* Washington, U.S. Govt. Print. Off., 1977. (95th Congress, 1st session. Senate. Report No. 95-466).

142. S. Res. 9, 93rd Congress, 1st session, as adopted by the Senate on January 6, 1973; the complete text of the resolution appears in U.S. Congress. Senate. Special Committee on the Termination of the National Emergency. *National Emergency.* Hearings, 93rd Congress, 1st session. Washington, U.S. Govt. Print. Off., 1973, pp. 95–99.

143. 41 Stat. 1359.

144. 66 Stat. c31.

145. U.S. Congress. Senate. Special Committee on the Termination of the National Emergency. *National Emergency.* Hearings, 93rd Congress, 1st session. Washington, U.S. Govt. Print. Off., 1973, p. 2.

146. See U.S. Congress. Senate. Special Committee on the Termination of the National Emergency. *Review and Manner of Investigating, Mandate Pursuant to S. Res. 9, 93d Congress: A Working Paper.* Committee print, 93rd Congress, 1st session. Washington, U.S. Govt. Print. Off., 1973, p. 4; this executive session transcript also appears in U.S. Congress. Senate. Special Committee on the Termination of the National Emergency. *National Emergency.* Hearings, 93rd Congress, 1st session. Washington, U.S. Govt. Print. Off., 1973, pp. 247–273.

147. *Ibid.*, p. 5.

148. *Ibid.*, pp. 9–10.

149. *Ibid.*, p. 10.

150. See *Ibid.*, pp. 7, 10.

151. See *Ibid.*, pp. 4, 5, 6.

152. *Ibid.*, p. 4.

153. See *Ibid.*, p. 12.

154. See U.S. Congress. Senate. Special Committee on the Termination of the National Emergency. *National Emergency.* Hearings, 93rd Congress, 1st session. Washington, U.S. Govt. Print. Off., 1973, pp. 10 (Rankin), 27 and 32 (Cotter), 93 (Casper), and 507 (Katzenbach).

155. See *Ibid.*, pp. 10 (Rankin), 56 (Cotter), 85–86 (Casper), and 747 (Griswold).

156. See *Ibid.*, pp. 10 (Rankin), 63–64 (Fisher), and 83 (Casper).

157. See *Ibid.*, pp. 10 and 11 (Rankin), 63–64 (Fisher), 85–86 and 93 (Casper), and 741 (Griswold).

158. The Special Committee's interim report is cited at Note 107,

*supra.*; by the time the panel issued its final report, cited at Note 109, *supra.*, the House had completed action on legislation creating the National Emergencies Act and the Senate Committee on Government Operations had concluded its hearings on the proposal.

159. See *Congressional Record*, v. 121, September 4, 1975: H8340–H8341.

160. See, for example, 10 U.S.C. 331-334, 50 U.S.C. App. 2401–2413, or, with regard to the controversy over the possibility of President Reagan sending American troops to El Salvador or Nicaragua, see 10 U.S.C. 712.

161. See 10 U.S.C. 671(b), 712, 3031, and 8031; the Special Committee's published compendium of emergency powers statutes is cited at Note 73, *supra.*

162. See 12 U.S.C. 1425a.

163. See 50 U.S.C. 456 and 1512.

164. Testimony of the author in U.S. Congress. Senate. Committee on Governmental Affairs. *Emergency Powers of the District of Columbia.* Hearings, 96th Congress, 2d session. Washington, U.S. Govt. Print. Off., 1980, pp. 18–19.

165. U.S. Congress. Senate. Special Committee on the Termination of the National Emergency. *National Emergency.* Hearings, 93rd Congress, 1st session. Washington, U.S. Govt. Print. Off., 1973, p. 752.

166. *Ibid.*, p. 753.

167. U.S. Congress. Senate. Committee on Government Operations. *National Emergencies Act.* Washington, U.S. Govt. Print. Off., 1976. (94th Congress, 2d session. Senate. Report No. 94-1168), p. 3.

168. *Ibid.*

169. This aspect of the Truman proclamation was related to the Special Committee in testimony by Dr. Adrian S. Fisher and in a portion of President Truman's memoirs appended to the panel's hearing record; see U.S. Congress. Senate. Special Committee on the Termination of the National Emergency. *National Emergency.* 93rd Congress, 1st session. Washington, U.S. Govt. Print. Off., 1973, pp. 65 and 477–491.

170. See New York *Times*, July 12, 1974: 8.

171. See U.S. Congress. Senate. Special Committee on National Emergencies and Delegated Emergency Powers. *National Emergencies and Delegated Emergency Powers.* Washington, U.S. Govt. Print. Off., 1976. (94th Congress, 2d session. Senate. Report No. 94-922), pp. 16–18.

172. See U.S. Congress. Senate. Special Committee on the Termi-

nation of the National Emergency. *National Emergency*. Hearings, 93rd Congress, 1st session. Washington, U.S. Govt. Print. Off., 1973, pp. 725–727 (Mathias) and 738–739 (Griswold).

173. See the codified version of the National Emergencies Act at 50 U.S.C. 1621 and 1631.

174. See 44 U.S.C. 1505(c).

175. U.S. Congress. House. Committee on the Judiciary. *National Emergencies*. Washington, U.S. Govt. Print. Off., 1975. (94th Congress, 1st session. House. Report No. 94-238), p. 15.

176. See U.S. Congress. Senate. Special Committee on National Emergencies and Delegated Emergency Powers. *A Recommended National Emergencies Act: Interim Report*. Washington, U.S. Govt. Print. Off., 1974. (93rd Congress, 2d session. Senate. Report No. 93-1170), p. 10.

177. See *Congressional Record*, v. 120, October 7, 1974: S18356–S18357.

178. See *Congressional Record*, v. 122, August 27, 1976: S14843–S14844.

179. See U.S. Congress. Senate. Special Committee on the Termination of the National Emergency. *National Emergency*. Hearings, 93rd Congress, 1st session. Washington, U.S. Govt. Print. Off., 1973, p. 528.

180. *Ibid.*, pp. 740, 752.

181. See E.O. 11490 in *Federal Register*, v. 34, October 30, 1969: 17567–17599, as amended by E.O. 11921 in *Federal Register*, v. 41, June 15, 1976: 24294–24336.

182. See U.S. Congress. Senate. Special Committee on National Emergencies and Delegated Emergency Powers. *National Emergencies and Delegated Emergency Powers*. Washington, U.S. Govt. Print. Off., 1976. (94th Congress, 2d session. Senate. Report No. 94-922), p. 37.

183. See U.S. Congress. House. Committee on Government Operations. *U.S. Government Information Policies and Practices — Problems of Congress in Obtaining Information from the Executive Branch*. Hearings, 92nd Congress, 2d session. Washington, U.S. Govt. Print. Off., 1972, pp. 2939–2994.

184. See Richard P. Pollock. The Mysterious Mountain. *The Progressive*, v. 40, March, 1976: 12–16; Robert Walters. Going Underground. *Inquiry*, v. 4, February 2, 1981: 12–16.

185. 87 Stat. 555.

186. 91 Stat. 1626.

187. See Harry S Truman. *Memoirs: Years of Trial and Hope*. New York, Doubleday and Company, 1956, pp. 419–420.

188. The passage from the Truman memoirs cited in Note 187, *supra.*, appears in U.S. Congress. Senate. Special Committee on the Termination of the National Emergency. *National Emergency*.

Hearings, 93rd Congress, 1st session. Washington, U.S. Govt. Print. Off., 1973, pp. 481–482.

189. See *Ibid.*, pp. 41–42.

190. See *Congressional Record*, v. 121, September 4, 1975: H8340–H8341.

191. See U.S. Congress. Senate. Special Committee on the Termination of the National Emergency. *National Emergency.* Hearings, 93rd Congress, 1st session. Washington, U.S. Govt. Print. Off., 1973, p. 742.

192. See U.S. Congress. House. Committee on the Judiciary *National Emergencies Act.* Hearings, 94th Congress, 1st session. Washington, U.S. Govt. Print. Off., 1975, p. 92.

193. See *Weekly Compilation of Presidential Documents*, v. 12, September 20, 1976: 1340.

194. U.S. Congress. House. Committee on the Judiciary. *National Emergencies Act.* Hearings, 94th Congress, 1st session. Washington, U.S. Govt. Print. Off., 1975, p. 32.

195. *Ibid.*

196. This situation is evident in terms of the execution of the obligation to conduct a review six months after a national emergency is proclaimed by the President; see *Congressional Record*, v. 126, May 14, 1980: S5340; *Ibid.*, May 15, 1980: E2440–E2441; *Ibid.*, November 20, 1980: S14785–S14786; *Ibid.*, November 21, 1980: H11191–H11192.

197. See *Congressional Record*, v. 126, July 24, 1980: H6457 (Danielson).

198. There is no indication in the executive communications section of the *Congressional Record* that such reports were ever received officially during 1980; informal checks with the White House, the Senate Committee on Foreign Relations, and the House Committee on Foreign Affairs by the author indicated that these reports do not appear to have been transmitted; a communique from the President in early December does not seem to meet the reporting requirement of the National Emergencies Act; see *Congressional Record*, v. 126, December 4, 1980: S15602–S15603; the required reports should have been transmitted within a 90-day period after mid-May and mid-November of 1980.

199. The recommendation appeared over two decades ago in J. Malcolm Smith and Cornelius P. Cotter. *Powers of the President During Crisis.* Washington, Public Affairs Press, 1960, p. 145; for endorsements of the proposal, see U.S. Congress. Senate. Special Committee on the Termination of the National Emergency. *National Emergency.* Hearings, 93rd Congress, 1st session. Washington, U.S. Govt. Print. Off., 1973, pp. 56 (Smith), 521 (Clark), and 747 (Griswold); the idea of a special panel also ap-

peared in U.S. Congress. Senate. Special Committee on National Emergencies and Delegated Emergency Powers. *A Brief History of Emergency Powers in the United States* by Harold C. Relyea. Committee print, 93rd Congress, 2d session. Washington, U.S. Govt. Print. Off., 1974, pp. 121–122.

200. President Carter's declaration of a national emergency (E.O. 12170), finding "that the situation in Iran constitutes an unusual and extraordinary threat to the national security, foreign policy and economy of the United States," appears in *Federal Register*, v. 44, November 15, 1979: 65729; it could be argued that a subsequent directive (E.O. 12211) pertaining to "the added unusual and extraordinary threat to the national security, foreign policy and economy of the United States created by subsequent events in Iran and neighboring countries, *including the Soviet invasion of Afghanistan*," (emphasis added) constituted an additional or second national emergency declaration responding to a new crisis in Afghanistan; see *Federal Register*, v. 45, April 21, 1980: 26685–26686.

201. See Jonathan M. Winer. The Iranian Assets Grab. *The Nation*, v. 232, January 17, 1981: 44–46.

202. See U.S. General Accounting Office. Report to the Congress of the United States by the Comptroller General. *Treasury Should Keep Better Track Of Blocked Foreign Assets*. Washington, November 14, 1980 (ID-81-01).

203. See U.S. Congress. Senate. Special Committee on National Emergencies and Delegated Emergency Powers. *National Emergencies and Delegated Emergency Powers*. Washington, U.S. Govt. Print. Off., 1976. (94th Congress, 2d session. Senate. Report No. 94-922), p. 10.

204. 56 Stat. 173.

205. 18 U.S.C. 1383.

206. See U.S. Congress. Senate. Special Committee on the Termination of the National Emergency. *Review and Manner of Investigating, Mandate Pursuant to S. Res. 9, 93d Congress: A Working Paper*. Committee print, 93rd Congress, 1st session. Washington, U.S. Govt. Print. Off., 1973, p. 3; U.S. Congress. Senate. Special Committee on the Termination of the National Emergency. *Emergency Powers Statutes: Provisions of Federal Law Now in Effect Delegating to the Executive Extraordinary Authority in Time of National Emergency*. Washington, U.S. Govt. Print. Off., 1973. (93rd Congress, 1st session. Senate. Report No. 93-549), pp. 9–10; U.S. Congress. Senate. Special Committee on the Termination of the National Emergency. *National Emergency*. Hearings, 93rd Congress, 1st session. Washington, U.S. Govt. Print. Off., 1973,

pp. 3-4; U.S. Congress. Senate. Special Committee on National Emergencies and Delegated Emergency Powers. *A Recommended National Emergencies Act: Interim Report.* Washington, U.S. Govt. Print. Off., 1974. (93rd Congress, 2d session. Senate. Report No. 93-1170), p. 2.

207.  18 U.S.C. 2152.

208.  The provision does not appear in the Special Committee's compilation of emergency powers statutes cited at Note 73, *supra.*

209.  See U.S. Congress. Senate. Committee on Government Operations. *National Emergencies Act.* Hearings, 94th Congress, 2d session. Washington, U.S. Govt. Print. Off., 1976, pp. 8-13.

210.  The provision is not even mentioned in the report of the Senate Committee on Government Operations, cited at Note 123, *supra.*

211.  U.S. Congress. Senate. Special Committee on National Emergencies and Delegated Emergency Powers. *National Emergencies and Delegated Emergency Powers.* Washington, U.S. Govt. Print. Off., 1976. (94th Congress, 2d session. Senate. Report No. 94-922), p. 10.

212.  *Ibid.,* p. 11.

213.  See, for example, 92 Stat. 3117, 3171; 92 Stat. 3289, 3319; and 91 Stat. 3351, 3381.

214.  See Frank Donner. The Terrorist As Scapegoat. *The Nation*, v. 226, May 20, 1978: 590-594.

215.  U.S. Congress. Senate. Special Committee on National Emergencies and Delegated Emergency Powers. *National Emergencies and Delegated Emergency Powers.* Washington, U.S. Govt. Print. Off., 1976. (94th Congress, 2d session. Senate. Report No. 94-922), p. 11.

216.  See Reorganization Plan Number 3 of 1978 in *Weekly Compilation of Presidential Documents*, v. 14, June 26, 1978: 1131-1133; E. O. 12127 in *Federal Register*, v. 44, March 31, 1979: 19367-19368; and E. O. 12148 in *Federal Register*, v. 44, July 20, 1979: 43239-43245.

217.  See Note 181, *supra.*

218.  See Note 182, *supra.*

219.  See Note 183, *supra.*

220.  See Note 184, *supra.*

221.  U.S. Congress. Senate. Special Committee on National Emergencies and Delegated Emergency Powers. *National Emergencies and Delegated Emergency Powers.* Washington, U.S. Govt. Print. Off., 1976. (94th Congress, 2d session. Senate. Report No. 94-922), p. 11.

222.  *Ibid.,* p. 12.

223.  *Ibid.*

224. *Ibid.*

225. *Ibid.*

226. *Ibid.*

227. *Ibid.*

228. *Ibid.*, p. 13.

229. *Ibid.*, p. 12.

230. *Ibid.*, p. 14.

231. See, for example, U.S. Congress. Senate. Committee on Governmental Affairs. *Sunset Act of 1980.* Washington, U.S. Govt. Print. Off., 1980. (96th Congress, 2d session. Senate. Report No. 96-865); U.S. Congress. Senate. Committee on Rules and Administration. *The Sunset Act of 1980.* Washington, U.S. Govt. Print. Off., 1980. (96th Congress, 2d session. Senate. Report No. 96-924).

232. See U.S. Congress. House. Committee on Rules. *Recommendations on Establishment of Procedures for Congressional Review of Agency Rules.* Committee print, 96th Congress, 2d session. Washington, U.S. Govt. Print. Off., 1980; U.S. Congress. House. Committee on Rules. *Studies on the Legislative Veto.* Committee print, 96th Congress, 2d session. Washington, U.S. Govt. Print. Off., 1980, especially pp. 756–802.

233. See Frederick M. Kaiser. Congressional Action to Overturn Agency Rules: Alternatives to the "Legislative Veto." *Administrative Law Review*, v. 32, Fall, 1980: 667–711.

234. With regard to the sunset proposal, see: Bruce Adams. Sunset: A Proposal for Accountable Government. *Administrative Law Review*, v. 28, Summer, 1976: 511–542; Bruce Adams and Betsy Sherman. Sunset Implementation: A Positive Partnership to Make Government Work. *Public Administration Review*, v. 38, January-February, 1978: 78–81; Eugene Bardach. Policy Termination as a Political Process. *Policy Sciences*, v. 7, June, 1976: 123–131; Robert D. Benn. The False Dawn of the Sunset Laws. *Public Interest*, No. 49, Fall, 1977: 103–118; Anthony R. Licata. Zero-Based Sunset Review. *Harvard Journal on Legislation*, v. 14, April, 1977: 505–541; Dan R. Price. Sunset Legislation in the United States. *Baylor Law Review*, v. 30, Summer, 1978: 401–462; Ron Randall. What's Wrong With Sunset Laws. *The Nation*, v. 224, March 19, 1977: 331–334; and Symposium. Controversy Over Proposed "Sunset" Legislation. *Congressional Digest*, v. 59, March, 1980: 67–96.

   With regard to the legislative veto proposal, see: James Abourezk. The Congressional Veto: A Contemporary Response to Executive Encroachment on Legislative Prerogatives. *Indiana Law Journal*, v. 52, Winter, 1977: 323–343; John R. Bolton.

*The Legislative Veto: Unseparating the Powers.* Washington, The American Enterprise Institute for Public Policy Research, 1977; Harold H. Bruff and Ernest Gellhorn. Congressional Control of Administrative Regulation: A Study of Legislative Vetoes. *Harvard Law Review*, v. 90, May, 1977: 1369–1440; Doyle W. Buckwalter. The Congressional Concurrent Resolution: A Search for Foreign Policy Influence. *Midwest Journal of Political Science*, v. 14, August, 1970: 434–458; Joseph and Ann Cooper. The Legislative Veto and the Constitution. *George Washington Law Review*, v. 30, March, 1962: 467–516; Cornelius P. Cotter and J. Malcolm Smith. Administrative Accountability to Congress: The Concurrent Resolution. *Western Political Quarterly*, v. 9, December, 1956: 955–966; Robert G. Dixon, Jr. The Congressional Veto and Separation of Powers: The Executive on a Leash? *North Carolina Law Review*, v. 56, April, 1978: 423–494; John B. Henry II. The Legislative Veto: In Search of Constitutional Limits. *Harvard Journal on Legislation*, v. 16, Summer, 1979: 735–762; Robert J. Ivanhoe. Congressional Oversight of Administrative Discretion: Defining the Proper Role of the Legislative Veto. *American University Law Review*, v. 26, Summer, 1977: 1018–1061; Jacob K. Javits and Gary J. Klein. Congressional Oversight and the Legislative Veto: A Constitutional Analysis. *New York University Law Review*, v. 52, June, 1977: 455–497; Carl McGowan. Congress, Court, and Control of Delegated Power. *Columbia Law Review*, v. 77, December, 1977: 1119–1174; Arthur S. Miller and George M. Knapp. The Congressional Veto: Preserving the Constitutional Framework. *Indiana Law Journal*, v. 52, Winter, 1977: 367–395; Note. Congressional Veto of Administrative Action: The Probable Response to a Constitutional Challenge. *Duke Law Journal*, v. 1976, May, 1976: 285–300; Glendon A. Schubert. Legislative Adjudication of Administrative Legislation. *Journal of Public Law*, v. 7, Spring, 1958: 135–161; Bernard Schwartz. The Legislative Veto and the Constitution — A Reexamination. *George Washington Law Review*, v. 46, March, 1978: 351–375; Geoffrey S. Stewart. Constitutionality of the Legislative Veto. *Harvard Journal on Legislation*, v. 13, April, 1976: 593–619; H. Lee Watson. Congress Steps Out: A Look at Congressional Control of the Executive. *California Law Review*, v. 63, July, 1975: 983–1094; and Lee F. Witter. The Legislative Veto: A Fight on the Horizon. *The Bureaucrat*, v. 9, Summer, 1980: 31–38.

235. U.S. Congress. Senate. Special Committee on National Emergencies and Delegated Emergency Powers. *National Emergencies and Delegated Emergency Powers*. Washington, U.S. Govt. Print.

Off., 1976. (94th Congress, 2d session. Senate. Report No. 94-922), pp. 15–16.

236. *Ibid.*, p. 16.

237. *Ibid.*

238. *Ibid.*, p. 17.

239. *Ibid.*, p. 16.

240. *Ibid.*, p. 17; since 1940, security classification policy for the departments and agencies has been established by executive order; see Harold C. Relyea. The Evolution of Government Information Security Classification Policy: A Brief Overview (1775–1973) in U.S. Congress. House. Committee on Government Operations. *Security Classification Reform.* Hearings, 93rd Congress, 2d session. Washington, U.S. Govt. Print. Off., 1974, pp. 505–597; that Congress may legislate in this policy area seems clear; see *Ibid.*, pp. 289–295; for recommendations in this regard, see: U.S. Congress. House. Committee on Government Operations. *Executive Classification of Information — Security Classification Problems Involving Exemption (b) (1) of the Freedom of Information Act (5 U.S.C. 552).* Washington, U.S. Govt. Print. Off., 1973. (93rd Congress, 1st session. House. Report No. 93-221), p. 104; U.S. Congress. House. Committee on Standards of Official Conduct. *Report on Investigation Pursuant to H. Res. 1042 Concerning Unauthorized Publication of the Report of the Select Committee on Intelligence.* Washington, U.S. Govt. Print. Off., 1976. (94th Congress, 2d session. House. Report No. 94-1754), pp. 43–44; U.S. Congress. Senate. Committee on the Judiciary. *Agency Implementation of the 1974 Amendments to the Freedom of Information Act.* Committee print, 95th Congress, 2d session. Washington, U.S. Govt. Print. Off., 1980, p. 36.

241. U.S. Congress. Senate. Special Committee on National Emergencies and Delegated Emergency Powers. *National Emergencies and Delegated Emergency Powers.* Washington, U.S. Govt. Print. Off., 1976. (94th Congress, 2d session. Senate. Report No. 94-922), p. 18.

## CHAPTER SEVENTEEN NOTES

1. I have established the following criteria for what I have termed "sound policy options," a concept that is referred to repeatedly in the paper: the policy must be creative, it must be formulated in an efficient manner, and it must satisfy Presidential needs. Creative policies are those which challenge existing or traditional policies, transcend immediate, short term concerns, and which

work toward the achievement of Presidential objectives. Efficiency is determined by the breadth and depth of data, the timeliness of its reaching the President, and its avoidance of departmental biases. Meeting Presidential needs is determined by the degree to which external factors, such as domestic political considerations, are factored in.

2. Of course not all of the writers have had the full benefit of twenty years of hindsight to draw from.

3. A thorough analysis of bureaucracy in general would require the gathering of data in fields such as communication theory, organizational theory, group theory, and decisionmaking theory. A thorough analysis of State would require at least some first hand experience.

4. Kennedy is used as a point of departure because it was during his Administration that international relations took on a new dimension with the emergence of Third World nations. Consequently fresh approaches to foreign policy were required, which, in turn, placed new demands on the foreign policy machinery.

5. Scholars, in their endless quest for originality and precision, have defined bureaucracy in a variety of ways. I will define it simply as a complex system of men, methods, and authority integrated to rationalize collective action.

6. Herbert Simon, *Administrative Behavior.* (New York: Free Press 1957), pp. 39–41.

7. Michael Crozier, *The Bureaucratic Phenomenon.* (Chicago: University of Chicago Press 1964), p. 194.

8. Ludwig von Mises, *Bureaucracy* (New Haven: Yale University Press, 1944) as cited in Lewis C. Manzer, *Political Bureaucracy* (Glenview, Ill.: Scott Foresman, 1973), p. 97.

9. See Charles S. Hyneman, *Bureaucracy in a Democracy.* (New York: Harper & Brothers, 1950), pp. 26–35.

10. Marshall Dimock, *Administrative Vitality.* (New York: Harper & Brothers, 1959), p. 23.

11. Alexander George, *Presidential Decisionmaking in Foreign Policy.* (Boulder, Colorado: Westview Press, 1982), p. 111.

12. What George described as occurring at a macro-level (i.e. the Executive Branch) is described here as occurring at a micro-level (i.e. State).

13. *The National Security Council, Jackson Subcommittee Papers on Policymaking at the Presidential Level*, Henry A. Jackson ed. (New York: Praeger Inc. 1965), pp. 169–171. Rockefeller had chaired Eisenhower's Advisory Committee on Government Organization from 1953–1960 and prior to that he served in the State Department.

14. Henry Kissinger, *The Necessity For Choice: Prospects For U.S. Foreign Policy* (Garden City, N.Y.: Harper & Bros., 1960), p. 345.
15. *The National Security Council, Jackson Subcommittee Papers* . . . , Henry A. Jackson ed., p. 35.
16. Leslie Gelb, "The Struggle Over Foreign Policy," *New York Times Magazine*, July 20, 1980, p. 34.
17. See Destler, I. M. *Presidents, Bureaucrats, And Foreign Policy.* (Princeton, N.J.: Princeton University Press, 1972).
18. This group included Walt Rostow, Carl Kaysen, Robert Komer, Michael Forrestal, and Bromley Smith.
19. Arthur Schlesinger Jr., *A Thousand Days, John F. Kennedy in the White House.* (Boston: Houghton Mifflin Co., 1965), p. 406.
20. *Ibid.*, p. 426.
21. Richard Nixon, *RN* (New York: Grosset & Dunlap, 1978), p. 340. It should be noted that this was a private deliberation of Nixon's. Publically he had endorsed State as the center of foreign policymaking.
22. See Henry Kissinger, *American Foreign Policy — Three Essays* (New York: W. W. Norton Inc., 1969) and *The Necessity For Choice: Prospects For U.S. Foreign Policy* (New York: Harper & Bros. 1961).
23. R. Gordon Hoxie, "The National Security Council," *Presidential Studies Quarterly*, Winter 1982, pp. 110–111.
24. Leslie Gelb, "The Struggle Over Foreign Policy," *New York Times Magazine*, July 20, 1980, p. 34.

## CHAPTER SEVENTEEN BIBLIOGRAPHY

Bacchus, William. *Foreign Policy and the Bureaucratic Process*. Princeton, N.J.: Princeton University Press, 1974.

Barron, Bryton. *Inside the State Department, A Candid Appraisal of the Bureaucracy*. New York: Comet Press, 1956.

Blau, Peter M. *The Dynamics of Bureaucracy*. 2nd ed. Chicago: University of Chicago Press, 1963.

Bloomfield, Lincoln. *The Foreign Policy Process*. New York: Sage Publications, 1974.

Crozier, Michael. *The Bureaucratic Phenomenon*. Chicago: University of Chicago Press, 1964.

Davis, D. H. *How the Bureaucracy Makes Foreign Policy*. Lexington, Mass.: Lexington Books, 1972.

Destler, I. M. "National Security Management, What Presidents Have Wrought," *Political Science Quarterly*. Winter, 1980–81.

_____. *Presidents, Bureaucrats, and Foreign Policy*. Princeton, N.J.: Princeton University Press, 1972.

Deutsch, Karl. *The Nerves of Government*. New York: The Free Press, 1963.

Dimock, Marshall E. *Administrative Vitality*. New York: Harper & Brothers, 1959.

Downs, Anthony. *Inside Bureaucracy*. Boston: Little, Brown, & Co., 1967.

Ford, Gerald. *A Time To Heal*. New York: Harper & Row, 1979.

Gawthrop, Louis. *Bureaucratic Behavior in the Executive Branch*. New York: The Free Press, 1969.

Gelb, Leslie. "The Struggle Over Foreign Policy." *New York Times Magazine*. July 20, 1980.

George, Alexander. *Presidential Decisionmaking in Foreign Policy*. Boulder, Colorado: Westview Press, 1982.

Halperin, Morton. "Why Bureaucrats Play Games." *Foreign Policy*. Spring 1971.

Hoxie, R. Gordon. "The National Security Council." *Presidential Studies Quarterly*. Winter 1982.

Hillsman, Roger. *To Move a Nation, The Politics Of Foreign Policy in the Administration of John F. Kennedy*. Garden City, N.Y.: Doubleday & Company Inc., 1967.

Inbar, Michael. *Routine Decision-Making, The Future of Bureaucracy*. Beverly Hills, Calif.: Sage Publications, 1979.

Jackson, Henry A. ed. *The National Security Council, Jackson Subcommittee Papers on Policymaking at the Presidential Level*. New York: Praeger Inc., 1965.

Kissinger, Henry. *American Foreign Policy-Three Essays*. New York: W. W. Norton Inc., 1969.

_____. *The Necessity For Choice: Prospects For U.S. Foreign Policy*. New York: Harper and Brothers, 1961.

_____. *The White House Years*. Boston: Little, Brown, Inc., 1979.

Landau, David. *Kissinger: The Uses of Power*. Boston: Houghton Mifflin Co., 1972.

Leacacos, John P. *Fires in the Basket, The ABC's of the State Department*. New York: World Publishing Co., 1968.

Schlesinger, Arthur Jr. *A Thousand Days, John F. Kennedy in the White House*. Boston: Houghton Mifflin Co., 1965.

Silberman, Laurence. "Toward Presidential Control of the State Department." *Foreign Affairs*. Spring, 1979.

Simon, Herbert. *Administrative Behavior*. New York: Free Press, 1957.

Simpson, Smith. *Anatomy of the State Department*. Boston: Houghton Mifflin Co., 1967.

*U.S. News & World Report*. "Tug of War Over Foreign Policy." June 19, 1978.

_____. "Behind the Disarray in Foreign Policy." Sept. 29, 1980.

Vocke, William C. ed. *American Foreign Policy, An Analytic Approach.* New York: Free Press, 1976.

Warwick, Donald. *A Theory of Public Bureaucracy: Politics, Personality, and Organization in the State Department.* Cambridge, Mass.: Harvard University Press, 1975.

## CHAPTER NINETEEN NOTES

1. Samuel P. Huntington, *The Common Defense* (New York: Columbia University Press, 1961), p. x.

2. See Robert E. Osgood, *NATO: The Entangling Alliance* (Chicago: University of Chicago Press, 1962).

3. General Bernard W. Rogers, "The Atlantic Alliance: Prescription For a Difficult Decade," *Foreign Affairs* 60 (Summer, 1982), p. 1152.

4. *Ibid.*

5. *Newsweek*, 19 April 1982, p. 31.

6. *The Economist*, "Without the Bomb," in *Atlantic Community Quarterly* 20 (Fall, 1982), pp. 201–09.

7. U.S. Congress, Congressional Budget Office, *Armed Ground Combat Modernization for the 1980s: Potential Costs and Effects for NATO* (Washington, D.C.: U.S. Government Printing Office, November, 1982).

8. Caspar Weinberger, *Annual Report to the Congress*, Fiscal Year 1984 (Washington, D.C.: U.S. Government Printing Office, 1983), p. 177.

9. Joshua Muravchik, *The Senate and National Security* (Beverly Hills: Sage Publications, 1980), pp. 45–6.

10. Norman Podhoretz, *The Present Danger* (New York: Simon & Schuster, 1980).

11. Michael R. Gordon, "Right-of-Center Defense Groups — The Pendulum Has Swung Their Way," *National Journal* (January 24, 1981), pp. 128ff.

12. Dick Kirschten, "The National Security Issue — A Matter of War and Peace?" *National Journal* (October 11, 1980), pp. 1688ff and Michael Gordon, "For the Pentagon's 'Minimal' Budget, It's Not Whether to Cut But How Much," *National Journal* (March 27, 1982), p. 544ff.

13. Stanley Hoffmann, *Dead Ends* (Cambridge: Ballinger, 1983), pp. 153–161.

14. See Paul M. Cole, "The American Nuclear Freeze Movement: Now and Five Years From Now," Draft chapter in forthcoming book on American peace movements (Washington, D.C.:

Georgetown University Center for Strategic and International Studies), pp. 42–46.

15. Leon Wieseltier, "The Great Nuclear Debate," *The New Republic*, 17 January 1983, p. 14.

16. *U.S. News & World Report*, 25 April 1983, p. 20.

17. John Fialka, " 'Congressional Military Reform Caucus' Lacks a Budget but Has Power to Provoke the Pentagon," *Wall Street Journal*, April 13, 1982 and Alton K. Marsh, "Military Reform Caucus Seeks Targets," *Aviation Week and Space Technology* (March 29, 1982).

18. Steven Canby, "The Alliance and Europe: Part IV, Military Doctrine and Technology" (London: IISS, Adelphi Paper 109, 1974); "The Winds of Reform," *Time* (March 7, 1983), pp. 12ff; and U.S. Congress, House, Committee on Foreign Affairs, *NATO's Future Role*, *Hearings*, 97th Cong., 2d sess., 1982.

19. James Fallows, *National Defense* (New York: Random House, 1981).

20. U.S. Congress, Senate, Senator Edward Kennedy Speech on the FY 1983 DOD Authorization Bill, 97th Cong., 2d sess. May 5, 1982, *Congressional Record*, p. S5115.

21. U.S. Congress, Senate, Senator Robert Byrd Speech on the FY 1983 DOD Authorization Bill, 97th Cong., 2d sess., May 6, 1982, *Congressional Record*, pp. S4644–53; "Budget Deficits," *Congressional Quarterly* (March 27, 1982), p. 661; and David Harris, "Understanding Mondale," *New York Times Magazine* (June 19, 1983), pp. 26ff.

22. U.S. Congress, House, Committee on Education and Labor, *The Defense Economic Adjustment Act*, *Hearing*, 97th Cong., 2d sess., 1982.

23. Joseph A. Pechman, ed., *Setting National Priorities: The 1984 Budget* (Washington: Brookings, 1982), pp. 1–22 and 79.

24. Congressional Budget Office, "Defense Spending and the Economy" (Washington: U.S. Government Printing Office, 1983), pp. xi–xvi.

25. After Maneuvering Is Over, 5% Defense Increase Likely," *Congressional Quarterly*, April 2, 1983, pp. 655ff.

26. Phil Gailey, "Arms Curb Sets Glenn Apart from Rivals," *The New York Times*, August 16, 1983, p. 17; "Cuts in Defense Spending Expected to be Difficult," *Congressional Quarterly* (November 20, 1982), pp. 2885ff; "Glenn: Another Liftoff," *Newsweek* (May 2, 1983), pp. 29ff; and Congress Decries Deficits, Weighs '84 Budget Revisions," *Congressional Quarterly* (February 5, 1983), pp. 243ff.

27. For a general critique of the "Maritime Strategy" as it compares

to the current "Coalition Defense," see Robert W. Komer," Maritime Strategy vs. Coalition Defense," *Foreign Affairs* 60 (Summer 1982), pp. 1124–44.

28. Conversation with Professor Walter Dean Burnham, Massachusetts Institute of Technology in Chicago, Illinois, September 2, 1983.

29. George Gallup, *The Gallup Polls: Public Opinion, 1972–1977*, Volume Two, (Wilmington: Scholarly Resources, pp. 1164–1165 and *The Gallup Report* (November, 1982), p. 17.

30. Timothy Clark, "After a Decade of Doing Battle, Public Interest Groups Show Their Age," *National Journal* (July 12, 1980), pp. 1136ff.

31. Dom Bonafede, "Issue-Oriented Heritage Foundation Hitches Its Wagon to Reagan's Star," *National Journal* (March 20, 1982), pp. 502ff.

32. Huntington, p. 176.

33. Harold Brown, *Thinking About National Security* (Boulder: Westview Press, 1983), p. 200.

34. Samuel Huntington, "Strategic Planning and the Political Process," *Components of Defense Policy*, Davis Bobrow, ed. (Chicago: Rand McNally, 1965), pp. 92–93.

35. Theodore Lowi, *The End of Liberalism* (New York: Norton, 1969), pp. 174–186.

36. Wallace Earl Walker, "Domestic Policymaking in the National Security State," Unpublished Paper delivered to the Northeastern Regional Meeting of the Inter-University Seminar on Armed Forces and Society, West Point, New York, April, 1983.

## CHAPTER TWENTY NOTES

1. 62 *The Congressional Digest* (November 1983), p. 288.

2. *Washington Post*, April 11, 1975, p. A17.

3. Letter from President Ford to Senator Eastland, quoted in John C. Cruden, "The War-Making Process," 69 *Military Law Review* (1975), p. 123.

4. *Congressional Quarterly Weekly Report*, October 29, 1983, p. 2221.

5. Robert F. Turner, *The War Powers Resolution: Its Implementation in Theory and Practice* (Philadelphia: Foreign Policy Research Institute, 1983), p. 73.

6. James Q. Wilson, *American Government: Institutions and Policies*, 2nd ed., (Lexington, Mass.: D. C. Heath, 1983), pp. 556–557.

7. Cruden, p. 110.

8. *The New York Times*, March 2, 1984, pp. A1, A11.

9. *Ibid.*, p. A11.
10. *Weekly Compilation of Presidential Documents*, Vol. 9, No. 43, p. 1286.
11. 77 L.Ed. 2d 317, 350.
12. *Washington Post*, June 28, 1983.
13. Turner, p. 38.
14. *Ibid.*, p. 17.
15. "Pacificus No. 1," in *The Papers of Alexander Hamilton*, ed. by Harold Syrett, vol. XV, 33–43 (New York: Columbia University Press, 1969) (emphasis added).
16. Robert Scigliano, "The War Powers Resolution and the War Powers," in Joseph M. Bessette and Jeffrey Tulis, eds., *The Presidency in the Constitutional Order* (Baton Rouge: Louisiana State University Press, 1981), p. 131. Compare *Federalist #78*, authored by Hamilton, with Section 3 of the *Second Treatise*, and compare the Declaration of Independence with the *Second Treatise*.
17. All references are to sections of the *Second Treatise*.
18. Aaron Wildavsky, "The Two Presidencies," in Aaron Wildavsky, ed., *The Presidency* (Boston: Little, Brown and Company, 1969), pp. 230–243.
19. Scigliano, pp. 133–140.
20. *United States* v. *Curtiss-Wright Export Corp.*, 229 U.S. 304 (1936).
21. Arthur M. Schlesinger, Jr., *The Imperial Presidency* (Boston: Houghton Mifflin Co., 1973).
22. *Korematsu* v. *United States*, 323 U.S. 214 (1944).
23. Patrick Henry, Speech at Virginia Ratifying Convention, in Cecelia M. Kenyon, ed., *The Antifederalists* (Indianapolis: Bobbs-Merrill, 1966), p. 244.
24. *Ibid.*, p. 167.
25. *Ibid.*
26. Alexander Hamilton, James Madison and John Jay, *The Federalist Papers* (New York: The New American Library, Mentor Books, 1961), p. 68.

# Index

6